P9-DFV-363

BOOK FORTY-FIVE
Louann Atkins Temple Women & Culture Series
Books about women and families, and their changing role in society

Plant Kin

Theresa L. Miller

A Multispecies Ethnography
in Indigenous Brazil

University of Texas Press ▼ Austin

The Louann Atkins Temple Women & Culture Series is supported by Allison, Doug, Taylor, and Andy Bacon; Margaret, Lawrence, Will, John, and Annie Temple; Larry Temple; the Temple-Inland Foundation; and the National Endowment for the Humanities.

Requests for permission to reproduce material from this work should be sent to:
Permissions
University of Texas Press
P.O. Box 7819
Austin, TX 78713-7819
utpress.utexas.edu/rp-form

♾ The paper used in this book meets the minimum requirements of
ANSI/NISO Z39.48-1992 (R1997) (Permanence of Paper).

Library of Congress Cataloging-in-Publication Data

Names: Miller, Theresa L. (Theresa Lynn), 1985– author.
Title: Plant kin : a multispecies ethnography in indigenous Brazil / Theresa L. Miller.
Description: First edition. | Austin : University of Texas Press, 2018. | Includes
bibliographical references and index.
Identifiers: LCCN 2017058303
    ISBN 978-1-4773-1739-6 (cloth : alk. paper)
    ISBN 978-1-4773-1740-2 (pbk. : alk. paper)
    ISBN 978-1-4773-1741-9 (library e-book)
    ISBN 978-1-4773-1742-6 (non-library e-book)
Subjects: LCSH: Canela Indians—Ethnobotany. | Cerrado ecology—Brazil. |
Sustainable living—Brazil. | Human-plant relationships—Brazil. | Traditional
ecological knowledge—Brazil.
Classification: LCC F2520.1.C32 M55 2018 | DDC 581.6/30981—dc23
LC record available at https://lccn.loc.gov/2017058303

doi:10.7560/317396

For Juliana Jilôt
Whose curiosity, strength, courage, and love for her multispecies family
made this book possible.

And for pànkrỳt ahkrare caprêc-re
The little red child bean who inspires care and affection
in a troubled world.

CONTENTS

LIST OF ILLUSTRATIONS

MAPS

DIAGRAMS

FIGURES

TABLES

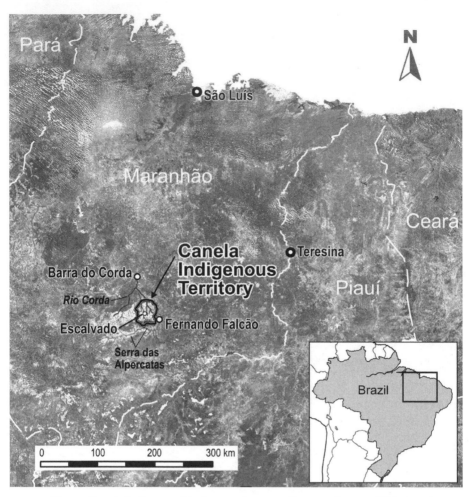

Map 1. Canela Indigenous Territory and surrounding area (source: Miller 2016).

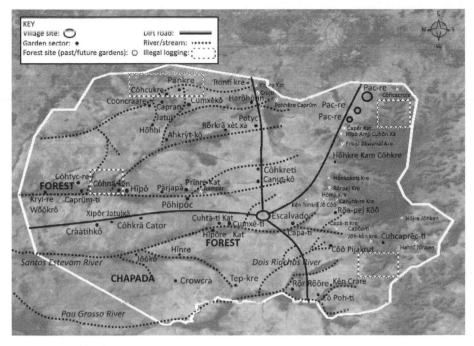

Map 2. Canela Indigenous Territory.

Toward a Sensory Ethnobotany
in the Anthropocene

Approaching People and Plants in the Anthropocene

It is no secret that people love plants. Over millennia, plant and human communities have become intertwined through processes of domestication, cultivation, and consumption. Plants are in our homes, our backyards, our gardens, our farms, and our food. They provide sustenance, solace, friendship, and health to human communities. As anthropology moves toward studies "beyond the human" (Kohn 2013:1), anthropological studies of plants and their relationships with humans are blossoming. Human care and even love for plants can be found across the globe, whether in backyard gardens in Mozambique (Archambault 2016) or England (Degnen 2009), Scottish therapeutic gardening programs (A. Jepson 2014), or Spanish botanical gardens (Hartigan 2015b, 2017). In Amazonia, plants are often integral to human communities and valued for their diversity—as found for the Huaorani of Ecuador (Rival 2016), Makushi of Guyana (Rival 2001; Daly 2016), and many Tupi-Guaraní communities (Balée 2013). A "plant turn" (Myers 2015:40; Hartigan 2017) is emerging, one that focuses on plant lives—including their sensory and communicative abilities, materiality, symbolism, and interrelations amongst themselves and with humans—in anthropology (Kohn 2013; Hartigan et al. 2014; Archambault 2016; Battaglia 2017; Hartigan 2017), philosophy (Hall 2011; Marder 2013), popular science (Chamovitz 2012; Haskell 2017), and plant science studies (Gagliano et al. 2012; Gagliano et al. 2014; Cahill 2015; Gagliano 2015; Gagliano and Grimonprez 2015).

Yet the ways in which people and plants come to know, care for, and perhaps love one another in multispecies communities remains less understood. While anthropology can grapple with human love and care for plants, "interviewing" the plants ethnographically remains a challenging endeavor (Hartigan et al. 2014), although there are recent sustained efforts to do so

(Hartigan 2017). For all we are learning about plant sensory perceptual abilities in the growing field of plant behavioral ecology (Biedrzycki and Bais 2010; Dudley et al. 2013; Cahill 2015), plants remain distinct entities from humans—"not lesser us" but rather a kind of "different-us" or "other-us" (Myers 2015:56). As such, perhaps we need to move toward a "planthropology," as Natasha Myers (2017:4) suggests, in order to get to know plants "intimately and on their own terms" and "to document the affective ecologies taking shape between plants and people."

Heeding the call for a planthropology, this book is a multispecies ethnography of people and plants in the Indigenous[1] Canela community of the Brazilian Cerrado[2] (savannah). It contributes to and expands upon the growing canon of literature in the plant turn by focusing on intimate, multi-sensory engagements among Canela people and plants, including their transformations over time and the ways in which people–plant engagements support multispecies care, survival, and well-being. For the Canela, plants are kin who are nourished and cared for throughout the plants' lives. How the Canela love their plant kin, and how that love supports multispecies care and well-being, is the focus of this book. Throughout the book, I examine the ongoing, creative, and caring work of making and growing multispecies kin in the changing circumstances of the Anthropocene epoch.

Through an approach I term "sensory ethnobotany," I take seriously Indigenous people–plant relationships over time and in myriad landscapes of the Brazilian Cerrado, a global biodiversity hotspot with high rates of endemic flora and fauna and native habitat loss (Myers et al. 2000). I explore the transformations of Canela human–environment and human–plant engagements over the past two centuries and the myriad ways in which the Canela, by loving and caring for their plant kin, are resisting and becoming resilient to present and future environmental challenges. Moreover, I envision possible futures for the Canela multispecies community in the threatened Cerrado, which is facing rapid environmental and climatic changes as the Anthropocene unfolds.

There are certainly numerous environmental challenges facing the Canela community of the twenty-first century. The Cerrado is considered one of the most biodiverse and most threatened biomes worldwide (Felfili et al. 2004), with over half of the region already deforested from activities such as logging, industrialized agriculture, and cattle ranching. It is expected to be severely affected by climate change, with rising temperatures and less rainfall estimated over the next half century (Bustamante et al. 2012). The northeastern region where the Canela territory is located is the epicenter of these present and future threats: it is considered Brazil's "newest agricultural hotspot" for industrialized soy and is expected to face the most extreme temperature and rainfall changes in the country (Bustamante et al. 2012, Gibbs et al. 2015:377). The Canela already are experiencing these threats. Illegal logging is increasing on their lands, bringing sociopolitical instability and violence in addition to deforestation of valued hardwood tree species. Industrialized eucalyptus and soy plantations are increasing in size nearby, threatening to erode soils and pollute waterways with pesticide runoff, and a rapidly expanding eucalyptus plantation is blamed already for drying out soils in Canela gardens in recent years. Meanwhile, drought and irregular rainfall are becoming an ever-present reality, contributing to uncontrollable fires during the dry season and a shorter and more unpredictable rainy season.

Eroded soils, depleted rivers and streams, deforested landscapes, uncultivable gardens, and the death and loss of diverse plant kin—is this the future the Canela face? Looking at the socio-ecological realities of the early twenty-first century Cerrado and the dramatic shifts in vegetation and climate expected to occur over the next few decades, a dire future for Canela people and plants could be on the horizon. Documenting the contemporary Canela life-world and how it has emerged over time through shifting human–environment engagements is, therefore, of pressing importance. Yet I am not undertaking "salvage" anthropology here, nor am I documenting "dying" interconnections among language, sociocultural patterns, and the environment (see Maffi 2001; Maffi and Woodley 2010). The Canela life-world is very much alive, seen in the complex categorization of eco-regions and garden areas; the complementarity of dualistic garden and soil "couples" that work together to support human and plant well-being; the aesthetics of landscape and education of affection for plant kin; and the intimate multi-sensory human–environment and human–plant engagements explored throughout this book. Rather, throughout this book I seek to understand how Canela human–plant engagements have transformed over time to become creative, caring relationships that promote survival and well-being. Moreover, I seek to understand the ways in which Canela people and plants continue to create, maintain, and pursue multispecies care in the Anthropocene, an epoch defined by uncertainty, instability, and loss for multispecies communities.

The Anthropocene is understood here as a phenomenological concept that is emergent and dynamic. Simultaneously geological, ecological, sociocultural, sociopolitical, and even cosmological, the Anthropocene is considered throughout this book as both an epoch definable and measurable in geological time and one that is "in formation . . . as generative as it is contested" (A. Moore 2015:1). In the geological sciences, the Anthropocene is defined by human activity[3] that has shaped the "socio-economic and bio-physical spheres of the Earth System," with global effects including rapid temperature increases, climate change, melting ice caps, rising sea levels, ocean acidification, deforestation, and biodiversity loss, among others (Steffen et al. 2015:82, 86–87). It increasingly is recognized as a new geological epoch that is "stratigraphically distinct" from the Holocene we have been living in over the past 10,000–12,000 years (Waters et al. 2016).[4] Debates continue over when the Anthropocene began,[5] with 1950 the currently favored date.[6] Conceptually, the Anthropocene invites new dialogues and research that connect the global, regional, and local; geological, biological, ecological, and sociocultural processes; and issues of political economy, political ecology, and environmental justice. In anthropology, new ways of understanding the concept and its emergence in the natural and social sciences are being explored. There are calls for greater recognition of the injustices and inequalities that are inherent to the Anthropocene through an Earth Stewardship framework (Ogden et al. 2013:341), calls to "question the terra-centric boundaries" of the Anthropocene and connect it to planetary systems (Olson and Messeri 2015:42), and calls for an Anthropocene anthropology that seeks to examine the concept critically in an open-ended conceptual framework (A. Moore 2016:1). Others question the conceptual usefulness of the Anthropocene and advocate for alternative or multiple -cenes (see Haraway et al. 2015): the Carbocene, Capitalocene, and Chthulucene, among others.[7]

With the plant turn, there is a call for considering the Planthroposcene, which Myers (2017:3–4) describes as "an aspirational episteme and way of doing life in which people come to recognize their profound interimplication with plants" in order to "make allies with these green beings." As a thought experiment, the Planthroposcene invites new ways of coming to know and understand plants as they interact with humans. The concept also has political ecological implications, as a way of situating human–plant relationships as central to planetary health, individual and communal survival, and local and global well-being. I draw from the Planthroposcene concept throughout this book to examine the intimate ways that plants and people engage with one another even as the environment and climate continue to change. While the Anthropocene is expected to bring major climatic shifts, environmental destruction, and loss for humans and nonhumans, the Planthroposcene concept suggests an opening for deepening our understanding of and alliances with plants—those diverse beings who give us food and shelter; take part in our ritual and everyday lives; and in some instances are connected to us through bonds of love and kinship. Although there are many ways that people and plants can come together or pull apart in the Anthropocene (or Planthroposcene), in this book I explore people–plant relationships through the lens of care, affection, and kinship, the primary ways that Indigenous Canela people and plants engage. As such, I draw from anthropological and science and technology studies of care (Despret 2004; Bellacasa 2011, 2015; Friese 2013; Atkinson-Graham et al. 2015; Kirksey 2015; A. Martin et al. 2015), particularly care amongst multiple species or "care of the species," as Hartigan (2017) explores. As a multispecies ethnography, this book explores the care and love for plant kin that Canela gardeners develop and maintain as well as the experiences of plants themselves, or what Myers terms "plant feelings" (Myers 2015). The "feelings" of people and plants that engender love, care, and affection amongst kin are sensory experiences—of humans handling, smelling, listening to, tasting, and responding to plants, and of plants responding to human touch and communicating in their own sensory ways of growth, movement, and chemical utterances that constitute much of plant "chemical language" (Gagliano and Grimonprez 2015:147). Through a framework termed sensory ethnobotany, this book hones in on these complex people–plant sensory experiences and the caring engagements they enable in an epoch—whatever "-cene" it may be called—wrought with ongoing transformations and change.

Approaching Sensory Ethnobotany

The sensory ethnobotany framework that I develop throughout the book takes seriously human and plant lived experiences and the valuation of these experiences to both humans *and* plants. Informed by plant science research on the behavioral and perceptual abilities of plants, anthropological research on multispecies assemblages, and ethnobotanical research on human classification and understanding of plants, sensory ethnobotany focuses on plant and human behavior, sensory capacities, and communication to examine the relationships between and among plant and human communities. It incorporates an analysis of the values and meanings of these relationships for humans and the sensory abilities of plants to respond to human value systems through processes of growth and development. Sensory ethnobotany is historical, focusing on the transformations and continuities of human and plant lived experiences and their relationships over time. How these multispecies relationships become valued or devalued over time and in diverse sociopolitical, socioeconomic, and sociocultural contexts are explored, bringing in a political ecological approach to human–plant encounters. Sensory ethnobotany is therefore an inherently interdisciplinary framework, drawing from anthropology, archaeology, phenomenological philosophy, botany, biology, historical ecology, and political ecology.

As anthropology questions the boundaries between human and plant lives with the plant turn and a planthropology (Myers 2017), so too is plant science questioning long-held assumptions about plant behavior and communication. The burgeoning field of plant behavioral ecology recognizes plant action as "behavior," which was typically seen as exclusive to animals, and explores plant responses to environmental events or changes (Cahill 2015). Recent studies have shown that plants exhibit "perceptual awareness, learned behaviors, and memory" (Gagliano 2015:3; Gagliano et al. 2014), that plants engage in "helping" activities of altruism and cooperation within and between species (Dudley 2015), and that plants can adapt to, communicate through, and alter mycorrhizal networks (Gorzelak et al. 2015). Studies of memory and learning show that plants, as non-neural organisms, have developed other mechanisms of acquiring, remembering, and learning information from their surroundings, such as through calcium signaling in their cells (Gagliano et al. 2014:69–70). Studies of plant communication reveal that plants communicate and interact within and between species through the emission of volatile chemicals and through visual displays involving shapes and colors (Gagliano and Grimonprez 2015:148). Meanwhile, plant kin recognition studies demonstrate the abilities of plants to recognize and respond cooperatively to kin within species through a variety of activities including changing root and stem growth and recognizing specific chemical emissions (Murphy and Dudley 2009; Biedrzycki and Bais 2010; Karban et al. 2014). Overall, plant behavioral ecology recognizes that plants are "highly sensitive organisms that perceive, assess, learn, remember, resolve problems, make decisions, and communicate with each other by actively acquiring information from their environment" (Gagliano 2015:1). The field of sensory ecology, primarily focused on animal behavioral ecology and evolutionary processes (Barth and Schmid 2001; Stevens 2013), also is beginning to include plants into studies of animal sensory capacities and systems (Stevens 2013, 2016).[8] Sensory ethnobotany draws from these recent developments to take into account new understandings of plant awareness, including what a plant knows, sees, smells, feels, hears, and remembers (Chamovitz 2012). It examines the unfolding knowledge of the sensory systems of humans and plants and the value systems associated with human–plant sensory engagements over time in diverse life-worlds.

While multispecies anthropology has been critiqued for a lack of attention to history, politics, and power (Bessire and Bond 2014), sensory ethnobotany focuses on historical processes and acknowledges the importance of power relations and inequalities between and among humans and plants as they emerge over time and space. In a sensory ethnobotany framework, the historical dimensions of human–plant relations and the connections between past and present humans and plants are developed and explored. Moreover, by focusing on the value and meaning of human–plant relationships to humans *and* plants, sensory ethnobotany is inherently a political ecological project, interested in understanding the aesthetic–moral valuation of sensory experiences and the ways in which these valuations shape multispecies social organization, kinship, and sociopolitical approaches to environmental use and management.

Sensory ethnobotany is therefore a dynamic framework, open to change and modification as new developments emerge regarding human and plant sensory capacities, human–plant relationships, and their valuation and transformations over time. It seeks to understand how multispecies lifeworlds have transformed over time and continue to change, particularly from environmental destruction and climatic changes in the Anthropocene (or Planthroposcene). It makes room for the diverse, creative ways that people and plants interact, come together, or push apart. Moreover, sensory ethnobotany allows for creative methods to be employed to come to know or "interview" plants (see Hartigan et al. 2014; Hartigan 2017) — especially by taking seriously Indigenous approaches to plants as kin, lovers, friends, supernatural entities, and mythical figures, as seen in the Canela life-world. Throughout the book, the creative sensory engagements between Canela humans and plants are taken seriously and explored in detail, including through the classification of land, soils, garden spaces, and plants; historical processes of coming to know and care for plants and gardens; traditional knowledge-making practices of educating affection for plants; gendered processes of making kin with plants; and shamanic communication with plants and Plant-People "master spirits."

Seen through a sensory ethnobotany lens, Canela human–plant engagements demonstrate the importance of plants to the sustainability, health, and well-being of human communities, and vice versa. Members of the Canela multispecies community rely on one another and develop sustained engagements in order to create and maintain the strength, happiness, and well-being (known by the Canela terms *ihtỳi* and *impej*) for both people and plants. As Myers (2017:3–4) points out, human futures "hinge on creating livable futures with plants." Plants can be our food, our source of income, our shelter, our comfort, our joy, and sometimes, our kin. Understanding plant-people engagements through sensory ethnobotany allows for a deeper analysis of the ways in which plants can provide human communities new opportunities for resilience to environmental and climatic changes. Resilience is understood here as an open-ended concept with multiple meanings in ecology, sociology, and economics (Brand and Jax 2007) that, overall, recognizes the ability of a socio-ecological system to "absorb disturbance and reorganize while undergoing change" (Walker et al. 2004:5). Yet while some socio-ecological studies of resilience have focused on a system's capacity to remain the same over time in "function, structure, identity, and feedbacks" (Walker et al. 2004:5) despite disturbances, there is also a recognition that "disturbance has the potential to create opportunity for doing new things" (Folke 2006:253). In sensory ethnobotany, resilience is a multispecies endeavor in which people and plants seek to manage and deal with "disturbances" to their socio-ecological worlds while simultaneously recognizing that "new things" can emerge that contribute positively to multispecies health and well-being—including new plant species, new types of gardens, new seed-saving and gardening practices, and new people. For the Canela, resilience can be understood as the expansion and growth of healthy, happy, and well multispecies families made up of diverse plants and people.

Human–plant alliances—made up of families or other types of social relations—are crucial to the Planthroposcene of the future (see Myers 2017). Through the sensory ethnobotany approach put forward throughout this book, the ways in which the Canela are making allies with diverse plants, even as the environment and climate continue to change, become clear. As such, sensory ethnobotany offers a new way forward for understanding human–environment engagements, biodiversity conservation, sustainability, and resilience in Indigenous life-worlds and beyond.

Introducing the Canela People

As a multispecies ethnography, this book includes both the Canela people and their plant kin as ethnographic subjects. The modern-day twenty-first century Canela have emerged as a robust, vibrant community of nearly 3,000 people and at least 300 types of plants living in a legally demarcated territory in the interior of Maranhão State, northeast Brazil (see maps 1, 2; Instituto Socioambiental 2018a).[9] The people speak an Eastern Timbira language within the Macro-Jê language stock, a major language group spoken by Jê Indigenous communities throughout northeast and central Brazil (Rodrigues 1999). The community refer to themselves alternatively as the Canela, an ethnonym originating from local Brazilian authorities, as the Ramkokamekra (literally "people of the tree resin grove"), and as the *mēhĩn*, or "people" in Canela (literally *mē* = plural, *hĩn* = flesh; William Crocker, personal communication; Nimuendajú 1946:12). Non-Indigenous outsiders, including local Brazilians and foreigners, are known by the term *cupēn*, meaning enemies, others, or outsiders, and typically are glossed as "whites" (*brancos/as*) in Portuguese. One of the poorest states in Brazil, Maranhão is home to numerous Indigenous territories, including Jê- and Tupi-Guaraní-speaking groups. Over half of the state belongs to Brazil's "Legal Amazonia" (*Amazônia Legal*) region and includes high, dense forests as well as savannah ecological zones. Along with other northeastern states, Maranhão is becoming a hotspot for industrial agriculture, causing rapid deforestation in both forest and savannah areas. The TI Kanela (*Terra Indígena Kanela*, in Portuguese, or Canela Indigenous Territory) is located in the Cerrado or savannah biome. It includes nine land types that the community categorizes, ranging from dense forests, to scrub-brush savannahs, to sandy *chapadas*. Although it constitutes only around 5 to 10 percent of the lands the Canela originally occupied prior to their "pacification" by non-Indigenous Brazilian settlers in 1814 (Nimuendajú 1946:64; Crocker 1994), the territory includes space for the main concentric circular village of Escalvado and dozens of gardening areas. Contemporary gardeners have developed a two-plot gardening system of maintaining plots in forest and riverbank areas simultaneously to provide a more constant supply of food throughout both the dry and rainy seasons.

The lives of Canela women, men, and children unfold through pathways throughout the territorial landscape, from village, to riverbank garden, to forest garden spaces, and back again. In the village of Escalvado, lives unfold in the concentric circular village layout of the ceremonial center and outer rings of houses. The village itself is divided into western (*pỳt cjêj xà*; "place where the sun sets") and eastern (*pỳt jú pôj xà*; "place where sun rises") sides, with those born into the western side categorized as *impej* (good, beautiful, true/original) and those born into the eastern side as the opposite, *ihkên* (bad, ugly, less true/original). Marriage patterns follow this division, with men from the eastern side marrying western-side women and vice versa. In this way, all Canela families are understood to include both the good and the bad, the beautiful and the ugly, with combined moral–aesthetic connotations (see also chapter 3, "Becoming Strong, Becoming Happy, Becoming Well"). Birth residence dictates membership into different moieties as well, with male moiety membership especially significant to sociopolitical and ceremonial activities throughout the annual ritual cycle (see Crocker 1990: 193–206; Miller 2015:119–125).

The village is also divided into gendered spaces—the outer rings of houses, which are considered female, and the male ceremonial village center. As a matrilocal community, women own the houses and are connected to their birth residences throughout their lives, either living with their mothers as adults or building their own houses nearby. Young boys remain in their mother's home until they are married, when they move into their wife's mother's home. Women's work and familial relationships are paramount in the matrilocal houses, where the primarily female activities of raising and caring for human infants and children, saving and caring for seeds and plant cuttings that are considered infants, and preparing and cooking food take place. Increasingly, women are giving birth at a younger age and having more children that reach adulthood than in the past (see Greene and Crocker 1994). A woman typically has her first child around fourteen to fifteen years old and has, on average, four to five children throughout her lifetime. With a growing population, there are now nearly three rings of houses encircling the ceremonial center (only one existed when the village was originally built in 1972). Houses range in style from the more traditional with thatched buriti-palm roof and walls, to an increasingly common thatched-roof and homemade adobe brick walls style, to houses made entirely of homemade adobe or even store-bought brick in the style of the non-Indigenous *cupēn*. Whatever the exterior appearance, houses typically are constructed as one large room where families of a woman, her husband, their daughters and sons-in-law, and grandchildren live together. At dawn and dusk, people start their days chatting behind or in front of the house before going about their daily activities, including working in the gardens. Families eat the evening meal inside or behind the house before settling in to sleep on sleeping mats woven from buriti palm fibers or in hammocks (a custom associated with Tupi-Guaraní groups). In charge of the cleaning, cooking, and childcare, women organize the households and strive to create spaces where happiness, health, and strength (encompassed in the Canela term *ihtỳi*) abound.

Radial pathways connect the outer rings of feminine houses to the inner masculine ceremonial center, in characteristic Timbira village organization (Azanha 1984). In the village ceremonial center, men form the leadership council that runs sociopolitical and ritual affairs, including organizing ritual festivities, communal work activities, occasional hunting trips (much less common than in the past); deciding cases of inter-familial justice such as divorce; and liaising with outsiders, including officials from the National Indian Foundation (*Fundação Nacional do Índio*; FUNAI), missionaries, and anthropologists. The exclusively male leadership council consists of all older men who are around forty years of age and above and is led by a chief (*pàhi* in Canela; *chefe* in Portuguese), between one and three vice-chiefs (*vice-chefes*), and the *pró-khãmmã*, a group of male elders belonging to the Lower moiety age set (Crocker 1990:369, 375). Those born into the Upper moiety age set can never form part of the *pró-khãmmã* group, just as women cannot participate in the leadership council as a whole. Although the concentric circular village is a hierarchical space where different power dynamics unfold, overall it is considered *impej* and essential for the survival and well-being of Canela individuals, families, and the life-world as a whole.

In addition to the village space, contemporary Canela women's, men's, and children's lives unfold in forest and riverbank garden plots. Although Canela subsistence livelihoods were more focused on hunting and gathering prior to sustained contact with non-Indigenous settlers in the early nineteenth century, over the past half century gardening has become the primary subsistence activity. Riverbank and forest gardens are considered complementary spaces that are both integral to the modern-day Canela life-world. Adult male and female couples typically are considered the joint owners of garden plots, yet women maintain the use rights of the plot upon the couple's separation or divorce. The locations of plots, especially in forest areas, are therefore usually passed down from mother to daughter. Through a gendered division of labor, women and men work together to maintain riverbank and forest gardens and care for their growing crops, whom they consider children. Along with the village space, complementary forest and riverbank garden spaces are also crucial to the well-being of contemporary Canela people and plants. In this book, I follow the lives of Canela women, men, and children and their relational pathways with one another and various nonhumans, especially plants, in village and garden spaces throughout the territorial landscape.

Introducing the Expert Gardeners

Certain individual people and plants form the backbone of this multispecies ethnography of the Canela life-world. Women form an integral part of this ethnography, since they are the primary caretakers of seed and plant cutting infants and growing crop children. Liliana[10] is a key actor—as an expert gardener, she is an authoritative voice on Canela gardening, agro-biodiversity maintenance, crop childcare, and human and plant well-being. Liliana loves her garden and the plants growing there. Each morning, she rises before dawn to visit her biodiverse plant kin in her gardens. Like all Canela subsistence gardeners, Liliana's crops are her children who need care and affection from their gardener parents through ongoing, intimate multi-sensory encounters. Since I first met Liliana and other Canela community members in 2011, they have shared with me their gardening expertise, complex eco-logical knowledge, and love for plant kin. As my adoptive mother, Liliana has housed, fed, cared for, and taught me as she has done with her three Ca-nela daughters. Literate in Portuguese and Canela, Liliana has experience working with outsiders. She participated for many years in anthropologist William Crocker's (2007) Canela diary program, which spanned five decades (1966–2013) and involved community members sending written and audio transcripts of their recollections of daily life (in Canela and Portuguese) to Crocker at the Smithsonian National Museum of Natural History in Wash-ington, DC. Liliana and her husband, João Miguel, maintain a household on the western side of the village with their daughter, Aline, her husband, Davi, and their eight children. From April 2012 to March 2013, and again during a visit in November 2017, I lived with the family of twelve in their thatched-roof house. Their other adult daughters, Nilda and Joaquina, live with their hus-bands and children in separate houses directly behind Liliana's in the second circle of village houses. Behind Liliana's house is a large outdoor cookhouse (a thatched-roof structure without walls) where the women of the family gather to prepare food, including the staple *farinha* (toasted manioc flour), and manioc–meat *beribu* pies reserved for ritual occasions. Animals wan-der in and out of Liliana's house, with chickens living in a corner inside the house and pigs snuffling around for food scraps near the cookhouse. In be-tween the cookhouse and her daughters' houses is Liliana's backyard garden, where she experiments with new crop species and varieties and maintains her favorite types of maize, beans, and squash. In addition to these village spaces, Liliana and her husband maintain large, biodiverse forest and river-bank plots that are adjacent to those of her daughters and sons-in-law. Lili-ana and her family members feature large in this ethnography, as they have much to teach about Canela gardening and human–plant engagements.

Liliana's sister Camila, another expert gardener within the community, is also a key actor. Camila lives next door to Liliana in her own family house with her husband, Wilmar, her classificatory mother (mother's sister), Belém, and her three adult daughters, sons-in-law, and grandchildren. Her situa-tion is unique in that both her husband and one of her sons-in-law are often traveling outside the Canela territory—Wilmar works for the FUNAI office in Barra do Corda, and her son-in-law Adriano is a college-educated politi-cal leader who ran for vice-mayor in the municipal elections in October 2012. Camila therefore runs her household and garden plots largely by herself and often visits them alone. Her unmarried children and grandchildren attend the local primary school and therefore visit the gardens less frequently than the adults do. With houses side by side, Camila and Liliana share everything from gardening advice, to seeds and plant cuttings, to beds for their children and grandchildren, who often swap houses for an evening. The closeness of these sisters' families is not unusual for the Canela, since one's mother and mother's sister are both called "mother" (*inxê* or *nàa*), and one's mother's sister's children are known as "siblings" (*khyê*).[11] Through these joint matrilocal families, women typically develop close relationships with one another and the female children in the family, passing on valuable knowledge such as gardening techniques and practices. Together, Liliana and her two sisters, Camila and Marlena, learned much of their gardening knowledge from their maternal family, including their grandparents, their classificatory mother Belém, and her husband Jacinto. In addition to living family members, Liliana and Camila's deceased relatives also play a role in this ethnography. These include their grandmother, Manuela Célia, who passed down seeds and gardening knowledge; their classificatory grandparent (a close relative), Dirceu, who was born a man, developed shamanic abilities and became a woman through embodied gendered activities and dress in their old age (see chapter 3, "Gendering Gardening: Traditions and Transgressions"); and their father, Paulo Eduardo, who was a well-known shaman with transformational abilities. Dirceu's experience of becoming a woman through dress and activities, especially saving and caring for seed infants, is a fascinating example of a rare transgression of the binary male and female gendered categories that become mapped onto embodied Canela gardening knowledge and human–plant relationships.[12]

While the central role of women to Canela plant caretaking is highlighted throughout the book, there are also many male key actors. The elder Fernando features prominently. He is an expert gardener with long-standing experience working with government officials and anthropologists, including William Crocker (1990). Literate in Canela and Portuguese, Fernando initially approached me in July 2011 with a desire to document Canela gardening knowledge and ethnobotanical classification (see chapter 4, "Categorizing Plants: Sensory Pleasures"). Fernando wears many hats—that of expert gardener, anthropological researcher, lead singer in ritual activities, and male elder who represents the Canela through travel outside the community. Fernando's initiative, hard work, and eloquence stand out and make him an ideal spokesperson to expound on the intricacies of Canela human and plant lives. Fernando lives in his wife Geralda's family home in the second circle of houses on the western side, along with their adult daughters, sons-in-law, and grandchildren.

Renato is another male key actor, known for his knowledge of Canela landscape management and his work outside the community. Fluent in Portuguese and Canela, Renato has lived in the nearby town of Barra do Corda and even served as a council member (*vereador*) in the local municipality of Fernando Falcão from 2000 to 2004. Having taken courses on environmental management and conservation, he is concerned over the environmental threats facing the Canela territory, including increasing instances of illegal logging and the expanding eucalyptus plantation near the territory, which has grown at least three times in size since its initial creation in 2011–2012. Unlike most Canela who have one or two different spouses throughout their lives, Renato has seven ex-wives (at last count in 2017) and therefore frequently moves between his mother's and his latest wife's household. Each time he has separated from a wife, she has maintained ownership over the forest and riverbank garden plots they maintained together. In 2012, for example, Renato had recently moved into his new wife's home in the outermost ring of houses on the village's eastern side. As the new son-in-law to his wife's family, he was responsible for demarcating the forest garden plots and assisting with the planting and harvesting in forest, riverbank, and backyard gardens. Younger than Fernando and Liliana, Renato often deferred to their expertise during our group meetings discussing the Canela life-world.

The group meetings also involved Wander, a man who is well versed in working with anthropologists and holds political sway in the male leadership council. His wife Vilma's home is in the first ring of houses on the western side and in 2013 was the only one in the main circle made entirely out of store-bought bricks in the *cupēn* style. These types of houses were becoming more common by 2017, but Wander was one of the first to embrace this style (and to have acquired enough funds through relationships with outsiders to purchase the bricks). Together, Liliana, Fernando, Renato, Wander, and I compiled the ethnobotanical lists of cultivated crop and native plant species and varieties found in appendices A and B through regular group meetings and periodic meetings and interviews with other Canela community members.

Leandro is another man who figures prominently as the elder expert storyteller. Leandro, who died in 2018 at about 95 years of age, worked with William Crocker throughout his fieldwork (1957 to 2011), including participating in the diary program (Crocker 2007). While I worked one-on-one with Leandro in 2012 and 2013, he recounted to me dozens of mythical–historical stories in Portuguese and Canela that feature throughout the book, including the mythical story of Star-Woman (Caxêtikwỳj), who introduced horticulture and biodiversity maintenance to the Canela community. Leandro's insight into the mythical and historical past is invaluable to understanding the transformations in Canela livelihoods over the past two hundred years of sustained contact with non-Indigenous outsiders.

While these six people—and their spouses, children, grandchildren, parents, grandparents, and other kin relations—are the key actors, many other Canela women and men feature throughout the book. In total, fifty Canela people took part in the interviews and surveys for this book during fieldwork conducted in July 2011, from April 2012 to March 2013, and in November 2017. I conducted ethnographic and ethnobotanical fieldwork using the qualitative and quantitative methods of participant observation, formal and informal interviewing, ethnobiological free listing (G. Martin 2004; Quinlan 2005), and ethnobotanical surveying. I consider anthropological fieldwork, and multispecies fieldwork in particular, to be a phenomenological exercise of following the unfolding pathways of Canela people and plants as they move throughout the territorial landscape. Similar to Veronica Stang's (2009:13) work with the Mehinaku of the Upper Xingu, my aim is to understand the phenomenological "flow of a person's experience." Yet as a multispecies ethnography, this book focuses on the "flows" or pathways of human *and* plant lives in the unfolding Canela life-world.

Introducing the Plant Kin

Through a sensory ethnobotany approach, in this book I follow the pathways of myriad Canela plants, including particular plant species and varieties that are key actors along with their human counterparts. From 2011–2017, my research assistants have identified 320 named plant kin living in the Canela territorial landscape. Of these, 266 are considered cultivated crop varieties belonging to at least 45 species, and 54 are categorized as native plants. Canela plant varieties are understood here as the "the smallest unit of perception and management of agricultural diversity" that receives a specific name and is the "object of a set of practices and knowledge" (Emperaire and Peroni 2007:763). While all plants are integral to the multispecies community, certain species and varieties emerge in key roles throughout this ethnography. The eight types of maize play key roles in their own ritual planting, growing, and harvest festivals, as do the fifteen types of sweet potato, eight types of squash, and other vined crops in the Hôxwa (literally "sharp pointed leaf") harvest festival. The seven types of sweet, nine types of bitter, and two types of half-sweet/half-bitter manioc, which are respectively categorized as feminine, masculine, and a blurred gender category of half-female/half-male, are crucial to understanding Canela multispecies gender and sexuality. Eighteen yam varieties display the importance of plant intentionality in the life-world, with two yam chiefs and four vice-chiefs leading and organizing the yam community in the garden space. Peanuts demonstrate the embodied connections among human gardener parents and crop children through the ritual restrictions gardener parents must follow while peanut children are growing. The twenty-eight types of rice display how crops introduced a century ago can multiply and become incorporated as authentically part of the Canela life-world, as can more recently introduced cultivated fruits such as banana, mango, watermelon, and papaya. Meanwhile, the fifteen types of gourd and two cotton varieties demonstrate the ways in which Canela coming to know cultivated crops can be lost over time if not maintained. And more than any other crop, the fifty-two types of *pànkrỳt* beans show the loving, affectionate parent–child relationships that develop between human gardeners and their bean seed infants as they are named, sorted, and saved.

Following the pathways of these plants as they entangle with one another and with their human caretakers leads to interesting explorations of multi-species love, kinship, friendship, and intentional capacities. The pathways of the yam chiefs anaconda yam (*krẽrô tekãjkãj/rorti*) and electric eel yam (*krẽrô pỳp-re*), for example, lead to comparisons of Canela human and plant animacy and social organization. The pathway of true/original maize (*põhy pej-re*) leads to the mythical figure of Star-Woman, the original Canela gardening expert who is beautiful, good, and true/original (*impej*), characteristics that this type of maize also espouses. The pathway of Guajajara tree bean (*pàt juhtõi-re pàrà-re/pryjĩ*) leads outside the Canela territorial landscape to the neighboring Tupi-Guaraní Guajajara group, from whom this varietal originates. Meanwhile, the pathway of red child fava bean (*pànkrỳt ahkrare caprêc-re*) leads to the loving, affectionate caretaking of human gardener parents for this aesthetically pleasing and much-adored seed. While these pathways may seem disparate, all are connected through an emergent "meshwork" (Ingold 2008) across time and space that includes and encompasses yams, garden layouts, maize, supernatural entities, other Indigenous peoples, beans, and Canela gardeners. Moreover, the Canela life-world orders and makes sense of these enmeshed entanglements through a focus on multispecies kinship and care. A sensory ethnobotany approach that focuses on the lived experiences of myriad humans, plants, and other non-humans allows for an untangling of the meshwork threads to explore the Canela life-world in both its messiness and order.

Following the Pathways of This Book

The pathways of the Canela life-world are entangled and interconnected over time and space, and each chapter of this book approaches a distinct set of relational pathways that together form the unfolding bio-sociocultural life-world. Chapter 1 follows the ethical–aesthetic pathways of valuing the changing landscape in the Brazilian Cerrado. It also explores the ways in which these distinct pathways form a life-world that unfolds in dualistic and triadic ways. As the Cerrado faces ongoing environmental destruction and climatic changes in the Anthropocene, the contemporary Canela continue to engage with and come to know their diverse territorial landscape. Canela women and men value the myriad eco-regions and soil types in their territory and seek out intimate, perceptual engagements with the land over time and in distinct spaces. Drawing from phenomenological approaches to the concepts of "aesthetics" and "landscape," in the chapter I put forward a Canela aesthetics of landscape through which certain human–environment perceptual relationships are aesthetically–ethically valued and made meaningful. These pathways of ethical–aesthetic value, I maintain, provide a way forward to approach environmental and climatic changes in the disappearing Cerrado biome. Chapter 2 follows the historical pathways of transformation and change in human–environment engagements that have created the modern-day life-world. In it, I examine how the Canela have come to classify, work with, and love a two-garden system of forest and riverbank garden plots. By exploring over two centuries of sustained contact with various non-Indigenous people (including Brazilians and foreigners), the pathways that have led to significant transformations of Canela lifeways become clear. Yet while the shift in Canela subsistence livelihoods—from semi-nomadic hunter–gatherers with intermittent gardening to subsistence horticulturalists with large, biodiverse gardens—is a result of structural violence from the outside, the modern-day love of gardens and gardening practices has become an authentically Canela way of understanding and becoming in the emergent life-world.

The modern-day love of garden spaces also entails loving and affectionately caring for the plants growing there. In chapter 3, the affectionate pathways of learning and knowing among people and plants are explored. I examine the ways in which elder and expert Canela gardeners, female and male, teach the younger generations how to affectionately nurture and care for crops, who are considered children. I maintain that through an embodied, gendered education of affection, Canela women and men are able to teach girls and boys how to "become with" (Haraway 2008) plants, the essence of successful gardening knowledge or knowing. Girls and boys learn how to engage perceptually with plants, who are intentional subjects, through everyday gendered gardening practices and ritual activities, including singing, food sharing, and food and sexual prohibitions that connect human and plant lives. These activities underscore and engender the multispecies kinship relationships among humans and plants as they live and grow with one another in forest and riverbank garden spaces. Moreover, these activities support human and plant happiness, strength, health (*ihtỳi*), and processes of becoming good, beautiful, true/original (*impej*), and holistically well.

Chapter 4 further explores these caring multispecies kinship relationships through an examination of the classificatory pathways of noticing, naming, sorting, and saving plant children. By focusing on the intimate perceptual engagements among human gardeners, seed and plant cutting infants, and plant children, the Canela are approaching ethnobotanical classification as a key aspect of crop childcare. As the environment and climate of the Cerrado continue to change, Canela gardeners are looking for new forms of crop childcare. The written ethnobotanical lists that Liliana, Fernando, Renato, Wander, and I created along with other gardeners are one such innovative form of contemporary crop childcare. While the practices and materials involving in list making originate from the outside, Canela gardeners are valuing and incorporating the lists into their highly transformational life-world on their own terms. These are living lists (Miller 2016), dynamic and open to new and changing human–environment engagements that are noticed, named, and categorized. The open-ended list making is another way that the multispecies love between Canela people and plants is manifesting itself and can provide new support for the survival and well-being of Canela multispecies families in the threatened Cerrado biome.

While understanding the pathways of gardener–crop engagements is integral to an examination of the transformational Canela life-world, other human–plant encounters also unfold in the Canela territorial landscape. In chapter 5, I follow the shamanic pathways of friendship, seduction, and danger with plants and their master spirits. Unlike the consanguinal parent-child engagements of gardeners and crops, shamans engage with plants and their master spirits in embodied and gendered ways as friends, lovers, and masters of dangerous elements. The relationships that predominantly male shamans develop with plants and Plant-People master spirits, I maintain, mirror human social relationships. Male shamans serve as friends and confidants to growing plants, as formal friends (*hapĩn*) to Plant-Men master spirits, and as "other husbands" (*mẽ mpyên-nõ*) to Plant-Women master spirits, who are similar to Canela human "other wives" (*mẽ prõ-nõ*). With heightened perceptual abilities that enable shamanic communication with and care for plants and Plant People master spirits, shamans serve as mediators between gardeners and plants and support human and plant well-being. Shamanic care for plants, while unfolding through distinct pathways, is therefore as crucial to the continuation of the unfolding Canela life-world as gardener–crop relationships are. I conclude the book with speculation on the multispecies futures that are possible for Canela people and plants in the Anthropocene. Through a sensory ethnobotany approach, I maintain that the ways that people and plants mitigate biodiversity loss and strive to maintain caring relationships becomes clear. While certain plants and landscapes may be drastically altered by environmental destruction and climate change, the ways in which Canela people and plants pay attention to, come to know, and care for one another provide ways to support multispecies survival and well-being. Although many futures could emerge through the speculative anthropology of climate change (see Whitington 2013:324–325), Canela multispecies resilience is possible—an outcome of loving and caring for plant kin in an unfolding world.

CHAPTER ONE

Tracing Indigenous Landscape Aesthetics in the Changing Cerrado

We have to preserve . . . now we are learning and seeing—look,
we have to keep planting and cultivating for our generation and the
future . . . In this way, people are remembering and planting . . .
We shall see.
—Fernando, May 2012

For the Indigenous Canela, the environment consists of a series of relational pathways that unfold between and among myriad human and nonhuman beings. These pathways and the value placed on them change over time, resulting from shifting sociocultural and ecological forms. "Preserving" ecological knowledge, as Fernando's above quote indicates, is grounded in shifting human–environment entanglements and subsistence patterns. No longer semi-nomadic hunter–gatherers with small garden plots as they were at the beginning of the twentieth century, the contemporary Canela primarily engage with the environment and landscape as sedentary subsistence horticulturalists. "Remembering and planting" and therefore valuing cultivated crops is becoming increasingly important to Canela understandings of and engagements with the environment or landscape. In this chapter, I examine the ethical and aesthetic value that the modern-day Canela place on the environment or landscape. In it, I put forward a phenomenological approach to landscape aesthetics that considers the emergent nature of the environment or landscape and the ways in which multi-sensory experiences among humans and nonhumans unfold to inform ethical and aesthetic value of the landscape. Tracing a Canela landscape aesthetic leads to an exploration of the Canela life-world as a whole and how it unfolds in dualistic and triadic ways. By integrating a phenomenological approach into structuralist studies of dualisms and triads in Jê-speaking communities, I maintain that the shape of the Canela life-world, including its dualistic and triadic patterns, emerges in new and interesting ways.

Understanding the environment or landscape as an unfolding, mutable series of human–nonhuman relationships helps inform an analysis of socio-ecological change in the Brazilian Cerrado, which is experiencing rapid rates of environmental destruction and likely will bear the brunt of further climatic changes in the Anthropocene. As the traditional and current homeland of the Indigenous Canela, the Cerrado and its changes have direct impacts on Canela engagement with and valuation of their dynamic life-world. With these socio-ecological realities of the changing Cerrado in mind, I describe what the Indigenous Canela aesthetics of landscape looks like in the twenty-first century. This includes an exploration of how the Canela classify and manage the nine eco-regions and ten soil types in their territory and how they are dealing with increasing environmental threats and destruction. I conclude with a discussion of resilience, namely what it means to live with, come to know, and value landscapes and human–environment engagements while experiencing ongoing environmental change. The Canela are already practicing multispecies resilience with their nonhuman counterparts, I maintain, by recognizing the continuity and dynamism of their landscape aesthetics and of the emergent life-world as a whole. In the rapidly changing Cerrado, this resilience is crucial to human and nonhuman survival and well-being.

Tracing a Canela Aesthetics of Land

Tracing a Canela landscape aesthetics involves engaging with phenomenological theoretical approaches to human (and nonhuman) interactions with and valuation of the land. Similar to phenomenological theory, especially that of Tim Ingold (2000, 2007a, b, 2012) and Vergunst et al. (2012), Canela understandings of an aesthetics of landscape focus on the unfolding processes of myriad human and nonhuman encounters that are valued and made meaningful over time in various territorial spaces. Phenomenological approaches typically focus on the environment or landscape as an emergent concept formed by ongoing human (and nonhuman) activity, namely embodied perceptual experiences. Indeed, in phenomenology, embodied perception holds the key to understanding the emergent world; as Maurice Merleau-Ponty pointed out ([1947] 1974:197), perception located in the body is the foundation of "all rationality, all value, and all existence." Moreover, through embodied perceptual experiences humans (and nonhumans) experience "how the world becomes a world" (Merleau-Ponty 1964:181). Philosopher Martin Heidegger ([1971] 2001:149, 178) similarly theorized the emergence of the world in terms of constantly "worlding" and gathering humans and nonhumans through processes of "dwelling" or "presencing" with the worlding world (see also Vergunst et al. 2012:3). Drawing from Heidegger, Vergunst et al. (2012:3) reject the traditional Western artistic approach to landscape as an "object of study" and examine landscape as a "way of reckoning—summing up—the temporal, relational qualities of the world." For Ingold, landscape is a "domain of entanglement" between and among humans and nonhumans, which are defined not as static entities but rather as "loc[i] of growth within a field of relations traced out in flows of materials" (Ingold 2006:14, 2013:8, 10–11). In this view, humans and non-humans are best understood by their active, relational processes—what they do and become over time. They are "biosocial becomings," emerging along certain "trajectories of movement and growth" (Ingold 2013:8–9; Ingold and Pálsson 2013; Pálsson 2013:27–28). The Canela similarly understand humans, nonhumans, and their environment as constantly becoming and co-constituting through multi-sensory, embodied relationships with myriad people, plants, animals, objects, and supernatural entities.

In a similar vein, rather than viewing the landscape as an external object to be visually observed and evaluated, Canela community members recognize their role in creating, shaping, and being part of the landscape through embodied, multi-sensory engagements. As Ingold (2012:197–198) points out, the term "landscape" originates from the Old English *landskap*, with *-skap* meaning "to shape," and is therefore situated in the historical context of the Medieval agrarian way of life. He argues that the term "earthy-sky-world" is more appropriate for describing the experiences of nomadic pastoralists and hunter–gatherers in their shifting surroundings (Ingold 2012:199). Yet for the modern-day Canela who are now subsistence horticulturalists, understanding landscape as "land shaped" is appropriate to explore how Canela people are shaping and creating the land in new and creative ways.

As the Canela engage with and shape the land, certain perceptual encounters between and among humans and nonhumans become meaningful and are appreciated for their beauty, morality, and originality—encompassed in the Canela term *impej*. Aesthetics in this sense is grounded in multi-sensory perceptual experiences, a focus that can be found in phenomenological approaches to perception and in aesthetic systems throughout the Amazon. In the phenomenological approach to perception that Ingold (2000:166–167) puts forward, beings, objects, or events are perceived for what they "afford" to human and nonhuman perceivers. Drawing from Gibson's ecological theory of perception, an "affordance" in this sense means what the environment offers or provides to the perceiver, with environment and perceiver existing in complementarity with one another (Gibson [1986] 2015:119–120). Meanwhile, Eduardo Kohn (2002, 2007, 2013) offers an approach to perception that is grounded in Peircean semiotic theory. In this approach, there is a focus on relationality and communication among humans and nonhumans, with the Amazonian environment consisting of a collection of human and nonhuman "selves" who engage in mindful and empathetic encounters (Kohn 2007:4). For Kohn, aesthetics is understood as a "system that attaches particular values to experience in ways that affect experience" (Kohn 2002: 70, 72). I draw from these approaches, and particularly Kohn's definition of Amazonian aesthetics, to understand Canela aesthetics as an ongoing series of relational, multi-sensory pathways between and among humans and non-humans that are subsequently valued and made meaningful by humans and nonhumans.

This working understanding of Canela aesthetics has a clear moral and ethical component, with certain moral and ethical valuation tied to particular perceptual experiences. Indeed, aesthetic experiences and ethical or moral values often are bound up together in Indigenous life-worlds. In Indigenous lowland South American communities, aesthetic and moral values are linked together in understandings of conviviality or "living well" (Overing and Passes 2000b), including the promotion of aesthetically pleasing and morally good social organization, village layout, individual embodied experiences and performances, and individual and communal work, among other concepts. For example, the Brazilian Kayapó connect aesthetic and moral value to bodily cleanliness, and an unclean or dirty body is understood as "aesthetically unbecoming, actively antisocial and even dangerous" to the individual and entire community (Turner 1995:149). Meanwhile, the Paraguayan Nivaclé tie together aesthetic value and morality in their understandings of village layout and embodied knowledge. Clean village paths are conceived as "aesthetic places" and their maintenance is integral to Nivaclé morality, with beauty of the path and the person linked to bodily knowledge of how to work together to maintain aesthetic–moral places in the community (Grant 2012:74–75, 78). In the Canela life-world, aesthetic and ethical–moral values also closely correspond. Aesthetic appreciation and moral goodness are connected in particular Canela human–nonhuman bodily experiences, work patterns (especially working in the gardens), and village and garden spaces throughout the territorial landscape.

A phenomenological aesthetics of landscape recognizes that aesthetics and ethics are integral to understanding the landscape, particularly when examining diverse communities' understandings of how land should be shaped and "bound up with ideas of appropriate relations and actions" (Vergunst et al. 2012:9). For Vergunst et al. (2012: 8), the "aesthetics of landscape" is "grounded in relations with landscape . . . closer both to the embodied person and to the flows of sociality within which they are living." This understanding includes a focus on the "folding" and unfolding practices that emerge through and in the landscape. That is, there is an emphasis on processes of landscape modification and change within complex human–environment systems and on the potentiality or immanence of engagements with the landscape and aesthetic–ethic valuation of such experiences. Taking this one step further to incorporate nonhumans (who may well be understood as "persons" in some contexts), the Canela aesthetics of landscape is understood here as a way of approaching the world in which notions of value flow from aesthetic–ethic embodied perceptual engagements between and among humans and nonhumans within and through the ever-unfolding landscape. For the Canela, the aesthetics of landscape is the primary way in which diverse humans and nonhumans approach and make sense of the life-world as it unfolds through complex and transformative processes.

Understanding the Canela Bio-Sociocultural Life-World

To live is to radiate.
—Canguilhem ([1965] 2008:113–114)

Canela landscape aesthetics emerges in an unfolding life-world composed of myriad people, plants, animals, supernatural entities, land types, village and garden spaces, and soils. The bio-sociocultural life-world of Canela humans, cultivated plants, and a variety of other beings consists of pathways on and through which humans and nonhumans grow, change, and live their intertwined lives. A life-world (or "meshwork" in Ingold's work [2007a, 2008]) is understood here as composed of various relational pathways between and among humans and nonhumans that unfold over time and in distinct places. This is a similar conceptualization as Georges Canguilhem's ([1965] 2008: 111–112) "milieu," which he understands as a dynamic "debate" between living organism and milieu, in that the living "makes the milieu for itself; it composes its milieu." In this view, a flexible "suppleness" of movement between organism and milieu are what constitute a "good" life, or what the Canela understand as being or becoming *impej*. The milieu, or life-world as it is understood here, takes shape by humans and nonhumans "radiating" along their developmental pathways (Canguilhem [1965] 2008:113–114). Gardening has become the quintessential relational pathway between Canela humans and nonhumans, as human gardener parents and crop children interact, care for, and support the strength and happiness of one another over time and in diverse spaces. Over time and across space, these diverse beings become embedded or "dwell" in the life world, in order "to make one's way through the world and make oneself at home in it" (Vergunst et al. 2012:3). Understood in this way, the Canela life-world is dynamic and transformational and is never wholly complete. While certain dualistic and triadic pathways have emerged as part of this life-world, as explored below, they continue to transform and change over time along with the myriad human and nonhuman beings that make up the emergent life-world.

Within the world that is continually coming into being, life processes of growth and decomposition are similarly emergent. Indigenous worldviews often emphasize the emergence of life (and death). For the Cree of North America, life is considered a "continuous birth" (Scott 1989:195). Similar understandings can be found throughout lowland South America, where processes of living and being alive are often understood as open and available to myriad beings that may not be included as "alive" in a Western framework (Praet 2013:192–193). For the Canela, life is understood not as a given state of being but rather as emergent through ongoing embodied effort on the part of humans and nonhumans. These "animist ontologies," as they are sometimes called, reflect an understanding of life "not as an emanation but a generation of being" (Ingold 2011:68–69). Yet "animist" understandings of life are often restricted and conditional, available by degrees of "animacy" that are hierarchically distributed among beings (see Praet 2013). Hierarchical animism, or a "scalar view" of animacy (Nuckolls 2010), can be found throughout Indigenous life-worlds and particularly in the Canela case. Canela "scalar animacy" hierarchically arranges the animacy or intentionality of living and deceased Canela (mẽhĩn) people, non-Indigenous white (cupẽn) people, animals, plants, Plant-People master spirits, other supernatural entities, and objects and artifacts. All of these beings and their interactions with one another make up the emergent life-world and possess varying degrees of life or animacy that change over time through processes of birth, growth, and decomposition or death. Unlike many other Indigenous communities in lowland South America and beyond, however, the Canela do not base their understandings of the living or animate on a shared "spirit" or "soul," as explored in chapter 5. Rather, the Canela understanding of life is similar to a phenomenological one—grounded in the active, embodied perceptual activities and capabilities of diverse humans and nonhumans while dwelling in the earth.

As the life processes of humans and nonhumans unfold in the Canela life-world, they are often conceptually organized in dualistic and triadic ways. Indeed, organizing the life-world in dualisms and triads is found among many

Jê-speaking communities. Studying Jê dualisms informed many twentieth-century ethnographies of groups such as the Xavante, Krahô, and Krĩkatí (see Maybury-Lewis 1967, 1979b; Lave 1979; Melatti 1979), and whether these dualisms formed triads initiated a well-known debate in structural anthropology between David Maybury-Lewis and Claude Lévi-Strauss. This debate was grounded in two contrasting approaches to Jê dualisms: that of Maybury-Lewis (1960, 1979c, 1989), who viewed oppositional pairs as "ideologically timeless and primordial" (Ewart 2013:22–23), and that of Lévi-Strauss (1963, 1995), who understood Jê binaries as inherently unstable and transformational and, therefore, open to forming triads. Through a structural anthropological approach, Lévi-Strauss (1963:151–152) maintained that Jê "concentric dualisms" formed "implicit triadisms," and in his later work expanded on the fluidity of dualisms into triads with his concept of "dynamic disequilibrium" (Lévi-Strauss 1995:63). The conceptualization of inherent triads in Jê dualisms is analytically robust from both a structural and phenomenological perspective, as it focuses on how conceptual systems change and transform over time. Moreover, conceptual dualisms transforming into triads is part of the lived experience of many Jê peoples. For example, for the Panará, the more "traditional" dual opposition between moieties in the ceremonial village center has shifted focus to an opposition between the young and the old in the village and between the Panará (*panará*, meaning "people") and Brazilian national society (*hipe*) (Ewart 2013:82). Together, these dualisms overlap and form a triadic structure of oppositional pairs within the village (young versus old, village center versus periphery) and that which lies beyond the "edge of the village," or the larger Brazilian society (Ewart 2013:235).

Many dualisms and triads shape the Canela life-world, as Crocker (1990: 183–193, 325–328) has explored. For the modern-day Canela, similar dualisms and triads as the Panará in relation to Brazilian national society and the territorial landscape have emerged. There is a key conceptual opposition between the *mēhĩn* ("people"; literally plural "us/we" + "flesh"), which refers to the Canela and other Timbira communities, and *cupēn* ("enemy, other, whites"), which refers to non-Indigenous Brazilians and foreigners. This opposition extends beyond living bodies to deceased "souls" that have distinct characteristics—the *mēkarõ* of the *mēhĩn* and the *pehjarohti* of the *cupēn* (see chapter 5). Understood as unequal, hierarchical, and fraught with violence, the *mēhĩn–cupēn* opposition maps onto living bodies, deceased souls, and the landscape. A triadic understanding of the landscape emerges, with village and riverbank spaces conceived as safer and more *mēhĩn*, forest gardens and forested eco-regions understood as more ambiguous spaces where both Canela and white people and souls spend time, and neighboring towns as the dangerous spaces where *cupẽn* people reside. Other overlapping dualisms forming triads also inform the Canela territorial landscape. The village ceremonial center and outer circles of houses are a dualistic pair, as are forest and riverbank gardens. When overlapped, a triadic relation emerges of village–riverbank garden–forest garden (see chapter 2, "Loving Forest and Riverbank Gardens in the Twenty-First Century," and diagram 4). This is similar to the triadic relationship among the central village circle or "cleared ground," the "peripheral waste land," and the surrounding environment or "virgin land" that Lévi-Strauss (1963:151–152) outlines. Yet unlike Lévi-Strauss's abstraction of "waste" and "virgin" lands, the Canela triad of village–riverbank garden–forest garden is a living landscape that is constantly used, managed, and maintained by humans and nonhumans. Other Canela dualisms and triads reflect living, embodied, perceptual experiences among humans and nonhumans. Dualistic *impej* and *ihkên* crop classification is a result of mythical, historical, and present-day engagements with crops, as are their transformations into triads of good, best, and regular yams; of good, bad, and worst manioc; and of good, bad, and regular crops in general (see chapter 4, "Noticing and Naming: Classifying Through Multisensory Experiences," and table 5).

Looking at Canela and other Jê dualisms and triads as a series of living experiences between and among humans and nonhumans can deepen an understanding of these life-worlds and how they unfold over time. While Lévi-Strauss (1963) long ago identified the transformational nature of Jê dualisms and triads, grappling with the dynamism of Jê life-worlds continues to be explored. Ewart (2013:235), for example, underscores the ways in which the dual organization of the Panará village is not static but rather the result of an ongoing process of construction as people build, modify, and tear down houses. Gardening also is considered an ongoing process of "making" garden plots and Panará people that are aesthetically–ethically valued (Ewart 2005). Despite this focus on process, Ewart maintains that Jê communities are focused on "being" rather than "becoming," and that "complexity lies in the social organization of what *is* the physically inhabited world" (Ewart 2013: 238; original emphasis). This structural approach obscures the phenomenological lived experiences of humans and nonhumans making and growing dynamic life-worlds. Instead, I maintain that what "*is* the physically inhabited world" is itself constantly unfolding and becoming through and alongside myriad human and nonhuman life pathways. In this view, the makeup of Jê life-worlds and their dualistic and triadic forms unfolds through intertwined biological and sociocultural processes over time and space.

Exploring the making of dualistic and triadic Jê life-worlds from a phenomenological approach can broaden an understanding of multispecies care and well-being. The specific dualistic and triadic forms that emerge are based on ongoing, intimate human–nonhuman relationships that are particularly valued and meaningful. These relationships often are grounded in care and affection, as well as the pursuit of individual and communal well-being. For the Panará, creating "beautiful" concentric circular gardens—divided in binary and tertiary ways—is based on valued engagements with the land and diverse crops that support community well-being (Schwartzman 1988; Ewart 2005). For the Canela, certain engagements with soil types have led to the dualistic classification of soil "couples" that are managed and cared for through gardening activities. Developing caring kinship relations with diverse crop children informs and maintains Canela dualistic and triadic classification of crops into good, best, bad, worst, and regular types. Meanwhile, shamanic engagements with Plant-People master spirits unfold in gendered dualistic ways, as male shamans develop formal friendships with Plant-Men and extramarital affairs with Plant-Women. Even village and garden spaces divided into binary and tertiary forms are the result of caring engagements with land types and other humans and nonhumans that inhabit these spaces. The Canela have developed unique ways of caring for, loving, and pursuing the well-being of diverse humans and nonhumans that play out in dualistic and triadic ways. Although the processes of making Jê life-worlds are distinct and varied, there tends to be an overarching emphasis on coming to know, categorizing in dualistic and triadic ways, valuing, and caring for others in the landscape.

Moreover, the composition of human–nonhuman entanglements in Jê life-worlds increasingly are being studied as avenues to support environmental sustainability, biodiversity conservation, and mitigation of and adaptation to climate change. Darrell Posey's landmark studies of the Kayapó displayed the complexity of their land management and environmental classification practices (Anderson and Posey 1989; Hecht and Posey 1989; Posey 2002). More recent studies of human–environment engagements in other Jê life-worlds similarly display their complexity and significance to conservation of local landscapes. Studies of Xavante and Krahô fire management practices demonstrate their importance to hunting and gardening activities and to conservation of Cerrado landscapes (Mistry et al. 2005; Welch 2015; Welch et al. 2013). Canela subsistence gardening lifeways, including fire management, similarly support conservation of the Cerrado's diverse eco-regions, soils, animals, and wild and cultivated plants. Through focusing on the ongoing processes that shape Jê life-worlds, including dualistic and triadic forms, their significance to environmental conservation becomes clear. And by focusing on caring for the environment and its nonhuman inhabitants in the unfolding life-world, the Canela provide new ways to understand conservation and sustainability that should inform policy making of future Cerrado conservation initiatives.

Understanding the Changing Cerrado

Approaching landscape as a series of continually unfolding human–nonhuman engagements that shape larger patterns of Indigenous life-worlds allows for an engaged political–ecological analysis of socio-ecological change in threatened environments such as the Cerrado. At around two million square kilometers, the Cerrado constitutes around 22 percent of Brazil's territory and is the largest savannah in the Neotropics (W. Jepson 2005:99; Simon and Pennington 2012:711). It has the most species richness and endemism of any Neotropical savannah and has the richest flora of the world's savannah regions, with over seven thousand known species (Klink and Machado 2005:707; Simon and Pennington 2012:711). It also covers three of South America's largest watersheds and contributes nearly half (43 percent) of Brazil's surface water apart from the Amazon (Strassburg et al. 2017:1). An ecologically diverse biome, the Cerrado boasts over seventy land systems identified based on climate, landscape, and soils (Felfili et al. 2004). The *cerrado sensu lato* eco-region is the "dominant savannah vegetation type" (Simon and Pennington 2012:712) and includes savannah woodlands, known as *cerrado sensu stricto*, closed woodlands known as *cerradão*, grasslands, gallery forests, swampy palm areas, and dry seasonal forests (Hoffman 2000:63; Felfili et al. 2004:38). Other land types include seasonal dry tropical forests and mesic gallery forests near riverbanks (Simon and Pennington 2012:712). Cerrado vegetation, particularly in the *cerrado sensu lato* eco-region, is well adapted to the severe dry season, nutrient-poor soils (compared with forested biomes such as the Amazon), and frequent wildfires and seasonal burning of slash-and-burn or swidden cultivation (Hoffman 2000:67–68). The Cerrado also has a long history of diverse human communities' presence in and modification of the environment. Indigenous communities have inhabited the region and managed the environment for centuries and most likely millennia. Archaeological evidence of Indigenous crop cultivation has been found in the Cerrado and neighboring regions. Remains of common bean dating from AD 1660–1738 (251 ± 39 BP) were found in the Cerrado of Minas Gerais State (Freitas 2006) and evidence of proto-southern-Jê villages and cultivation of maize, squash, manioc, and bean dating from AD 1280–1430

(670–520 BP) were found in the southern Santa Catarina State (Corteletti et al. 2015). Paleobiolinguistic research of Indigenous linguistic terms for cultivated crops such as bean, maize, and manioc also indicates the longevity of Indigenous landscape use and management in the region. For example, the oldest southern Jê linguistic terms for common bean date from AD 75 (1875 BP) and AD 129 (1821 BP) for both maize and manioc (Brown et al. 2013, 2014a, b). These communities most likely engaged with the biome's various eco-regions through village construction, trekking, hunting and gathering expeditions, and slash-and-burn horticulture in ways that are similar to and differ widely from historical and present-day Indigenous landscape management. Overall, the Cerrado has long been a place where diverse biological, ecological, and sociocultural patterns have unfolded and intertwined, making it a unique part of Brazil and the world.

Considered one of the most biologically rich and most threatened biomes in the world (Felfili et al. 2004), the twenty-first century Cerrado is in flux. Conservationists categorize the Cerrado as a global biodiversity hotspot, meaning that it has exceptional rates of species endemism and native habitat loss (Myers et al. 2000). Over the past half century, over half of the Cerrado has been deforested by logging, cattle ranching, and industrialized agriculture (Klink and Machado 2005; Lima 2014; Françoso et al. 2015). While rates of deforestation have fluctuated annually, by 2005 around 880,000 km² of the Cerrado had been deforested, with around 500,000 km² converted into pasture with invasive species of African grasses (Klink and Machado 2005: 708). From 1990 to 2010, the percentage of natural vegetation cover (including trees and other wooded lands) in the Cerrado decreased from 53.1 to 47 percent (Beuchle et al. 2015:121). It is now estimated that only 19.8 percent of the biome remains "undisturbed" by deforestation, agribusiness expansion, and infrastructure development (Strassburg et al. 2017:1). If the current deforestation rate of around 1.5 percent per year continues, it is estimated that by 2050 up to 60 percent of native flora and fauna habitat will be destroyed in the Cerrado biome and up to 90 percent in central Maranhão State where the Canela territory is located (Feeley and Silman 2009:12383).

With deforestation rates that are two to three times higher than the Amazon and a lack of government initiatives to halt deforestation, the Cerrado has been characterized as a zone of environmental sacrifice in comparison with the Amazon (Sawyer 2009:150–151; Oliveira and Hecht 2016:269). Concerted conservation efforts largely have focused on the Amazon, such as the ten-year soy moratorium (2006–2016) during which soybean traders agreed to refrain from purchasing soy grown on deforested lands. The soy moratorium had an immediate effect, with deforestation for soy decreasing to only around 1 percent of expansion in the Amazon by 2014 (Gibbs et al. 2015: 377). Meanwhile, in the Cerrado where the moratorium did not apply, soy expansion continued unabated, fluctuating between 11 and 23 percent from 2007 to 2013. Deforestation due to soy production drastically increased in the northeastern region of the Cerrado, including Maranhão, Piauí, Tocantins, and Bahia States. Considered "Brazil's newest agricultural hotspot," the northeast and eastern Cerrado experienced "nearly 40 percent of total soy expansion (2007–2013) [that] occurred at the expense of native vegetation" (Gibbs et al. 2015:377).

Climate change is another threat to the Cerrado and to the northeastern region in particular, bringing hotter temperatures and less rainfall (Bustamante et al. 2012). With agricultural expansion producing high rates of carbon dioxide emissions (80 percent of Brazil's total emissions in 2005 [Lapola et al. 2014:27]), deforestation for agriculture and climate change are bound up together through emergent processes of corporate-led neoliberal capitalist growth. Studies indicate that the northeast, Brazil's poorest region, will bear the brunt of both agricultural expansion and climate change in the country. In addition to experiencing continued deforestation and habitat loss from soy and other monocrops, the northeastern region of the Cerrado is most at risk for drastic climatic shifts. Climatic modelling estimates that in the next hundred years temperatures in the northeast Cerrado will rise between 4° and 6° C and precipitation will decrease by up to 70 percent (Bustamante et al. 2012:663–664). Deforestation, habitat loss, and climate change could make the Cerrado in fifty or one hundred years' time unrecognizable, especially for communities such as the Canela who live in the northeastern region with the direst environmental and climatic predictions. Sacrificed for the Amazon by conservationists, abandoned to corporate agricultural interests, and continuously threatened by climate change, the formerly vibrant Cerrado has become a disappearing biome.

The plight of the Cerrado recently has garnered attention by Brazilian governmental agencies and multinational organizations, leading to projects such as the World Bank–funded Sustainable Cerrado Initiative for 2009–2014 (GEF 2016). Also in 2009, the Brazilian Ministry of Environment established the Action Plan for Preventing and Controlling Deforestation and Fire in the Cerrado, which aims to reduce deforestation and subsequent greenhouse gas emissions in the Cerrado by 40 percent by 2020 (MMA 2016). The Brazilian government also initiated a National Vegetation Recovery Plan in 2012 that aims to restore 12 million hectares of native vegetation by 2030 throughout the country (MMA 2018). Other proposed initiatives for Cerrado conservation include Strassburg et al.'s (2017) "Greener Cerrado" scenario, which combines more efficient land-use management for soy and cattle, extending protected areas in the biome, and undertaking more ecological restoration programs.

Recent studies also are documenting the ways in which Indigenous territories and protected areas contribute to halting deforestation in the Cerrado. Although Indigenous territories and protected areas account for only 4.1 and 8.3 percent of the Cerrado, respectively (Klink and Machado 2005: 709; Françoso et al. 2015:36), both have been found to effectively reduce habitat conversion for agricultural expansion (Carranza et al. 2013). Studies indicate that expanding and better managing protected areas could lower deforestation rates in the Cerrado (Françoso et al. 2015), although others point out that establishing protected areas without halting agricultural expansion elsewhere continues to "discourage traditional production systems" in the biome (Eloy et al. 2016:510). Indeed, local and Indigenous communities living in and near protected areas and demarcated Indigenous territories are continuing to pay attention to, engage with, and often sustainably manage Cerrado landscapes even as they continue to change.

Yet while establishing protected areas and promoting ecological restoration can offer demonstrable support to halting deforestation, respecting communities' traditional subsistence livelihoods and territorial boundaries is paramount to long-term sustainability. Indigenous communities with long-standing ties to their environments (and legal title to their lands) have been shown to sustainably manage the local landscape, including its biological and ecological diversity, better than areas that are not under Indigenous management. For example, Welch et al. (2013:381226) found that over four decades, the landscape management practices, including controlled burning for traditional hunting, of the Jê-speaking Xavante in the Cerrado of Mato Grosso State "maintained the integrity of the cerrado landscape and sustained vegetational recovery" better than that of adjacent lands, which were not managed by Indigenous peoples and became fodder for agribusiness development. In another study of the Xavante, researchers found that Xavante communities exhibited a "closer link" with biodiversity than the non-Indigenous settlers living in the same region of the Cerrado (Marimon and Felfili 2001:567). Comparing Xavante and settler uses of various plant species in the *pau brasil* (*Brosimum rubescens* Taub.) forests, researchers found that Xavante communities value the forests as a whole, having multiple uses for many different species and expressing concern for conservation efforts, while the settlers primarily are concerned with logging the forests for commercial use (Marimon and Felfili 2001:566–568). The Canela similarly manage and maintain the ecological and biological diversity in their territorial landscape in ways that are distinct from their non Indigenous neighbors (*cupõn*) and are concerned over environmental destruction orchestrated by these neighbors (see "Understanding Illegal Logging and Other Threats" below).

It is in this context of a rapidly changing Cerrado biome that the unfolding twenty-first century Canela life-world emerges. A product of global capitalist accumulation and global climatic shifts, the changes wrought on the Cerrado will deeply affect the Canela and the ways they engage with and value the landscape. Yet the Canela aesthetics of landscape is resilient and open to new ways of paying attention to and understanding the environment as it changes. Moreover, Canela classification of and engagement with the environment could help prevent further environmental destruction, if policy makers and conservation practitioners begin taking seriously Indigenous knowledge-making (epistemological) and world-making (ontological) practices.

Approaching the Canela Territorial Landscape

Understanding Eco-Regions, Garden Sectors, and Soil Types

Canela life unfolds in the changing Cerrado landscape through daily engagements with the local flora and fauna in diverse eco-regions. People admire the vast, open savannah dotted with scrub bushes, small thick trees, and termite mounds, and they often comment upon the beauty of these vistas. Crocker (1990:188; personal communication) describes how Canela community members felt despondent after they were forced to relocate temporarily to the gallery forests of the Guajajara Indigenous territory in 1963, as they longed for the "beauty of the savannahs." Liliana, a child at the time, similarly recounted to me that her grandmother longed for what she called the "open Cerrado" while living in the Guajajara "live forest" area (see chapter 2, "Gardening: A Brief History, 1814–Present"). The Cerrado landscape is considered *impej*, that which is beautiful, good, and true/original. Through careful attention and aesthetic–ethical appreciation of the landscape, Canela women and men recognize the beauty and goodness of multiple land types or eco-regions. Indeed, aesthetic appreciation of the savannah and classification into distinct eco-regions is common among Jê-speaking Indigenous communities. The Kayapó, for example, identify fourteen types of what researchers termed "agricultural" land (Anderson and Posey 1989; Hecht and Posey 1989; Posey 2002:188), and the Xavante recognize eight environmental zones (Marimon and Felfili 2001:566).

Table 1. Classified eco-regions in the Canela territory

Canela name	Portuguese translation	English translation
Põ	Chapada	Type of dry, sandy area
Pàrkô	Chapada fechada	In between sandy and forested area
Irom	Cerrado	Savannah
Ivẽntũm	Mato vivo	"Live forest"; forested area
Iromtũm	Mato velho	"Old forest"; more mature trees
Pjêhtũm	Terra velha	"Old land"; similar to iromtũm
Hipêj	Capoeira	"Old" second-year garden area
Coh-cahêhnã	Beira do brejo	Riverbank area
Caxàt-re kô	Mato verdadeiro	"True forest"; "forest that grows by itself"

The Canela classify their territorial landscape into nine distinct eco-regions that roughly correspond with the Cerrado *sensu lato* regions described above (see table 1). The *irom*, or savannah, consists of more open grasslands and is said to "protect" the native animals who live there, including peccaries (*crôre* in Canela; *Pecari tajacu* L.), coati (*Nasua*), tapir (*Tapirus*), and red brocket deer (*veado-mateiro*; possibly *carà* in Canela; *Mazama americana* [Erxleben]). Canela men occasionally go on hunting expeditions in this eco-region, although with less frequency than in the past. In addition to the many animals that typically reside in this eco-region, there are also numerous trees and plants that the Canela classify as native to the savannah. Fernando, Liliana, Renato, and Wander identified twenty-four plant species that are native to the *irom* eco-region. These include hardwood trees that have become targets for illegal logging, including white ipê (*tu-re pàr jaka-ti; Tabebuia roseoalba* [Ridl.] Sandwith), black ipê (*Tu-re pàr tyc-ti; Handroanthus impetiginosus* [Mart. ex DC.] Mattos), *sucupira* (*cuhtà pàr, Bowdichia virgilioides Kunth*), and *maçaranduba* (*caprãn jõõ pàr; Manilkara huberi* [Ducke] A. Chev); see appendix B. Male hunting expeditions also traditionally take place in the *pàrkô*, or closed *chapada*, eco-region, which hunters consider "half-forest." With some tree cover, the *pàrkô* is home to herds of peccaries, which men traditionally hunt with bows and arrows (or shotguns nowadays). Armadillos (*awxêt; Euphractus sexcinctus* L.) often give birth under the trees and brush, as Fernando explained. Gardening sometimes occurs in the closed *chapada* as well, owing to the region's clay soils, which are adequately fertile for cultivating crops.

Meanwhile, the open *chapada*, or *põ* in Canela, is known as being especially fertile and welcoming to a wide diversity of native flora and fauna. Fernando, Liliana, and Renato described the *põ* eco-region as "preserving everything," including wild animals and plants, as well as cultivated crops. It is also known for being especially beautiful. Looking out onto sandy hills covered with native *chapada* grasses (*ahtu*) one afternoon in June 2012, Renato remarked upon how *impoj* (meaning beautiful, good, and true/original) the *chapada* vistas are. Renato and others also described the *chapada* as being particularly *impej* after the burning (*queimada*) occurs later in the dry season, when shoots of brilliant green grass contrast with the blackened earth. This visually striking scene combined with the intermingled smells of burnt wood and fresh grass provide striking and memorable multi-sensory experiences of aesthetically appreciating the *chapada* landscape. Animals that live in the *chapada* include the native Pampas deer (*po*; *veado-campeiro*; *Ozotoceros bezoarticus* L.), the ema, a species of large native bird (*māā*; *Rhea americana* L.), a smaller native bird (siriema; Cariamidae), a South American fox (*xoti*; *Pseudalopex* sp.), and a native hawk (*hàc*). Fernando, Liliana, Renato, and Wander identified twenty-two plants native to the *chapada* (see appendix B). These include many trees that provide seasonal fruit harvests to complement Canela garden produce, such as two types of *chapada* cashew (*ahkrỳt-re*; *Anacardium occidentale* L.), piqui (*prīn pàr*; *Caryocar coriaceum* Wittm.), two types of *puçá* (*crītīn-re pàr* and *crotot-re pàr*; *Mouriri* Aubl.), bacuri (*cǔmxê pàr*; *Platonia insignis* Mart.), *mangaba* (*pênxôô pàr*; *Hancornia speciosa* Gomes), and *jatobá vaqueiro* (*tecrêj pàr*; *Hymenaea* sp.). With its sandy soil, the *pô* can sustain some cultivated crops, and families can maintain garden plots in this eco-region if they desire.

Forested eco-regions are better suited for gardening than the *chapada*, owing to their more fertile soils. The three different types of forested eco-regions—the *ivēntǔm*, *iromtǔm*, and *pjêhtǔm*—are all classified as forest, and gardeners describe them as "serving well" for gardening. However, the *ivōn tǔm*, or live forest type, is considered the ideal eco-region for cultivating forest garden plots. It can provide many years of garden plots with its fertile soils, and the plots typically require only two rounds of burning and slashing. It is more densely forested, and similar to the *irom*, has hardwood trees such as types of ipê and *pau d'arco* (*Handroanthus impetiginosus* [Mart. ex DC.] Mattos) that have become desirable to loggers (see "Understanding Illegal Logging and Other Threats" below). While garden plots are also maintained in the *iromtǔm* and *pjêhtǔm* eco-regions, these are older areas with more mature trees that are consequently more difficult to fell for cultivation. The *coh-cahêhnǎ* riverbank eco-region is considered to have the most fertile soils, which are ideal for riverbank garden plots. Gardeners identified eight native plants and trees belonging to the riverbank, including a type of wild "potato of the riverbank" (*mrīti krô*) and those that are also planted in riverbank and backyard gardens, such as buriti (*crowa pàr*; *Mauritia flexuosa* Mart.) and *buritirana* (*crowarà pàr*; *Mauritiella* sp.). Canela families therefore typically maintain plots simultaneously in one of the forested eco-regions and in the *coh-cahêhnã*, following the contemporary Canela dual forest and riverbank gardening system. Fernando described this eco-region as "feminine" in that it "grows, sustains, and protects" the crops planted there. While other eco-regions are not described in terms of gender, categorizing the riverbank as feminine is similar to other Canela gendered categorizations of the territorial landscape and of crops, especially manioc (see chapter 4, "Noticing and Naming: Classifying Through Multi-sensory Experiences").

In addition to forest and riverbank eco-regions suitable for gardening, the Canela also classify as an eco-region the *hipêj*, which refers to areas of old second-year garden plots that already have been cleared and do not have any more forest. While only a few new crops are typically planted in the *hipêj* eco-region, women frequent these areas to collect bitter manioc roots that were planted during the previous year. Bitter manioc roots (*manaíba* or *maniva* in Portuguese) also feed paca (*Cuniculus paca* L.) and agouti (*Dasyprocta*) rodents long after gardeners leave the area to lie fallow. In this way, Liliana described how the *hipêj* "sustains" the wild animals that come to feed there. The old garden areas can be found throughout the territory, especially nearby the forested eco-regions where new first-year forest garden plots are demarcated. The true forest, or *caxàt-re kô* eco-region, is found throughout the territory but mainly in the southeast. These areas are known as "forests that grow on their own," in that they can regenerate quickly and grow into beautiful hardwood forested spaces. People recount thrilling tales of the eco-region's distinctive inhabitants, including jaguars and supernatural entities.[1] The *caxàt-re kô* is available for gardening, but it is a more time-consuming activity here than in other areas because of its rapidly growing forests. Demarcating a new garden plot here is not impossible yet takes at least five consecutive rounds of burning and slashing to complete. Couples therefore prefer to maintain gardens in other eco-regions where demarcating is less labor-intensive.

Together, the nine eco-regions comprise the entire Canela territory. The main village of Escalvado is located in between the *ivẽntũm* forest and *põ chapada* eco-regions and is usually categorized as being in the *chapada* itself. Meanwhile, there are also dozens of garden sectors (*seitores da roça* in Portuguese) spread throughout various eco-regions where Canela families maintain plots. Fernando, Liliana, Renato, and Wander identified fifty-six past, current, and future garden sectors (some of them classified as forest sites that have been or will become garden sectors) throughout the territory, with nine main garden sectors for forest gardens (see table 2, map 2). Most of the sectors where forest gardens are cultivated lie in the northeast, where there is a particular area of *ivẽntũm* forest, and in the northwest, where part of the põ (*chapada*) area lies. There are some other popular forest garden sectors in the southwest as well, such as Capà-ti (Cabiceiro do Ponto). Riverbank garden plots can be cultivated near any riverbank, although they are typically located in the center or center–south of the territory, within easy walking distance to Escalvado village. The main rivers within the territory are the Dois Riachos (Two Streams), Pau Grosso (Thick Stick), and Santos Estevam, in addition to other smaller streams. The Pau Grosso and Santos Estevam rivers eventually join past the Canela territory to form the Corda River, after which the town of Barra do Corda is named.

Gardeners value the garden sectors for their ecological diversity and widely distributed geographic locations. They provide spaces in which the dual-plot gardening system can be maintained year after year, including fallow periods. In addition, the dozens of garden sectors allow for matrilocal families to maintain adjacent plots. While each adult couple typically owns one forest and one riverbank garden plot, families often choose to cultivate plots next to each other in the same garden sectors. As the head of her family, Liliana explained that maintaining adjacent garden plots is important so that her husband, daughters, sons-in-law, and grandchildren continue to help each other and so that no one forgets their familial ties. Liliana's maternal classificatory grandparents (her mother's sister and her husband) maintained plots in four main forest garden sectors, and she now refers to having garden "properties" (*propriedades*) in these areas, which are Põhipôc (Campestre), Cumxê-ti Kat (Baixão Preto), Potyc (Brejo dos Bois), and Capà-ti (Cabiceiro do Ponto) (see map 2). The Capà-ti sector in the southwest is another preferred forest garden location for Liliana's extended family. Liliana's sister Camila prefers to maintain her family's forest plots in this sector, close to those of Liliana and her family. The family manages riverbank plots in various locations nearby the village, and each household maintains a backyard garden as well. Other families have other preferred garden sectors, often depending on previous generations' gardening locations. For Fernando's wife Geralda, the favorite garden sector is Côhnã-kẽn (Passagem de Pedra) in the northwest quadrant of the territory. Walking or bicycling to this garden sector with his sons-in-law, Fernando surveys the soil quality to decide the exact location of a new forest garden.

Indeed, gardeners typically choose the locations of their plots based on eco-region, garden sector, and soil type. The Canela classify ten different types of soil that are grouped into pairs (see table 3). While each pair can sometimes be found in the same eco-region, the soils are not paired according to geographical location but rather because they work together as

Table 2. Garden and forest sectors in the Canela territory

Orientation	Canela name	Portuguese name
	Main forest garden sectors	
Center–east	Prĩnre Kat	Pé de Piqui
Center–north	Põhipôc	Campestre
Center–south	Capà-ti	Cabiceiro do Ponto
	Cuhcaprêc-ti	Brejo Vermelho
Center–west	Cumxê-ti Kat	Baixão Preto
North	Caprũm-ti	Baixão Fundo
	Côhnã-kẽn	Passagem de Pedra
	Hĩpô	Lagoa do André
	Kryi-re Wôôkrô	Aldeinha
	Other garden and forest sectors	
Center	Canut-kô	Baixão dos Pomba
	Côhkreti (Pypypkô)	Baixão da Raposa
Center-east	Rampàr	N/A
	Ahkrỳt-kô	Cajueira
	Potyc	Brejo dos Bois
	Rõrkrã xêt xà	Côco Queimado
Center–south	Cahỳhk-re Kre	N/A
	Capà-ti Kre	N/A
	Capêr Kat	João Vicente
	Capôc-ti Jõh-kên kre	N/A
	Côô Pijakrut	N/A
	Hahhĩ Jõhken	N/A
	Hĩpô Amji Cuhõn Xà	Lagoa do Pinó
	Hôjre Jõhken	N/A
	Hômji Kre	N/A
	Rõa-pej Kôô	N/A
	Rõrpej Kre	N/A
Center–west	Hĩnre	N/A
	Hĩpôre	Lagoinha
East	Capran Jatuj	Estaleiro
	Côhcukre	Baixão da Ladeira
	Côôncrààre	Baixão Seco
	Crujti	N/A
	Cumxêkô	Bacuri
	Harôhôhn	Curicaco
	Kàj-re Kat	Pé de Borrachinha
	Pànkre	N/A
	Pohhêre Caprũm	Baixão
	Ronti kre	Suçuarana
North	Côhtyc-re	Baixão Escuro
	Crààtihkô	Sambaiba

Table 2. Continued

Orientation	Canela name	Portuguese name
Northeast	Hõhhi	Buzinal
	Pàrjapà	N/A
	Xipôr Jatujxà	Maria Oliva
	Côhkrã Cator	N/A
	Crowcrà	Buriti Seco
	Cuhtà-ti Kat	Baixão Sucupira
	Jôôkô	Cabeleiro do Antonião
	Tep-kre	Formosa
South	Hõhkre Kam Côhkre	N/A
	Hônkokoti Kre	N/A
	Kên Tohkrã Jõ Côô	Estiva
	Printi Jikwa-xàhkre	N/A
	Côhcacroje[1]	Soturna
Southwest	Cô Poh-ti	Pau Grosso
West	Kên Cràre	Galerinha
	Rõr Rõõre	Cocalinho

[1] Rented by *cupẽn*

a "couple." As Fernando explained to me, the soils are "couples" (*casais; amji catê* in Canela) similar to a husband and wife or "friends" (*companheiros*). He compared the soil couples to paired mythical figures in mythic storytelling such as Sun and Moon, who create Canela humans and are formal friends (*hapĩn*; often translated into *companheiros* in Portuguese; see chapter 3, "Becoming Strong, Becoming Happy, Becoming Well"). Fernando also likened soil pairs to the married couple of Caxêtikwỳj (Star-Woman), the mythical figure who introduced horticulture to the Canela community, and her Canela husband Tyc-ti (see chapter 2, "Learning from Star-Woman: Origins of Horticulture and Biodiversity Maintenance" and appendix C). In a conversation in August 2012, Fernando explained the complementarity of soils and of everything in the Canela life-world:

> Fernando: On earth, everything is a couple. As with Moon and Sun, Sun and Moon, like a type of spouse or *companheiro*.
> Me: Are the soils *companheiros*?
> Fernando: Yes, just as Morning Star [Star-Woman] and Small Star [Tyc-ti] are also *companheiros*, it is like this. Here on earth, these soils that we are talking about, they are all types of couples, and that is why things begin like this. They help one another, as with human beings — the wife helps the husband, and the husband helps the wife.

Table 3. Classified soil types in the Canela territory

Soil couple type	Canela name	Description
Oppositional	Pjê kên	"Weak soil" unsuitable for gardening
	Pjê pej	"Good soil" found mainly in ivẽntũm
Oppositional	Pjê-rerec	"Very soft soil"
	Pjê tỳj	Hard clay; less suited for cultivation
Complementary	Amcó	Fertile soil in coh-cahêhnã
	Awpêê	Especially fertile soil in coh-cahêhnã
Complementary	Pjê caprêc	Red clay soil found in surrounding hills
	Pjê xôm	Sandy soil mainly in põ; suitable for some crops
Complementary	Awrerec	Fertile "soft earth"
	Carẽc	"Mud rain"; watery clay; suitable for gardening

The soil couples help one another in different ways, depending on whether they are considered oppositional (*amji kajnã*) or complementary (*amji catê*) pairs.[2] For example, *pjê pej*, literally good soil, and *pjê kên*, literally weak soil, are an oppositional pair that help one another through their differences. While *pjê pej* is found mainly in the *ivẽntũm* forested eco-region and is ideal for cultivating many crops, *pjê kên* is its opposite—it is considered "weak" or "bad" (*kên*) soil that cannot sustain gardens and can be found anywhere in the territory. *Pjê pej* also responds well to fire, and according to Fernando and Renato, it is even better for cultivation after the burning (*queimada*) performed before planting a new garden. Compared with its oppositional pair of weak/bad soil, the good soil is identified as clearly superior. Gardeners therefore can use this opposition to their advantage by identifying and avoiding areas with weak soil while seeking out areas with good soil. Liliana uses this strategy when planning new forest gardens by looking at and feeling the soils in *ivẽntũm* live forest and *pjêhtũm* old land eco-regions to determine whether they are *pjê pej* or *pjê kên*. The soil couple of *pjê-rerec* and *pjê tỳj* are also an oppositional pair. *Pjê-rerec*, which literally means very soft earth, allows for some crop cultivation, while *pjê tỳj*, meaning hard earth or hard clay, is not used for gardening.

Other soil couples work together through complementary pairings. The pair of *pjê caprêc* or red clay and *pjê xôm* or sandy soil are both suitable for crop cultivation, albeit in different ways. Both the clay and the sand are complementary and are said to "secure" the growing crops, according to Fernando. While both types can be found in some of the forested eco-regions, *pjê caprêc* mostly is located in the hills surrounding Escalvado village and can sustain some crops. *Pjê xôm* typically is located in the *põ* or *chapada* and can sustain types of cashew, coconut, squash, and common bean. Gardeners often use the *pjê xôm* soils to grow crops they are not currently cultivating in their new first year forest or riverbank plots. During the 2012–2013 gardening season, for example, Liliana decided to cultivate a second-year *hipêj*, or old garden, in the Capà-ti (Cabiceiro do Ponto) garden sector owing to the area's *pjê xôm* soil. Feeling the soft, sandy soil in her hands, Liliana determined it was *pjê xôm* and would be relatively fertile for growing varieties of squash and common bean, especially the type of Guajajara tree bean (*pàt juhtõi-re pàràre/pryjĩ*; pigeon pea; *Cajanus cajan* (L.) Millsp.) that is a family favorite. Another complementary pair that is said to "secure" cultivated crops is *carẽc*, a whitish clay, and *awrerec*, or soft earth. Both types of soil are wetter than the other couples are, with *carẽc* having a muddy consistency and *awrerec* resembling the irrigated soil created by the non-Indigenous *cupẽn*. *Awrerec* is especially fertile, and varieties of banana, sugarcane, pineapple, squash, rice, and sweet potato grow well in it. Fernando described the fertility of *awrerec* as similar to a woman who produces many children, in that it produces abundant harvests of cultivated crop children. While the *carẽc* clay is not described as being as lush or productive as *awrerec*, with its wet consistency the clay supports crops in ways that are similar to its complementary pair. By far the most fertile soils, however, are the complementary pair of *awpêê* and *amcó* soils found in the *coh-cahêhnã* riverbank eco-region. Fernando similarly described this pair as "feminine," producing crops as fertile women birth children. Gardeners maintain that this soil pair is the best for gardening, or in Fernando's words, "the most principal [soils] we have." *Awpêê* in particular is known for "protecting" Canela gardeners and "helping with survival," as Fernando described. Crops can be planted and harvested earlier in it than in the soils of the forested eco-regions. *Amcó* is akin to its pair and can sustain squash, watermelon, maize, banana, sugarcane, and sweet and bitter manioc. Liliana described the *amcó* and *awpêê* soil couple as "working together" to produce abundant harvests in the *coh-cahêhnã* riverbank eco-region. During the planting seasons of riverbank gardens in 2012 and 2017, Liliana chose areas that had both *awpêê* and *amcó* soils. By using this soil couple, Liliana assured me, gardeners and their families will "have food all the time" and "never experience hunger."

Through these complex classification schemas of eco-regions, garden sectors, and soil types, the Canela aesthetics of landscape becomes clearer. Through classification, the Canela are valuing and giving meaning to engagements with the environment that are particularly salient in their unfolding life-world. The primacy of gardening and human–plant engagements in the twenty-first century Canela life-world is reflected in the community's categorization of the landscape. With types of land and soil identified, named, and categorized based on their ability to sustain gardens, it is clear that gardening is the lens through which modern-day Canela perceptually engage with, make sense of, and value their territorial landscape. And while other activities such as traditional hunting expeditions continue to affect and influence Canela landscape aesthetics, gardening has become the primary way in which Canela women and men discuss and relate to the land. Appreciating and valuing the land through gardening has allowed for a robust and vibrant categorization schema that can be adaptable and resilient in the face of environmental change and destruction. By noticing, categorizing, and managing the nine eco-regions, ten soil couples, and dozens of gardening sectors, Canela gardeners are paying attention to diverse spaces in the territorial landscape and becoming attuned to how they are changing over time, for better or for worse.

Understanding Illegal Logging and Other Threats

The environmental destruction and change affecting the entire Cerrado biome, and especially the northeastern region, is emerging in distinct ways in the Canela territorial landscape. Concerns include cattle ranching, illegal logging, agricultural expansion, and drought. The southeastern part of the territory is described by Canela community members as an "at-risk" or "invaded" area threatened by cattle ranching and illegal logging. In 2012, the garden sector known as Côhcacroje, or Soturna in Portuguese, was being rented out to non-Indigenous families for cattle ranching and agriculture. While individual involvement in this endeavor and its legality remain unclear, it is not uncommon for property lines and documents to be forged in rural areas of Brazil through activities known as *grilagem* (see Campbell 2015). Whether Canela political leaders were aware of the rented areas is also unknown, as I was advised against asking these sensitive questions at the afternoon male political meetings in the village center. Certain community members informed me that illegal logging also was occurring in the southeast region in 2012–2013 and that both the Canela political leadership and local FUNAI officials were aware of these activities. By 2017, these activities had increased fourfold. From 2012–2017, loggers invaded areas in the southeastern, eastern, southwestern, and northern parts of the territory (see map 2). Loggers were removing valuable hardwood tree species in all of these areas, including *ipê, pau d'arco, sucupira, jatobá* (*Hymenaea* sp.), and *maçaranduba*. In more than one instance, loggers entered the territory without permission to cut down and remove trees in the dead of night. The most recent area that has been logged since July 2017 is in the richly forested *ivẽntũm* eco-region with long-standing forest gardens that are no longer safely accessible. The operation was and continues to be run by local non Indigenous *cupōn* (with the assistance and/or permission of a few Canela community members.) Owing to the real dangers involved, I have caught only a glimpse of these activities, although I can estimate that the logging operation is a widespread network stretching across Maranhão State and possibly into neighboring Piauí State. The illegal supply chain of these logs stretches from the Canela territory to sawmills in the nearby town of Barra do Corda. From there, it is possible that the wood is shipped to furniture makers in Maranhão, and finally arrives for sale in outdoor furniture markets found in the town of Timón in Maranhão and its sister city, Teresina, across the Parnaíba River in Piauí. During conversations in 2012–2013 and 2017, Canela community members were troubled by the continued illegal logging and its implications for territorial integrity, worrying that there is a "danger of losing land" this way. They also maintained that the male leadership council was concerned about these activities. However, they explained that acting to halt illegal logging or even discussing it was "life threatening" to anyone involved, including themselves, FUNAI officials, and myself. High rates of assassinations of environmental activists, including Indigenous peoples, throughout Brazil attest to these dangers (Global Witness 2015). In Maranhão, violence against and assassinations of Indigenous people protecting their lands have skyrocketed. Recent violence includes the brutal attack of members of the Gamela community, who are struggling for legal recognition of their traditional territory, by local ranchers in April 2017 (Watts 2017); the murder of a married couple from the Jë-speaking Gavião-Pykobjë community, who were run over with logging truck in March 2017 (Melo 2017); and killings of Tupi-Guaraní-speaking Guajajara community members by loggers and their associates throughout 2016 (Milanez 2017). Since 2010, at least five members of the Tupi-speaking Ka'apor community defending their lands from illegal logging also have been killed, and continued threats are made against community members (Greenpeace Brasil 2016). Since violence of this kind is met regularly with impunity in Maranhão, Indigenous communities and their advocates continue to engage in a dangerous dance with loggers and their associates. Canela engagements with the territorial landscape, and especially the *ivēntūm* eco-region, are therefore fraught—on the one hand seen as a beautiful live forest to be aesthetically valued and gardened, and on the other seen as a dangerous deforested space to be avoided whenever possible.

Other environmental threats remain on the periphery of the Canela territorial landscape at present yet could bring potentially devastating effects to Canela subsistence lifeways. Soy plantations are encroaching nearby, including onto the neighboring Apaniekra Indigenous territory, which lies only 45 km west of the Canela (Crocker, personal communication; Rizzo de Oliveira 2005, 2014). Industrialized soy agriculture is known to cause soil erosion and water depletion (Altieri 2009; Eloy et al. 2016). Runoff from fertilizers and agrochemicals pollutes waterways, leaving high levels of phosphorus and nitrogen (Altieri 2009:5). Nutrient enrichment causes algal blooms, depleting oxygen in water and leading to "dead zones"; in soils excess nitrogen can lead to less diversity of plant species (Horrigan et al. 2002: 446). Runoff pollution and exposure to high levels of phosphorus and nitrogen also can affect human health negatively (Wolfe and Patz 2002), although there is a paucity of research on these issues for Brazilian communities living near soy plantations (Garrett and Rausch 2016:484). Whether the Apaniekra and Canela will experience these consequences of living near soy remains to be seen, although expansion of soy agriculture is likely to continue in the agricultural hotspot of the northeast Cerrado (Gibbs et al. 2015).

Eucalyptus plantations are even closer to the Canela territory. In 2012, a Japanese multinational corporation established a eucalyptus plantation known as Fazenda Escondido on the road between Barra do Corda and the Canela Indigenous territory, approximately 35–40 km away from Canela lands. By 2017, the plantation had been sold to a Brazilian company and had increased at least threefold in size, including an on-site plant that makes charcoal from the felled eucalyptus trees.[3] Community members have been concerned about the plantation's impact on the area's water supply and wild animals. Renato, who has taken classes on environmental issues, noted his concern that the soils would become "dried out" from the eucalyptus trees, and other community members have expressed similar concerns about eucalyptus negatively affecting the soils and exacerbating drought. Renato also stated that the plantation's agrochemicals (agrotóxicos) were killing off the wild game in the region. As with soy, eucalyptus is known to cause soil erosion, water depletion, and biodiversity loss in areas surrounding plantations (Ribeiro 2008; Lúcio et al. 2014; Eloy et al. 2016). Canela community members are recognizing these changes, which could dramatically affect their subsistence gardening patterns.

Canela gardeners also are concerned about droughts, which are increasingly affecting gardening seasons. Since 2012, the Cerrado of northeast Brazil has been experiencing a drought that has resulted in irregular rainfall and temperatures. Unusual rainfall during both the rainy and dry seasons has impacted Canela gardening patterns and crop harvests. During the rainy season of 2015–2016, there was a severe period of practically no rainfall, resulting in Canela community members losing some of their crops that became dried out in forest and riverbank garden spaces. The drought may have affected ritual activities in 2012–2013 as well, including a maize planting ritual that occurred much earlier in the season than usual (see chapter 3, "Celebrating Plant Lives: First Harvests"). Moreover, in 2017, the rainy season started much later than usual, causing gardeners to burn new garden plots months after they typically do so. The drought also has caused increasing incidents of uncontrollable fires both within and outside the Canela territory. With climate change likely bringing hotter temperatures and less rainfall, Canela gardening patterns may experience further adjustments in the years and decades to come.

Nevertheless, the Canela persist in their intimate engagements with and appreciation of the Cerrado landscape. Categorizing and living with the nine eco-regions, fifty-six garden sectors, and ten soil types, Canela community members continue to remember, pay attention to, and value their territorial landscape. Through an aesthetics of landscape, the Canela are able to recognize environmental threats and destruction of their valued environments. Addressing the threats they face requires cooperation and shifting value systems at local, regional, national, and global scales, in order to incorporate and take seriously Canela landscape aesthetics in the changing Cerrado in real and meaningful ways.

Becoming Resilient: Living with and Valuing the Land

As the Cerrado landscape continues to face environmental destruction and climatic changes, what are the possibilities for future human–environment and specifically human–plant engagements? In the Anthropocene epoch, Haraway (2016) calls for humans and nonhumans to "stay with the trouble" of environmental change, destruction, and loss through multispecies care and relatedness. With multispecies kinship and social relations integral to many Indigenous life-worlds (LaDuke 1999; Tallbear 2011), paying attention to Indigenous ontological world-making practices can lead to better care of our "damaged planet" (Haraway 2016:98). The Canela landscape aesthetics approach to caring for diverse plant kin in the local Cerrado landscape therefore can teach us how to keep alive myriad human–environment engagements throughout the world. And through the sensory ethnobotany theoretical–practical framework that I put forward throughout the book, we can understand better the specifics of Canela multispecies care, resilience, and resistance.

The Canela recognize and value the diversity of their territorial landscape, including the native flora and fauna growing and living in diverse eco-regions and soil pairs. Through an aesthetics of landscape, the Canela come to know and appreciate their nonhuman counterparts, including animals, plants, soils, and lands. Canela humans and nonhumans are practicing multispecies resilience, as they live with and value one another. From a phenomenological approach, the Canela are shaping or "worlding" their life-world—by repeatedly following relational pathways of meaningful human-environment perceptual engagements over time and space.

Yet other actors are shaping their life-worlds as well in competing and destructive ways. Multinational corporations, the national and local Brazilian government, illegal logging cabals, and local cattle ranchers are crafting other worlds in the same territorial landscape based on strikingly different value systems. Nonhuman entities also take part in these competing life-worlds. Phosphorus and nitrogen seep their ways into streams and rivers, eucalyptus and soy plants quench their thirst at the expense of local flora, native hardwood trees are killed and maimed, cattle wander past makeshift fences, and wild game are poisoned by pollutants. The world-making practices of neoliberal capitalist accumulation are notoriously leaky, seeping into other life-worlds through processes of extraction, destruction, and often violence. In this sense, the Cerrado has become a "leaky" environment (e.g., Haraway 1991; Alexander 2002), with myriad human–nonhuman engagements taking place and seeping into the soils, lands, flora, fauna, and people with lasting effects.

But life in the "capitalist ruins" (Tsing 2015) is not without hope. There are spaces where multispecies engagement and care continue to emerge (see, e.g., Nading 2012; Tsing 2015; Archambault 2016; Haraway 2016). Within the disappearing biome of the Cerrado, the Canela have created their own space of multispecies resilience, where human–environment and specifically human–plant engagements are pursued and valued. In conservation ecology and studies of socio-ecological systems, "resilience" is understood as the ability of a system to undergo change, self-organize, and have the capacity for learning and adaptation, including following "disturbance-driven change" (Walker et al. 2002, paraphrasing Holling 1973). Expanding on this concept through a phenomenological perspective, multispecies resilience is understood here as the ability of humans and nonhumans to create, interact, collaborate, and adapt in an unfolding life-world that is continuously changing. Canela multispecies resilience is therefore embodied in their ongoing, intimate engagements with the land, soil, flora, and fauna throughout their territorial landscape. Feeling sandy soils, visually appreciating sweeping *chapada* landscapes, smelling freshly burned earth and new grass, tasting newly harvested fruit from the forest, listening to the river flow while digging into the wet soils — are all embodied acts of multispecies resilience, of becoming with, knowing, and caring for the Cerrado landscape. The native vegetation of the Cerrado also may be engaging in processes of resilience. A recent statistical modelling study estimates that the Cerrado has a "good capacity for recuperation . . . against the anthropic pressure of agricultural expansion exercised against it" (Lima 2014:47; my translation).

Multispecies resilience necessarily involves both humans and nonhumans as they collaborate with one another to maintain valued relationships and learn to adapt and value new relationships that emerge from destructive processes in the Cerrado of the Anthropocene. In this sense, multispecies resilience is also resistance to the destruction of the Cerrado. By continuing to live with, value, and understand the eco-regions, soils, animals, and plants in their lands, the Canela are keeping their highly adaptable life-world living. And by regenerating themselves, the scrubby bushes, grasses, woody plants, and hardwood trees of the Cerrado are participating in the Canela life-world and adapting to its changing circumstances in resilient ways. Together, Canela people and plants continue to carve out spaces for themselves in the changing Cerrado. Canela multispecies resilience offers a way forward for sustainable use and management of the Cerrado that is simultaneously new and old, a result of past and present human–environment engagements and their adaptations over time. Policy makers, governmental officials, and conservationists should take seriously Canela multispecies resilience if the Cerrado is to survive (and perhaps even thrive) in the Anthropocene.

CHAPTER TWO

Loving Gardens: Human-Environment Engagements in Past and Present

The hard worker creates two gardens—one in the fresh area [riverbank] and another in the center [forest area]. Those who enjoy working [do it this way]. They will not need anything, for they will have everything. [. . .] It is as people say—those who like gardens, who love gardens, who adore gardens, will do it this way, with two gardens.
—Fernando, July 2012

Understanding Indigenous Landscape Transformations

In the modern-day Indigenous Canela life-world, people love to garden. Women and men enjoy talking about their forest and riverbank plots and the distinct variety of crops they are planting, tending, and harvesting in each. After the sun sets in the evening, families often sit in woven plastic chairs known as "spaghetti chairs" (*cadeiras espaguete*) in front of their thatched-roof houses and update each other on the garden and its produce. Which crops are feeling happy (*ihtỳi*) and are growing well, and which ones are floundering? Is it time for the men to begin the burning of new garden plots in the forest and near the riverbank, or for the women to hang the vines of the myriad common bean and fava bean varietals from maize stalks or manioc sticks? While discussing the future of their gardens and crops, women often sort through their diverse saved seeds, admiring and commenting on the brilliant colors and patterns of their seed children. Men typically smoke tobacco while lounging in hammocks, resting before another day's work creating and maintaining the large gardens their families desire.

This nightly rhythm centered on the gardens and their diversity is relatively new for the Canela. Until the mid-twentieth century, the community frequently relocated their villages and maintained a semi-nomadic lifestyle. Although the ancestors of the Canela maintained gardens in the early nineteenth century and most likely earlier (Ribeiro [1819] 1841:187), the plots were smaller with less variety of crops, and families usually planted one plot at a time. In this chapter, I explore the transformations that have occurred in Canela gardening practices over the past two hundred years that the community has inhabited the geographical region where their current legally demarcated territory is located. In particular, I examine how the Canela have shifted from being semi-nomadic hunter–gatherers with small garden plots to become twenty-first century subsistence horticulturalists who love to cultivate large, biodiverse gardens in forest and riverbank areas.

The history of transformations in Canela ways of life over the past two centuries has been fraught with violence, famine, disease, and socioeconomic and sociopolitical marginalization. The structural violence that has wreaked havoc on Indigenous livelihoods and landscapes throughout Brazil continues to inform Canela engagements with their environment today. In this chapter, I examine the past and present violence and inequality faced by the Canela from a combined phenomenological sensory ethnobotany and political ecology perspective. That is, I focus on the lived experiences of past and present Canela humans and nonhumans (especially plants) as they have shaped and maintained their environment or landscape while recognizing that these experiences have been informed by wider local, regional, and global forces resulting in territorial dispossession, violence with impunity, environmental destruction, and socioeconomic and sociopolitical marginalization and exploitation (see Nabhan et al. 2011; Bell et al. 2015). While resulting from larger processes of structural inequality, the transformations of Canela gardening practices are understood by the community today as authentically Canela ways of dealing with and resisting these inequalities and as ways of continuing to engage with the environment on their own terms. Indeed, Canela resistance to and resilience from marginalization and exploitation can be seen in their pursuit of ongoing, intimate engagements with their environment and specifically with gardens and cultivated plants.

The transformations of Canela gardening are explored in three main contexts: in the history of territorial land rights and subsistence strategies from 1814 to the present; in the contemporary dual garden system; and in the origin of horticulture mythic story in its various forms. The increased importance of gardening to individual people and to the community at large becomes clear in all three contexts. Historical and ethnographic accounts display how the lifeways of past Timbira and Canela communities changed over time to incorporate new gardening practices and a wider variety of crops, as well as an overarching appreciation for subsistence horticulture as a way forward for the community. The experiences of modern-day gardeners, meanwhile, demonstrate how Canela women and men value and love the dual garden system, which enables greater nutritional and economic self-sufficiency and promotes happy (*ihtÿi*) and well (*impej*) Canela people and plants. Finally, elder storytellers' modifications to the Star-Woman mythic story over the past century underscore the contemporary significance and authenticity of Canela gardening practices and biodiversity maintenance. I maintain that the sensory ethnobotany approach, which highlights phenomenological embodied experiences between and among people and plants, can best account for these transformations in Canela engagements with the environment over time.

Gardening: A Brief History, 1814–Present

Historical records of the Canela and related Timbira groups are scarce, especially those that provide descriptions of subsistence patterns and environmental management practices. The first mention of the Timbira in Portuguese written accounts dates from 1728 (Annaes da Biblioteca e Archivo Público do Pará, 1902–1913). Around this time, Portuguese colonial authorities and settlers began engaging in frequent warfare with the Timbira communities whose lands they were trying to invade. Forming groups known as *bandeiras*, the settlers began encroaching onto Timbira territories in the interior of present-day Maranhão and Piauí States, near the Parnaíba River. Warfare continued for the remainder of the eighteenth and into the early nineteenth centuries. Timbira groups often defeated the *bandeiras*, although they also suffered many defeats. Between 1793 and 1801, the Capiecrans, the ancestors of the modern-day Ramkokamekra-Canela, experienced heavy losses through battle and the kidnapping of women and children (Nimuendajú 1946:32; citing Ribeiro [1815] 1848). By 1810, the *bandeira* groups had claimed and settled a large area in southern Maranhão. As anthropologist Curt Nimuendajú (1946:3) notes, this era was the "classical period of the *bandeiras*" that was largely documented by Francisco de Paulo Ribeiro, an "eyewitness and occasional participant" of the settlers' activities. Indeed, Ribeiro's accounts ([1815] 1848, [1819] 1841, [1819] 1849) provide the most detailed descriptions of the *bandeiras* and of Timbira lifeways in the early nineteenth century. He describes the battles between the two groups, as well as the methods the settlers used to gain territory if warfare failed. These included signing false treaties with Timbira groups and subsequently massacring and/or selling the community members into slavery. According to Ribeiro ([1819] 1841; my translation), "the Indian wars were due to the colonists' craving for slaves rather than the need to open up new territories."

Not only were Timbira communities fighting battles with the non-Indigenous *cupēn* (the "enemy" or "other"), they also engaged in inter-tribal warfare in the eighteenth and early nineteenth centuries. Crocker and Crocker (2004:11) estimate that there were around thirty to fifty Timbira tribes, each with a population of around one to two thousand, that lived between the eastern Parnaíba and western Tocantins Rivers during this time. Accounts of inter-tribal skirmishes are prevalent in Canela oral history, as William Crocker documented in the late 1950s and early 1960s. According to his elder research assistants, Timbira groups both attacked one another and formed trading partnerships, although any alliance was tenuous and easily broken (Crocker and Crocker 2004:11). Attacks involving the weaponry of wooden clubs and bows and arrows typically took place during the dry season, as bows and arrows were said to not function well in the heavy rains of the rainy season (Crocker 1978).

Frequently engaging in warfare on multiple fronts, Timbira groups lived semi-nomadically and seasonally. In the dry season, they "wandered" on extended hunting and gathering treks. Ribeiro ([1819] 1841:187–188; my translation) describes their mobile trekking practices, including the types of game they hunted and native fruits they gathered:

> They roam, wandering in the district that belongs to them during all the dry summer weather, it being in this season that they properly use the game and fruit of their lands. [. . .] Their order of traveling is the following: at daybreak, a column of the young men [walk], and at a certain distance they divide themselves into two or three convoys, gathering fruits. They return to join each other at a certain point, and begin the hunt for game in this way: they surround them [the game] with fire created by lighting the dry grasses of a certain portion of the fields, leaving open a small space as a doorway, in front of which they can wait for the traffic of animals that, affected by the same fire, gather in the center . . . they gather cobras, lizards, locusts, turtles, agouti, paca, deer, ema, and some other animals that are more or less abundant depending on the area burned and the nature of the land. They also collect many fruits, such as the *curití*, juçara, bacaba, *sapucaia*, *piquí*, *mucajuba*, mangaba, *guabiroba*, bacuri, *puçá*, cashew [*caju*], *araçá*, and in some abundance the coconut of the wild palm. . . . They are also used to eating a root or vine that they call *cupá*, which is fairly meaty, although it lacks flavor that excites the appetite.

In the rainy season, they moved to settlements in order to cultivate small garden plots. Ribeiro ([1819] 1841:187, 190) recounts that the Timbira used stone axes to demarcate new plots and cut down trees and brush and describes their gardening activities:

With the first rains, they march to their settlements [*povoações*], where a few people have remained, keeping guard and tending to the infirm. Then they prepare a little land in which they are accustomed to growing potato, peanut [*mendubís*], and *catité* or *zaburro* maize. In the meantime, as the planted crops are growing in the cover of winter, they eat the crops of the last year that were saved in individual sacks [*paiões*] that each family kept hidden for themselves. In the months of May and June they gather the harvest, which they save in the same way for the next year, and then they leave the settlements to go enjoy once again the fields and provisions that nature has prepared for them.

Although the plots were small and only included a few different crops, it does appear that the gardens were important to eighteenth- and early nineteenth-century Timbira subsistence patterns, providing new and stored food for the rainy season. Nevertheless, Ribeiro emphasizes the importance of the mobility of trekking to Timbira men and women, in contrast to the semi-sedentary lifestyle of maintaining large garden plots of today. Although the community usually would construct a "perfect" concentric circular organization of shelters to spend the night, cook, bathe, and sing and dance, they typically began "marching" onward again the next morning. Ribeiro ([1819] 1841:189] notes that "there are very few occasions that they happen to stay two consecutive nights in the same place."

Whether this mobile lifestyle was a preference, the result of already frequent warfare, or both, it was exacerbated by the "peace" treaties Timbira groups began signing in the 1810s. In 1814, the Ramkokamekra-Canela (called the Capiecran by Ribeiro) under their chief Tempé accepted a treaty with a settlers' group on the condition of receiving assistance in attacking their enemies, the Fox (Ĉa'kamekra or Tsoo-khãm-më-khra) tribe (Ribeiro [1815] 1848:43; Nimuendajú 1946:32). The community relocated to the outskirts of the non-Indigenous Buritizinho settlement in 1815 and abandoned their usual hunting, gathering, and gardening activities. Left to fend for themselves for subsistence, Canela men and women began taking heads of cattle and crops from settlers' gardens. The settlers responded in what Ribeiro describes as "the worst way of all"—luring the Canela to the town of Caxias on the border of Maranhão and Piauí States, which was experiencing a smallpox epidemic, with the false promise of another attack against the Fox tribe (Ribeiro [1815] 1848:44). Once there, the community experienced devastating disease and violence. For the Canela, it was "a terrible state of formal subjection, hanging them by their torsos, striking them and their wives . . . even taking the life of some" (Ribeiro [1815] 1848:44). Not long after, the remaining community members fled to the Alpercatas hills (*Serra das Alperca-tas*) in the interior of Maranhão State (see map 1).

According to Canela oral history, the nearly decimated community scattered in and around the Alpercatas hills from around 1816–1817 until around 1840 (Crocker, personal communication). Reduced from a population of thousands to around one hundred by 1820 (Crocker and Crocker 2004:11), the remaining community members were struggling to survive. Crocker's elderly research assistants in the 1950s described the dismal conditions of Canela lifeways while the community was in hiding. Even obtaining water from a nearby stream was difficult, since an individual had to leave the relative safety of the hills and risk exposure to the settlers (Crocker and Crocker 2004:16). At some point between 1820 and 1835, the community created a settlement farther north of the Alpercatas on the Porcos stream, although it is unclear how long they remained here. Around 1835, Luis Domingo Kawkhre became the first Canela chief appointed by the non-Indigenous authorities, and in 1840 the authorities allowed the community to settle near the Alpercatas hills (Crocker 1990:10,). Chief Kawkhre led the establishment of a village in the southeast region of their modern-day territory. Called Pac-re (Little Scorpion), it is known as the first village of the Canela with both historical and mythical origins. It had a concentric circular layout characteristic of Jê and Timbira communities. In a 1958 survey of old village remains, Crocker's research assistants Antônio Diogo and Paolo Adriano described Pac-re as the place where the Canela "lived first" after the period of wandering (Crocker, personal communication). In mythic storytelling, Pac-re is the village from which all Timbira groups originate. While other Timbira groups eventually dispersed from the place, the Canela remained and marked the area as their territory. Historical records indicate that other Timbira groups such as the Mud (Karë?katêyê) and Boar (Krôô-re-khãm-më-?khra-re) peoples joined the Canela community around this time (Crocker and Crocker 2004:11–12). Indeed, the contemporary Canela consider themselves the descendants of five Timbira groups: the Ramkokamekra (Möl-tûm-re), Piranha (Apaniekra), Mud, Boar, and Fox peoples. They call themselves and other Eastern Timbira groups by the term *mẽhĩn* ("people;" *mẽ* = plural; *hĩn* = flesh).

The newly formed community of multiple Timbira groups continued to relocate village sites frequently throughout the nineteenth century. They moved from Pac-re to a site farther east called Khén-Té-Kô-Kacwërë (Area Where Stream Pierces Through Mountain). In the 1850s or 1860s, the community relocated to a village south of the original Pac-re site called Padre-Katôk-Tsà (Place Where Priest Fired Gun), named after a Catholic priest who visited the area and "baptized" the community. The remains of both these sites, including the concentric circular layout, were still visible in the late 1950s (Crocker, personal communication). By the 1870s, Zé Cadete Pal-khre (Hole in Foot) became the new chief and relocated the community to a new village known as Akhã'tu (Soft Surface/Body). Antônio Diogo recounted during Crocker's 1958 old village survey that his grandparents lived here when they were in their twenties.

From the 1880s to the early 1900s, the Canela established multiple villages in the same region where the modern-day village of Escalvado is located. In the early 1880s, they lived in Ahkrã-Khã-Tỳi (Hard Ground) village. Antônio Diogo was born here, and a new chief, known as Major Delfino Kôkaipó, took power. The next village site was called Pjê Xôm (Sandy Soil/ Earth), and Delfino remained the chief of the community. By the mid-1890s, however, another competing village was formed nearby with Colonel Tomasinho as chief (Crocker 1990:10). Delfino then moved his followers to a second village called Ahkrã-Khã-Tỳi in the early 1900s, and the Fox people, the Canela community's former enemies, joined Delfino and his followers here around the same time. The incorporation of the Fox people was not entirely harmonious, however. In 1903, some community members executed a Fox man for witchcraft, which led to a further split between the villages of Delfino, who had Fox relatives, and Tomasinho (Nimuendajú 1946:239; Crocker and Crocker 2004:21–22). After briefly relocating to a site called Kupá-Khĩa (*Kupá* Vine Oven), where Antônio Diogo's son Manuel Diogo was born, Delfino and his followers moved farther east to the Bois stream (Crocker, personal communication). Tomasinho and his followers also moved east to the Pombo stream. The two Canela villages remained two streams apart for nearly a decade, until the early 1910s.

While the Canela and other neighboring Timbira communities were able to relocate their villages frequently across a wide range of territory from 1840 onward, territorial disputes with non-Indigenous ranchers and settlers were not uncommon. Without legally demarcated lands, the Indigenous groups' subsistence and survival continued to be at stake. In 1913, the Arruda rancher family took matters into their own hands by massacring the entire community of the Khéncatêjê people, a Timbira group living nearby the Canela in the southwest. Fearing for their own lives, the two Canela communities scattered into the Alpercatas hills until it was safe to return to their lands. Chief Tomasinho died during this time, and by 1915 Delfino had reunited the Canela in one village on the Raposa stream (Crocker and Crocker 2004:24).

The reunited community remained on the Raposa stream until the early 1920s, when Delfino died and Faustino Ropkhà became chief. In 1922,

Faustino established a new village called Mac Pàra (Mango Tree) on the Santo Estevão stream in an area known as Ponto, near the Escalvado area. The community also maintained a secondary settlement called Kro-ré-khré (Peccary) nearby, possibly as an area for gardening. When the German Brazilian anthropologist Curt Nimuendajú first visited the Canela in 1929, he found them living in Mango Tree village. He was adopted into the family of the deceased chief Delfino's son and was given Delfino's Canela name of Kôkaipó. Nimuendajú continued to visit the community over the next few years, in 1930, 1931, 1933, 1935, and 1936 (Nimuendajú 1946:33). During this time, he documented numerous aspects of the community's lifeways, including their subsistence practices. Although the Canela continued to relocate to a new village every few years, their subsistence patterns were becoming more horticultural and semi-sedentary than in centuries past. The group had also increased in population, from around one hundred in the 1820s to around three hundred in the 1930s (Nimuendajú 1946:33). Nimuendajú (1946:64) notes that numerous external forces affected the transformation of Canela subsistence lifeways:

> It was grim necessity that drove the natives to create a new basis of subsistence. The reduction of the tribal territory to one-twentieth of its former extent; the encroachments of Neobrazilian cattle on even this residual habitat; and the use of firearms in hunting by Neobrazilians and, to some extent, also by the Indians caused such diminution of big game that hunting rapidly lost its economic significance.

By the 1930s, Canela gardening practices had changed considerably from a century earlier. Garden plots typically were located near riverbanks, and individual families occasionally maintained two separate plots simultaneously. The matrilocal system of garden ownership and gendered division of labor were important facets of gardening practices, both of which still exist today. Every adult married woman and some unmarried women owned a plot, and women from the same family typically planted gardens that adjoined one another. Women were responsible for weeding and harvesting most crops, men for clearing land for a new garden plot, and both women and men planted crops together. The available tools had changed as well, with gardeners using metal axes acquired from non-Indigenous settlers throughout the nineteenth century (Nimuendajú 1946:59–60).

In addition, gardens included a wider variety of crops than those documented by Ribeiro ([1819] 1841) in the early nineteenth century. Nimuendajú documented numerous crops that the Canela divided into "aboriginal" and "introduced" after contact with settlers. These divisions still hold today, albeit with certain modifications over time (see chapter 4, "Expanding Multispecies Families"). Aboriginal crops included maize (*põhy*), yam (*krẽrô*), sweet potato (*jàt*), bitter and sweet manioc (*kwỳr* and *kwỳr cahàc*), horse bean (the *pànkrỳt* category of today), gourd (*cuhkõn cahàc* squash of today), bottle gourd (*cuhkõn*), ground nut (peanut, *caahy*), cotton (*caxàt*), annatto (*pym*), arrowroot, and the edible *kupá* vine. Introduced crops included various fruit trees such as mango, papaya, and banana; sugarcane, cayenne pepper, tobacco, the *tingí* fish poison vine, and rice (Nimuendajú 1946:58). Although gardens remained primarily for subsistence, surpluses of manioc and rice were sometimes sold and traded in nearby towns. In 1930, for instance, the Canela brought "horse loads" of manioc flour from their gardens to "save" the townspeople of Barra do Corda from famine, an act which obliged the townspeople to "acknowledge publically [*sic*] that the Indians had planted considerable crops" (Nimuendajú 1946:61).

Nevertheless, Canela lifeways remained precarious, subject to environmental conditions, disease, and the continued threat of violence and encroachment by non-Indigenous settlers and ranchers. In 1934, a lack of remaining timber for construction and the onset of a measles epidemic forced the Canela to move farther downstream the Santo Estevão, to a village site called Baixão Preto. Shortly thereafter, in 1935, a smallpox epidemic ravaged the community and claimed Chief Faustino. The community then split into two different settlements on the Bois and Pombo streams in the east. When Nimuendajú returned in 1936, he encouraged the competing villages to reunite at a new village site on the Raposa stream, in between the Bois and Pombo streams (Nimuendajú 1946:33). The village was named Kô'kaipó-Katol-Tsà (Place Where Curt Nimuendajú Returned), with Doroteo Hàktoo-khot as chief of the newly reunited community. Thus, Nimuendajú's presence had a noticeable impact on Canela settlement patterns, seen especially in his involvement in the 1936 relocation.

The Indian Protection Service (*Serviço de Proteção aos Índios*, SPI) agents who came to the Canela after Nimuendajú, directly contributed to the further circumscription of Canela territory and development of more sedentary lifeways. In 1938, the SPI agent Castelo Branco visited the Canela and encouraged them to move back to the Ponto area on the Santo Estevão stream. He established the first Ponto village and adjacent SPI post, the remains of which Crocker visited as part of his old village survey twenty years later (Crocker, personal communication). Ranchers and settlers were encroaching onto the Ponto area during this time (and indeed onto most areas where the Canela established villages). Castelo Branco defended the Canela from these advances and convinced the non-Indigenous people to relocate their settlements elsewhere, thereby carving out a small territory for the Canela (Crocker, personal communication). In 1940, SPI agent Olímpio Cruz established a second Ponto village to the southeast, in closer proximity to the stream and the SPI post. He remained at the post until 1947, and afterward a number of SPI agents passed through (Crocker 1990:74). While the SPI agents acted in accordance with their mission to "protect the Indians" from often violent land disputes, they also pursued the larger SPI policy goal of "facilitating the economic integration of … [Indians] in the final stages of de-Indianization" (Devine Guzmán 2013:32; citing a teacher from the 1940s Canela SPI school). Indian Protection Service agents established schools to teach Portuguese and the rhetoric of the "civilized" Brazilian nation–state, and they provided the community with manufactured goods such as cloth, shotguns, gunpowder, and staple foodstuffs (Crocker and Crocker 2004:29; Devine Guzmán 2013:31). Hunting and gathering activities also were discouraged, and these practices already had been waning owing to the ongoing circumscription of the Canela territory.

By the mid-twentieth century, SPI policy shifted from complete acculturation to the "improvement" of Indigenous peoples through a focus on "self-reliance" (Devine Guzmán 2013:114, 136). For many Jê communities, including the Canela, this policy resulted in a focus on commercialized agricultural projects in order to become economically "productive" members of Brazilian national society (Ávila 2004; Devine Guzmán 2013:114). As Crocker and Crocker (2004:29) note, however, by the mid-1950s, the Canela had become accustomed to relying on the SPI for many manufactured goods and foodstuffs. Moreover, the male leadership council was not able to organize the younger male age groups to cultivate large commercial garden plots. While commercialized agriculture did not take off during this time, the Canela continued to maintain smaller garden plots for subsistence. Ponto remained the main village site throughout the 1940s and into the early 1950s. After Chief Doroteo's death in 1951, however, a split in the leadership developed between Pedro Gregorio Kaaràkhre as chief of Ponto and Alci Kapêltuk as chief of a competing village at Baixão Preto. Initially a temporary gardening settlement, the Baixão Preto village was made official in 1955 with its own SPI agent and post. When Crocker first conducted fieldwork in 1957–1958, he moved between the two villages and was adopted into families living at both sites (Crocker, personal communication).

By the early 1960s, the Canela had occupied Ponto village for over twenty years, demonstrating the community's shift to a more sedentary way of life. The population had also increased to around 400 people (Crocker 1990:58). Additionally, the development of Baixão Preto from a gardening settlement into a full-fledged village site indicates the increased importance of gardening to Canela lifeways, with the political situation allowing families to remain nearby their garden plots in the area's fertile soil. Garden sites also were located on the Pombo, Raposa, and Bois streams to the east, which families from both Ponto and Baixão Preto visited frequently (Crocker, personal communication). It is unclear when the contemporary practice of maintaining both a riverbank and forest garden plot began, although Crocker mentions each at different points in his extensive writings (Crocker 1990:95; Greene and Crocker 1994; Crocker and Crocker 2004:59).

In 1963, however, a dramatic event forced the Canela to abandon their villages and gardens. It began when a Canela woman, Maria Castelo Khêê-kwỳj, claimed that her unborn fetus was the sister of Awkhêê, the mythical figure who established the current unequal relationship between the Canela (mēhĩn) and the non-Indigenous cupēn.[1] Upon her daughter's birth, Maria Castelo claimed, Awkhêê would return and initiate a "new world order" dominated by the Canela instead of the cupēn (Crocker and Crocker 2004: 30–31). In preparation for this messianic event, a faction of the community engaged in an ongoing festival period of ritual dancing, singing, and feasting, taking cattle from nearby ranchers' farms for the feasts. As a result, in mid-1963 the ranchers attacked the Canela, burning down their villages and attempting to massacre the community. My research assistant Fernando, a young man at the time, described how men, women, and children escaped through a nearby stream after ranchers killed a few community members. My adoptive mother Liliana, then a child, remembered that families were forced to abandon their garden plots and leave behind many of their saved seeds and cuttings. Indian Protection Service agents helped to diffuse the violence and led the Canela to the neighboring territory of the Tupi-Guaraní-speaking Guajajara, where they remained until 1968.

During fieldwork in 1964, Crocker found the Canela to be initially "demoralized" upon their relocation to the forested Guajajara territory (Crocker and Crocker 2004:32). Soon after, however, the community established villages and garden plots in the fertile gallery forest soils. The political factionalism continued, with Pedro Gregorio establishing a larger village next to the SPI post, and Alci creating a smaller settlement farther upstream. Afraid to venture far from the post or the villages, families created small garden plots behind their houses (Crocker, personal communication). Many crop varietals were lost in the forced relocation, including those of maize, cotton, and peanut (Crocker 1990:95). Some types of corn must have been saved, however, since photos taken by Crocker show that the plants thrived in backyard gardens during this time. Canela families acquired other crops from the Guajajara, especially Guajajara tree bean (*pàt juhtõi-re pàràre/pryjĩ*), which is now a community wide favorite.

Despite this readjustment onto Guajajara lands, most families longed for the Cerrado landscapes, with their wide-open vistas, scrubby brush, and savannah grasses. Liliana, for example, recounted that her family was frightened by the gallery forests and missed their savannah garden plots. By 1968, small family groups began returning to the savannah and established four or five settlements throughout the territory. According to Liliana, most of the abandoned garden plots were empty, the crops having died out or been stolen by settlers. Some types of bitter manioc and pineapple remained in certain garden areas, particularly in the Põhipôc garden sector (see map 2). Bitter manioc varietals were still growing in the plot of Liliana's family because a *cupẽn* "friend" (*compadre*) had protected them from theft during the family's absence. With less crop diversity overall, though, Canela gardeners were left with an uncertain subsistence future. The political situation was similarly uncertain, with multiple settlements led by different men vying for the chieftainship. In 1972, Pedro Gregorio eventually solidified his authority through sponsoring a Khêêtuwajê festival (the first in the male initiation ritual complex) in the Escalvado area. The community reunited in Escalvado, creating a large concentric circular village that they continue to inhabit today.

As the Canela settled into Escalvado as their main village, they simultaneously were maintaining numerous garden plots throughout the territory in various garden sectors (*seitores da roça*). Ranchers and settlers continued to encroach on their lands, however, especially to the east of Escalvado where the ranchers had initially instigated the attempted massacre less than a decade earlier. In the early 1970s, various government agencies began the process of legally demarcating the Canela territory. These included FUNAI, which replaced the SPI in 1967, the Ministry of Justice, and the National Institute of Colonization and Agrarian Reform (*Instituto Nacional de Colonização e Reforma Agrária*). Over the next decade, government workers came to establish the official boundaries of the Canela territory, including areas in the east where encroachment by ranchers was rampant. The demarcation process was completed in 1982, establishing the Canela Indigenous Territory (TI Kanela) of 125,212 hectares (Instituto Socioambiental 2018a). With a newly legal basis to the land, including the village, dozens of garden sectors, and areas for the occasional hunting activities that still occurred, the community was surviving and thriving. A population boom occurred throughout the 1970s and 1980s, with an increase from 437 in 1970 to 836 in 1988 (Greene and Crocker 1994). Canela families were relying on garden produce more than ever before, and cultivating more than one garden simultaneously was becoming more common. Nevertheless, periods of what is called "half-hunger" (*meia-fome*) affected many people during the rainy season when the forest garden produce had been depleted. As a result, it was common for men, women, and sometimes entire families temporarily to relocate to nearby non-Indigenous settlers' farms for work as seasonal laborers.

Indeed, from the 1970s to the 1990s, Canela interaction with (and dependence on) non-Indigenous outsiders became increasingly common. In addition to government workers visiting to demarcate the territory, FUNAI agents established a post, primary school, and infirmary adjacent to the main village circle. The National Health Foundation (*Fundação Nacional da Saúde*) also established a health post in the 1990s (Crocker and Crocker 2004: 35). Missionaries from the Summer Institute of Linguistics (SIL) lived in Escalvado from 1968 to 1990, working on a Canela dictionary and translating the Bible into Canela (Popjes and Popjes 1986). Crocker continued periodic fieldwork visits throughout the 1970s and 1990s, bringing gifts of manufactured items and money that some families began to expect and rely upon. As access to the village became easier for outsiders through the construction and maintenance of roads, the Canela also were able to visit nearby non-Indigenous towns to purchase manufactured goods such as cloth, soap, foodstuffs, cooking oil, beads, and gardening tools. These relationships with the *cupẽn* were often based on an unequal power structure that continued to marginalize the Canela, creating and reinforcing an ongoing cycle of dependence on non-Indigenous people for education, healthcare, religious instruction, money, and manufactured goods.

It is therefore not surprising that smaller messianic movements predicting the reversal of *cupẽn–mẽhĩn* relations continued to occur throughout the 1970s, 1980s, and 1990s. The messianic approach focused on mythical transformations of social relations with outsiders at the expense of maintaining ongoing engagements with the local environment. In the 1970s messianic movement, for example, the leader Marcelo convinced community members to abandon their garden plots and move to a small forest settlement to await the return of Awkhêê. Marcelo claimed that the mythical figure would reverse his previous mandate that the Canela live in poverty while the whites became rich (see Miller 2015:107–111) and transform the *mẽhĩn* into rich and powerful *cupẽn*. The movement began during the slash-and-burn and planting periods of creating new gardens and many families therefore left their plots with few if any crops planted. A young mother at the time, Liliana participated in the movement, leaving behind her large forest garden full of growing maize and rice varietals in the Põhipôc (Campestre) garden sector. After a period of ritualized feasting, singing, and lovemaking, Marcelo declared that Awkhêê would return the following morning. Liliana re called that his followers painted themselves with body paint and spent the night singing ritual songs from the Pep Cahàc male initiation festival period. When the mythical figure failed to appear, the movement quickly ended and community members slowly returned to the main village and their garden plots. The gardens were mostly empty, however, and as a result many families experienced hunger that season.

A similar situation occurred in 1982, when Reinaldo, the leader of another messianic movement, told the community that garden work no longer mattered because the world would soon end. Reinaldo demanded harvested crops and hunted game as gifts and encouraged an ongoing festival period of singing, dancing, feasting, and playing soccer over working. He even threatened to "stop the rain" in garden plots if anyone continued cultivating them, since he claimed to control the weather. In 1997, the messianic leader Nilton also told the community to stop working because they were only "waiting for death" and the end of the world to come. Similar to Marcelo, he encouraged the community to remain painted with ritual body paint and maintain an ongoing festival period in preparation for the coming apocalypse. This movement incorporated Christian elements as well, with Nilton in possession of a magical Bible that came from the sky and made him powerful.

While many people often participated in the messianic fervor of these movements, an alternative approach emerged that focused on resisting dependence on outsiders through direct engagement with the environment, in the form of subsistence gardening.[2] During the 1982 movement, for example, Liliana and her family returned to their garden plot away from the frenzy in the village. Despite Reinaldo's threats of stopping the rain, Liliana recounted that there were heavy rains that year and her family's gardens produced abundant harvests. As her classificatory father Jacinto told her at the time, "if the world ends, it ends, but I want to keep working in the garden." Similarly, during the 1997 movement Liliana and her family continued maintaining their garden plots, as did other community members and their families.

Both the messianic and subsistence gardening approaches emerged out of a historical context of structural violence, sociopolitical and socioeconomic marginalization, and continued dependency on outsiders in numerous ways. As Rizzo de Oliveira (2007:209; my translation) argues, the "messianic expectation" of the Canela "emerged through their need to understand the processes of change within which they were inserted." However, I maintain that the messianic movements presented a more passive approach of waiting for cosmological intervention that would change the community's socioeconomic and sociopolitical circumstances. Subsistence gardening, meanwhile, offered the Canela a way to actively assert their independence from outsiders and create their own present and future through engaging with the local Cerrado landscape and providing food for one's family.

In the twenty-first century there remains an ongoing tension between concerted Canela efforts to shape their own life-world and their continued dependence on outsiders for political support, institutional religious backing, monetary assistance, and support of territorial integrity, among other things. Some community members have become involved in local politics in the township of Fernando Falcão, while others are taking part in the activities of local missionaries, including a German family from the Christian Evangelical Mission of Brazil and a Brazilian woman from the Assembly of God church based in Belém, Pará State. Many older men and women receive retirement payments from the government (*aposentadoria*), and many younger women receive monthly payments through Bolsa Família, a conditional cash transfer program that benefits poor women with young children who fulfill certain health and educational requirements. While Bolsa Família funds often provide much-needed cash to women for purchases such as soap, clothing, and foodstuffs in neighboring towns, there are also cases of the debit cards being used as collateral against debts to cattle ranchers, furthering dependence on and indebtedness to *cupẽn* outsiders (Miller 2013). In addition, Canela community members are once again relying on various government agencies to demarcate a second Canela territory of around 100,000 hectares that encircles the current TI Kanela. Known as TI Kanela Memortumré, the territory was legally identified in 2012 but still needs to be declared and "homologated" (*homologada*) to gain legal title, a process that can take years to complete (see Instituto Socioambiental 2018b).

Yet dependence on outsiders is only part of the emergent Canela life-world. Subsistence gardening plays an increasingly important role in the survival, resistance, and resilience of Canela people, plants, the environment or landscape, and the life-world as a whole. Gardens are larger than in the past and include a wider variety of crop species and varieties. A dual plot system of maintaining gardens in both forest and riverbank areas simultaneously has developed, which enables families to maintain a more constant supply of food throughout the year (as the next section discusses). Thus, Canela gardeners are no longer dependent on the seasonal work in *cupẽn* farms during the rainy season that they relied upon in previous decades. Moreover, Canela women and men of today identify themselves as gardeners, and the community at large values and appreciates the hard work involved in maintaining the large, biodiverse, and beautiful (*impej*) plots that families desire.

Although Canela gardening practices have undergone numerous transformations over the past two centuries, the modern day community views gardening as an authentically *mehin* activity in which Canela women and men can take pride. The subsistence gardening approach continues to provide a way for community members to resist dependence on and assert equality with the non-Indigenous *cupẽn*. During a conversation in May 2012, my research assistant Renato explained the importance of gardening as resistance to ongoing inequality and structural violence:

> The custom of the Canela in times past . . . at the end of the last century [nineteenth century], was that not all the Canela worked hard before; only a few people worked. This was because the young people were always having a festival, or making love to women. But today I am seeing the way of the Canela . . . like here, with your mother Liliana. In addition to a little money [she receives] sometimes, she is going to the garden every month to create a large garden. Why does she want to create a large garden? In addition to a large garden, people are planting and preparing things well. [. . .] So the garden is important here for us. As Liliana said, if we do not put in gardens, what will happen here? Today, in all of Brazil, I do not know which government—that of Lula or of Dilma or before, but they [the government] almost finished off the race of Indigenous peoples in all of Brazil. But, through policy, they cannot finish off the Indigenous race. [. . .] Today we are still preoccupied with creating gardens. Why? To not suffer from hunger. Because having rice, beans, fava beans, maize, peanut—then one can survive.

Loving Forest and Riverbank Gardens in the Twenty-First Century

Cultivating plots in both forest and riverbank areas has become the primary way that the contemporary Canela practice horticulture. The majority of families cultivate plots in both areas, and many of them also maintain small gardens in backyards behind their houses. Located in different land types with distinct soils, forest and riverbank gardens have distinct planting, tending, and harvesting schedules that overlap throughout the year. Gardeners maintain that the overlapping cycles ensure a constant supply of food throughout the year. Cultivating two gardens is the best defense against hunger or half-hunger (*meia-fome*), which can occur during part of the rainy season in December and January when the forest garden produce mostly has been depleted. Hunger is associated with feelings of weakness and sadness, known by the term *ihpêc*. Conversely, being satiated with food creates feelings of happiness and strength, or *ihtỳi*. While preparing meals in the cooking area behind her house, Liliana frequently would explain to me the importance of maintaining two gardens simultaneously. With both forest and riverbank gardens, as well as a small backyard garden she uses for experimenting with new crop species and varieties, Liliana repeatedly said that she "does not let the family suffer from hunger" and ensures they have food "all the time." She also emphasized the connection between gardening and happiness, strength, and being or becoming well in a holistic sense (*impej*). As she told me once in October 2012, "the gardens are the same as the father or mother of people. Without gardens, I would be sad [*ihpêc*]! Where would I do my work; where would I find food to eat?" During an interview in May 2012, my research assistants Renato and Wander reiterated this point. Renato explained that he creates new gardens to prevent "suffering from hunger," and Wander maintained that large garden plots help the Canela survive:

> This is how we are surviving [with gardens]. If people do not have gardens, it is a sad thing [*ihpêc*]; without any happiness [*ihtỳi*]. But, up until now, I am thankful that people are going to learn more how to . . . have this courage, to have more of a mind and an idea to work more in the gardens. So that our people can maintain themselves; so that this Canela family can survive well!

By providing a constant supply of food throughout the year, the dual gardening system helps maintain the happiness and strength of Canela families, and in Wander's words, helps them to "survive well."

Dual gardens are also conceptually significant in the modern-day Canela life-world. Jê-speaking communities are known in the ethnographic literature for the dual organization of their spatial and symbolic worlds (Maybury-Lewis 1979b). As Maybury-Lewis (1979c:2) pointed out, it was Nimuendajú who initially "stressed that dual organization was the key to the understanding of the Jê-speaking peoples." Drawing from Nimuendajú's initial suggestion, numerous anthropological studies have focused on the dualities in Jê kinship, social and spatial organization, ritual, and exchange (Da Matta 1973, 1982; Melatti 1978, 1979; Lave 1979; Maybury-Lewis 1979a, c; Seeger 1981, 1989; Lea 1986; Coelho de Souza 2002, 2004; Falleiros 2005). While the dualistic concentric circular organization of the Canela village is common in past and present Jê-speaking communities, the dual gardening system of forest and riverbank plots is a more recent conceptual dualism unique to the Canela that has emerged over the past half-century.

Forest and riverbank gardens are understood as a "couple" (*casal; amji catê* in Canela) that help each other, similar to a married man and woman and to the five soil couples that work together to increase soil fertility (chapter 1, "Approaching the Canela Territorial Landscape"). My research assistant Fernando described the connection between forest and riverbank gardens in this way during a conversation we had in July 2012:

> The gardens that we talk about are a couple, a garden couple [...] This is why I say that the gardens are like spouses — because you create one near the riverbank, in the fresh area, and afterward you create another one in the center [forest area]. You plant this first one near the riverbank during the month of August, and the other in the center you plant in November, December, or January, and you will not have any problems. [...] To have only one garden is nothing!

Similar to a husband and wife who work together for the well-being of the family unit, so too do forest and riverbank garden spaces promote well-fed, strong, and happy (*ihtỳi*) families. The forest and riverbank garden couple complement each other with their distinct territorial locations and soil types, gardening techniques, planting, growing, and harvest seasons, and diversity of crops planted in each area.

Forest gardens are located in forest sectors (*seitores da roça* in Portuguese) throughout the territory. Fernando, Renato, and Liliana named and located dozens of forest garden sectors in the maps they drew, with the majority of them located to the east and north of Escalvado village (see map 2). The most popular land types for forest gardens are the live forest (*ivẽntũm*) areas spread throughout the northwest and northeast quadrants of the territory, as well as the old forest (*iromtũm*) and old land (*pjêhtũm*) types. The live forest is especially favorable owing to its fertile *pjê pej* soil. According to Fernando and Liliana, this type of soil responds particularly well to fire during the slash-and-burn season and can produce an abundant harvest. Gardeners also sometimes plant forest gardens in the sandy *chapada* (*põ*) areas to the north of Escalvado, and in the true forest (*caxàt-re kô*) areas to the south. While there are no standardized property rights to these sectors, forest garden areas typically are passed down through the matrilocal family, with daughters continuing to garden in areas where their mothers and grandmothers cultivated. Each adult male and female couple typically cultivates a forest garden near those of other couples in the wife's family. For example, Liliana's three daughters and sons-in-law rotate their forest gardens in four different sectors that the matrilocal family has been using for at least three generations — the Põhipôc (Campestre) and Cumxê-ti Kat (Baixão Preto) areas in the north, Capà-ti (Ponto Velho) in the south, and Potyc (Brejo dos

Bois) in the east. If a couple separates, the forest plot and its produce usually remain in the hands of the woman and her family. While many couples remain together throughout their lives, Renato has married and separated from at least seven women in Escalvado (as of late 2017). After every separation, he moved out of his ex-wife's home and ceded the gardens he had cultivated to her and her family. Without a spouse, Renato returns to his mother's household and cultivates gardens in the areas where she has her familial connections. Fernando, Liliana, Renato, and Wander all agree that this system of forest garden inheritance is relatively new, a byproduct of the sedentary lifestyle the Canela have been living since 1972.

Riverbank gardens, on the other hand, are not passed down through matrilocal family lines in the same way. While couples tend to cultivate these plots nearby those of their family, choosing the location of riverbank gardens is a more fluid and flexible process. A gardener couple typically selects a riverbank garden in an available area of the riverbank land type (*coh-cahêhnã*) within a short walk (fifteen minutes to an hour) from Escalvado. Liliana's riverbank gardens in 2012–2013 and 2017, for example, were only a twenty-minute walk away from her house to the west of the village. Most of these plots are located next to streams that form the Santos Estevam or Pau Grosso Rivers in the northwest of the territory. Other riverbank gardening areas are available further east near the Pombo, Raposa, Bois, and Curicaco streams, although these are much farther from the village and are not the preferred areas to maintain a riverbank garden. The *awpêê* and *amcó* pair of soil types in the *coh-cahêhnã* riverbank land type are more fertile than forest garden soils, and cultivated crops grow faster here than in the forest areas.

New forest and riverbank garden plots are both called *pùl-tuwa* (*roça*) during the first year of planting, growing, and harvesting crops. During the second annual cycle, a plot is known as an old garden (*hipêj* or *pùl-wej*; *capoeira*), which is also a categorized type of land. By the third year, the same plot is an older garden (*caxàt-re kô*; *roça mais velha*).[3] In a second-year old garden, gardeners tend to the bitter manioc varietals that were planted the previous year, and some experts such as Liliana and her sister Camila plant more varietals of bitter and sweet manioc, fava bean, and common bean. Nothing new is planted in a third-year garden, although women typically continue to visit the area to collect bitter manioc. After the third year, gardeners leave older plots in both forest and riverbank areas to lie fallow for seven or eight years before cultivating the land again. The plot is not completely out of use during the fallow period, however, since many gardeners continue to collect fruit from trees planted during the first gardening cycle. Fernando and Liliana, for example, maintain varietals of cashew (*ahkrỳt*), banana (*pypyp-re*), orange (*ràràj*), and mango (*mac*) in their fallow garden spaces, all of which begin bearing fruit after five to seven years. An average Canela couple therefore attends to eight different garden spaces during one annual cycle—the new, old, older, and fallow gardens in forest and riverbank areas.

While all of these spaces are important to Canela gardeners, the new forest and riverbank gardens have particular significance as the complementary garden couple. They complement each other in terms of size, with forest gardens being much larger than riverbank plots, which are constrained on one side by a river or stream. In early May, the eldest male of the family and his sons-in-law demarcate new plots in both areas. As the eldest male in his family, Fernando instructs his sons-in-law to delineate the rectangular plots over the course of a few days, using machetes to clear away the brush and mark the plots' boundaries. According to Fernando and Renato, the ideal size for a forest garden plot is three *linhas* long and five or six *linhas* wide (approximately 0.85 × 1.4–1.7 hectares). Some families demarcate plots that are as much as seven *linhas* long (approximately 2 hectares) if they have many male family members or can pay men outside the matrilocal unit for their labor with gifts or money. Fernando and Renato attribute the rectangular shape and form of measurement they currently use to their non-Indigenous neighbors (*cupẽn*). Liliana maintains that gardens are sometimes demarcated as circular plots, which is similar to the Jê-speaking Panará, who are known for their concentric circular garden organization (Ewart 2013). This organization is rare, however, and could be unique to Liliana and her family. Canela gardeners today overwhelmingly prefer the rectangular spatial organization for forest and riverbank plots.

Forest and riverbank gardens are also complementary in their slash-and-burn cycles. In forest areas, multiple rounds of slashing and burning occur from May to September. In May, June, and July, men cut down the hardier forest trees, which can take several days to fell using a steel axe. Women and children clear away smaller brush and debris with machetes. The entire family often relocates to a temporary shelter in the forest to conduct this work, and they periodically return to stay there throughout the forest garden season. At the height of the dry season in early to mid-August, men and older boys begin the initial burning (*queimada*) of the forest plots, which typically lasts around two days. Women rarely accompany men to this first burn, but they do pay close attention to the skies for signs of smoke from distant forest plots. Upon seeing the smoke, Liliana describes how a woman should signal that the burn is happening by sweeping the ground and pounding an empty wooden mortar with a pestle in front of her house. According to Liliana, these activities help ensure a successful burn and growing season in forest garden plots. After the first burn, women and children slash the burned debris while men clear it from the plot. For plots cultivated in the live forest (*ivẽntũm*) areas, a second round of burning and slashing is necessary in late August or early September. In the denser true forest (*caxàt-re kô*) areas in the south, new plots require four or five burn-and-slash cycles. Fernando maintains that all burning should be completed by late September, before the first rains of the rainy season begin in early October.

Meanwhile, demarcating and felling trees in a new riverbank plot is much less time-intensive. The tree species in these areas tend to be smaller and have softer wood, and gardeners tend to clear away less vegetation in these areas. As Fernando and Renato explain, leaving the trees, grasses, and other vegetation growing near the riverbank helps prevent erosion and maintains a barrier between the river and the garden plot. Because riverbank plots are typically within easy walking distance from the village, families can visit the areas frequently without relocating to temporary shelters. In addition, riverbank plots usually require only one round of burning and slashing. Men perform the burning for two days at the end of July, and the entire family then slashes and clears away the burnt debris. If a second burn-and-slash cycle is needed to sufficiently clear the plot, it occurs in early August.

Riverbank gardens are therefore ready for planting much earlier than their forest garden counterparts, and the two planting, growing, and harvesting cycles complement each other by providing food at different times of the year. The two plots also have distinct garden layouts within which specific crop species and varieties can flourish. Over the course of many interview sessions, Fernando, Liliana, Renato, and Wander provided templates for the layout and schedule of riverbank and forest plots. The templates display the ideal form of the dual gardening system. In reality, individuals and families shape and modify these templates depending on their specific circumstances, including the current needs of their human (and plant) families. In chapter 3, I examine how particular expert gardeners Liliana, Camila, and Fernando and their families creatively expand upon these templates. Here I focus on the ideal riverbank and forest plot, in order to shed light on the material and symbolic complementarity of the two gardens.

In the ideal riverbank garden (see diagram 1), planting begins in mid-August. First, the gardener couple plants fruit trees near the riverbank to serve as a buffer between the river or stream and the garden. In Fernando's 2012 riverbank plot, for example, he and his wife Geralda planted buriti palm trees near the riverbank. Banana varietals are also a popular choice. Next to the trees at the riverbank's edge, the gardener couple plants sweet manioc by placing cuttings of mature roots (*maniva* or *manaíba*) in the ground at

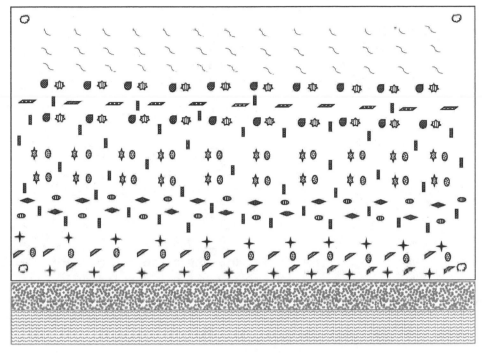

Diagram 1. Riverbank garden layout.

regular intervals, yet more haphazardly than rows. Men and women typically plant crops such as manioc together. Men dig the holes with a digging stick made from the *critin-re* native tree, and women place the cuttings or seeds in the holes. The gardener couple also plants varietals of species that grow particularly well in the fertile riverbank soils, including maize, fava bean, common bean, rice, squash, watermelon, yam, sweet potato, and sugarcane. Liliana explains that fava bean varietals often are planted near sweet manioc at the river's edge, so that women can hang the growing fava vines from the sweet manioc sticks. In the middle of the plot, fava bean and maize varietals are planted in juxtaposed horizontal rows, also in order to hang the fava vines from the maize stalks as they grow.

If the riverbank plot is large enough to accommodate the long vines of sweet potato, the gardener couple intercrops sweet potato varietals with common bean "on the vine" (*feijão de corda*) varietals near the riverbank side of the plot. They intersperse fast-growing rice varietals throughout the entire plot as well. At the end of the plot furthest from the riverbank, gardeners plant yam varietals in one row and varietals of squash and watermelon in separate holes next to each other in another row or two. Many couples, in-

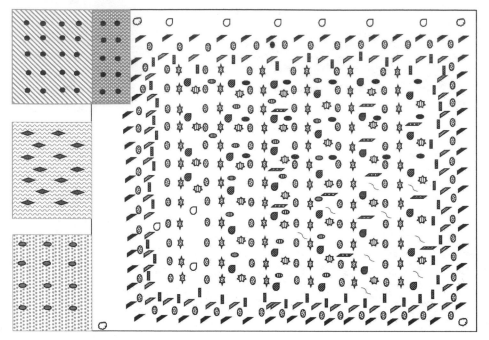

Diagram 2. Forest garden layout.

cluding Fernando and Geralda, line the outer edge of the plot with two or three rows of the *tepja-re* vine, which takes two to three years to mature. The vine is used to stun fish and eels, especially the electric eel (*poraquê*; *Electrophorus electricus* L.), in the water so that they can be easily collected and killed. It is also common to plant a type of inedible fava bean known as *pànkrỳt cahàc-ti*, or cobra fava (literally translated as "large common fava"), in the four corners of the rectangular plot. According to many gardeners, including Fernando, Renato, Liliana, and Wander, the strong smell of the plant deters snakes from entering the garden and biting humans.

The ideal layout of a forest plot is more complex, since a wider variety of species and varieties can be planted in the larger plots and distinct soils of forest areas (see diagram 2). While much of the planting in forest gardens takes place during the rainy season from October to January, it is possible to plant certain crops earlier in the year. Some couples, including Liliana and her husband, plant yam varietals interspersed in the center of the garden as early as June or July. Other families choose to plant an early crop of maize, yam, and/or sweet manioc in between the two burn-and-slash cycles in September. Maize and yam varietals are spread throughout the plot and sweet manioc is planted in straight rows. According to Fernando, September is

Caahy / peanut	●	Cuhkõn / gourd	⏝
Jàt / sweet potato	◄►	Praxĩ / watermelon	✺
Krĕrô / yam	▱	Pypyp-re / banana	✛
Pàt juhtõi-re / common bean not "on the vine"	0	Tepja-re / *tingi* fish poison vine	⤸
Pàt juhtõi-re / common bean "on the vine"	⬭	Cobra fava – to repel cobras	⬡
Pàt juhtõi-re pàràre/pryjĩ / "Guajajara tree bean"	⬭	Vegetation left growing next to riverbank	⣿⣿⣿⣿
Pànkrỳt / fava bean	◍	River/stream	〜〜〜
Põhy / maize	✡	Separate garden for varieties of peanut	⧄⧄⧄
Arỳihy / rice	▮	Separate garden for Caahy capa-re peanut variety	▨▨▨
Bitter manioc	◤	Separate garden for varieties of Jàt / sweet potato	〰〰〰
Sweet manioc	◸	Separate garden for varieties of Pàt juhtõi-re / common bean that are not "on the vine"	⣿⣿⣿
Cuhkõn cahàc / squash	◗		

Diagram 3.   Key for diagrams 1 and 2.

also a good time to plant watermelon and squash in adjacent parallel rows in the middle of the garden, as long as gardeners are mindful to leave space for both species' long vines. Gourd (*cuhkõn; Cucurbita* spp.) and bottle gourd (*cuhtõj; Lagenaria siceraria* [Molina] Standl. and/or *Crescentia cujete* L.) can be planted in one corner of the plot during this time as well, again leaving space for the vines, which can interfere with the growth of rice and bitter manioc. Unlike the riverbank plot, the *tepja-re* fish poison vine is intercropped with other species in the middle of the forest garden. When the rainy season begins in October, the gardener couple typically plants separate rows of bitter and sweet manioc around the edges of the rectangular plot. Fruit trees can be planted around this same time as well. In November, gardeners plant maize, fava bean, slow-growing rice varietals, and a portion of the common bean crop.

Paying attention to crop growth rates is crucial in forest plots. For example, Fernando and Liliana explain that common bean should be planted in stages, as the vines grow too quickly and crowd the garden if planted all at once. The four "on the vine" common bean varietals can be intercropped at different times throughout the forest plot, while Guajajara tree bean (*pàt juhtõi-re pàràre/pryjĩ*) should be planted in a horizontal row or rows in one section of the garden. They also maintain that rice should be planted around the edges of the plot first, and once it begins to bud, then maize can be planted. As in the riverbank plot, maize and fava bean are planted together in rows, leaving enough space between each hole for the maize to develop large stalks and ears. Older gardeners teach the younger generation about the close connection between maize and fava bean, which Fernando described as a "protective" and helpful relationship of mutual growth and abundance.

Other crops do not grow well together with different species and must therefore be planted in separate mini-gardens next to the main forest plot. Peanut, for example, should be planted in two separate mini-gardens — one for the *caahy capa-re* variety and the other for the three remaining peanut varietals. Sweet potato varietals, typically planted in December, also require a separate mini-garden, as do the nine varieties of common bean that have particularly lengthy vines (see appendix A for the full list of common bean varietals). While December marks the end of the main planting season, certain crops such as varietals of fast- and slow-growing rice can be planted well into January if desired. If gardeners are trying to space out crop harvest times even further, they can plant bitter manioc and common bean varietals as late as February.

While crops are growing, female gardeners manage and tend to the multiple crop species and varieties through regular visits to riverbank and forest plots. These are predominately female activities, although male gardeners sometimes accompany their spouses on the visits, especially to the more distant forest gardens. Liliana and her sister Camila explain that women generally visit their riverbank gardens on a daily basis, as the crops growing here require more care and attention than those in the forest plots. In the early morning, shortly after sunrise, it is common to see groups of women from the same family walking in the direction of the riverbanks to visit their plots. Liliana and Camila sometimes visit riverbank plots alone if their daughters are occupied with household activities. Once there, they survey the garden space, pulling out weeds and hanging the vines of vined crops such as fava and common bean. Although forest gardens do not require daily care, Fernando, Renato, Liliana, and Wander tell me that they should be visited at least every few days or once a week at a minimum. If left for longer periods of time, forest vegetation can quickly overtake a forest plot and its produce. Women often stay at the temporary shelters nearby the plot for days at a time during a particular weeding or tending period. During these longer stays, a woman is usually accompanied by her daughters, sisters, and mothers,[4] and sometimes her husband, father, and sons will visit as well. It is more unusual for a woman to visit a distant forest plot by herself, although some women such as

Camila do so out of necessity. In 2012–2013, Camila's daughters attended the primary school in the village and her husband and son-in-law were involved in local politics, leaving little time for them to visit forest gardens with her. By 2017, her daughters were all married and finished with school and therefore had more time for gardening activities with their mother.

Certain crops that are planted in forest plots, such as peanut, require special care and attention. When Liliana chooses to plant peanut varietals in a separate mini-garden, she carefully weeds the space without disturbing the seedlings, as this can lead to an ant infestation that destroys the crop. Rice growing in forest plots also requires special attention. As the wide variety of rice varietals begin to ripen in April or May, native parakeets (*krẽ-re*) and other types of birds can eat the entire crop in a matter of days. The *krẽ-re* birds especially "enjoy" eating the crop, the elder storyteller Leandro tells me, because they are transformed Canela people according to a mythic story. During this time, men bring their shotguns to the forest garden to scare away the birds and save the rice crop. Since women are more attuned to the daily and weekly rhythms of the plot, they often inform their male relatives when the birds are coming. One morning in late April 2012, for example, Liliana instructed her son-in-law Davi to visit their conjoined forest plots with his shotgun and scare away the birds. He rode off on his bicycle, shotgun in tow, and the family enjoyed an abundant rice harvest later in June.

By paying attention to the life cycles of their growing crop children (which I explore further in chapter 3), women gardeners become acutely aware of the harvest times of different species and varieties. The overlapping harvests in riverbank and forest plots complement one another and provide an ongoing supply of food throughout the year. For example, maize in the riverbank plot is typically ready to harvest by November or December, when much of the planting season is still underway in the forest plot. Fast-growing rice varietals can be harvested around the same time, and if a couple chooses to plant a second round, the second harvest takes place in February or March. Certain varietals of sweet manioc typically mature earlier in January. The timing of these riverbank harvests is crucial, providing food during the middle of the rainy season when half-hunger would typically strike a family with only a forest garden. Most of the other crops planted in riverbank plots are also ready for harvest in February or March, including sweet potato, fava bean, common bean, squash, and watermelon. In April and May, gardeners usually harvest some of the bitter manioc they planted eight months to a year before near the riverbank's edge.

In forest plots, the early harvest season typically begins in February or March, although the occasional early crop of maize is sometimes harvested in December. Families usually harvest sweet potato, watermelon, maize, and fast-growing rice varietals in late February and early March. The community as a whole also performs two separate rituals to celebrate the first harvests of sweet potato and other vine crops (known as the Hôxwa) and then maize (known as the Põhy Prỳ-re). By April, May, and June, most of the other crops in forest plots are ready for harvest, including slow-growing rice, fava bean, common bean, and squash. Yams, peanuts, and gourds have longer maturation periods and are usually harvested in June or July.

Harvesting manioc, largely the staple food crop, can occur practically any time of the year in both forest and riverbank plots. Canela gardeners categorize manioc into types of sweet, bitter, and half-sweet/half-bitter manioc that have widely different maturation periods. Most sweet manioc varietals mature in only five months, while most bitter manioc varietals take a year to mature and produce the best-tasting *farinha* (toasted manioc flour). One bitter manioc variety, tortoise arm bitter manioc (*kwỳr pakran-re* or *kwỳr caprãn jũkee*), takes a year and a half to mature fully, and strong vine bitter manioc (*kwỳr hêhtyi*) matures in three years. Hugging vine manioc (*waíputre*), one of the two varieties that Canela gardeners classify as half-sweet/half-bitter, can remain in the ground for an impressive five years before harvesting. Women are responsible for paying attention to the locations and growth rates of their manioc crops in new, old, and older riverbank and forest plots. Expert gardeners such as Liliana and Camila therefore space out the planting of diverse manioc varietals to ensure a frequent supply of the crop throughout the year.

Women typically harvest crops with their husbands, with groups of women, and often with the entire family. Men sometimes harvest crops in male-only groups as well, especially rice or manioc in larger forest gardens. These larger crops occasionally are taken to sell in markets in nearby non-Indigenous towns. In June 2012, for example, my adoptive relative Magdalena paid for additional manual labor outside her family and the use of village trucks to harvest her large manioc crop, which she and her female relatives then processed into sixty large bags of *farinha*, each weighing 20–30 kilos. She intended to use some of the crop for festival periods in which her daughter was performing as a *wuh-tỳ* female ritual associate (see Crocker 1990: 105–106) and the rest to sell within and outside the community. While some people sell or barter their surplus food crops to other Canela community members outside their family, it is still relatively uncommon to sell produce to the non-Indigenous *cupẽn*. Overall, gardening is primarily a subsistence activity that can usually sustain a Canela family throughout the year when practiced in dual forest and riverbank plots.

The complementarity of forest and riverbank gardens is material—

composed of overlapping yet distinct land types, soils, garden layouts, and types and life cycles of crops   and symbolic, composed of the dialectical conceptual relationship between the two. Fernando, Liliana, Renato, Wander, and other gardeners consistently referenced each garden in relation to the other. Soils in the riverbank are understood as more fertile only in relation to the slightly less fertile soils of forest plots. Similarly, the locations and sizes of each plot refer to one another, with riverbank gardens closer yet smaller, and forest gardens farther away yet larger. Gardeners frequently compare their work in the two plots, saying that tending to crops in riverbank plots is easy compared with the difficult work of maintaining a forest garden. Overall, the conceptual dualism of forest and riverbank gardens for contemporary gardeners emphasizes the interdependence of both spaces. As a garden couple, they work together and fortify one another, bringing happiness, strength, and an overall state of well-being (*impej*) to both people and plants. Conversely, having only one garden plot in the modern-day lifeworld is cause for sadness, weakness, and being or becoming unwell (*ihkên*). As Fernando pointed out, "to have only one garden is nothing!"

In the modern-day Canela life-world, however, the dual gardening system does not exist in material or symbolic isolation. Riverbank and forest gardens are material–ecological spaces and conceptual categories in relation to Escalvado village, which is arguably the material–symbolic center of the Canela community where much of life unfolds. When drawing maps of the territory, Fernando and Renato consistently drew Escalvado first then added the riverbank and forest garden sectors in relation to the village. Similarly, Liliana, Camila, and their daughters discussed their daily and weekly routines in all three spaces in relation to one another. Working in the gardens is compared to working in the house in the village, just as tending to crops near the riverbank is compared to taking care of crops in forest gardens. During one of our conversations in October 2012, Liliana explained that "I take care of my gardens. I protect them, same as I do with my human family. Just as when I have dishes, I wash them; when I am at home, I do not let garbage remain in my house." Here she is comparing clearing gardens of debris and keeping them clean to cleaning her house and the materials within it. In another conversation in July 2012, Liliana compared the dual gardens her daughter Nilda was in charge of cultivating that year. Her family always takes care of a "garden near the riverbank, and another in the center [forest area]," Liliana maintained. The lives of contemporary Canela women and men unfold in all three spaces as they move between the village, riverbank garden, and forest garden areas in order to support the well-being of themselves and their human (and plant) families.

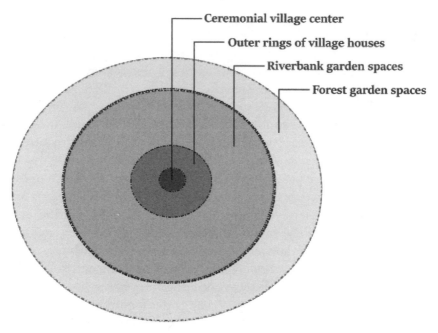

Ceremonial village center

Outer rings of village houses

Riverbank garden spaces

Forest garden spaces

Diagram 4. Triadic structure of village–riverbank garden–forest garden.

This triadic structure of the Canela territory unfolds from two concentric dualistic pairs—the ceremonial center and outer rings of houses in the village and the complementary areas for riverbank and forest gardens, the latter of which geographically and conceptually encircle the former (see diagram 4). The conceptual and geographical arrangement of the village-riverbank garden–forest garden triad accords with Lévi-Strauss's (1963:131) theory of Jê concentric dualisms forming implicit triads and with Crocker's (1990:325–328) observations of Canela dualisms and triads in linguistic associations and conceptual thinking (see also chapter 1, "Understanding the Canela Bio-Sociocultural Life-World"). Seeing as the emphasis on cultivating dual riverbank and forest gardens is a relatively recent phenomenon that is connected to the more sedentary lifeways of Escalvado village, it is clear that the triadic spatial organization of the territorial landscape is also a relatively recent addition to the life-world over the past forty-five years. Nevertheless, each of these three spaces is seen as integral to the Canela life-world and its future. The riverbank and forest gardens, when combined with the village space, provide a means for Canela women and men to feed their families, become happy, strong, and well, and develop intimate engagements with the growing crops and the garden spaces that they truly love and adore.

Learning from Star-Woman: Origins of Horticulture and Biodiversity Maintenance

One afternoon in June 2012, I was lounging in my hammock in my mother Liliana's house, taking a break from the hot sun and festivities of the week-long Pep Cahàc male initiation ritual period (see Crocker 1990:274–275). Liliana called to me in her typical way: "Toaxêkwỳj, *vem cá!* [Toaxêkwỳj; come here!]"[5] Our elderly next-door neighbor Leandro had come over to visit me, as I was interested in recording his versions of the vast array of Canela mythic stories. Over the course of a few months, we recorded twelve different long-form mythic stories, which Leandro told in Portuguese with Canela vocabulary. On this first day, the then-eighty-nine-year-old Leandro wanted to begin with the mythic story of Star-Woman (Caxêtikwỳj) who introduced horticulture to the ancestral Canela community. He had learned the story from his very old grandfather Lauriano when he was still alive. The origin of horticulture myth is common among Jê-speaking communities, with either Star-Woman or a mythical mouse or rat introducing maize and other crop species to the human community (Wilbert 1978:209–227; Ewart 2013: 205–207). For the Canela, the Star-Woman mythic story is particularly conceptually significant to modern day community members. As Renato stated during one of our conversations on biodiversity maintenance, "even today, we continue learning from Star-Woman." Fernando, Liliana, and Wander agreed, explaining that Star-Woman taught the Canela people (*mëhĩn*) the plant categories and "indicated the names" of the diverse species and varieties that gardeners cultivate today. Indeed, nearly every crop species and variety grown today is attributed to Star-Woman, other than those that are categorized as introduced by non-Indigenous outsiders (*cupẽn*; see chapter 4, "Expanding Multispecies Families"). Overall, there is an intimate connection between Star-Woman and contemporary gardening practices, including agro-biodiversity maintenance.

By defining horticulture as an ancestral Canela activity with mythic origins, the Star-Woman myth gives authenticity to modern-day gardening activities and preferences. The story itself has transformed over time to incorporate the historical context of Canela gardening and its modern-day appreciation and valuation. Here I compare the version Leandro told me with those recorded by Crocker (1990) and Nimuendajú (1946). The basic schema of the story in all three versions is as follows: Star-Woman comes down from the sky in the form of a frog and then transforms into a beautiful woman with long hair. She introduces herself to a Canela man called Tyc-ti (literally "black and large"). She then shows Tyc-ti and his family crops growing nearby the village and demonstrates how to process and consume the newfound food. Prior to her arrival, the community ate rotten wood and was unware that the plants in their local landscape were edible. After showing the community how to grow, process, and consume the crops, Star-Woman returns to the sky, usually taking Tyc-ti with her. Gardeners today associate the Morning Star (*Estrela Dalva*) with Star-Woman and a smaller nearby star with her husband.

Within this basic structure, certain transformations of the mythic story have emerged over the past eighty years. The most notable modifications are the incorporation of multiple crop species and varieties, the increased emphasis on multi-sensory, embodied engagements with crops and processes of ecological learning, and the inclusion of relations with outsiders (the *cupēn*). While it is possible that earlier recorded versions left out these aspects, it is clear that they have become integral to the modern-day version. In the version recorded by Nimuendajú in the 1930s (1946:245), for example, Star-Woman shows only maize to the ancestral Canela. She shows Tyc-ti that the corncobs growing near the riverbank are edible, although he is suspicious of the newfound food. After Star-Woman harvests the ears of corn, she processes them into large maize pies (*beribu*) wrapped in wild plantain or banana leaves (*acahôc pej* in Canela; *Heliconia* sp.) and teaches the community how to eat the pies instead of rotten wood. *Beribu* pies are a significant ceremonial food for the modern-day community, although they are typically made out of manioc. According to Nimuendajú (1946:62), the Canela community of the 1930s associated four types of maize with Star-Woman: true/original maize (*pōhy pej-re*), large white maize (*pōhy jaka-ti*), mixed-color maize (*pōhįto'rómre*), and *pōhįkreakáre*. The first three types are currently cultivated today, although mixed-color maize is known as *pōhy tohrom-ti* (large mixed-color maize). The fourth type possibly refers to the small maize (*pōhy kryi-re*) type that contemporary gardeners cultivate. When Crocker (1990:302) recorded mythic stories in 1975, the elder storytellers with whom he worked maintained that Star-Woman showed people a wider variety of cultivated crops and gathered fruits, including "corn, other vegetables, *buriti* palm fruits, and, in effect, all foods except wild game . . . these new foods had always existed in the wild, but the Canela did not know they were edible" (Crocker 1990:304).

In Leandro's version, he discusses the diversity of crops that Star-Woman showed the Canela, including all types of corn, sweet potato, sweet and bitter manioc, and the fruits of tucum, buriti, and *mangaba* native trees. Contemporary gardeners directly attribute other species and varieties to Star-Woman as well. Liliana maintains that the "painted" varieties of fava bean, some of her favorites, have been in Canela gardens since Star-Woman's arrival. Renato, meanwhile, states that the ancestors cultivated "all the seeds" after Star-Woman's initial discovery of horticulture.

In addition to the growing number of crops included in the mythic story over time, there is also a greater emphasis on the multi-sensory, embodied ways that Star-Woman engages with the environment and the ancestral community, in order to show them the plentiful agro-biodiversity in the local landscape. The versions recorded in Nimuendajú (1946) and Crocker (1990) do not include detailed explanations of how Star-Woman sees, touches, tastes, and processes crops or how she transmits this knowledge to the people. Leandro, however, focuses on the multi-sensory engagements between and among Star-Woman, Canela people, and plants. When Star-Woman shows her husband the fruits of tucum and buriti trees, for example, Leandro focuses on the visual appreciation and taste of the newfound food:

> The next morning, at seven in the morning, Caxêtikwỳj said to her husband, "let us go bathing. Bring the large basket." They came to the stream and saw a large amount of tucum fruit [rônti xô or ronre xô in Canela; *Bactris setosa* Mart.] "Pick this tucum," Caxêtikwỳj told Tyc-ti, and he did so. She began chewing it, and asked him, "Are you going to eat it?" "No, if I eat that, I will die," Tyc-ti answered. He did not want to eat it; he became angry. "No, you will not die. This is what feeds you; it is your food. I am going to find everything for you to know about," Caxêtikwỳj told him. She gave him the tucum fruit, and he chewed it, swallowed it, and found it tasty. Once they were in the water, there were many buriti [*crowa pàr*] palms next to the stream. Caxêtikwỳj gave the buriti fruit to Tyc-ti for him to taste it as well. Again, Tyc-ti said, "I am not going to eat this because it is raw, and very red." Caxêtikwỳj told him, "no, it is not raw; it is fruit, buriti fruit! People are not accustomed to eating it; you do not know. I am still going to find other fruit in the *chapada*, and in the forest." Caxêtikwỳj gave Tyc-ti the fruit for him to swallow, and he liked it. She made juice and showed him how to drink it.

Although Tyc-ti is not initially willing or able to see or taste the fruits as food, through his intimate relationship with Star-Woman he learns how to engage with tucum and buriti fruits in new sensory ways. Similarly, Leandro describes how Star-Woman teaches Tyc-ti and the entire community to appreciate maize through sight, taste, and smell:

> Another day, Caxêtikwỳj took Tyc-ti to a different stream. They went into the stream, and there were many ears of corn falling into the

water. Tyc-ti asked her, "What is in here, these tall stalks and big ears?" "It is maize!" Caxêtikwỳj told him. "This is what I am discovering for you all to know about. Let us go to the village, to show people." They had to roast it, because it was still raw. There were so many ears of corn, and they arrived to the house with all the ears. Caxêtikwỳj's sisters-in-law were seated, and she told one of them, "my sister-in-law, this is food; it is an ear of corn. I am going to roast it for you to see." Caxêtikwỳj said this; she had this knowledge. Together, they made a grater to grate the ears of corn. Then, they made a fire, roasted the ears, and ate them. All the sisters-in-law were chewing the food. "Are you seeing it; is it tasty?" Caxêtikwỳj asked. It was so tasty! "You have never seen this; it was I who discovered it, and I still have other things to discover," Caxêtikwỳj told them. "The fruits of the riverbank, and there are other plants too." Caxêtikwỳj grated the ears of corn, made an earthen oven, and brought the maize husks with her as well. She wrapped the grated maize meal in the husks, covered them, and baked them in the oven. When it started smoking, she opened the oven. Everyone smelled the nice smell of the maize *beribu* pie, and thought it was beautiful [*impej*].

Through these sensory experiences mediated by Star-Woman, the Canela ancestors develop embodied gardening skills and practices, expanding their corpus of ecological knowledge and active knowing. Star-Woman is the original gardening expert who shares her knowledge with Canela men and women through multi-sensory engagements with growing crops in riverbank and forest areas of the territorial landscape. In Leandro's version of the story, Star-Woman shows people the native fruits and maize varietals near the river or stream, as well as *mangaba* fruits, sweet potatoes, and sweet and bitter manioc growing in forested areas. When Star-Woman shows the community the *mangaba* fruits in the forest, she also demonstrates the specific techniques necessary to create an earthen oven (*khĩya*):

Another day, Caxêtikwỳj said, "let us go to the forest so I can show another fruit to you." It was *mangaba* [*pênxôô pàr*]; it was a large, tall tree with fruit this size [about the size of a fist]. Caxêtikwỳj was in the forest and presented the *mangaba* tree to the people, saying, "This is for you all to know about and to eat. Stop eating rotten wood; that is not food! This is the food that I came here for everyone to know about." An Indian climbed up the tree to cut down the fruit, and it fell to the ground. They collected all of it. Caxêtikwỳj herself showed them how to do everything—how to make the earthen oven. They dug a hole and arrived with the *mangaba* fruit. "Light this earthen oven," Caxêtikwỳj told them, and when they heated up the stones, Caxêtikwỳj took off the stones and put water in the hole. She heated it up, and put in the fruit, which turned soft that very moment. When she was done teaching them, Caxêtikwỳj took away the cooked fruit and returned to the village. They made the food, ate it, and enjoyed it. "[Look at] all of my discoveries of these fruits of the forest! Stop eating rotten wood now; do not remember it anymore," Caxêtikwỳj told the people.

Here, Leandro emphasizes Star-Woman's discoveries in the forest (versus the riverbank) and her creation of the earthen oven, which nowadays is seen as an authentic Canela way of cooking that is used primarily for ritual activities. By reiterating Star-Woman's command to stop eating rotten wood, Leandro is also highlighting the new era of Canela lifeways and subsistence patterns that Star-Woman's discoveries initiated. In another part of Leandro's story, the focus shifts to the gendered aspects of gardening knowledge when Star-Woman teaches women about sweet potato:

On another day, she said, "let us go again to the forest, so that I can show you another fruit." She took only women with her, and there were many of them. They arrived in the forest, and there were many sweet potato vines, right there in the forest. She started digging up the sweet potatoes, and the women took them back to the village. They made another earthen oven and baked the sweet potatoes, and after cooking them, they were soft as well. All the teachings of Caxêtikwỳj, everything that she taught them, the ancestors learned as well.

The focus on gender extends to Star-Woman's teachings on the categorization of manioc:

Another day, Caxêtikwỳj showed them sweet manioc in the forest. There was so much of it! They harvested the sweet manioc, and they ate it—it was tasty. Caxêtikwỳj showed them bitter manioc too, and told them, "This bitter manioc is not for making *beribu* pies. The sweet manioc is feminine, and the bitter manioc is masculine. You cannot make pies with the bitter manioc, only with the sweet manioc—[because] it is a woman. Bitter manioc is a man; it is bitter, and if you make pies with this, it will kill you and you will die. You have to grate it, squeeze it in the *tipití* [*tap-ti*], and make *beiju* [a type of pancake] or *farinha* [toasted manioc flour] with it and you can eat it this way." She showed all of these crops for the Indian to know about. Slowly, they became accustomed to this new food; they began to know about it until they knew everything well.

The categorization of feminine sweet manioc and masculine bitter manioc, as well as a blurred gender category of half-female, half-male for the half-sweet/half-bitter types, is a significant aspect of contemporary crop classification practices (see chapter 4, "Noticing and Naming: Classifying Through Multi-sensory Experiences"). In these ways, Leandro's story shows how Star-Woman is understood as the originator of nearly all modern-day gardening activities, preferences, and knowledge. She is responsible for the focus on multi-sensory, embodied engagements with a wide diversity of crops; for specific planting, tending, harvesting, and processing techniques; for the conceptual division between riverbank and forest areas; for the gendered division of certain gardening activities; and for crop categorization and naming. Once Star-Woman has passed along her vast knowledge of plants and horticulture to the ancestral Canela community, she returns to the sky with her Canela husband:

Caxêtikwỳj told her husband, "I am going now. I only came to show this food to you all for you to learn about it. Now I already showed you everything. I am going to return to the sky." Tyc-ti did not want to let her leave. "I am going with you," he said. "No, you are not," she told him. Nevertheless, he convinced her, and Caxêtikwỳj took Tyc-ti with her to the sky. She told him, "let us go together. They already found the fruits in the forest, and the food from the crops as well. They will make gardens and harvest the crops—the *maniva* [roots] of sweet manioc. They will plant sweet potatoes, and buriti, and watermelon, and all the seeds." Caxêtikwỳj went into the sky with her husband.

While the contemporary version of the story focuses on the originality of modern-day gardening practices and agro-biodiversity as directly linked to Star-Woman, it also includes the role of outsiders (*cupẽn*) in attempting to destroy these practices. Neither Nimuendajú (1946) nor Crocker (1990) mention the involvement of non-Indigenous outsiders in their recorded versions of the mythic story. In Leandro's telling, however, outsiders figure prominently after Star-Woman distributes maize pies to the entire community:

People [the *mēhĩn*] said, "Caxêtikwỳj is finding this food for us to know about! We are going to cut down the maize tree; it is very tall and is heavy with ears of corn." The next morning . . . the Indian [*mēhĩn*], he never learned to be intelligent, he did not know, and he asked the

Christians [*cupēn*] to cut down the maize tree. The Christians took the largest ears of corn, and left the smaller ones for us. That is why the whites plant maize with large ears, and the Indians plant maize with smaller ears, because the Christians stole the large ears and left the smaller ones.

When asking the non-Indigenous outsiders for their assistance, the ancestral Canela are unaware that they might be betrayed. This type of scenario is found throughout the two-hundred-year history of *mēhĩn–cupēn* relations, as described in the first section of this chapter. The outsiders' theft of the larger and arguably better crops is almost always included in the modern-day telling of the Star-Woman story. Liliana listened to Leandro's storytelling that afternoon in June 2012, and in the evening, she recounted her grandmother Manuela Célia's version of the theft. According to her, the *cupēn* stole giant maize stalks, manioc roots, and bushels of rice in front of the Canela, who did not prevent the theft because they "did not know anything." Liliana maintained that the non-Indigenous neighbors had taken all the good crops from the Canela, who had been too defenseless to stop them. The contemporary Star-Woman story therefore sheds light on the interpretation of historical, mythical, and current-day inequalities as simultaneously resulting from blatant theft perpetrated by non-Indigenous outsiders and from a lack of Indigenous knowledge. At the same time, by celebrating the vast ecological knowledge that Star-Woman shares specifically with the Canela community, the story enables the Canela to value and appreciate their own modern-day gardening practices.

Although Star-Woman is understood as the discoverer of nearly all crop species and varieties, two other mythic stories describe alternative origins for particular crops. In one story, the mythical figure of Giant Armadillo (Awxêti) introduces peanut, sweet potato, and a few types of maize to the Canela warrior Pàrpajõi-te. In another story, the mythical figure of Macaw (Pàn) shows annatto trees (*pym* in Canela; *urucum* in Portuguese; *Bixa orellana* L.) to a Canela man, the seeds of which are made into a bright red paste for body painting. Canela gardeners commonly reference these figures when discussing the particular crops with which they are associated. Fernando, for example, told me the story of Giant Armadillo on two separate occasions when we were discussing modern-day varietals of peanut and sweet potato. In another conversation, Renato maintained that Giant Armadillo was a "hard worker" who gave peanut and sweet potato to the *mēhĩn*, and for this reason, the Canela continue to cultivate these crops today. Even today, he said, armadillos living in the local landscape enjoy eating the sweet potato crop growing in forest gardens. When discussing varietals of annatto, Fernando and Renato agreed that the Canela had received annatto trees from Macaw, and that macaws living in the forest today continue to paint their feathers with the brilliant red paste made from annatto seeds.

Leandro's versions of these stories emphasize the embodied ecological knowledge that Canela people have learned from intimate engagements with mythical figures, similar to his telling of Star-Woman. For example, Leandro describes the encounter between Giant Armadillo and the Canela warrior in the following way:

> Pàrpajõi-te traveled again. Afternoon arrived, and he came to Giant Armadillo's [Awxêti's] garden. Pàrpajõi-te entered his house and sat down. Giant Armadillo arrived and was afraid of Pàrpajõi-te, and Pàrpajõi-te was afraid as well, because Giant Armadillo is huge. They both were afraid of each other. Giant Armadillo said, "let us sleep here together. You will lay next to the fire on one side, and I will lay on the other side. We will talk until dawn ...
>
> "I am going to sleep now," Pàrpajõi-te said, "but I will not bother you." "Nor will I bother you," Giant Armadillo responded. "We are going to be real friends, *kêt-ti* [grandfather/uncle] and *tàmtswè* [named grandchild/nephew]." Giant Armadillo put sweet potatoes in the ashes of the fire, and when they were cooked, he took them out and gave one to Pàrpajõi-te for him to eat. Pàrpajõi-te ate it, and found it tasty. "Tomorrow I will give you seeds [and cuttings] to take with you and plant in your garden. This here is good food. Feed yourself with seeds," Giant Armadillo said. In the morning, Giant Armadillo and Pàrpajõi-te entered into an agreement with each other. They did not fight. Giant Armadillo packed up some seeds [and cuttings] for Pàrpajõi-te, giving him sweet potato, peanut, pink maize, white maize, and red maize. Giant Armadillo packed up all of these seeds for him.

By including Canela kinship terms, Leandro is underlining the intimate relationship that Giant Armadillo and the Canela warrior have developed through the embodied activities of eating, sleeping, and visiting gardens together. Although they initially fear one another as strangers with different bodies (human and more-than-human), Giant Armadillo establishes himself as the grandfather or uncle of Pàrpajõi-te, which is traditionally an expert–novice relationship. In this way, Giant Armadillo can share his embodied ecological knowledge of various seeds and cuttings with the Canela warrior.

In the story of Macaw, a similar process of embodied learning through intimate trans-species encounters occurs. After getting lost in the forest one night, a Canela man meets Macaw, who offers to show him the way back to the village. On the way, Macaw shows the man a grove of annatto trees. Leandro describes the discovery:

> They came close, and arrived at the grove of *urucum* trees. There were many trees, large *urucum* trees. They were very large in the forest. Macaw said to the man, "this *urucum* that you all do not yet know about, this is mine. We paint it on our bodies; it is very red." Then he showed the man how to use it. "Break some off, for when you arrive in the village, and show [the seeds] to the women. Bring the women here to take some and paint it on their bodies."
>
> In the beginning, the ancestors did not know about this *urucum*; they only knew how to use [a certain rock] as paint. It is also red, and you can paint with it like *urucum,* but it is not very red. Macaw discovered the real *urucum* for the man, and the man took two branches of the tree with him. He came to the road and walked to the village. Everyone came together, asking, "where have you been? Where did you spend the night?" "I lost my way back to the village, but I have arrived now. Macaw showed me where the village was and the road to it, and I came back," the man said. "Look, this is called *urucum* [*pym*]! This is the real macaw's *urucum* that Macaw showed me. There is a grove of trees in the middle of the forest. Tomorrow, I am taking all the women there to break off the branches and use [the seeds] to paint our bodies." This is how Macaw showed the Indians *urucum* for them to use.

By showing the man how to paint his body with the thick bright red paste, the more-than-human Macaw engages with the human Canela man in multi-sensory ways—mainly through sight and touch. Overall, the embodied processes of ecological learning that Canela ancestors experience with Star-Woman, Giant Armadillo, and Macaw inform the ways in which modern-day gardeners teach younger generations, as I explore in chapter 3.

In addition to providing the basis for modern-day environmental knowledge transmission, the mythic stories give meaning and value to contemporary gardening practices in the face of ongoing inequality with and dependence on the non-Indigenous *cupẽn*. Just as the non-Indigenous people are said to cultivate larger crops than the Canela, they also are known to maintain larger gardens and storehouses and to have greater access to farm machinery. In spite of these seemingly unequal gardening practices, the Canela value their own activities and diversity of cultivated crops. Over breakfast of coffee, *farinha,* and eggs one morning in June 2012, Renato described the importance of mythic stories such as that of Giant Armadillo to contemporary Canela gardeners and compared the mythical origins, hard work, and expert knowledge of Canela gardeners to that of the non-Indigenous *cupēn*:

> Giant Armadillo [Awxêti] was cultivating peanut [*caahy*]. He was cultivating sweet potato, and even today we have sweet potato and peanut, because of Giant Armadillo. He was a hard worker who cultivated all these crops. Then the giant one [Pàrpajõi-te], who liked to hunt in the forest, received these seeds. And this is why he brought back the seeds to his people. Even today, you can see that peanut and sweet potato still exist, that diverse crops still exist. After the arrival of the Portuguese, they began killing the Indians—attacking and attacking them—until today, when the white men [*cupēn*] have their stored crops; their big warehouses in which they store various seeds. Nowadays, with machines that do the work, I do not even know how many hectares of maize, peanut, and sugarcane [they have]. They even plant watermelon out of season, without rain, because of irrigation. So things remain the same [as they were in the past], as we are still seeing today. [...] Now it is June, and they [the whites] have watermelon without water. But us *mēhĩn*, since we work with manual labor—not like the *cupēn* are doing—all the time the *cupēn* do not understand our culture and they say, "the *mēhĩn* are lazy." But it is not the truth! *Mēhĩn* are hard workers! They can work in the middle [forest garden plots] and suffer from hunger! They can do log racing, like they are going to do today. [Unlike the whites], the *mēhĩn* grow their gardens for food! That is why the story of Giant Armadillo is very important.

As Renato eloquently states, inequality with and dependence on non-Indigenous outsiders remain significant aspects of contemporary Canela experiences. Yet gardening activities, agro-biodiversity maintenance, and their mythical–historical origins provide material and symbolic resistance to continued structural violence. The central role of the horticultural mythic stories of Star-Woman, Giant Armadillo, and Macaw in the current Canela life-world demonstrates the community's attempt to value and make sense of their place in the local landscape despite the structural violence that forms part of their past and present experiences.

Gardening as Resistance

Over the past two hundred years of sustained *mēhĩn–cupēn* relations, myriad transformations of Canela gardening activities have taken place. Gardening practices have changed in response to outside forces such as warfare, disease, land encroachment and loss of territory, violence, governmental involvement, and socioeconomic and sociopolitical marginalization. The semi-nomadic trekking lifestyle with small garden plots that Ribeiro ([1819] 1841) described in the early nineteenth century became less viable after the community was nearly decimated from violence and disease and as their lands were forcibly taken from them by non-Indigenous settlers. With less territory available for hunting and gathering, gardening became more important to Canela nutritional needs, as seen in Nimuendajú's (1946:58) descriptions of garden plots with a wide variety of crops both aboriginal to the *mēhĩn* and introduced by the *cupēn* outsiders. With the advent of government involvement through the SPI post and its agents, the community gradually shifted to a more sedentary lifestyle of remaining in one village for multiple years, which replaced the mobility of frequent village relocation of the past. The ranchers' backlash to the 1963 messianic movement temporarily increased their mobility and led to a decline in the agro-biodiversity that Canela gardeners were beginning to maintain and appreciate. From the 1970s onward, however, Canela lifeways have become increasingly sedentary with Escalvado as the main village site, and gardening continues to gain importance, especially with the development of the dual plot system.

Structural violence and inequality underlie all of these transformations in Canela subsistence patterns. Nevertheless, modern-day gardeners view gardening as an authentically Canela practice that they can value and appreciate. The community loves the contemporary dual garden system and its material and symbolic complementarity. Mythic stories attest to the originality of this love and appreciation for gardening, agro-biodiversity, and the transmission of multi-sensory, embodied gardening knowledge. Although it may have been, as Nimuendajú (1946:64) states, "grim necessity that drove" the Canela to become subsistence horticulturalists, in the contemporary Canela life-world working in and maintaining multiple large, biodiverse gardens brings happiness and overall well-being to oneself and one's family. In this sense, gardening is a *choice* (albeit a structured one)—the decision to work hard and become happy, strong (*ihtÿi*), and overall well (*impej*) and the decision to resist inequality with and dependence on outsiders through providing sustenance, happiness, and well-being to one's human (and plant) family.

Loving and caring for forest and riverbank gardens is an act of resistance to ongoing structural violence that continues to affect the community. Indeed, in the twenty-first century Canela life-world, dependency on and inequality with non-Indigenous people remains commonplace, seen especially in processes of rampant political corruption, exploitative creditor–debtor relationships, and violence with impunity.[6] Environmental destruction and change is becoming another threat to Canela lifeways. Illegal logging is currently occurring throughout the territory, and between 2012 and 2017 loggers illegally removed valued hardwood trees from at least four areas within the TI Kanela. A eucalyptus plantation created in 2012 on the road to Escalvado village continues to expand its reach, contributing to deforestation near the territory and encroaching on the community's water supply. Soy plantations similarly are encroaching on the neighboring Apaniekra Indigenous territory, which lies only 45 km to the west of the Canela territory. Additionally, climatic and ecological modelling indicate that the Cerrado will become drier, hotter, and experience rapid habitat loss for native plants over the next decades (Feeley and Silman 2009; Bustamante et al. 2012).

Despite these challenges, community members describe themselves as able to survive and thrive through gardens and gardening work. As Wander eloquently stated during one of our meetings in May 2012:

> I think that gardens are important. In the first place, I want to say that the garden is the mother of the people [mēhĩn]. The garden is our defense; it is my defense. To me, gardens are about surviving well. Secondly, having a garden . . . and having much produce helps us escape from misery. We have never completely escaped from this misery, but we have not completely died away either. Because we always have some gardens.

Surviving and thriving through gardening is a phenomenological experience, grounded in ongoing, intimate engagements with diverse soils, crops, and people in forest and riverbank plots. The importance of these embodied engagements to gardening practice and learning how to garden is emphasized in mythical storytelling, especially the origin of horticulture myth with Star-Woman's expert, multi-sensory teachings. Loving gardens incorporates all the senses, as gardeners see the beauty of green buds shooting through the freshly burnt earth, smell the earthy soil, handle the growing bean vines, listen to the rustling leaves in the winds of the dry season, and taste the newly harvested crops. In this view, Canela resistance to inequality is itself a multi-sensory experience, with forest and riverbank gardens providing the spaces for Canela women and men to create and maintain their own emergent life-world full of well-fed, happy, and thriving people and plants. By focusing on the lived engagements among the Canela, their ancestors, and the environment over time, a sensory ethnobotany approach reveals that resistance to oppression can be ecological and phenomenological, as well as political. Gardening as ecological, phenomenological, and political resistance is one of the most significant transformations of the Canela life-world over the past two centuries, and one that hopefully will continue to help the community survive and thrive in the wake of environmental and climatic shifts of the Anthropocene.

CHAPTER THREE

Educating Affection

Becoming Gardener Parents

I take care of [my crops] this way, same as my daughters! Same as at
home, I take care of my crops this way. I have to clean and clear [the
garden]. If I do not take care of them, they are no good. [. . .] I do not leave
them. I have to pay attention, so that the crops stay [in the garden] for us.
I have to keep the garden clean.
—Camila, July 2012

Parenting Plants: Skills, Practice, Process

Becoming a parent to plants in the Canela life-world is an ongoing, lifelong
process involving practicing an embodied, multi-sensory skill set. Girls and
boys learn how to develop these skills through frequent visits to forest and
riverbank garden spaces with their adult female and male elders. In this chapter, I explore the transmission of multi-sensory, embodied gardening knowledge across generations of Canela gardeners through what I term an education of affection. The education of affection expands on Tim Ingold's (2000)
"education of attention" concept, which highlights the "enskilment" of novices through verbal and nonverbal showing, and draws from other work on
enskilment and apprenticeship (Lave 2011; Marchand 2014), to incorporate
multi-sensory, embodied, and gendered experiences between gardeners
and plants that are subsequently valued and made meaningful through long-
term practical processes. Educating affection, I maintain, is the primary way
in which Canela girls and boys come to know garden spaces, cultivated crop
children, and the unfolding life-world as a whole.

Camila's quote above underscores the key elements in the Canela education of affection explored in this chapter. Firstly, there is the focus on crops
as children with agentive capacities—they can see, listen to, and eat with
their gardener parents, and as Camila intimates, they will physically relocate
to another garden if their gardener parents mistreat them for long periods.
Secondly, there is a recognition that care and affection are the cornerstones
of human–plant engagements. Gardening *is* caretaking—there is no sub-

stantial difference, and it is impossible to discuss or learn about gardening in the Canela life-world without extensive conversations and practical lessons on how to affectionately care for and nurture a diversity of plant children and seed infants. Thirdly, Camila's quote emphasizes the importance of certain embodied and gendered skills that younger gardeners must learn from older generations that are essential to crop childcare. These skills include planting, visiting, tending to, cleaning and clearing, harvesting, and saving seeds and cuttings for women and girls and demarcating new plots, burning debris, and assisting with planting and harvesting for men and boys. Fourthly, gendered skill sets require long-term practice through intimate, multi-sensory encounters with crops in forest and riverbank garden spaces. Fifthly, and finally, Camila emphasizes the processual aspect of gardening knowledge, grounded in paying attention to garden spaces and crop children throughout their lives. All five of these elements of educating affection are explored throughout this chapter. The last three elements—embodied, gendered skills; multi-sensory practice; and process—deserve further fleshing out here.

Canela girls and boys develop gardening skills through individual, multi-sensory, and embodied experiences. Whether boys are looking for signs of smoke and smelling a newly set fire when burning debris or girls are hearing their grandmothers' advice about plant caretaking and handling crops, Canela children learn how to garden by engaging multiple sensory modalities. Becoming a skilled Canela gardener and learning how to engage with multiple crop species and varieties is akin to Trevor Marchand's (2014:185) study of English woodworkers who engage with wood in sensory ways based on the material's diverse grains, colors, odors, figures, and densities. Marchand (2014:183) points out that the embodied skills of woodworking "grow in response to, and in relation with, the total working environment of tools, machinery, materials, fellow carpenters, and clients," and thus he argues that training "*grows* the body and mind of the learner" (Marchand 2014:185; author's own emphasis). Similarly, in this chapter I explore the ways in which Canela boys and girls develop embodied skills that "grow" alongside their own "working environments" in forest and riverbank spaces involving elder women and men, myriad cultivated crops, different soil types, and gardening tools such as digging sticks and woven baskets. "Growing" embodied skills involves long-term practice, as novices learn how to improvise and work in relation to the tools and environments at hand. For woodworkers, becoming skilled is "measured by one's ability to respond creatively, solve problems and incorporate new information" (Marchand 2014:183). Canela gardeners, I maintain, also emphasize creativity and improvisation as they practice and "grow" their gardening abilities, with young children encouraged to play and use their imagination in garden spaces and expert gardeners valued for their experimentation and incorporation of new crop species and varieties (see chapter 4, "Expanding Multispecies Families").

Growing skills through practice is processual, and educating affection is an ongoing process that constantly is unfolding as Canela adults, children, and plant children come to know one another and garden spaces through intimate sensory experiences. It takes many seasons of watching their elders from an early age and later participating themselves for Canela boys to learn how to set a fire for a new garden plot and girls to learn which weeds should be cleared during tending visits. Jean Lave's (2011:154) approach to apprenticeship as a series of relational processes is particularly relevant here, especially her focus on the "historical processual coming to be" of human beings and the knowledge or knowing they develop over time. Reworking the traditional concept of "apprenticeship" as someone who does not know learning from someone who does (E. Goody 1989:234), Lave (2011:156) suggests that "we are all apprentices, engaged in learning to do what we are already doing." This chapter draws from Lave's understanding of learning and knowledge acquisition as a processual becoming in order to shed light on seemingly obscure processes of learning how to garden. Indeed, Canela gardening knowledge is not straightforwardly passed down through verbal instructions from experts who know to novices who do not know. Rather, Canela girls and boys learn much of their embodied gardening skills through indirect, nonverbal showing by their elders, as Ingold (2000) emphasizes, and through their own experiences of doing "what they are already doing"—visiting and playing in garden plots and assisting their elders in diverse garden-related tasks that form part of everyday experiences. Moreover, this conceptualization of apprenticeship allows for a more nuanced understanding of expert knowledge as dynamic and processual, open to new skills and practices over time. As I demonstrate in this chapter, Canela gardeners who are known experts in the community recognize the limits of their knowledge and are constantly learning through improvisation and creativity. The mark of an expert gardener is not possessing a fixed set of transmittable verbal knowledge but rather the ability to pay attention to, adapt, and learn from ever-changing plant children, soil and land types, and environmental factors such as weather and climate. It is this attention and adaptability to change that will enable Canela gardeners and their processual knowing to become resilient in the face of climate change in the Cerrado.

While recognizing the importance of skills, practice, and process in Canela gardening knowledge broadens an understanding of Canela education, it is also essential to examine the fundamental significance of affection to human environment and human plant engagements in the Canela life world. I devote particular attention in this chapter to learning, knowing, feeling, and gendered becoming with plants to highlight the affectionate encounters that Canela girls, boys, women, and men develop with plant children over time. Educating affection supports the happiness, strength, and overall well-being of people and plants, encompassed in the Canela terms *ihtỳi* and *impej*. Understanding what these concepts mean to Canela people and plants is therefore crucial to deepening an examination of educating affection and becoming kin to plants. Moreover, I maintain that educating affection is grounded in making kin of plants. Drawing from Haraway's (2016) understanding of "making kin" of multispecies others, and from Ingold and Hallam's (2014) "growing-in-making" concept of human–nonhuman relationships, I argue that Canela gardening knowledge transmission is centered on multispecies kinship relations of care and affection. Expanding on Amazonian theories of sociality and conviviality (e.g., Overing and Passes 2000b) to incorporate plant kin, I maintain that Canela gardeners are caretaking, making, and growing their families into multispecies human–plant assemblages that enrich and enliven the emergent bio-sociocultural life-world.

Learning, Knowing, and Feeling with Plants

Understanding Plant Children

In the contemporary Canela life-world, cultivated crops are considered children in need of nurturing care and affection. Camila's quote clearly demonstrates this connection through her recognition that she "cares for her crops" in the same way as her human children. Liliana also repeatedly described her motherly connection with gardens and crops during our many conversations, at one point stating matter-of-factly: "Seeing as I have gardens, I remember them and enjoy them, same as having a baby in my arms. I take good care of my gardens; I protect them, same as my human family." While women are the primary caretakers of growing plants, men also consider themselves fathers of plant children. Fernando often described himself as the father of the crops growing in his garden and explained the importance of caring for plant children by gardener mothers and fathers during a conversation in August 2012:

> People take care of plants the same as they do [with] people. If one does not take care [of the plants], the brush overtakes them, and they

become very angry and sad, as human children do. Nowadays, the mother uses perfume and has to cut her hair and paint [herself] with *urucum* and *pau de leite*, and they say that the [crop] child will grow quickly. She paints herself, and they say that it is pure happiness [for the crops]!

As Fernando explains, crop children are emotional, intentional actors whose happiness is paramount to successful gardening practices. Weeding brush and cleaning the garden space, which are predominately female activities, are forms of plant childcare that help crops to grow quickly and become strong and happy. Effectively burning and clearing new garden plots, which are male activities, also bring happiness to crops, as does ritual singing performed by female and male gardeners (see "Singing to Plants: Plant Feelings" below). Learning how to keep crop children happy and prevent them from feeling angry and sad are crucial components of gardening knowledge transmission. Younger generations learn how to engage in parental acts of care and affection that adults, particularly women, also shower onto their human children. Environmental phenomena including the sun and rain assist with parental caretaking of growing plant children as well. Fernando describes how the sun protects and helps the plants and how the rain is another kind of "mother" to the crops, feeding and sustaining them with water as a mother feeds her baby breast milk.

Crop children are similar to human children yet are even more dependent on their gardener mothers and fathers throughout their life course. In the same conversation, Fernando compared the needs of human and plant children:

When he [the human child] is grown up, his mother does not have to take care of him anymore, for he takes care of himself. With cultivated crops, the garden owner him- or herself takes care [of the crops]. When they are already grown, the gardener still cares for them.

Because of this continued dependency on gardener parents throughout the life course of plant children, gardening is an especially intensive process that necessitates ongoing acts of caretaking until harvesting, and further caretaking ensues to save seeds and cuttings, which are considered infants or fetuses (as I explore in chapter 4, "Saving: Motherly Love and Agro-Biodiversity Conservation"). Canela children must therefore learn how to care for plants throughout the growing cycle, and girls in particular must learn how to save and care for seed and plant cutting infants.

While plants are considered children throughout their lives growing in garden spaces, when they are harvested they have matured into adults at the end of their natural life cycles. Shamans with heightened perceptual abilities are able to see the adult crops in this late stage of life, just as they can see the Plant-People master spirits of every crop species and variety (see chapter 5). The well-known shaman Paolo Eduardo, for example, informed his daughter Liliana that varietals of bitter manioc left in the ground for two to three years appeared to him as old people who had already had children and grandchildren of their own. Fernando similarly explained to me that harvestable crops already have passed through adulthood and their lives have ended, so people can consume them "without problems." Canela families do not eat plant children, Fernando further explained, but rather the recently deceased adult plants, and Fernando maintained that this is "normal" behavior for humans to undertake. Liliana agreed, telling me that mature crops ready for harvesting are the "same as being dead," and being eaten by humans is their natural next step. Crop lives are cyclical, however, in that saved seeds and cuttings from last season's harvest are considered fetuses and infants that eventually will develop into crop children in garden spaces once again. By conceptually separating their roles as caring, affectionate parents of saved seed and plant cutting infants and growing plant children and as consumers of harvested dead adult plants, Canela gardeners such as Liliana and Fernando are able to emphasize the gardener parent–crop child relationship. Rather than solely understanding gardening as cultivating foodstuffs to be consumed, male and female gardeners focus on the intimate realities of "becoming with" (Haraway 2008)—that is, living, growing, loving, maturing, and even dying with—plants in forest and riverbank gardens. They pass on the importance of these experiences with plant children to their human children, and the cycle of caring for and nurturing crops through multi-sensory, embodied encounters continues.

Learning with Fire

Learning and knowing about gardens is grounded in multi-sensory perceptual experiences with garden spaces, soils, and the plant children growing there. Different tasks sometimes emphasize certain sensory experiences over others, but on the whole there is a recognition that gardening is a multi-sensory endeavor for both people and plants. Boys and girls learn how to employ their senses in gardening tasks, and plants respond in turn through their continued growth and happiness. In order to complete the male tasks of demarcating and burning a new plot, boys learn how to engage with garden spaces and soils from their male elders in the family. A boy initially learns how to measure and delineate a garden plot from his older male relatives in his natal home and later on develops his techniques through working with his father-in-law and male relatives in his wife's family. By watching his maternal grandfather, father, and uncles (the husbands of his mother's sisters) cut away the brush and by participating himself, a Canela boy learns the embodied skills necessary to wield a machete and a steel axe to cut down hardier forest trees. While women and girls sometimes participate in later rounds of cutting away the brush, known as *coivara* in Portuguese, boys and men undertake the first round of *coivara* when they are demarcating the boundaries of a new garden plot in forest and riverbank areas. Boys learn from their elders how to measure the rectangular plots by *linhas* (see chapter 2, "Loving Forest and Riverbank Gardens in the Twenty-First Century") and cut away brush and small trees to delineate the size of the plot. Different land types require different amounts of slashing and burning for new plots. Through the embodied practice of handling machetes and axes, boys learn that the *chapada* grasses (*ahtu*) are easier to slash away than the sturdy trees in the true forest (*caxàt-re kô*) land type and that the brush next to the river must be maintained to avoid erosion in riverbank plots.

After slashing, the *queimada* burning must be performed on new plots. This is an especially important gardening task that boys must learn from their male elders, for performing it badly can lead to uncontrolled fires, causing damage to one's own and others' gardens. Indeed, with drought and irregular rainfall making uncontrollable fires more likely, learning how and when to manage and light fires effectively (*cuhỳ* = fire; *ihpôc* = to light fires) is becoming even more critical to the Canela life-world. The eldest male in the family typically advises the younger men and boys when and how to perform the burning, as Fernando describes:

> When the *queimada* is arriving, you tell your son-in-law and grandson, you all meet up, and you take them there [to the garden plot]. You tell them, "we are going to clean the area around the garden, and afterward we will burn the garden. If we burn it as it is now, the fire will keep burning into the forest and that will be harmful. That is why we are making a barrier so the fire does not pass through." We do this work [of cleaning], and another day we set the fire, and the fire will not pass through [the barrier]. If people do not do this and simply set fire to the garden, the fire will pass through the garden and go far, far away, and it will burn of its own accord.

With these verbal instructions, the boys in Fernando's family learn how to create a barrier with larger brush and felled trees to prevent the fire from spreading beyond the boundaries of their garden plot. Boys must also learn how to determine the best time for the burn, which Fernando and Wander informed me should take place at the height of the dry season in early-to-mid August for the forest plot and slightly earlier in late July for the river-bank plot. The timing of the burn is crucial so that, according to Fernando, the land and plant debris burn well and do not remain "raw" or untouched by fire.

To determine whether the fire is burning successfully, Fernando teaches his younger male relatives to experience it in multi-sensory ways — by seeing the smoke from afar and by "smelling the burn—one stays nearby to see if the smell is good [and] will give sustenance to the crops." Smelling the scent of burning is a particularly effective way of learning how to gauge the fire and its effects, and Fernando says the scent "gives happiness" to gardeners. Boys learn from their male elders that the fire helps the soil and assists the crops to grow abundantly once they are planted. Through verbal guidance and nonverbal showing from their elders, as well as through individual perceptual experiences — especially sight and smell — Canela boys learn how to engage with and manage fire in their families' garden plots. Once married, a young man brings these embodied skills with him to the gardens of his wife and her family.

In this sense, Canela boys are using multiple sensory modalities to learn about fire and, I maintain, to learn *with* fire. Through developing skills of distinguishing different smells of fire, recognizing the various ways that the burn visually appears, listening to the crackling flames, and feeling the freshly burnt soil to make sure it is ashy rather than "raw" and unburnt, boys are engaging directly with fire and its effects. With the assistance of their male elders, boys grow embodied skills with fire and come to know it intimately. Many studies have demonstrated fire's benefits to the soil in slash-and-burn cultivation (e.g., Hoffman 2000; Hecht 2003; Lehmann et al. 2003) and detailed fire ecology among Indigenous and traditional groups world-wide (Fowler and Welch 2015; Laris et al. 2015; Petty et al. 2015). The use of fire among Jê-speaking groups also has received recent attention, including a focus on Xavante male transmission of fire ecology knowledge that is similar to the Canela (Welch et al. 2013; Welch 2015). For the Canela, however, there is a specific emphasis on sensory perceptual experiences in learning about, or with, fire. Moreover, while the soil and land are thought to benefit from a good burning, Canela gardeners benefit from and appreciate fire as well. As Fernando explained, smelling a successful burn brings happiness to male gardeners, one of the many ways that gardening practices bring happiness and strength (*ihtyi*) and overall well-being to people and the soils, lands, and plants with whom they engage. By learning with fire through intimate sensory experiences, Canela boys also become happy and strong, and over many seasons of embodied practice, they develop into men who can pass along the verbal and nonverbal knowledge of fire to future generations.

Tending and Visiting: Coming to Know Plant Children

While boys are learning with fire, girls are learning how to tend to crop children while they grow. Nimuendajú (1946:60) remarked that these activities were "almost a wholly feminine job" in the 1920s and 1930s, and this remains the case today. Occasionally, older men tend to crops, but this is typically the purview of expert gardeners who undertake cultivation projects beyond the scope of normal gardening practices (as seen in Fernando's case explored below in "Cultivating a Happy Life: Fernando"). Women are the primary caretakers of most growing crops, and they often bring their children with them to forest and riverbank garden plots. Frequently, entire female work parties consisting of an elder woman, her adult daughters, and her granddaughters visit the plots and occasionally spend nights there together. My sister Aline, for example, often takes different combinations of her eight children with her to harvest manioc in her forest and riverbank plots. Her eldest daughter, Aliciane, has developed a particular appreciation for manioc cultivation, accompanying her mother to harvest the crops and helping with the toasting of manioc flour (*farinha*) on the oven behind the house. Learning how to care for growing crops involves verbal instructions, particularly those pertaining to the food and sex prohibitions associated with specific crop growing cycles described in "Understanding Human–Plant Bodily Engagements" below. Most women remember receiving specific instructions from their grandparents on how to raise plant children successfully. Liliana, for example, explained how her sister Camila's gardening expertise stemmed from paying attention to the advice of their grandparents:

> She heard enough—the advice of Dirceu [grandparent], Jacinto [father], and Manuela Célia [grandmother]. Dirceu was a talker; they spoke so loud! We were all afraid and obeyed their words. [...] These things that Dirceu explained to us, she remembered well! I did not remember, but she did!

Although Liliana certainly does remember her grandparents' verbal instructions (she has recounted their advice to me numerous times), her emphasis on Camila "hearing" the advice underscores the sensory component of verbal teaching and learning. Listening to elders is an important aspect of

Canela knowledge transmission, including their advice, instructions, and storytelling. Indeed, it is commonly thought that only elders should engage in oral mythic storytelling because of their age and expertise—and that younger generations will meet an untimely death if they tell mythic stories before they are sufficiently old enough. Verbal instructions of gardening practices in particular have a mythical importance, seen in Star-Woman's lengthy pronouncements on crop cultivation, harvesting, and processing, as explored in chapter 2. While there are many verbal instructions that women pass on to younger female relatives, here I focus on hanging vines, one of the most important and common activities in plant caretaking. Elder female gardeners such as Liliana and Camila verbally instruct their daughters and granddaughters to care for vine crops by hanging the vines while they are growing. In particular, they maintain that fava bean and maize should be planted next to each other so that the fava vines can be hung from the maize stalks. Liliana tells her granddaughters that fava bean and maize "work well together" in this way. She advises them to visit the fava vines daily to ensure they remain hanging and do not drop on the ground, because fava does not bear fruit on the ground.

Nonverbal showing also plays an important role in plant caretaking. For example, girls receive hands-on embodied experience hanging the vines of fava bean varietals, the four common bean "on the vine" varietals, and sometimes the vines of yam varietals (depending on space and personal preference). Girls learn how to drape the yam and common bean vines on nearby fruit trees or manioc sticks. Liliana and Camila show the girls how to hang fava bean vines gently from manioc sticks, buriti tree saplings, or maize stalks. If the fava bean vines begin wrapping around the maize stalks or manioc sticks as they grow, the women express their satisfaction that the girls have correctly hung the vines to encourage this interdependent growth. While squash and watermelon vines are typically not draped over other crops, Camila and Liliana show their younger female relatives how to relocate these vines to another area in the garden if they are interfering with other species' development. Tubers such as sweet potato and yam and roots such as manioc do not need as frequent attention, yet women and girls still visit these crops frequently to survey their growth and remove weeds nearby. Showing girls how and when to remove weeds nearby certain crops is an important practice. Liliana teaches her granddaughters how to delicately remove weeds growing nearby peanuts in their separate mini-garden without disturbing the plants themselves. Drawing her cloth skirt (pano) between her knees and kneeling on the soft earth, Liliana carefully pulls out the small grasses and weeds that crop up near the peanut plants, while her youngest granddaughters watch and the eldest kneel down to participate in the weeding. Verbal instructions are unnecessary in these instances, since girls can mirror what their elders are doing and learn to "do what they are already doing," to paraphrase Lave (2011).

Overall, girls learn the importance of making regular trips to visit garden plots. Plant caretaking involves frequently visiting garden plots and spending time with various crop species and varieties through tending and weeding. Keeping garden spaces clean and tidy is an essential task for female gardeners. As Liliana often tells her grandchildren: "I cannot leave the crops to become overgrown by the forest and become ugly . . . I have to clean; I have to walk [there] every day. Seeing as I have a garden, I cannot stay put." Moreover, frequently visiting gardens to tidy the space and tend to crops brings happiness to plant children. Girls learn from their mothers, maternal aunts (who are also called "mother," *inxê*), and maternal grandmothers that crops are children whose happiness is paramount to abundant harvests. Elder gardeners maintain that developing intimate, affectionate relationships with crops through multi-sensory perceptual experiences is the best way to care for plant children. These sensory experiences include tending, weeding, tidying the plot, and simply visiting crop children to spend time with them (and ritually sing, as the following section describes). Women typically visit their garden plots as frequently as possible, regardless of whether they have a specific task to perform, in order to maintain the affectionate relationships they have developed with their crops. For example, my naming-aunt (*tùy*) Ivanete frequently visits her family's forest garden plot despite its long distance and the fact that she often burns her feet in the hot sand during her walk there. Spending time in the garden with her crops, especially her favorite yam varietals, including anaconda yam (*krẽrô tekãjkãj/rorti*), outweighs the great physical discomfort she endures to be there. Ivanete experiences happiness and strength by affectionately engaging with her yam children, which in turn brings them happiness and well-being. The younger women in her family have learned from her example, and neighboring families comment on how much time all the women spend in their adjacent forest plots. Through her hard work and attentive care, Ivanete's garden produces a bountiful and diverse yam harvest appreciated by the community, and she sets an example for younger girls learning how to affectionately spend time with the crops growing in their families' gardens.

Ivanete's example demonstrates the reciprocal nature of gardener mother–plant child relationships that promote the happiness, strength, and well-being of both people and plants. As with male gardeners who find happiness with a fire that burns "well," female gardeners become happy, strong, and well from intimate visits with their crops that include tending, weeding, and tidying. Yet while both men and women consider themselves the fathers and mothers of growing crop children, these relationships play out in distinctly gendered ways. Men maintain a greater distance with their crop children that mirrors their relationships with human children, with whom they typically play a more peripheral role than mothers do. In general, fathers are not involved actively in human childcare unless they are teaching specific lessons to their sons or younger male relatives pertaining to building houses, demarcating and burning garden plots, hunting, fishing, and ritual activities. Traditionally, fathers even are prohibited from holding their newborn children until they are around six months old (although many men disregard this restriction nowadays). Nevertheless, men display their care for human children through building and maintaining houses, traditionally providing hunted game meat and fish to eat, and teaching important father-son gardening lessons. Similarly, gardener fathers build the homes of crop children through demarcating and burning a new garden plot in which crop children reside and by providing meat for the food sharing ritual with crops described below (see "Sharing Food with Plants").

In contrast, women's gardening roles focus specifically on intimately nurturing and caring for plant children, similar to their roles as mothers to human children. Becoming a mother to human and plant children involve similar processes of embodied coming to know and developing caring affection. Female gardeners often make direct comparisons between human and plant childcare. Liliana and Camila tell their daughters and granddaughters that tending a garden is similar to the duties of keeping house and looking after infants and small children, likening weeding and cleaning the plot to sweeping and tidying their thatched-roof houses. Liliana clearly explained her motherly relationship with crops the following way:

> As the female garden owner [dona da roça], I am the same as the mother of people . . . I have to protect my work; I cannot lose the work that I have. What I do in the gardens is my obligation—I have to care for [the crops] same as I care for my family.

Coming to know plant children is therefore centered on learning to care for them as nurturing mothers. Just as girls learn how to become mothers to human infants and young children through spending time with them, paying attention to their needs, and keeping them tidy, safe, and happy, so too do girls learn embodied practices to support the needs and promote the happiness of plant children. Girls become mothers to plants by learning from verbal instructions and nonverbal showing from their female elders, as well as through their own sensory experiences. Through these processes of educating affection, girls learn how to engender nurturing relationships with their plant kin, which are essential to gardening in the twenty-first century Canela life-world.

Singing to Plants: Plant Feelings

Another key component of plant caretaking and learning to garden involves ritually singing to growing crop children. Singing ritual songs (cânticos; increr xà in Canela) to a variety of crop species and varieties in the garden brings them happiness, which in turn enables them to grow abundantly. Indeed, ritual singing brings plant feelings to the fore more than other gardening activities. While ritual singing in the garden space is an activity that both women and men can undertake, women are more likely to sing to crop children during their frequent visits to forest and riverbank plots. The songs are similar to those sung in the communal harvest rituals described below (see "Celebrating Plant Lives: First Harvests"), yet there are important differences. Rather than celebrating the end of the crop's natural life cycle and its relationship to the entire community as in harvest rituals, songs sung in the garden space usually include words of encouragement to and affection for growing crops from individual gardener mothers and fathers. The squash song (cuhkōn cahàc mā increr-xà), for example, is sung by individual female or male gardeners to their vine crops, including squash, watermelon, sweet potato, fava bean, common bean, and yam, as well as to sweet and bitter manioc. After the Hôxwa sweet potato harvest festival takes place at the height of the rainy season in January or February, a gardener typically visits her garden to sing this ritual song to the growing crops. Fernando described to me how the crops "run" or "walk" toward the singer to listen closely and appreciate the words of the song, which are meant to bring happiness and strength to the crops and thereby encourage their growth. Peanut varietals (caahy) also require a song to encourage their growth and remind them of the garden owners' caretaking and affection. In the separate mini-garden on the side of the forest plot where peanuts should be planted, the female or male gardener grabs the peanut vines and sings to them, telling them to grow and be happy. The growing peanuts are said to listen to the advice of their gardener mother or father and flower shortly thereafter. Without the gardeners' singing, Fernando explained, the growing plants become sad and weak, thereby making it difficult for them to produce an abundant harvest. The crops "need an owner to take care of them . . . to sing and clean the garden," Fernando maintained. Renato agreed that ritually singing to crops is crucial for successful gardening, and that the singing even improves soil fertility. Both men teach younger generations the importance of ritual singing to attend to crop children's feelings and encourage their growth.

This affectionate encouragement toward plants is seen clearly in the lyrics of the gourd song (*cuhkôn mã increr xà*), which is intended for all varieties of gourd (*cuhkôn*) and bottle gourd (*cuhtôj*). As Fernando explained, the song tells a story and gives an explanation to the gourds about how their gardener parents will care for them. Singing the song in Canela, Fernando then translated the lyrics into Portuguese and provided additional description (which I have translated into English here):

> "Grow now, to make me happy; the day that you are grown, I am going to harvest you and take care of you, because inside of you I am going to store all the seeds to plant next, [and] I am going to bring water in you. This is why I am singing this song to you, to make you happy." [...] They say that the gourd hears it—it could be the mother or the father who sings it . . . they say that the gourds will hear it and their fruits will begin blossoming. Then, when it is already realized, the mother or father . . . suspends the leaf and grabs the vine, same as with young people . . . the gourd is like a child.

Liliana chimed into this conversation, adding that "only the gourds listen" to this song, indicating that crop species and varieties need to be specifically addressed in order to hear their gardener parents' singing and feel happy as a result. Modern-day gardeners maintain that the embodied skill set of promoting crop children's happiness through ritual singing has been passed down from the ancestors and must be taught to future generations to support abundant harvests. Therefore, while Fernando often worries over the loss of gourd varietals because their use as storage containers has been largely replaced by manufactured plastic containers (see chapter 4, "Writing: Plant Childcare in the Twenty-First Century"), he continues to teach the gourd song to the younger generation in the hope that it encourages the cultivation of gourd children. In this sense, girls and boys learning how to sing ritually promotes agro-biodiversity, as they practice and perform different songs to ensure the happiness and continued cultivation of diverse crop species and varieties.

Young boys and girls also learn that singing in the garden is a multisensory activity for both people and plants, involving aural, visual, and tactile embodied skills. Not only do gardeners sing and crops listen; gardeners also emphasize to their younger relatives the importance of looking at and touching the crops. Crop children in turn enjoy being seen and handled by their gardener parents during the ritual singing. Fernando showed me how he picks up and suspends the crops' vines in the air while singing the squash song and peanut song and how he dangles gourd vines and leaves during the gourd song. He maintained that these activities "please" the growing squash and gourds. Squash varietals also enjoy being rubbed with red *uru-cum* (annatto) paste while they are growing, and this activity strengthens the vines and squash fruits. Learning how to appreciate the visually striking bright red paste, along with the intimate handling of vines and singing words of encouragement, demonstrates the human education of affection toward plants that is ever present in Canela gardening knowledge transmission.

While these songs for squash and other vine crops, peanuts, and gourd are sung and passed down by male and female gardeners, certain ritual songs are intended for specific mother gardener–plant child encounters. Liliana described songs for squash and yam that typically are sung only by women. She shared the songs with me while we were alone inside her daughter's house one afternoon, away from the men who usually joined our research group on most mornings and afternoons. Men are not forbidden from hearing or learning the song lyrics, but Liliana made it clear that the songs are part of a corpus of specifically women's knowledge and should be passed down through generations of female gardeners. Liliana, for example, learned the women's squash song (*cuhkōn cahàc mā increr xà cahāj*) from her grandmother Manuela Célia, and in this instance passed it on to me, her adoptive daughter. The song typically is performed by an older woman in the forest or riverbank garden space after the squash varietals have been growing for two or three months but have not yet fruited. First, the older woman whispers, and then her voice steadily rises to a yell as she calls for the squash and its vine to pay attention. Next, she describes her motherly role to the crop child. Liliana sang the verses to me in Canela (my translation into English here):

> Vine! Vine! [whispered]
> How are you, squash seed?
> How are you, squash seed?
> Listen to me, squash; you are going to have much fruit
> I am your mother and I protect you.

As with other ritual songs, the singer handles the crop child's vines while singing. She also strips one of the leaves and places it near the vine during the song. These activities, Liliana assured me, "please" the squash child. It listens to the song, recognizes the gardener as its mother, becomes happy from the intimate interaction, and consequently will produce an abundant harvest. Women continue singing and performing other rituals throughout the squash's life cycle, especially if the crop is failing. Liliana explained how if the squash flowers fall and shrivel up (which is usually blamed on a menstruating woman visiting the garden; see "Understanding Human–Plant Bodily Engagements" below), the female garden owner should visit the garden with *urucum* seeds in her hand, all the while singing, "squash, do not die!" These ongoing singing rituals throughout the squash growing season highlight the specific caretaking work of female gardeners and the importance of girls practicing these embodied skills over many seasons. Through processual practice, girls learn not only the song's lyrics but also the specific habits and preferences of their particular squash children. Are they happy with one round of singing, or do they need the supplementary visit with *urucum* seeds and extra rounds of singing? Do the squash children appreciate being rubbed with *urucum* paste, and do they prefer being sung to by their gardener mother or father? The ritual singing, combined with tending, weeding, and visiting activities, help girls to become attuned to the feelings of the crop children in their families' gardens.

Girls also learn a women's yam song (*krẽrô mã increr xà cahãj*) intended to please yam children. When she was a girl, Liliana's grandmother Manuela Célia taught her that long ago the yam vines became dried out during the dry season and for this reason, the ancestor women "discovered" this song. The song can be sung by an individual woman in her garden while planting the yam cuttings and/or by a group of women in the village later in the growing season. When sung during planting, the song pleases the yam cuttings and encourages their growth. If female gardeners notice their yam vines shriveling or drying later in the season, a group of women will "become animated" and decide to sing a version of the song in the village, as Liliana described. The group of women begin singing late at night, while slowly walking around the main street in front of the first circle of village houses. In this version, the song's lyrics change slightly to address the dried-out vines and foliage directly. The lyrics describe how the women have just discovered that the yam vines are dried out and how they are asking the vines to stay alive and continue growing. Through these two separate rounds of individual and communal ritual singing, the women are demonstrating their motherly affection for the yam crops and their commitment to plant caretaking throughout crop life cycles. Moreover, the communal female ritual singing (known as *hõkre pôj* in Canela; see Grupp 2015) displays the power of motherly care for crop children en masse, something that women typically do not showcase in other ritual ceremonial activities that take place in the village. While men and boys learn ritual songs and are expected to perform them for the crops growing in their gardens, through ritual singing women and girls develop unique gendered relationships of nurturing care with their squash, yam, and other crop children. Ritual singing enables women and girls to become distinctly in touch with plant feelings in ways that men and boys do not typically pursue. Learning how to garden is therefore an embodied, gendered process that the following section explores in more detail.

Understanding Gendered Multispecies Bodies

Understanding Human–Plant Bodily Engagements

Educating affection for plants is an embodied endeavor, and as such it involves understanding and conforming to certain food and sex restrictions that are tied to human and plant life cycles. As Fernando, Liliana, and others described, the food and sex restrictions (*më ipiyakri tsà* in Canela; *resguardo* in Portuguese) have been passed down from the ancestors and are integral to being and becoming *impej*—good, beautiful, true/original, and well in a holistic sense. The restrictions are gendered and form an important part of both male and female human life cycles. For boys and men, there are restrictions during the ear-piercing ritual, a series of activities during the male ritual initiation complex, and when becoming a skilled hunter, log racer, ritual singer, or shaman, as chapter 5 describes (see "Becoming a Shaman: Engagements with Nonhumans"). The ear-piercing ritual for adolescent boys involves food restrictions, including avoiding "heavy" (*hū-ti/py-ti* in Canela) foods, and restrictions from touching blood, for both the boy and his maternal naming uncle (*kêt-ti* or *kêt-re*), who is typically the one to pierce his nephew's (*tàmtswè*) ears.[1] Here, the shared restrictions underscore the embodied connection between nephew and naming uncle, which begins at the nephew's birth and is solidified and maintained throughout their lives, especially through membership in certain moiety groups, which is determined by one's naming uncle (see Crocker 1990:193–209). During the Pep-yê festival period, one of the three male initiation ritual periods (see Crocker 1990: 272–273; Miller 2015:122–123), the food and sex restrictions enable boys to learn and develop new embodied skills. Older boys are interned in their mothers' houses for around six months, although they have more freedom of movement in the final month. While interned, the boys must bathe in outhouses nearby, refrain from sexual intercourse, and avoid heavy foods such as game meat. Fernando explained that the only "true" foods the "imprisoned" boys should consume are sweet potato, peanut, the true/original maize variety (*pōhy pej-re*), two types of red rice (small red fast-growing rice and small red slow-growing rice [*arỳihy caprêc-re kênpei* and *arỳihy caprêc-re* kênpôc]), and *farinha seca* (dry toasted manioc flour). By undertaking these restrictions, Fernando and Renato maintained that boys make themselves "beautiful" (*impej*) and open to learning hunting, log racing, ritual singing, or shamanic skills, which in turn require further restrictive periods to maintain. Adolescent girls, meanwhile, traditionally undergo individual restrictive periods in their mothers' houses during their first menstruation, following the same diet as that of the Pep-yê interned boys. While the restrictions enable boys to become strong and powerful sociopolitical leaders, shamans, and hunters, for girls the period serves to strengthen them to visit and work in garden plots. In this way, girls' bodies are prepared specifically for crop childcare, whereas boys' bodies are prepared for traditional male roles, even those that no longer serve an everyday purpose, such as becoming a skilled hunter.

Although restrictions for adolescents highlight gender differences, women and men face similar food and sex restrictions once they conceive a child together, including throughout the woman's pregnancy and until the infant is around six months old. During this time, the mother and father of the fetus (and subsequently infant) are prohibited from engaging in sexual intercourse and from eating numerous heavy foods, including various meats. While a woman is pregnant, she and her husband typically consume only rice, especially small red fast-growing rice and small red slow-growing rice, the latter of which is usually made into *mingau*, a type of porridge. These two types of rice are considered the best, most beautiful, and truest/most original (*impeaj to impej*; see chapter 4, table 5), which makes eating them especially beneficial to the parents' and child's well-being. Ignoring the prohibitions, Liliana, Fernando, Renato, and Wander explained, is "dangerous" for the health and well-being of both parents and their growing child owing to the intimate connection that is developing among all three bodies. Girls and boys learn about the restrictions and the dire consequences of disregarding them from their female and male elders.

Younger generations learn that consuming prohibited foods affects the infant's bodily health once it is born and that eating different types of restricted foods leads to specific health issues for the infant. According to Liliana, Fernando, Renato, and Wander (following advice commonly found and taught throughout the community), eating different meats will cause various bodily ailments for the newborn baby. If a pregnant woman or her husband eats pork or beef, for example, the baby will have a wound on its head, and eating grilled meat or cow tongue will give the baby a wound on its tongue. Similarly, eating the tripe or liver of a cow is prohibited because it will give the baby a stomachache or diarrhea. A pregnant woman should refrain from eating chicken until the baby can walk, although Liliana mentioned that this prohibition is followed less frequently than in the past. The couple also should avoid eating wild game, for it will lead to various problems for the infant: deer meat will give the baby sores on its skin; paca meat will make the baby "thick" or unhealthily fat; coati meat will give the baby itchy or "uncomfortable" skin; and porcupine meat will make him or her unhealthily skinny. Some prohibitions are aimed specifically at the husband and highlight his embodied connection with the newborn. For example, the husband should refrain from eating potato buds during the woman's pregnancy, as these will make the baby have a wounded or sore nose once it is born. Other food restrictions are meant to safeguard the mother's health during her pregnancy, and disregarding these prohibitions can negatively affect her bodily well-being. A pregnant woman also cannot eat potato buds because she will develop a spotted backside, and if she eats the meat in a *beribu* manioc–meat pie she will develop spots on her face, or her face will turn completely black once she gives birth. There are also certain activities that a pregnant woman should refrain from doing, including touching a wooden spoon to her mouth for it will cause a delayed birth and sleeping heavily or during the day because this will lead to "problems" with the baby, as Liliana maintained. She passed on this advice to her daughter Joaquina during her pregnancy in the spring of 2012, and both Joaquina and her husband Vítor closely followed the food prohibitions throughout her pregnancy and into their daughter's first few months.

Once the baby is born, the restrictions change and lessen in severity as time goes on, reflecting the changing connection among mother, father, and infant bodies. There are certain restrictions immediately following the baby's birth and until the umbilical cord falls off. Being fathers themselves, Fernando and Renato explained that the father should remain lying down inside the house and consume only rice porridge, and that both the mother and father refrain from bathing the "upper half" of their bodies. After the cord falls off, Fernando explained, the father rubs a leaf from the *hotreỳun* plant on the infant's body and makes tiny bracelets out of the fibrous leaf for the baby to wear. These activities are thought to protect the baby from developing an illness or pain caused by the parents' consumption of heavy foods. Despite this embodied act of protection for the baby, the new parents should still refrain from eating the prohibited heavy foods, including meat, and sweet foods such as sugarcane, mango, banana, papaya, and most other fruits, for these items will give the baby diarrhea or stomach pains. The father continues eating only rice until the infant is around six months old so the child will "grow fast and be strong," as Fernando described. Meanwhile, the new mother can begin eating cow meat in order to produce milk for her infant, as Liliana advised Joaquina when she gave birth in July 2012. When the baby is around two months old, the mother's diet can include common bean and fava bean, and by three months, Liliana explained that she can eat "almost anything" except for especially heavy and fatty meats such as pork and wild game. Not only are the diets different for new fathers and mothers but so is the physical connection with the infant. While the mother constantly is holding and cuddling her baby, the father traditionally cannot hold his child until he or she reaches six months of age. Additionally, neither parent should visit the garden plots until the infant is six months old, because the souls (mēkarōn) of deceased Canela, who normally reside in forested areas near and inside garden plots, can harm the baby (see chapter 5). Joaquina and Vítor strictly followed these restrictions after their daughter was born at the beginning of the gardening season and were therefore unable to create a new garden plot or visit old ones during this time. They relied on Liliana and her husband to maintain garden plots and share her garden produce, thereby highlighting the importance of the matrilocal family unit to support and care for human (and plant) family members. Through these various restrictions, which are distinctly gendered to reflect the particular embodied mother–child and father–child relationships that develop over time, human children become healthy, strong, and well.

There are similar gendered, embodied connections among gardener mothers, fathers, and plant children as those among parents and their human children. Plant children, therefore, also require their human gardener parents to undergo food and sex prohibitions to become happy, strong, and healthy and to grow abundantly. While assisting with gardening tasks for their family plots, girls and boys learn about these restrictions through verbal instructions from their elders. As with human children, only the female and male garden owners or parents of plant children will undertake the restrictions while crops are growing. Girls and boys learn about the restrictions through verbal instructions from their elders in the house, yet they will not experience these particular embodied tasks until they own garden plots themselves as adults, typically after marriage and the birth of their first child. That couples usually do not maintain their own forest and riverbank gardens until the birth of their first child (when the marriage is solidified through a marriage ritual; see Miller 2015:128–131) underscores the connection between human and plant parenting. After learning and undertaking the restrictions for the human child, and participating in acts of caring, affectionate parenting, it follows that young women and men will be better prepared to affectionately care for their plant children.

Since plant children are myriad and diverse, there are specific restrictions that gardeners should follow when growing different crop species and varieties, especially those of fava bean, peanut, yam, maize, squash, and gourd. Liliana, Fernando, Renato, and Wander agreed that planting and tending to fava bean varietals requires the most care from gardener parents, including following certain restrictions. Gardeners should plant fava bean seed infants with clean hands, for example. While the plant children are growing, male and female gardeners must refrain from eating certain meats, similar to restrictions for the mothers and fathers of human fetuses and infants. Disregarding the food prohibitions also has similarly negative effects on plant bodies. If gardeners eat the liver of any animal it will inhibit an abundant fava harvest, and eating tripe will dry out the fava bean pods and lead to an insect infestation in the garden. Camila told me that while her fava bean varietals are growing, "I do not eat the fat from any animal—pig, paca liver, peccary . . . [otherwise], the fava will not give a good harvest." She also explained that smoking tobacco next to the growing fava bean or bitter manioc will make the crops "bitter" and inedible and will make bitter manioc have stronger "poison" than usual (referring to the root's toxic levels of cyanogenic glucosides). There are other restrictions that tie gardeners' bodies to more than one crop species or variety. For example, when gardeners intercrop fava bean with bitter manioc and hang the fava vines from the manioc sticks, they should refrain from eating animal tails, for this will prevent the two crops from successfully growing together. Here there is an embodied connection among various multispecies kin—including men, women, and diverse fava bean and bitter manioc varietals.

At other times, the restrictions focus on certain bodily characteristics of crops themselves. Peanut varietals (*caahy*) planted without their shells require strict restrictions during planting and growing seasons, while peanuts planted with their shells do not necessitate any restrictions.[2] While the reasons behind this gardening regulation are unclear, it points to the importance of crop bodies—shelled or unshelled—in their relationships with humans. Planting peanuts without their shells is a delicate process, as Fernando and Liliana described. The gardener should not touch the peanuts with her bare hands, for this will cause ants to attack the crop; instead, she places the peanuts on a piece of bark from the *critin-re* tree (the same tree from which digging sticks are made; see chapter 2, "Loving Forest and Riverbank Gardens in the Twenty-First Century") and transfers them directly into the hole. There are also prohibitions against gardener mothers and fathers eating heavy foods such as meat and fish until peanut children flower and mature. Wander explained to me that eating meat during this time, even if one washes one's hands after the meal, will "affect" and "cause harm" to the peanuts. He maintained that a gardener shows his or her "respect" for the peanut crop by undergoing these restrictions.

Other crops also deserve respect and care from their gardener mothers and fathers through food prohibitions, and violating the restrictions consequently causes bodily harm to the crop children. If a gardener eats native *macaúba* (*ronhàc*) or bacuri (*cŭmxê*) fruits while growing yam varietals, for example, the yam tuber and/or vine will become rounded and hard, like the shape and consistency of these fruits, and will not produce a good harvest. Eating *macaúba* also is prohibited when growing maize varietals, as the corn kernels will become rounded and inedible. According to Liliana and Camila, consuming *macaúba* fruits during the planting and growing seasons will ruin all the crops growing in the garden, making them similarly round, hard, and inedible. They agreed that gardeners also should refrain from eating animal fat while growing gourd children and from eating pork fat while growing squash children, as this will inhibit the squash vines' growth.

In addition to food restrictions, the physical condition of a gardener and certain physical activities can have a negative bodily effect on growing crop children. A woman who is menstruating or pregnant should avoid visiting the garden space and specifically being near varietals of bitter and sweet manioc, sweet potato, squash, and common bean. The presence of a menstruating woman can cause all growing crops to "dry out" and is therefore "dangerous" for the plants' well-being, as Liliana and others explained. If a menstruating woman spends time in the center of the garden plot where bitter manioc is usually planted, the manioc roots will become rotten and putrefy, and sweet potato will become dried out and inedible if she visits its mini-garden next to the forest plot. Pregnant women also should avoid visiting the center of the garden and the areas where squash and common bean varietals are growing, as they will cause the flowers of these species to die, preventing the fruits from maturing. When some of Liliana's squash crop in her backyard garden did not produce fruit in May 2012, for example, she speculated that the crop had failed because her pregnant daughter, Joaquina, or granddaughter, Patrícia, had walked too close to the growing plants. The physical activities of having sex, defecating, and talking loudly or fighting also are thought to upset and bring harm to crop children. Camila and Liliana recounted how their grandparent Dirceu instructed them to "respect the garden" and its crops by refraining from having sex there. Ignoring this restriction, Dirceu told them, causes the plants to "putrefy." Defecating in or immediately nearby the plot also is prohibited because, according to Liliana and Fernando, the plants "dislike the smell." Camila added that her grandparents taught her to avoid talking loudly or fighting with family members in the garden space, as this will upset the crops. Extending the parent–child embodied connection between gardeners and plants even further, Fernando described how physical traits can be "passed down" from the gardener parent to his or her plant child. Someone who has good, strong teeth, for example, should plant the maize crop so that it too develops "beautiful teeth," or rows of kernels. If a gardener with bad teeth plants maize, the ears of corn may develop "failed" kernels that are unsuitable for consumption.

Connecting embodied activities of human gardeners—including eating certain foods, engaging in sexual intercourse, visiting gardens in specific bodily states, and even the ability of passing on physical traits—to the development and growth of cultivated crops shows how seriously Canela gardeners take multispecies kinship in the contemporary Canela life-world. Indeed, the restrictions for parents of both human and crop children shed light on the embodied and consubstantial nature of Canela parenting and caretaking of people and plants. The foods that parents consume have a direct bodily effect on their human child, so much so that eating prohibited foods results in physical injuries, illnesses, or discomfort for the infant, while refraining from such foods and eating only rice makes the child physically strong and healthy. The parents' embodied activities such as engaging in sexual intercourse, bathing, and visiting garden plots also affect the growing human child. In the same way, gardener parents can negatively affect their plant children if they eat prohibited foods, carelessly handle seeds, or have sexual intercourse in forest and riverbank garden spaces, while refraining from these activities and affectionately caring for the crops helps them become strong (ihtỳi) and beautiful and well (impej) in a holistic sense.

Just as the prohibitions for pregnant mothers and their male partners, which are common throughout lowland South America (see Rival 1998), continue after the child is born, so too do the restrictions for gardener parents continue throughout the natural life cycle of the growing crops. Although the restrictions for new parents of human children eventually lessen and end after the child reaches around six months old, the embodied link between mothers, fathers, and children remains through the conceptualization of sharing the same blood (caprôô) throughout their life courses (e.g., Crocker and Crocker 2004:94) and through multi-sensory, consubstantial engagements of living, eating, working, and sleeping together. Gardeners create and maintain similar multi-sensory embodied connections with their plant children, and the restrictions also become less stringent as crops mature from seedlings in need of extra care and affection to adults in old age who are harvested and transformed into foodstuffs. In these ways, Canela parenting of humans and plants emerges as an unfolding series of multi-sensory encounters in which Canela women and men are involved in the processual "making-in-growing" or "growing-in-making" (Ingold and Hallam 2014:5) of human and plant children. By learning about the food and sex restrictions from an early age, Canela girls and boys are able to prepare for their eventual roles becoming parents of people and plants. Moreover, the continual restrictions for each season of planting, tending, growing, and harvesting crop children, as well as for each pregnancy (although with less severity after the first child), highlights the continual becoming of Canela multispecies parenthood. Girls and boys will become parents to people and plants many times over, and each time the embodied connections with their multispecies kin will be solidified and maintained through the ritual restrictions tied to human and plant lives.

Sharing Food with Plants

Learning how to become a gardener mother or father also traditionally involves ritually sharing food with plant children in the forest or riverbank garden space. Along with ritual singing and food and sex restrictions, sharing food is another ritual display of care and affection for growing crop children. While the food-sharing ritual is performed less frequently than in the past, some gardener couples and their families still hold a ritual feast with their crops after they have planted all the seeds and cuttings in the garden plot. Typically, the eldest male of the family and his sons-in-law hunt and kill a game animal in the forest, so that they can serve this meat to their newly planted crops. The entire family then visits the garden together, including the elder female and male gardening couple, their daughters and sons-in-law, and grandchildren. The women cook the meat into *beribu* manioc pies in a large earthen oven (*khiya*) and then share the food with the crops. Boys and girls who participate in the ritual with their elders therefore learn the embodied skills necessary to hunt game and prepare *beribu* pies, respectively. They also learn the importance of the food-sharing ritual for crop childcare and growth, as Fernando described:

> It is like this: when the garden owner cultivates everything ... he has to look for animals—deer, ema, peccary—and bring them there [to the garden]. They say that we must help the things that were planted—bitter manioc, maize, rice. The garden owner says, "I will look for animal [meat] for our children in the garden to grow quickly." [The crops] are the same as children. That is why one has to clear the brush inside

the garden; one cannot leave lots of brush near the plants. When cared for well, the crops say, "our father is taking good care of us and that is why we are going to grow well; we are going to become large for our father."

As Fernando explained, the growing crop children eat the manioc–meat pies alongside their human family. All the crop species and varieties are said to eat together during the meal, and the meat pies help them to grow abundantly. Since *beribu* pies traditionally are reserved for ritual celebrations and considered a delicious delicacy, sharing them with the plant children displays the importance of sating their appetite and helping them to grow.

Camila's family, for example, continues to recognize the importance of ritually feeding the crop children every year after they have finished planting. Her son-in-law Edson usually hunts agouti, armadillo, paca, or deer in the distant forest regions and then brings the game meat to the forest garden plot. Camila and her three daughters prepare the meat into *beribu* pies, and the entire family, including the plant children, feast on the food together. When asked why she maintains this ritual, Camila explained to me that the crops "need to eat the meat" to grow well and produce a larger harvest. She also maintained that the crops "become happy" from the shared feast. Liliana, Fernando, Renato, and Wander concurred with this explanation, adding that the crops "grow like humans" and therefore need the meat to develop, just as Canela human children need. Additionally, they described the food-sharing ritual as a way to "thank" the crops for growing and staying in their garden plots. Since unhappy crops can relocate physically to a different plot, as observed by shamans with heightened perceptual abilities (see chapter 5), gardener parents are grateful to crop children who are satisfied with their treatment and choose to stay and grow abundantly in their garden plots. Although people who do not possess shamanic abilities cannot visually see the crops eating or moving to a different plot, shamans inform the community that the crops feast on the meat and become happy and satisfied from this ritual meal. Through this act of commensality, gardeners can be sure that their crops will feel well cared for and part of the multispecies family.

Girls and boys learn that all crop species and varieties need the meat that is shared with them during the food-sharing ritual to assist with their growth and development. Craving meat to appease their appetites is another way that crops are understood to be "the same as people," as Fernando described. Yet gardener parents also teach the younger generations that sweet manioc varietals "desire" meat more than other crop children because they are categorized as feminine in mythic storytelling and modern-day ethnobotanical classification. Based on gardening knowledge passed down from the mythical figure of Star Woman, sweet manioc varietals are considered feminine with traditionally female characteristics, including being "sweet, very beautiful, calm, and soft." Fernando explained, "that is why, in the past, we only called sweet manioc *impej-re* [little good one], because they say it is good and beautiful. [. . .] They say that the hunter told his wife, 'go find *impej-re*; grate it, and save it for us to make *beribu* [manioc–meat pies].'" Similarly, only women should prepare sweet manioc "because it is feminine," according to Fernando, especially when made into dough for *beribu* pies. Another feminine attribute of sweet manioc is its desire for meat. Fernando teaches younger generations of gardeners that "sweet manioc likes to eat meat, because it is like a woman, [it is] feminine, who does not go hunting for meat, but waits [at home]" for her husband or son-in-law to bring meat, whether it is wild game or cow meat purchased from local cattle ranchers. Sweet manioc varietals similarly wait for their human families to bring them meat to eat together in garden spaces, thereby engaging with human gardeners through gendered, embodied experiences of desire and taste.

While varietals of bitter manioc and half-sweet/half-bitter manioc also consume meat during the food-sharing ritual, their encounters with gardeners are distinctly based on the different gendered categories they occupy. Bitter manioc varietals are known for traditionally masculine attributes including being "bitter, dangerous, fierce, ugly, and bad" (*ihkên*) as well as "brave, valiant, and courageous." Similar to men who kill hunted game, masculine bitter manioc varietals kill wild animals with their toxic levels of cyanogenic glucosides (that human gardeners remove through intensive processing prior to consumption). One type, black hair bitter manioc, is *ihkêãn-re*, or the "worst, most dangerous, ugliest, and fiercest," and requires many days of processing to remove the higher level of toxins found in its roots. Gardeners encounter the masculine bitter manioc varieties with caution, carefully removing their toxins by using a *tipití* [*tap-ti* in Canela] made out of woven buriti palm to squeeze out the poison or by soaking the roots in the stream to make wet toasted manioc flour (*farinha d'água*). Meanwhile, the two types of half-sweet/half-bitter manioc (hugging vine manioc [*waiputre*] and not-bitter manioc [*kwỳrxênti*]) exhibit both female and male characteristics and fall into a blurred gender category that is "in the middle" of masculine and feminine. Similar to feminine sweet manioc, the half-sweet/half-bitter types are good and pretty (*impej*), yet they have "very thick and long" roots that are akin to bitter manioc varietals, according to Fernando. Both types have "middle" levels of toxicity—the tapioca of hugging vine manioc is considered poisonous yet the pulp is not, and the pulp of not-bitter manioc is said to have a small amount of poison that requires minimal processing prior to consumption. Gardeners recognize the uniqueness of the blurred gender manioc and seek out both types to save, grow, and consume. Hugging vine manioc, in particular, is considered to be "stronger" and more aboriginal than other types, and Liliana maintained that it is the chief of all manioc due to its strength. With their gendered female, male, or even half-female/half-male bodies, then, manioc crop children engage with human gardeners in distinct ways. Gendered embodiment is therefore not only relevant for understanding human gardening experiences but also for gleaning insight into the experiences of growing crop children, especially manioc. Learning gendered lessons themselves, girls and boys also learn the importance of gender to crop children's experiences in the education of affection.

In addition to gaining insight into gendered crop experiences, the food-sharing ritual teaches Canela girls and boys the importance of commensality to creating and maintaining kinship ties with both humans and nonhumans. Processing and eating food together, especially manioc, is an important part of creating and maintaining consubstantial bonds among people throughout Indigenous lowland South America (see Passes 2000; Heckler 2004; Emperaire and Peroni 2007). It is well-known that commensality supports sociality or "conviviality" of human communities in the region (Overing and Passes 2000b) and brings together families and communities worldwide (Kerner et al. 2016). Yet the role of nonhumans in commensality is less understood, either as eaters or as foods being eaten. In the food-sharing ritual, humans and plants connect through the embodied acts of sharing and eating food together. Human gardeners show their willingness to incorporate plant children into their families by visiting the plants' home, the garden space, and offering desired foodstuffs to them. While women and men already have begun developing caring relationships with their crop children through saving seeds and cuttings, demarcating and burning-and-slashing new plots, planting, tending, singing, and engaging in ritual restrictions, the ritual of sharing food solidifies and maintains the parent–child connection. Moreover, younger girls and boys learn that crops are children to be fed, just as human children are. And just as feeding, sharing food, and eating together are essential to caring human kinship relations in the region (Fausto and Costa 2013), ritual commensality is crucial to plant caretaking and the multispecies kinship ties that are the hallmark of the twenty-first century Canela life-world.

Celebrating Plant Lives: First Harvests

While educating affection for crops focuses mainly on caring for plant children (and seed and plant cutting infants, explored in chapter 4), gardeners also teach younger generations how to respect and care for mature adult plants at the end of their natural life cycles. Through harvest rituals, the lives of specific crop species and varieties are celebrated and honored by the human community at large. As with gardening activities, harvest rituals are gendered, with men and women performing distinct embodied roles that they pass on to younger generations of boys and girls. Many crop species and their varieties are celebrated ritually at the end of their lives with different types of harvest festivals. There are community-wide celebrations for the first harvests of fava bean, squash, sweet potato, cultivated cashew fruit (*ahkrỳt*), native *chapada* cashew fruit (*ahkrỳt-re*), and buriti (*crowa*) fruit. There is also a larger harvest festival for sweet potato and all vine crops (known as the Hôxwa) as well as planting, growing, and harvest festivals for maize.

The first harvest rituals are exclusively male, performed by the elders of the lower moiety age-set within the male leadership council (*pró-khãmmã*; see chapter 1, "Introducing the Canela People"; Crocker 1990:375) who taste the crops to ensure they are "safe" for the rest of the community to consume. Those who are not part of the council, including children, young adults, and women, are forbidden from eating the crop before it is tested and approved by the male elders. Typically, the women from whichever family that collects the first harvest will process, prepare, and present the crop to the male elders in the ceremonial center for the taste test. For example, in the first harvest ritual for fava bean in May or June, the women prepare a dish of fava bean, with rice or baked into a *beribu* pie, in the morning and present it to the men sitting under the shade of the mango tree in the ceremonial center in the afternoon. Once the men have eaten the fava bean dish and declared it safe, the council will "liberate" the crop by allowing the entire village to harvest and consume the fava bean varietals growing in their garden plots. The first harvest ritual for squash requires the same performance, with the women of the family cooking and presenting the squash for the male elders to consume in the ceremonial center, and the subsequent liberation of the crop. During the sweet potato first harvest ritual, women present cooked sweet potato to the male elders, who slowly chew it while drinking water. This technique is said to help the men to determine whether the crop will make them ill. If the tasting is successful, then the crop is liberated until the end of the season, when consumption of sweet potato varietals is once again restricted to the male elders. Cultivated cashew is also restricted twice, at the beginning and end of the harvest season. The women of the family whose garden produced the first harvest give the raw cashew fruit to the elders, who liberate the crop until its consumption is restricted to older males at the season's end.

In addition to celebrating cultivated crops at the end of their lives, there are also rituals associated with the first harvest of the semi-domesticated *chapada* cashew and buriti native fruits. Anyone in the community can choose to bring the first harvest of *chapada* cashew to the male elders when it ripens in September. After listening to a ritual song associated with the fruit, the men taste the crop and liberate it for the rest of its fruiting season. There are ritual songs associated with the buriti fruit first harvest ritual as well. The entire community sends a basket of the buriti fruit to the ceremonial center for presentation to the male leadership council. Before testing the fruit, the appointed elders of the council sing five ritual songs—one each facing each cardinal direction (east, north, south, west in that order), and the fifth song in the middle of the ceremonial center. The entire council then consumes the fruit, signifying that it is liberated until the end of the fruiting season, when it is available only to the older men. Whether honoring cultivated or semi-domesticated crops, the first harvest rituals underscore the embodied connection between elder men and "elder" crops at the end of their natural life cycles.

Meanwhile, women and younger girls and boys suffer negative embodied consequences if they seek out connections with harvested crops that have not yet been liberated by elder men. Similar to the ritual food and sex restrictions described above, there are prohibitions against eating the crop before it is liberated by the male elders, and violating the prohibition results in bodily suffering. Anyone who eats fava bean or squash varietals before they are liberated will be bitten by various insects, and young people who hide fava bean or squash crops from the male leadership council will develop "spines" on their skin that publicly mark them as violators. The consequences for young men and women who violate the norms for the sweet potato harvest are more severe than for other crops, which is attributed to a mythic story in which a young woman, either pregnant or with a newborn child, transforms into an old woman after eating sweet potato. Thus, as Fernando and Renato explained, young people who eat sweet potato during one of the restricted periods also will age immediately, developing wrinkled skin and grey hair. Young people who eat the cultivated cashew fruit while it is restricted, meanwhile, will develop spots all over their faces, yet only after having two or three children. And while the buriti fruit is prohibited, the young women or men who eat it will become emaciated or be attacked by an insect or arachnid, such as a spider, scorpion, ant, or mosquito. These bodily consequences demonstrate the role that gender and age plays in human–plant engagements pertaining to first harvest rituals. Celebrating adult plants becomes the exclusive purview of elder men, while women, girls, and boys are punished for trying to seek out engagements with mature plants through harvesting, collecting, storing, or eating.

While women participate in the Hôxwa (literally "sharp pointed leaf") festival to celebrate sweet potato and all vined crops, men once again take center stage in the ceremonial activities. The Hôxwa festival takes place in February or March when sweet potato varietals are typically ready to harvest, and it is considered an "animated," enjoyable ritual comparable to Brazilian Carnival, which is celebrated around the same time of year. Its central component is the sweet potato song (jàt mã hàhkrihkrit) and associated dance that men perform in the village ceremonial center. The male lead singer coordinates the singing, using his gourd maraca to keep the beat. Women also participate in the singing, albeit behind the men on the outskirts of the ceremonial center. As with the ritual singing performed by individual female and male gardeners in garden plots, the communal male and female singers tell the sweet potato varietals they are their children who must grow fast and well. According to Liliana, Fernando, Renato, and Wander, the song "helps the sweet potato grow well" for seasons to come, and it benefits other vine crops as well, including watermelon, which is harvested around the same time, and squash, fava bean, some types of common bean, and yam, which are harvested later in the year. As Fernando explained, fava bean and squash do not require communal ritual singing during their first harvest rituals because they have already "listened" to and become "happy" from the sweet potato song. Through animated singing and dancing, the Hôxwa festival is said to make both people and vine crops feel "happy" and "well."

The ritual festivities for maize similarly highlight male-embodied connections with maize varietals during planting, growing, and harvest seasons. In the planting ritual, the male ritual "owner" (dono; cu-te to hõ tekjê; see Grupp 2015) of maize[3] presents maize seeds and performs the maize song (põhy jacrer) to the male leadership council in the ceremonial center. Although typically performed in November or December before the maize planting season in forest garden plots, in 2012 the maize owner Sílvio performed the ritual in July to correspond with the riverbank garden planting season. Wrapping kernels of large red-yellow maize (põhy caprêc-ti) into a cloth bundle, Sílvio presented them to the council and sang the maize song in six parts (three performed slowly, three quickly). The lyrics tell the story of a maize plant that is angry with a female gardener and is humiliating her while she is working and harvesting another maize plant. Traditionally, male moiety groups also perform rituals during the song, although this did not take place while Sílvio sang.[4] The next day, Sílvio planted the same maize kernels from the ritual in his riverbank plot, making sure to refrain from eating beforehand. As with the first harvest rituals, the ceremony and subsequent planting by the maize ritual owner liberates the crop, allowing the entire community to plant maize at their leisure. Fernando pointed out that the maize ritual owner can choose to bring any varietal of maize to the ceremony, and that regardless of his choice, the ceremony brings happiness to all types of planted maize.

During the maize growing season, men perform other ritual songs for maize and undertake ritual log racing, a common component of many ceremonial events. The maize log races are a series of ritual races between the upper and lower age-set male moiety groups using logs cut in the ceremonial corn style (see Crocker 1990:100). Men sing a pair of complementary (or coupled) ritual songs that reference the log races—the *pōhy jōpī jacrere* song, which is sung during the end of the dry season in September (if the maize is planted early in riverbank plots), followed by the *ahtyc mā ahkra* (literally the Black Regeneration moiety song), performed at the beginning of the rainy season in November or December. The growing maize plants can "hear" and become "happy" from the songs the men sing, as Fernando explained. Shamans often tell people that the maize plants walk from the gardens to the ceremonial center to listen to the singing. Even the logs cut in the ceremonial corn style can hear and become happy from the singing, which celebrates the logs' roles in the ritual racing activities.

Happy and strong from the singing, the maize crops will produce an abundant harvest that is celebrated through another male-led ceremony. Since the maize children are thought to become sufficiently happy from the ritual singing while growing, singing during the harvest festival is not necessary. The maize harvest festival typically occurs after the Hôxwa in February or March, although it took place in November 2012 while Sílvio was the maize owner because of his early planting in the riverbank. Sílvio harvested the first maize crop from his garden, crushed the ears of corn into a powder, and served it to the group of male elders who try first harvests. Once they tasted it and approved the crop as safe, the entire community was allowed to harvest the maize in their gardens. In the afternoon, the male lead singer called young men to the ceremonial center to play a game known as *pōhy prỳ* (literally "maize shuttlecock"), which involves tossing shuttlecocks made from ears of corn into the air without letting them fall on the ground. Sílvio and his family made the shuttlecocks for the harvest ceremony, and all the male moiety groups played together until late in the afternoon. The game, according to Liliana and others, is meant to increase the maize harvest, and Crocker (1990:100) notes a relationship between how many times the shuttlecock is tossed without hitting the ground and the abundance of the harvest. As with the planting and growing ceremonies, the harvest festival is intended to make the maize kernels happy and promote successful maize harvests for years to come.

Through these harvest rituals (and the planting and growing rituals for maize), men and women display distinctly gendered, embodied connections to their crops. While women take on the primary caretaker role for plant children through individual everyday activities in garden spaces, men emphasize their own relationships with harvested adult crops through communal ceremonial activities in the village center. Elder men in particular seek out and maintain intimate relationships with mature elder crops through communal sensory experiences of tasting, touching, and singing to them. This is in contrast to elder women's individual experiences of handling vines and singing to growing crop children in forest and riverbank gardens. The exception is maize, which men ritually celebrate throughout its life and not solely when it has reached elder status. The ceremonial importance of maize has been well documented in Jê-speaking communities (see Miller 2010 for a detailed review). In the Canela life-world, distinct embodied, multi-sensory relationships develop among men and maize crops during planting, growing, and harvesting. Elder men visually appreciate the maize kernels during the planting ritual, male moiety groups sing to the growing crop and handle logs stylized as corncobs, elder men taste the newly harvested adult maize, and younger men playfully toss the corncob shuttlecocks in the harvest ritual. The maize rituals are exclusively male and even involve disparaging female gardeners' connections to maize in the ritual planting maize song. Through these embodied interactions with maize, men are displaying the crop's value to the community while simultaneously emphasizing their own ceremonial and political power. Whereas women have arguably more relative power and more intimate experiences with crops in the garden plots and houses, men are empowered by the communal rituals in the ceremonial village space. Moreover, the crops men celebrate become more valued and meaningful owing to their association with male ceremonial power. All the crops that are celebrated ritually by men are considered especially valuable to male and female gardeners, and their varietal diversity is supported and maintained by the community at large. As with other human–plant embodied gendered experiences, the male multi-sensory encounters with plants that are pursued and celebrated in the harvest festivals are integral to educating affection. Boys learn from their elders that relationships with mature crops are just as important as those with crop children and that they too will have the opportunity to engage with valuable crop elders after reaching adulthood.

Gendering Gardening: Traditions and Transgressions

Through the ritual activities of food and sex restrictions, ritual singing and food sharing in garden spaces, and harvest rituals in the village space, women and men develop and maintain intimate, embodied experiences with cultivated crops. These experiences are clearly gendered, with female and male bodies interacting with plants in distinct ways. Female bodies are expected to develop intimate relationships of nurturing motherly affection throughout the course of crop children's lives. While male bodies should engage affectionately with crop children as fathers, they also are expected to communally celebrate and honor prestigious crop elders at the end of their lives. These strictly defined gender roles are integral to the Canela life-world. Female and male roles and spaces are considered complementary to one another, each one essential to the creation and maintenance of the concentric circular village, the moiety system, the family, and the dual garden plot system.

Yet what happens if these traditional gender roles are transgressed? While uncommon, there are instances of people actively transgressing, in embodied ways, the traditional gender roles into which they were assigned at birth. One well-known example is that of Liliana's grandparent, Dirceu, who was born a man yet is said to have become a woman in their old age. Dirceu engaged mainly in male gendered activities throughout childhood and adulthood, including serving in the army in the nearby town of Barra do Corda as a young person and developing shamanic perceptual activities that are typically acquired by men. Yet Dirceu also engaged in some traditionally female activities, including doing chores in their mother's house and even occasionally wearing the cloth skirt (pano) that girls and women wear. Liliana also recalled seeing Dirceu "lying with men" while she was a young girl, indicating that perhaps Dirceu engaged in same-sex sexual activities at the time (which is not openly discussed or accepted in the Canela life-world). As an elderly person, Dirceu fully adopted female dress, mannerisms, and embodied activities. By wearing the cloth skirt, assisting with household chores, and participating in the predominately female activity of seed saving, Dirceu transgressed traditional gender norms and was considered to become a woman by community members (literally *mam hũmre hapuhna cahãj* in Canela, or "man who transformed into a woman"). Liliana explained that by following the "law of women" (*lei das mulheres*) in bodily appearance and experiences, Dirceu developed female characteristics. Dirceu continued to participate in some traditional male activities, such as remaining married to a woman and living in the wife's home, thereby underscoring the ambiguity of Dirceu's embodied position. Similar to the half-male/half-female category of manioc, Dirceu occupied an in-between space in the Canela life-world. And just as the half-male/half-female types of manioc have similar characteristics as feminine sweet manioc, including being *impej* (beautiful, good, true/original), so too was third-gendered Dirceu considered to be more akin to the feminine than the masculine through their embodied experiences. Saving seeds was one of the primary ways that Dirceu established femininity and was therefore able to engage intimately with seed infants as a surrogate crop mother (or a third-gendered category of half-mother, half-father). Even when transgressing gendered norms, then, interacting with plant children necessitates some sort of gendered embodied position.

There are limits to acceptable transgressions of gendered bodies in the Canela life-world, however. There are a few other instances of men developing feminine embodied aspects (and perhaps becoming a third-gendered category), including a man who dressed with a cloth skirt around the same time as Dirceu. However, women typically are prohibited from developing masculine characteristics. In one example, a young unmarried woman began dressing in masculine shorts and a t-shirt and singing ritual songs in the main village street, an activity reserved for male ritual singers. Unlike Dirceu and the other man, who were tolerated and eventually even accepted by community members, the young woman was chastised by the male leadership council and prohibited from continuing her transgressive dress and embodied activities. Dirceu's third-gender position remains distinct among the Canela and according to Liliana was possible only on account of Dirceu's elderly age, having already fulfilled the traditional male activities of hunting, becoming a shaman, demarcating and burning garden plots, marrying, and procreating with women. Indeed, it was in old age that Dirceu publically became a woman; as a young person, only close family members, including Liliana, knew about Dirceu's dressing in cloth skirts and lying with men. Overall, boys and girls are expected to learn and become enskilled in specific tasks based on their gendered birth assignment. While it is a fluid, dynamic process of learning how to become with plants, educating affection is limited by sociocultural gender norms that become imprinted on human and plant bodies. Learning from their elders which embodied activities are considered "feminine" or "masculine," younger girls and boys interact with their multispecies human and plant kin in these distinctly gendered ways.

Caretaking of Plant Children: The Experts

Learning how to garden and becoming with plants is a generalized process of developing everyday skill sets and ritual practices, yet there are also distinct activities that girls and boys learn from particular gardening experts in their families. Gardening experts embody the ethos of educating affection, in that they pursue and seek out affectionate, nurturing engagements with a wide diversity of crop children in forest and riverbank plots. The three expert gardeners discussed here are well-known in the community for their large, biodiverse gardens that produce abundant harvests. They are generally admired for their gardening expertise and sought after to exchange seeds and cuttings. Expert gardeners recognize that their knowledge and expertise is contingent and dynamic, ever-expanding and changing due to new experiences with their plant kin each gardening season. Moreover, experts maintain that their enthusiasm and affection for crop children and garden spaces is paramount to gardening knowledge and expertise. Without plant caretaking, gardening would be a fruitless exercise, bound to fail as unhappy crop children would be unable to develop into abundant harvests. Through the experiences of expert gardeners Liliana, Camila, and Fernando, the importance of educating affection for plants becomes clear.

Diversifying Crops Is Our Strength: Liliana

More than other gardeners, Liliana is known for maintaining a wide diversity of crops in her forest and riverbank garden plots. Renato often told Liliana she was the "only woman [gardener] who cultivates so many things." Fernando and Wander, meanwhile, once explained to me that Liliana was the "Dilma Rousseff of gardens," likening her gardening prowess to the leadership capabilities of Brazil's first female president. Other Canela gardeners single out and admire Liliana for her gardening expertise and enthusiasm, especially her cultivation of many different crop species and varieties. Neighbor women often visit Liliana's house to discuss gardening techniques and to acquire some of her diverse varietals through exchange. Those who visit her garden plots are struck by their biodiversity. When the Canela tractor driver, Dorival, visited Liliana's forest plot in early 2013, for example, he expressed his appreciation for the tall fava bean vines, telling her his heart "beat very fast" upon seeing the beautiful vines. When Liliana and I visited her forest garden with other community members in November 2017, everyone commented on its beauty and biodiversity. Community members were impressed with the diverse manioc varietals she had recently planted, exclaiming "*impej!*" as they handled the varietals' distinct leaves and sticks. Liliana herself attributes her expertise to the teachings of her maternal and paternal classificatory grandparents, who showed her various gardening techniques and gave her seeds and cuttings of varietals that she continues to cultivate today. In turn, Liliana passes along this knowledge and appreciation of biodiverse gardens to her daughters and grandchildren.

One of the most important aspects of Liliana's gardening prowess is her knowledge of which crop species and varieties grow best in different garden plots. Through experiential showing by her grandparents and decades of personal experience planting gardens, Liliana has developed her own techniques and practices that correspond with and deviate from the more general practices outlined in chapter 2. In the riverbank plot, Liliana maintains that squash, watermelon, banana, maize, and bitter and sweet manioc produce abundant harvests in the fertile *amcó* soil type. She also likes to plant true/original sugarcane (*cãn peaj-re*) and the fish poison vine (*tepja-re*) in the riverbank garden. For banana varietals, Liliana initially plants the saplings in riverbank plots and after a few years relocates the trees to her and her daughters' backyard gardens to allow more space for their growth. She also maintains a large grove of cashew trees in the riverbank plot, the different varietals of which she proudly shows to neighbors, family members, and myself (see figure 1). Some species, such as annatto, are grown mainly for ceremonial purposes. In October 2012, Liliana planted true/original annatto (*pym peaj*), the seeds of which are boiled down to make a brilliant red body paint that she needed for her grandsons who were participating in the following year's Pep-yê male initiation festival period. With proper care and tending, Liliana assured me these trees would continue to bear fruit for nine years, thereby providing many seasons of rich red body paint.

Liliana's preferences of where and when to plant different species and varieties shed light on her creativity and experimentation in garden spaces. In the forest plot, Liliana advises her family to plant yam and common bean varietals twice per year. While the adult couples of the family plant most crops together, Liliana likes to plant the second crop of yam varietals by herself, an unusual practice for a Canela gardener. Being well attuned to the dry and rainy seasons in the Cerrado, Liliana is flexible with her planting schedule and waits to plant varietals of squash, sweet potato, and peanut until the heavy rains arrive in November or December. The beginning of the heavy

Figure 1. Liliana with a large red cashew in her riverbank plot, August 2012.

rains also determines when she plants maize varietals, which can be as early as November or as late as February. Liliana maintains that December is the best month for planting rows of sweet and bitter manioc cuttings, and she and her family plant fast-growing rice at the end of the month, which Liliana prefers over the slow-growing varietals. For fava bean, Liliana experiments with different schedules, planting varietals in December, January, and February to gauge which crop gives the most abundant harvest in May or June.

Her flexibility and creativity are especially apparent in the backyard garden space, where she easily can experiment with planting schedules and with small crops of new species and varieties. In the backyard plot, Liliana typically plants her favorite varietals of different species, including of fava bean, common bean, maize, squash, sweet potato, and papaya and banana fruit trees. While many Canela families maintain some sort of backyard garden, Liliana's is larger and more biodiverse than the average backyard plot. If Liliana is curious about the taste or successful harvest of a recently acquired species or variety, she will test it in the backyard plot. In May and June 2012, for example, Liliana was growing a small amount of coriander that she had acquired from whites (cupẽn) in the nearby town of Barra do Corda. She also planted the seeds from tomatoes that I brought from Barra do Corda for her to cook (she enjoys trying out new cooking techniques as well).

Liliana's desire to increase agro-biodiversity by incorporating "new things" (coisas novas) as she calls them highlights her openness to dynamic gardening knowing, including learning about new crops and practices from both insiders (mẽhĩn) and outsiders (cupẽn). Liliana repeatedly explained that experimenting with and incorporating new species and varieties into garden plots was "the most important thing" for her. She values new crops for their own attributes, such as a distinctive color or taste, and most importantly because they contribute to the overall spectrum of biodiversity in her gardens. When surveying the growing crops in her gardens, Liliana finds it beautiful to see many species and varieties together. She actively pursues the cultivation of as many species and varieties as possible. This includes an impressive collection of dozens of the fifty-two named fava bean (pànkrỳt) varieties; five types of cashew trees; six maize varieties; multiple varieties of sweet potato, yam, manioc, maize, and squash; and multiple varieties of more recently introduced fruit trees (papaya, mango, banana, and orange). She actively acquires new varieties through exchange within and outside the Canela territory and occasionally through the discovery of new crop types in her garden plots (see chapter 4, "Expanding Multispecies Families"). For example, in December 2012, Liliana planted seeds of the four new maize varietals that her son-in-law Vítor had acquired at a government-sponsored seed exchange with other Jê-speaking communities. Explaining why she planted the new varietals immediately after acquiring them, Liliana told me that she "enjoys the new maize—it is pretty [*impej*]."

Maintaining and increasing overarching agro-biodiversity is Liliana's main pursuit, and she therefore cultivates varietals she enjoys and desires, as well as those she actively dislikes. Liliana maintains certain types of sugarcane, maize, peanut, and yam because they are considered the "most beautiful" (*impeaj to impej*) and directly associated with the mythical figure of Star-Woman (see chapter 4, table 5).[5] Other varieties are actively maintained for their visual beauty, such as cobra bitter manioc (*kwỳr awari*), which produces an appealing bright-yellow *farinha* (toasted manioc flour). Liliana also devotes space in her gardens for especially delicious varietals, including Guajajara tree bean (*pàt juhtõi-re pàràre/pryjĩ*), large bright red bean (*pàt juhtõi-re intep-ti*), large dry squash (*cuhkõn cahàc cràà-ti*), large white sweet potato (*jàt jaka-ti*), and small red parrot tail sweet manioc (*kwỳr caprêc-re/krỳi-re japỳ*). Still other varieties are cultivated for times of food insecurity—tortoise arm bitter manioc (*kwỳr caprãn jũkee*), for example, can remain growing in the ground for one and a half years and therefore serves as a food storage to be used in times of shortage. Additionally, Liliana continues to cultivate distasteful large white membrane true/original yam (*krẽrô pej caxwỳn jaka-ti*) and large brown-violet membrane true/original yam (*krẽrô pej caxwỳn kukum-ti*), both of which have an especially bland taste and are said to produce lesions in a person's foot when consumed. Although these yams are categorized as *impej* (good, beautiful, true/original) in Canela ethnobotanical classification, they are informally known as *ihkên* (bad, ugly, less true/original). Explaining why she continues to grow varietals that are bad, less delicious, and cause bodily harm, Liliana alternatingly told me that cultivating as many species and varieties as possible helps "defend" her family from hunger, that she should maintain the knowledge passed down from her grandfather about "all the seeds," and that she enjoyed the beautiful diversity growing in her garden plots. In addition to providing food security, the less delicious yams therefore contribute to Canela gardening knowledge and overall agro-biodiversity. Moreover, the distasteful yams are understood as crop children in need of nurturing care and affection. Liliana's enjoyment and appreciation of her ever-expanding multispecies family of diverse crop children, including both the *impej* and *ihkên*, forms an integral component of her fluid, dynamic gardening knowing.

Liliana cares for her diverse plant children through frequent visits to tend, weed, and ritually sing to them. While Liliana and her daughters regularly visit their adjacent forest plots together to tend and interact with their crop children, she occasionally visits the garden by herself, an unusual activity for a female gardener. Liliana spends her time surveying all the crops and attending to individual species and varieties that may need her care. Many of her visits to the forest plot are spent hanging fava bean, common bean, and yam vines on nearby maize stalks or manioc sticks. She also observes the mini-gardens of sweet potato, other types of common bean, and peanut maintained at the edge of the forest plot. As is commonly the case, Liliana takes extra care when planting peanut and avoids weeding it while growing, since this can lead to ant infestations that destroy the crop. Additionally, during her visits Liliana determines whether animals have entered the garden space. She can tell when an armadillo has eaten some of her sweet potato varietals, for example, and knows when parakeets (*krẽ-re*) will attempt to eat most of her rice varieties before the harvest. She advises her male relatives of the birds' imminent arrival so that they can scare away the birds with shotguns. To repel snakes from entering, Liliana plants the native *fava da cobra* plant that resembles fava bean, since snakes are said to dislike its pungent smell. By observing animals and taking steps to prevent their entry into the garden space, Liliana is caring for and protecting her human and plant family members.

In turn, the affectionate care that Liliana gives to her diverse crop children promotes the happiness and strength (*ihtỳi*) of both people and plants. As the mother (*inxê*) of crop children, in Liliana's words, she is responsible for supporting their happiness and strength, and these activities consequently bring her feelings of happiness and strength. Moreover, growing happy, strong, and diverse crop species and varieties results in bountiful harvests, which will provide food security (and strong, happily fulfilled bodies) for Liliana's human family members. Liliana's gardening expertise is therefore grounded in caring, affectionate experiences that lead to strong, happy, and holistically well (*impej*) plant and human families. In this way, Liliana's diverse multispecies family has survived and thrived for decades. It will continue to thrive in new and dynamic forms as her daughters and granddaughters carry on Liliana's embodied teachings of the importance of crop diversity for overall well-being.

Mothering Crops: Camila

Camila is another gardening expert whose expertise is grounded in mothering her crop children. The quote at the beginning of the chapter highlights Camila's devotion to caring for her crops just as she cares for her daughters and grandchildren. As Liliana's younger sister, Camila learned much of her

Figure 2. Camila weaving a basket in the space between her house and Liliana's, May 2012.

gardening knowledge from the same elder family members and from Liliana herself. Yet Camila has developed her own gardening practices as the elder of her own family. Neighbor women admire Camila's diverse crop species and varieties, particularly her rice collection, during visits to her house in the main village circle, next door to Liliana's house (see figure 2). Camila typically has many bushels of rice drying from the house rafters, and her diverse rice varieties were often the ones I photographed for ethnobotanical surveys. Camila's forest and riverbank garden plots are also biodiverse, typically including varieties of yam, squash, watermelon, bitter and sweet manioc, fava bean, common bean, rice, maize, and peanut. She enjoys planting common bean varietals in her second-year old gardens (*hipêj*) to give them extra space to grow, and she is particularly fond of growing peanuts, which she plants in a separate mini-garden near the forest plot.

Showing her enthusiasm for gardening, Camila explained that she plants crops anywhere she desires, including forest, riverbank, and backyard garden spaces. Camila's backyard garden is a unique space where she nurtures biodiverse crop children that are both aboriginal and introduced to the community (see chapter 4, "Expanding Multispecies Families"). In 2012, Camila was maintaining native species such as *cajá* (*pyyrija*; *Spondias mombin* L.) saplings and the trees of *pitomba* (*hyjorore*; *Talisia esculenta* Radk.), *tuturubá* (*capôcre*; *Pouteria macrophylla* [Lam.] Eyma), and *jenipapo* (*pôl-ti*; *Genipa americana* L.), whose fruits are used to make a semi-permanent ritual black body paint. Camila also seeks out species that originate outside the Canela territory, including mango, papaya, and banana trees, which have been part of Canela gardens for decades, as well as more recently introduced jackfruit (*potukà*; *Artocarpus heterophyllus* Lam.), guava (*cwaj-jap*; *Psidium guajava* L.), and tamarind (*pôj kôc-jôjre cahàc*; *Tamarindus indica* L.) saplings and tomato plants. In November 2017, Camila was growing many of these same species and varieties, as well as various types of common bean and squash, the vines of which were beginning to twist around the new wooden fence she had built around the backyard garden's perimeter to keep out village animals, including pigs, chickens, dogs, and cats.

Similar to Liliana, Camila appreciates the new species and varieties growing in her backyard garden for their overarching diversity. In addition, the backyard garden is an ideal place where Camila easily can bring happiness to both crop and human children. She can carefully tend to the newly introduced crop children daily while they are saplings, paying attention to their needs and desires as a learning opportunity for future growing seasons. Meanwhile, the mature trees provide ripe fruits to the human children in her family and those of her neighbors. One hot, dry afternoon in August 2012, for example, Camila's grandchildren and children from nearby houses climbed up her *pitomba* tree and joyfully gorged themselves on its newly ripe fruits. Juice dripping down their faces, they happily chattered and sang during their feast, offering me one of the small, rounded green fruits as I passed by. The sheer joy of these children demonstrates the happiness that Camila's backyard garden brings to human children, which is borne out of Camila's nurturing care for the fruit tree children as they grow.

Camila takes seriously her nurturing affection for growing crop children in backyard, riverbank, and forest plots. To show that she is attentive to the plants' needs, Camila remains quiet while planting and tending to them. Unlike the typical Canela gardener, she does not ritually sing to her crops but rather spends time quietly cleaning and weeding the garden space to ensure that the crops are happy and will not relocate to a better-managed garden. While acknowledging that it is hard work, Camila takes pleasure in gardening activities and typically stays at her forest plot every other week. Sometimes her daughters accompany her, but similar to Liliana, Camila often visits the plot by herself and expresses her happiness at spending time in the garden space. She is proud of her gardening prowess and hard work, and especially of the fact that her usually abundant harvests "do not let hunger arrive" at her doorstep.

While the garden space generally brings happiness to gardeners, there are times when sadness prevents one from visiting and working in the gardens. After Camila's classificatory father Jacinto passed away during the main planting season in November–December 2011, for example, she was too sad to plant many crops in her forest plot. By April 2012, Camila still was spending many days at home and infrequently visited her gardens. Liliana explained that the sadness caused by their father's death prevented Camila from working and led her to "mope about" the house, a sign of her feeling weak and sad (*ihpêc*).[6] Liliana also was saddened by his loss and planted slightly less crop varieties than usual, although she avoided the malaise that affected Camila by continuing to visit and work in the happy garden space. In this way, the garden creates and reinforces feelings of strength and happiness for Canela gardeners. Conversely, avoiding the garden space when feeling sad or weak only reinforces those feelings, making it harder for someone like Camila to visit the garden and recover feelings of happiness (*ihtỳi*). Fortunately, when the 2012 planting season began, Camila had recovered from her *ihpêc* state and happily cared for her crops. Expressing her affectionate feelings for her crops to me later that year, it was clear that Camila had re-established her motherly role toward crop children. She vowed never to leave them, perhaps referencing her previous weak and sad state. Camila's transformation from *ihtỳi* to *ihpêc* and back again to *ihtỳi* demonstrates the emergent, unfolding nature of gardening knowing and educating affection for crops. Even an expert gardener such as Camila can be confronted with serious setbacks that affect her gardening prowess. Yet as time passes, she can regain her strength and happiness and engage with crop children once again.

Cultivating a Happy Life: Fernando

Expert gardener Fernando also expresses his happiness and satisfaction while working in his biodiverse garden plots. He views the gardens as places that give sustenance and provide for a "happy life." While Canela women are the primary caretakers of growing crops, men occasionally play a more engaged role throughout the annual forest and riverbank gardening cycles. Fernando is unique for a Canela man, as he is actively involved in all aspects of gardening, including demarcation, planting, tending, and harvesting along with his wife, Geralda, and their family members. As a skilled gardener and former hunter, Fernando has expert knowledge of the eco-regions, soil types, and native flora and fauna in the Canela territory. He is especially aware of how wild animals interact with growing crops in garden spaces. In the second-year-old garden areas, for example, Fernando knows that wild peccaries and paca and agouti rodents feed off the bitter manioc left growing there. He also informs his grandchildren that after a *queimada* (burning) in a new garden plot, animals come to eat the buds of newly sprouted *ahtu* and *woporore* native *chupudu* grasses. For Fernando, having old and new gardens feed wild animals in this way is essential to the preservation of the animals and of nature in general. He takes particular pleasure in knowing that the gardens are providing the animals with new food, as he maintained that the animals "enjoy and need to eat new things" as much as humans do. Thus, for Fernando the garden plots and their produce sustain and give enjoyment to animals as well as to humans.

As with Liliana and Camila, Fernando's emphasis on the enjoyment and necessity of "new things" translates into an appreciation for and maintenance of crop species and varietal diversity. He and his wife cultivate a wide array of species and varieties in their forest plot and exceptionally large riverbank plot. In both plots, the couple grows bitter and sweet manioc, squash, sweet potato, watermelon, yam, fava bean, common bean, rice, maize, and peanut. Fernando experiments with species that are not commonly grown in garden plots, including native buriti (*crowa pàr*), bacaba (*caper; Oenocarpus bacaba* Mart.), and açaí (*têrêrc; Euterpe* sp.) trees and *tucum da chapada* (*ronre*), which is made into twine for beaded necklaces and ceremonial belts (*krãn-re*), among other ritual items. In his backyard garden, Fernando also grows varieties of mango, papaya, lime, and orange. And in 2017, Fernando had established a backyard plot of thriving large white sweet potato (*jàt jakati*) and large purplish-black sweet potato (*jàt tyc-ti*), which the young girls in my family and I admired as we walked to the stream to bathe. His enthusiasm for gardening and biodiversity maintenance even extends beyond the confines of traditional garden spaces to include a grove of cashew tree varieties that he manages near his house and to a communal grove of buriti and bacaba trees behind the eastern side of the village, a project that he initiated (see figure 3).

Fernando and Geralda also maintain crop varieties that few other families cultivate, including yam that multiplies (*krẽrô teamjijapê/tum pram*), small basket yam (*krẽrô kaj-re*), large mixed-color maize (*põhy kror-ti*), hairy tail maize (*põhy jĩire*), and small jaguar bean (*pàt juhtõi-re kroro-re*). Fernando prefers particular varieties for their taste, physical appearance, and/ or for their usefulness in the garden space. He appreciates large mixed-color maize, for example, for its beautiful kernels that are mixed white, brown, and black, while small basket yam has an interesting shape similar to a woven basket (*kaj*). As with Liliana and her family, Fernando also enjoys growing cobra bitter manioc because of the beautiful and delicious yellow *farinha* it produces and because he likes to hang growing fava bean vines from the sturdy sticks of this manioc varietal. Fernando seeks out and maintains new

Figure 3. Fernando in the buriti and bacaba tree grove, April 2012.

or rare varieties because they are different and will add to his overall crop collection, regardless of their taste or beauty. For example, he sought out and acquired hairy tail maize from the government agency EMBRAPA[7] (*Empresa Brasileira de Pesquisa Agropecuária*), and he continues to cultivate it despite the fact that it is not especially tasty. Similar to Liliana, Fernando values a wide spectrum of agro-biodiversity in his garden plots more than a particular variety's individual traits.

Additionally, over the years, Fernando has become actively involved with outsiders, including governmental functionaries, nongovernmental development workers, missionaries, and anthropologists, and in one of his many leadership roles he advocates for biodiversity maintenance in Canela gardens. Fernando expressed to me many times his concern over youths who were "no longer remembering" how to garden and the subsequent biodiversity loss related to this forgotten knowledge. To address his concerns for the community, Fernando worked with the nongovernmental organization CTI (*Centro de Trabalho Indigenistas*) on a project in the 1990s to grow jackfruit and *cupuaçu* (*Theobroma grandiflorum* [Willd. ex Spreng.] K. Schum.) trees, the fruits of which were intended to be processed into juice and commercialized. While the commercial aspect of the project fell through, Fernando continues to maintain the fruit trees that CTI gave the Canela community.[8] In 2012, Fernando met with representatives of FUNAI and EMBRAPA at their offices in Brasília concerning the recovery of lost crops and received seeds of large grey maize (*pōhy jiproh-ti*) and *kupá* (*Cissus* L.) vine cuttings that he brought back to the community. Canela gardeners have all but abandoned growing *kupá*, even though Nimuendajú (1946:58) recorded it as an "aboriginally known" species. Fernando also supported and sent Canela representatives to a government-sponsored seed exchange among Jê-speaking Indigenous communities that took place in Pará State in September 2012, wherein the representatives brought back four new types of maize. Through these various engagements with outsiders, Fernando has been able to better maintain and even increase the biodiversity of his own and others' garden plots. Other gardeners therefore know and respect Fernando as an expert gardener who can interact successfully with various outsiders (*cupẽn*) to acquire new crops that are subsequently incorporated into Canela (*mẽhĩn*) gardens.

According to Fernando, a biodiverse and abundant garden is essential for a Canela person's happiness, as it "quenches" the desires in one's life. In his view, garden work "fortifies" people by providing food and by promoting overall happiness and well-being. Thus, for Fernando, maintaining and acquiring diverse crop species and varieties from within and outside the territory is "necessary for life." As he eloquently explained:

> The gardens are important for survival! Because the gardens sustain us ... [they] satisfy life [and] give happiness and contentment to life. Without gardens, it is like a person without eyes, without hands, and without feet. A person without eyes does not see anything, without hands does not do anything, and without feet does not walk, and [therefore] does nothing. That is why we should be hard workers ... for us to produce, feed ourselves, and live! Without crops, one becomes weak and near death. [...] However, rice, *farinha*, squash, bean, sweet potato fortify. The garden is important for these things.

By comparing a Canela person without a garden to someone without eyes, hands, or feet, Fernando underscores the embodied aspects of physical garden work, as well as of consuming crops that fortify human bodies. In this way, the metaphor sheds light on the importance of gardens and the expert knowledge that maintains them to embodied survival and well-being for individuals, families, and the entire multispecies community. For Fernando does not limit his understanding of gardening to promote a happy life to Canela people alone; rather, he acknowledges that crops are similarly deserving of happy, fulfilling, and fortifying life experiences. He identifies crops as being "similar to children" in that they require constant care and attention to bring them joy and to ward off feelings of sadness. Fernando likes helping crop children to live well and be happy through caretaking activities such as hanging fava bean vines, an activity that the fava bean itself enjoys. While care and affection for growing crops is not limited to expert gardeners, their activities and preferences demonstrate ideal multispecies human–plant relationships more than other gardeners. Moreover, the gardening expertise of a few gardeners, when passed along to younger generations, promotes happiness and well-being for generations of multispecies Canela families.

Becoming Strong, Becoming Happy, Becoming Well

Why am I interested in gardens? Because gardens give sustenance. The garden makes me happy [ihtỳi] all the time, every day. If I lacked a garden, before long I would become weak. Do you know why? Because for me, the garden is the most important [thing], and it gives a lot of strength. Seeing as I have gardens, I am happy! I sleep well, and every day at daybreak, I am awake [and] already remembering the work in the garden that I want to do to protect my life.
—Liliana, May 2012

Through eating [crops], this abundance is blood. Because [when one] eats well, one becomes strong and very big and beautiful, very beautiful [impej] indeed! That is why the garden is important. For survival. When people eat well, they become very strong!
—Renato, May 2012

As an education of affection, gardening exemplifies the connection between the Canela concepts of ihtỳi (happiness, strength, health) and impej (good, beautiful, true/original). These are embodied concepts that together form Canela understandings of being or becoming well in a holistic sense. Both humans and nonhumans experience embodied states of ihtỳi and impej, and their opposites—ihpêc, meaning sadness, weakness, and illness, and ihkên, that which is bad, ugly, and less true/original. People are constantly inquiring over others' current embodied states of becoming well or unwell. The common greeting when meeting someone is, "Apej?" (literally, "are you impej [good/well]"?) The other person typically responds with "impej," meaning "I am good/well", "ipej," meaning "I was unwell but now I am better," or "ihkên," meaning "I am unwell," such as while a woman is menstruating. The two concepts can be intensified, through the augmentatives impeaj to impej (best, most beautiful, truest/most original) and ihkêãn-re (worst, ugliest, least true/ original). Being or becoming impej and ihkên can also refer to behavior. Fernando explained that behaving in an *impej* manner means "being generous," while those who behave in an *ihkên* way "mistreat" others. The pursuit of becoming *ihtỳi* and *impej* is an ongoing process throughout one's life, subject to changing physical and emotional states and various interactions among humans and nonhumans.

Experiencing these embodied states is gendered, based on Canela women's and men's pursuits and activities throughout their lives. Women typically emphasize the embodied *ihtỳi* states they experience through frequently visiting and working in garden spaces, which over time can lead to becoming *impej*. Liliana often described forest and riverbank gardens as places of respite "where there is no sadness; everyone is happy [and] strong all the time, doing all the work." The garden space, she repeatedly maintained, "gives her strength" and "defends" her and her family from hunger as well as from sadness, weakness, and "unhealthy" malaise (*ihpêc*). Liliana also directly linked garden work and its lack to the concepts of *ihtỳi* and *ihpêc*, as she explained during one of our conversations in October 2012:

Liliana: *Ihtỳi* is strength, hardness . . . and weakness is *ihpêc*. The correct word—*ihpêc-re*—very weak, weakness.

Me: Does *ihtỳi* mean being healthy too?

L: Yes, it is health.

Me: And when a person is *ihpêc*, is he or she ill?

L: [He or she] has a problem, an illness. There are some people who do not undergo *resguardo* [food and sex prohibitions], and they too are *ihpêc xà*—sad, because they did not undergo the strict diet. [. . .] This person . . . only creates weakness—he/she does not like to walk, does not like to become strong. [. . .]

Me: Is the person who is strong also *impej*? Is there a connection between *ihtỳi* and *impej*?

L: Yes, *ihtỳi* is linked to the most beautiful word, *impej*.

Me: And *ihpêc* is linked to *ihkên*?

L: Yes, they are not well—weak and sad. *Ihtỳi* is strong, happy—not feeling sadness. [. . .] Working in the garden and preparing food before the weakness arrives; preparing everything beforehand—in this way the weakness does not come. However, *mẽ ihpêc xà* creates weakness all the time . . . people become weak, unmoving, and quiet inside the house. These people do not enjoy speaking, nor playing; they only foster anger and speak badly about others. [. . .] Those who feel strong have the courage to do everything to survive, and suffering does not stay near them. They do the same as a chicken who takes care of her family—clearing away rubbish, getting food for the children—the father and mother of the family do the same things as the chicken who cares for her chicks, and these bad things do not enter! In my understanding, this is very important.

Here there is a strong emphasis on frequently visiting and working in garden spaces to become *ihtỳi*, *impej*, and overall holistically well. Similar to a chicken who cares for her chicks, Liliana works hard in the gardens to feed and care for her human and plant families. Recognizing that the opposite cycle of becoming sad, weak, ill (*ihpêc*), and eventually *ihkên* is possible through lack of garden visits and work, Liliana strives to courageously continue gardening to prevent suffering for herself and her human and plant kin. In another conversation, Liliana underscored the importance of waking early to visit the gardens to avoid weakness:

Seeing as I have gardens, I awake at four o'clock in the morning to prepare things, to prepare breakfast to give me strength. We prepare the food, and by four or five in the morning, we are going to the garden. Since I am far away from the [forest] garden this year, I cannot become softened with weakness! I have to have the courage to wake up [early].

Waking early and requiring little sleep is also linked to processes of becoming *impej* through food and sex restrictions (see chapter 5, "Becoming a Shaman: Engagements with Nonhumans"). Indeed, the benefits of undergoing food and sex restrictions are often compared to those of garden visits and work, in that both are ongoing processes that support becoming good, beautiful, true/original (*impej*) and holistically well. The food and sex restrictions that female and male gardeners undergo while their crop children are growing doubly underscores the connections among restrictions, gardening, and human and plant well-being.

Men also recognize the importance of gardening and garden spaces to Canela happiness, strength, health, and well-being. Yet because they are not the primary caretakers of growing crop children, they often emphasize other gardening activities that connect *ihtỳi* and *impej* concepts rather than predominately female garden work. Renato described gardens as spaces where people become strong and happy through many activities, including working, conversing, making love, and staying healthy and avoiding illness. In the above quote, he also emphasized the consumption of harvested crops as integral to states of becoming strong, happy, and *impej*. Although the entire community consumes garden produce, the male emphasis on crop consumption seen here reflects their domain over certain harvested crops, which only elder men can consume before first harvest rituals liberate the crops for women and children (see "Celebrating Plant Lives. First Harvests," this chapter). Nevertheless, Renato's statement that abundant garden harvests are "blood" that make people "strong" and "beautiful" overtly refers to all the Canela, including men, women, and children. Moreover, this underscores the embodied significance of maintaining garden plots, as they satisfy people's appetites and help male and female bodies become *ihtỳi*, *impej*, and well overall.

Crops themselves also experience embodied states of happiness, strength, health, and wellness, and their opposites. Gardener mothers and fathers observe crop behavior to determine what embodied states they are experiencing—crops that are feeling *ihtỳi* will grow fast and abundantly, while those that are feeling neglected or *ihpêc* will wither and dry out and often relocate to another family's garden plot. Crop children directly express feelings of happiness or sadness to their shamanic friends, who then communicate their needs and desires to gardener parents. The Plant-People master spirits also advocate for crops' ability to be or become *impej* by communicating with the shaman in gendered ways (see chapter 5). In these ways, crop well-being is supported and maintained in the Canela life-world.

While people and plants pursue embodied states of *ihtỳi* and *impej* throughout their lives, they also are categorized as *impej* or *ihkên* based on birth or existence. People are categorized as *impej* or *ihkên* based on their matrilocal birth residence, as outlined in the mythic story of Sun (Pỳt) and Moon (Putwre). In the story, Sun and Moon are formal friends (*hapĩn; compadres*) who come down from the sky and each create children in their likeness. Sun is *impej* and engages in activities to help the Canela, while Moon is *ihkên* and continuously hinders Sun's activities and their benefits to people. When they make children, Sun creates *impej* people to live on the western side of the circular village (*pỳt cjêj xà*; "place where the sun sets"), while Moon creates *ihkên* children to live on the eastern side (*pỳt já pôj xà*; "place where sun rises"). The storyteller Leandro described the origin of Canela people the following way:

> They went to the stream. Sun said, "we are going to make our children. Let us go to the stream." Sun jumped into the stream, and two children came out. Their hair was beautiful—smooth, and very white! Moon also jumped into the stream, and two children came out—with ugly, unruly hair! Moon said, "let us trade our children, *compadre!*" Sun responded, "no, these are my children! You keep your children, and I keep mine."

Fernando similarly described the origin of Canela people:

> They say that Moon's children do not have smooth, shiny hair, but Sun's children have shiny hair. Sun invited Moon to the stream. Then, Sun said, "*compadre*, let us create our children!" "Yes, it is good!" said Moon. "Look, look over there," Sun said. He dove into the stream, came out, and his child came out with him, accompanying him. Sun did this a second time, and again; four times he did this, and he created four children. Sun told Moon, "*compadre*, do it too!" Moon dove into the stream, and his child came out with him, but with ugly/untidy [curly] hair. Moon dove, created another one, and they all had the same hair. "All is well; we both created four children," Sun said.... They say that Moon's children have ugly/unruly hair, and Sun's children are much prettier!

The conceptual division of *impej* and *ihkên* people and village spaces shapes marriage and residence patterns in the contemporary Canela life-world. A man who is born on the western side must marry a woman on the eastern side and move into her family's home to avoid committing incest, and vice versa. *Impej* and *ihkên* people exhibit similar characteristics of the mythical figures from whom they are descended. Fernando explained that Sun's children are "more similar" to Sun and are more beautiful, better, and sometimes even more truthful than Moon's uglier, lesser children. Indeed, people living on the western side of the circular village (Sun's children) often joke about easterners being "liars" and not as "pretty" as they are descended from Moon.

When used as categories of people, the concepts of *impej* and *ihkên* are less dynamic and fluid than when they are embodied states of becoming. Both westerners and easterners can become *impej* through embodied activities such as gardening, but it remains the case that those born on the eastern side will be categorized as *ihkên* throughout their lives. Yet while there is an aesthetic–moral hierarchy of *impej* over *ihkên*, both concepts and categories of people are necessary and integral to the Canela life-world. Overall, the concepts are "the same size" according to Fernando, with *impej* being only "slightly better." Both categories of people and village spaces are necessary for the reproduction and continuation of the Canela life-world. Through kinship and marriage, every Canela family is both *impej* and *ihkên*, composed of family members from western and eastern sides. The necessity of *ihkên* elements in the life-world also emerges in ritual activities such as the Fish festival, which is sponsored by the *mēhkin* male ritual group. The group is categorized as *ihkên*, and their primary role is to bring this "bad" element into the festivities by making jokes and generally being "liars and deceivers," according to Fernando (see Crocker [1990.189, 275–276] for a more comprehensive analysis). In myth, ritual, kinship and marriage, and village layout, there is a recognition that both good and bad elements are essential to the continuation of the unfolding Canela life-world. And whether categorized as good or bad, Canela people can and do pursue the embodied state of becoming *impej* or well through intimate engagements with human and non-human others.

Cultivated crops are similarly able to pursue embodied states of becoming *ihtỳi* and *impej* while simultaneously being categorized as *impej* and *ihkên* (and their augmentatives, *impeaj to impej* and *ihkêän-re*). Rather than being connected to Sun and Moon, *impej* and *ihkên* cultivated crops are linked to the mythical figure of Star-Woman and her Canela husband Tyc-ti, respectively. As chapter 4 ("Noticing and Naming: Classifying Through Multisensory Experiences") describes, certain crops are linked directly to Star-Woman and categorized as *impej* and *impeaj to impej*. These include types of maize, *pànkrỳt* (fava) bean, squash, yam, sweet manioc, half-sweet/half-bitter manioc, rice, annatto, sugarcane, and mango. Meanwhile, all types of bitter manioc and one type of inedible fava bean are linked to her husband Tyc-ti and categorized as *ihkên* and *ihkêän-re*. Similar to the categories of people, crop species and varieties categorized as *impej* and its augmentative are understood as being more beautiful, better, truer, and more original than others, while the *ihkên* or *ihkêän-re* types are uglier, worse, and less true/original. In addition, there is a third category of "regular" (*cahàc*) crops that overlaps with the good and bad categories.

Regardless of whether they are good, bad, or regular, all categories of crops were introduced by Star-Woman and are seen as essential to crop childcare and agro-biodiversity maintenance in the contemporary life-world. Season after season, gardeners continue to cultivate and interact with as many types of good, bad, and regular crops as possible. All types are crop children in need of nurturing care and affection, and maintaining a diversity of crop children is paramount. Liliana exemplifies this pursuit of affection toward diverse crop children in many ways. For example, she continues to cultivate large white membrane true/original yam (*krêrô pej caxwỳn jaka-ti*) and large brown-violet membrane true/original yam (*krêrô pej caxwỳn kukum-ti*), which include both *impej* and *ihkên* characteristics (see Miller 2017). These two yams are categorized simultaneously as *impej* in Canela ethnobotanical classification, known as vice-chiefs in yam social organization and informally known as *ihkên* due to their bland taste and the lesions they are thought to cause on people's feet. The yams underscore the existence of both good and bad qualities in the Canela multispecies community and highlight the ways in which *impej* and *ihkên* concepts overlap and intertwine. Similarly, Canela human behavior is often described as fluctuating between "a little good and a little bad" (Crocker 1990:188), with both qualities part of Canela human experience. Recognizing both the goodness and badness of these yams, Liliana maintained that she "cannot leave them" behind by ceasing to cultivate and save them. Maintaining many different crop children, including those that are good, bad, and regular, in the garden is "beautiful this way," Liliana stated. Fernando similarly described the importance of maintaining diverse crops, both good and bad (see Miller 2017:333):

> There is everything; everything that we cultivate. It does not make a difference; we cultivate everything. There [in the garden], there is no difference. [. . .] Also, *ihkên* varieties; we also plant them. We cook them, we use them, we consume all the varieties.

For both people and plants, diversity itself—including everything that is good, better, bad, worse, and regular—is valued and meaningful as being *impej* overall. Moreover, all human and plant children—including children who behave "naughtily" (Crocker 1990:188) and bad yams that cause bodily harm—deserve a chance to grow and become happy, strong, healthy, and well in the Canela life-world.

Pursuing happiness, strength, health, beauty, goodness, and overall well-being is not limited to the Canela. Indeed, other Jê-speaking communities approach the pursuit of well-being in similar ways. For example, the Panará of Pará State also conceive of well-being and its lack in terms of two pairs of interconnected concepts: *suakiin* ("energetic, sociable") and *suangka* ("lazy, unsociable"), and *inkiin* (that which is "beautiful") and *nangka* (that which is "ugly"; Ewart 2013:176). Panará people who are *suakiin* paint themselves with body paint, work collectively, talk together, and have "increased overall intersubjective availability" (Ewart 2013:178) that plays out in distinctly gendered ways. Collective gardening work supports being *suakiin* and overall well-being, especially clearing garden plots and harvesting peanuts (Ewart 2008: 513–514). Cultivating peanuts in the middle of concentric circular garden plots in particular promotes well-being, as a "critical indicator of living well" (Ewart 2005:23; my translation). Those Canela gardeners who feel *ihtỳi* similarly seek out more "intersubjective" engagements with other human gardeners and with their nonhuman plant children, and these engagements are gendered as well, with women interacting with saved seeds and growing plants in affectionate ways that are differentiated from male gardeners' relationships with cultivated crops. In the same way as a Canela person who is feeling *ihpêc* will remain "immobile and quiet inside the house," as Liliana described, a Panará person who is *suangka* will stay "indoors or out of sight behind the house," manifesting his or her sadness in a "withdrawal from intersubjective engagements" and a "radical reduction in spatial movement" (Ewart 2013:179). Panará people often become *suangka* while mourning the death of a kinsperson, just as Camila experienced an *ihpêc* state that prevented her from leaving the house or visiting the gardens while grieving her classificatory father's death (see "Mothering Crops: Camila," this chapter).

While there are striking similarities between the Canela and Panará concepts, two key differences emerge. Firstly, the Canela understanding of *ihtỳi/ihpêc* and *impej/ihkên* as embodied states of becoming differs from the Panará, who conceptualize *suakiin* as the "basic condition of being Panará when life is good," and *suangka* as a "state that is acquired . . . the basic absence of *suakiin*" (Ewart 2013:179). While the Canela concepts are embodied states that a person works toward becoming over time and in diverse spaces in the territorial landscape, the Panará concepts appear to be understood as fixed by either their presence or absence in Panará individual and communal life. For the Canela, becoming strong, happy, healthy, good, beautiful, and well or their opposites involves ongoing, active engagement (or disengagement) with others in the life world. Secondly, the Canela approach well-being from a multispecies perspective, recognizing that human–nonhuman engagements are central to becoming well and attributing states of *ihtỳi*, *ihpêc*, *impej*, and *ihkên* to their nonhuman counterparts, especially plant children. While the Panará approach relations with certain crops such as peanuts in ways similar to parent–child relationships (Ewart 2005), whether they connect pursuing multispecies engagements with well-being for humans and nonhumans remains unclear. Indeed, while the human pursuit of well-being or conviviality has been well documented throughout lowland South American Indigenous communities (see Overing and Passes 2000b; Griffiths 2001; Santos-Granero 2015), the ways in which nonhumans participate in these processes is less understood. The Canela approach to multispecies kinship and care is a clear case of pursuing well-being for humans *and* nonhumans, specifically plants, which could be similarly found elsewhere throughout the region and in other Indigenous life-worlds worldwide.

Making and Growing with Plant Kin

In the Canela life-world, gardeners are "making kin" as Haraway formulates it (2016:102–103) — creating "kinds-as-assemblages" of humans and various plant species and varieties that are bound together through caring, nurturing engagements of kinship. Care and sociality, especially in the context of living well, are commonly found in ethnographies of Indigenous lowland South America. Overing and Passes's (2000a:14) "conviviality," for example, emphasizes the affective experiences of everyday activities such as hunting, gardening, gathering, and preparing food (Overing 2000:67; Passes 2000: 100). Creating and maintaining conviviality is a combined aesthetic and moral endeavor. It is seen in the pursuit of living together with kin in the same village, as is common across the region (Rivière 1969; Schwartzman 1988; Gow 1991, 2000; Santos-Granero 2000;), and working together in collective groups, as discussed by Schwartzman (1988:71) for the Panará and Griffiths (2001:249) for the Uitoto, among others. This "moral economy of intimacy" among human kin, as Viveiros de Castro (1996:188–190) described it, is often contrasted with the "symbolic economy of alterity" that encompasses many human engagements with nonhumans, especially animals and supernatural beings, through a modicum of affinity and predation.[9] Understanding Amazonian sociality through these two modes obscures a number of human and nonhuman relationships, as Santos-Granero (2007) explored in his article on Amazonian notions of "friendship" among non-kin and between shamans and supernatural beings. In addition, it is important to consider how nonhumans contribute to and participate in conviviality. For the Canela, the pursuit of conviviality includes multispecies kin-making, wherein families of humans and plants are constantly made through intimate, caring, and embodied processes of living, working, eating, and being together. Multispecies conviviality includes multi-sensory, affective experiences among and between women and men, girls and boys, and a diversity of crop children, as well as various animals, soils, and land types. Canela relationships between gardeners and cultivated plants is therefore one of kinship, consanguinity, and affection—all of the hallmarks of living well within the "moral economy of intimacy." Since becoming with nonhuman others is increasingly recognized as integral to Indigenous lowland South American communities, it would be beneficial to consider the role of nonhumans, and especially plants, in studying intimacy and care among other peoples in the region.

It also would be beneficial to connect studies of Amazonian (multispecies) sociality and conviviality with those of environmental management and knowledge transmission. The concept of educating affection explored in this chapter addresses this intersection by focusing on various human–plant engagements that unfold over time and in distinct spaces and that contribute to the overall well-being of the emergent life-world. As an ongoing process, educating affection is grounded in human and plant life courses and creative world making practices. That is, educating affection is about processes of human and plant "making-in-growing" and "growing-in-making," as Ingold and Hallam (2014:5) describe, or what Haraway terms "making-with" our "companion species" (Haraway 2008, 2016:58), in that people and plants are co-constituting one another through embodied encounters of growth and commensality that create and maintain kinship ties. In the unfolding Canela bio-sociocultural life-world, human and plant kin are constantly growing-in-making themselves and their relationships with one another—through gardening practices of burning, slashing, tending, and weeding and through various ritual activities (singing, food sharing, food and sex restrictions, and harvest ceremonies). As girls and boys learn how to garden, they develop alongside and become entangled with plants, so much so that human and plant happiness, strength, and well-being become reciprocal and mutually constitutive. These entanglements will have to shift over time, as the environment of the Cerrado becomes hotter and drier from predicted climatic changes. Yet Canela gardeners, who persistently pursue affectionate multispecies engagements, are well equipped to "stay with the trouble" and remember, pay attention to, and make space for plant kin in highly transformational times on a "damaged planet" (Haraway 2016:98). Anthropologists, ethnobotanists, and environmental scientists would do well to learn from the Canela education of affection in order to come to know other diverse plant kin in changing climates.

CHAPTER FOUR

Naming Plant Children

Ethnobotanical Classification as Childcare

Categorizing Plants: Sensory Pleasures

Fernando first introduced himself to me on a particularly hot afternoon in July 2011. Standing under the scant shade that the thatched roof of my sister's house provided, Fernando enthusiastically showed me his typewritten list of thirteen different yam names in Canela and Portuguese. He told me about the importance of horticulture, including its cosmological origins in Star-Woman, the mythical figure who introduced gardening to the community. He lamented the loss of certain crop varieties in recent years. As I returned to my sister's house from bathing in the stream the following morning, I found Fernando waiting for me again, this time with a live chicken huddled under his arm. Chicken in tow, he took me to his wife's house in the inner circle of houses. Nestled between large sacks of rice from a recent harvest sat the old typewriter on which he had written numerous lists of cultivated plant names, including those for types of maize, sweet potato, manioc, and bean. "I am old and knowledgeable, and when you come back you should work with me," he told me. He wanted to document the names of Canela cultivated crops in a systematic way and to perhaps recover some varietals that had been lost over the years. Giving me the typed paper list of yams, Fernando implored me to return in order to work on expanding the lists together.

As Fernando demonstrated during this first visit, Canela gardeners seek out and find enjoyment in listing the names of their crops. During subsequent interviews and conversations, I noticed the enthusiasm of gardeners whenever they were asked to list the different kinds of crops they grew. While conducting a survey in June 2012, one of the participants, Lorena, noticed that one of her favorites was missing from the list of yam varietals. "There is no pig testicle yam (*krẽrô crô cre*) listed here!" she eagerly called out in Canela. She described the appearance and texture of the yam (with Liliana translating into Portuguese for me) as small, round, and very hairy—a fitting description for its name, we all agreed, laughing. A few days later, another survey participant, Noemi, noticed that mixed-color peanut (*caahy kror-ti*) was missing from the lists. She described her love of this uniquely colored varietal and its origin, as she had brought it back with her after visiting a relative in a Krĩkatí village, another Jê-speaking community. Listing the names and noticing the absence of favored types was an enjoyable activity for these women as they described the multi-sensory experiences involved in their preferences. Crop classification draws from sensory experiences, many of which are pleasurable—that of feeling the texture and enjoying the taste of a yam varietal or visually appreciating a type of peanut's striking colors and smell as one roasts it over the fire.

In this chapter, I maintain that Canela crop-naming practices consist of multi-sensory, embodied experiences with a variety of nonhumans in the life-world, including seeds, cuttings, cultivated and wild plants, animals, and soils. There is a Canela "pleasure of naming" as people "*notice* the diversity of life," similar to that described by Anna Tsing (2010:192; emphasis author's own) in the herbarium at Copenhagen University's Botanical Museum. Unlike herbarium specimens, however, seeds and cuttings in the Canela life-world are named and loved as alive, growing fetuses or infants. I examine the ways in which ethnobotanical classification, including naming and saving seeds and cuttings, is part of Canela plant childcare. Naming crops is a caring, affectionate act, as Canela gardeners draw from a variety of multi-sensory experiences in the life-world to give names that reflect the individuality and significance of their diverse crop children. Similar to naming a Canela human infant, naming a seed or cutting is an important step in the recognition of a plant's inclusion in the Canela life-world and its potential to become an intentional actor with whom one can engage through sustained acts of care and affection. This especially can be seen in gardener mothers' interactions with the fifty-two types of named *pànkrỳt* bean children. I maintain that the relationships that emerge between Canela women and their bean infants exhibit the multispecies care or "multispecies love" (Tsing 2010:201) that has become the hallmark of contemporary Canela ethnobotanical classification. In this way, the Canela ethics or aesthetics of multispecies care supports agro-biodiversity conservation, as gardeners name and nurture as many plant children as possible in their garden plots.

Classifying and naming plants is an inherently dynamic process that is constantly changing owing to agro-biodiversity loss, maintenance, and increase. Similar to other lowland South American Indigenous communities

(Rival 2001; Balée 2013), Canela gardeners display an overarching preference for diversity in their gardens. They therefore actively seek out new plant infants and children to adopt into their multispecies families. New crops typically are acquired through exchange with neighboring Indigenous communities, as seen in Noemi's peanut exchange. There are indications that introgression with crop wild relatives also may be occurring. I examine the ways in which new categories, species, and varieties of plants are incorporated into Canela gardens to add to the overall diversity of garden plots. Over time, these adopted plants become transformed into authentically Canela plant children and are valued as such.

The recent creation of written ethnobotanical lists is another way that the dynamism of plant-naming practices is made manifest. Documenting Canela plant naming in written form is a creative, participatory process that I have developed with Fernando, Liliana, Renato, and Wander (and with periodic input from other gardeners). The first of their kind for the Canela, the written ethnobotanical lists represent the transformation of Indigenous plant-naming practices that traditionally have been passed down orally. This is an intentional transformation of knowledge about and engagements with plants, spearheaded by the Canela gardeners themselves as a new way to pursue and safeguard ecological knowledge and agro-biodiversity maintenance. Writing down the names of seed and plant cutting infants, I maintain, is a new embodied act of plant childcare that gardeners hope will keep their plant children alive for future generations. The active transformations of Indigenous ecological knowing and people–plant relationships, as seen in the adoption and naming of new plant children and of new naming practices, display the resilience of Canela gardeners in the wake of rapid environmental and climatic changes that are occurring throughout the territory and the Cerrado biome.

Noticing, Naming, Sorting, and Saving

Noticing and Naming: Classifying through Multi-sensory Experiences

Categorizing and naming crops is an "art of noticing" (Tsing 2010:192), of paying attention to the shapes, colors, sizes, textures, tastes, smells, and sounds that describe or are associated with the plants themselves. Through attentive and affectionate multi-sensory experiences, gardeners develop crop categories and their boundaries. These are informed by past and present experiences of humans and nonhumans, including the Canela ancestors, the mythical figure of Star-Woman, modern-day gardeners, and the

Pànkrỳt ahkrare

Pànkrỳt ahkrare caprêc-re

Pànkrỳt ahkrare kuctỳi tyc

Pànkrỳt càà pê-xuùre

Pànkrỳt carêntohkà pó

Pànkrỳt catêc-re hy

Pànkrỳt cuhkryt-ti

Pànkrỳt cupēkwỳj

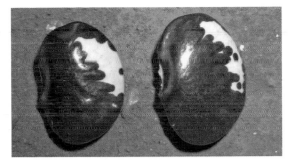

Pànkrỳt hàc jarati

Pànkrỳt hipêj cre

Pànkrỳt hipêj cre catia

Pànkrỳt hipêj cre jarkwa tep

Pànkrỳt pyytà

Pànkrỳt tàtà-re

Pànkrỳt tàtà-ti

Pànkrỳt tatap-re

Pànkrỳt têhtê cahàc

Pànkrỳt tic-re intep-re

Pànkrỳt tic-re tep-re

Pànkrỳt tic-ti catia ita

Pànkrỳt tohcaiwêu jipro-re

Pànkrỳt tohcaiwêu-re

Pànkrỳt tohcaiwêu-re catia ita

Pànkrỳt tohcaiwêu-re tep-re

Pànkrỳt tohcaiwêu-ti (pàn jahkat)

Pànkrỳt tyc-re

Pànkrỳt tyc-ti

Pànkrỳt xôn

Pànkrỳt xôn-ti

plants themselves, especially those received through exchange or those that newly "appear" in the garden space (explored in the following section). As the experiences of Lorena and Noemi in the ethnobotanical surveying show, Canela gardeners meticulously identify and name each varietal in order to place it in the overarching category or sub-category to which it belongs. These categories roughly correspond to Berlin's (1992) taxonomic ranks of "generic," "specific," and "varietal" forms (see table 4). I use the term "variety" here in accordance with Emperaire and Peroni's (2007:763) definition of the term as "the smallest unit of perception and management of agricultural diversity" that receives a specific name and is the "object of a set of practices and knowledge."

The complexity of Canela ethnobotanical classification has developed through noticing and paying attention to the emergent bio-sociocultural life-world. Canela gardeners' use of "generic" categories, "specific" subcategories, and different "varietals" draws from paying attention to the ecological, sociocultural, and cosmological aspects of growing crops' lives. Noticing the differing maturation periods of rice (arỳihy), gardeners divided it into the subcategories of fast-growing (arỳihy kênpei), which takes five months to mature, and slow-growing (arỳihy kênpôc), which takes around eight months to harvest. They divide manioc into sweet (kwỳrỳre) and bitter (kwỳr cahàc) types based on the level of toxicity from cyanogenic glucosides, which is common among lowland South American Indigenous communities (Rival 2001; Emperaire and Eloy 2008; Rival and McKey 2008). Yet Canela gardeners also identify a unique third category of half-sweet/half-bitter manioc that is only "partly" toxic. Through noticing particular qualities of these three types of manioc, gardeners identify them by gender as well. Sweet manioc is feminine, being "calm, sweet, and beautiful," while bitter manioc is masculine, being "ugly, brave, and fierce," as Fernando described. The two half-sweet/half-bitter types are in-between, displaying characteristics that are half-female and half-male. From a cosmological perspective, the sweet and half-sweet/half-bitter types are likened to the mythical Star-Woman and are impej, meaning that which is true/original, good, and beautiful (see table 5). As Fernando explained, they resemble Star-Woman in appearance and taste, being as "beautiful, light-skinned, and sweet" as she was while on earth. Conversely, bitter manioc is ihkên, that which is "less true/ less original, bad, and ugly," and is directly linked to Star-Woman's large, darker-skinned, "ugly" Canela husband, Tyc-ti, whose name literally translates as "big and black." One varietal in particular, black hair bitter manioc (kwỳr tyc-ti/kwỳr krã jimoctyc) is directly linked to Tyc-ti and his thick black hair and is categorized as ihkêãn-re, meaning the "worst, ugliest, least true/

Table 4. Canela plant-naming categories

Canela category ("generic")	English translation	Canela subcategory ("specific")	English translation	Number of "varietals"
		"Aboriginal"		
Ahkrỳt	Cashew	—	—	8
Arỳihy	Rice	Arỳihy kênpei	Fast-growing rice	14
		Arỳihy kênpôc	Slow-growing rice	14
Caahy	Peanut	—	—	5
Caxàt	Cotton	—	—	2
Cuhkōn	Gourd	—	—	12
Cuhkōn cahàc	Squash	—	—	8
Cuhtōj	Gourd	—	—	3
Jàt	Sweet potato	—	—	15
Krērô	Yam	Krērô pej	True/original yam	4
		Krērô cahàc	Regular yam	14
Kwỳr	Manioc	Kwỳrỳre	Sweet manioc	7
		Kwỳr cahàc	Bitter manioc	9
		Waíputre; kwỳr xenti	Half-sweet/half-bitter manioc	2
Pànkrỳt	Fava bean	—	—	52
Pàt juhtōi-re	Common bean	—	—	18
Pōhy	Maize	—	—	13
Pym	Annatto	—	—	4
		"Introduced"		
Ahkrôhti-xô	Passionfruit	—	—	2
Bacat	Avocado	—	—	2
Cãn	Sugarcane	—	—	6
Cwaj-jap	Guava	—	—	2
Hyhcuxwa-re	Sesame	—	—	2
Mac	Mango	—	—	9
Mamão	Papaya	—	—	4
Potukà	Jackfruit	—	—	2
Praxĩ	Watermelon	—	—	5
Prôprô	Pineapple	—	—	2
Pypyp-re	Banana	—	—	9
Ràràj	Orange	—	—	2
Rĩm	Lime	—	—	3
Rõrti	Coconut	—	—	3
Têc-rà cahàc	Acerola	—	—	2

Table 5. Canela crop categorization of "good" (*impej*) and "bad" (*ihkên*) crops

Crop	English translation
"Good" (*impej*) crops	
8 types of *pōhy*	8 types of maize
4 types of *krêrô pej*	4 types of true/original yam
All 52 types of *pànkrỳt*	All 52 types of *pànkrỳt* bean (fava)
All 7 types of *kwỳrỳre*	All 7 types of sweet manioc
Arỳihy jaka-re kênpei	Small white fast-growing rice
Cãn peaj-re	True/original sugarcane
Cuhkōn cahàc pej	True/original squash
Kwỳr xênti	Not-bitter half-sweet/half-bitter manioc
Mac peaj-re	True/original mango
Pym peaj	True/original annatto (*urucum*)
Waíputre	Hugging-vine half-sweet/half-bitter manioc
"Best" (*impeaj to impej*) crops	
Arỳihy caprêc-re kênpei	Small red fast-growing rice
Arỳihy caprêc-re kênpôc	Small red slow-growing rice
Krêrô pỳp-re	Electric eel yam
Krêrô tekãjkãj/rorti	Anaconda yam
Pōhy pej-re	True/original maize
"Bad" (*ihkên*) crops	
8 types of *kwỳr cahàc*	8 types of bitter manioc
Pànkrỳt ihkên	Inedible "bitter" bean (*fava amarga*)
"Worst" (*ihkêãn-re*) crop	
Kwỳr tvc-ti (kwỳr krã jimoctvc)	Black hair bitter manioc

original, and fiercest/most dangerous." Many other crop categories and varietals also are linked to Star-Woman, including all fifty-two types of beans
in the *pànkrỳt* category (translated as *fava* in Portuguese and belonging to
multiple species); eight types of maize; and one varietal of rice, squash,
sugarcane, mango, and annatto, respectively. Five varietals are especially associated with her and are *impeaj to impej*, meaning the best, most beautiful,
and truest/most original. These include true/original maize (*pōhy pej-re*), two
types of rice, anaconda yam (*krêrô tekãjkãj/rorti*), and electric eel yam (*krêrô
pỳp-re*). Fernando explained to me that the most beautiful types of maize
and yam are especially delicious and sweet and have white kernels and pulp,
similar to Star-Woman's demeanor and her beautiful, long white hair.

Yams in particular have a strong cosmological association with Star-
Woman. In addition to the two best yam varietals, the subcategory of true/
original yam (*krêrô pej*) is good (*impej*) and directly associated with her. These

good and best yams lead yam sociopolitical organization, which mirrors that of the human community in the village space. Anaconda yam and electric eel yam are the yam chiefs, and the four types of true/original yam are the vice-chiefs. Together, these six varietals govern the regular yam (*krêrô cahàc*) sub-category and organize yam social relations in the garden space. Gardeners such as Liliana notice the chiefs' ability to "strengthen" the other varietals when planted in the middle of the entire yam crop. By paying close attention to the activities and characteristics of their crops, including rice growth rates, manioc toxicity levels and gendered characteristics, the cosmological likenesses of many crops to Star-Woman or Tyc-ti, and yam sociopolitical organization, gardeners are able to incorporate the intimate details of plant lives into their crop categorization practices.

Naming individual crop varieties also sheds light on the lives of native animals and plants in the local Cerrado landscape. Generations of Canela gatherers and hunters have paid attention to and classified the plants they collect for food and medicine and the animals they hunt and fish. Gardeners in turn have applied this attentive knowledge of nonhumans in their environment to cultivated crop names. A number of cultivated crop names reference sensory experiences with native plants from throughout the distinct territorial land types, including the forest, riverbank, and *chapada*. *Hônxôti* leaf slow-growing rice (*arỳihy hônxôti kênpôc*; *Oryza sativa* L. or *Oryza glaberrima* Steud.) resembles the native forest plant, *hônxôti*, whose leaves appear and feel dried out when they ripen. *Capa-re* plant peanut (*caahy capa-re*; *Arachis hypogaea* L.) has a similar appearance as the *capa-re* plant that grows near riverbeds. Grey *ahtu* grass sugarcane (*cãn ahtu/jiprore*) resembles a type of grass commonly found in the *chapada* in its length and shape, and small *piqui* mango (*mac prĩn-re*) has a similar rounded shape and smell as the native *chapada piqui* fruit (*Caryocar coriaceum*). To name these cultivated crops, gardeners have drawn from a variety of sensory experiences including visually appreciating a native plant's appearance in shape or size, feeling its dried-out texture, and smelling and tasting its sweet fruits.

Many crop names also reference game animals found in forest spaces. The native Pampas deer (*po* in Canela; *veado-campeiro* in Portuguese; *Ozotoceros bezoarticus*), still occasionally hunted, is referenced in the names for common Cerrado deer fava bean (*pànkrỳt po cahàc*) and Cerrado deer toe-nail annatto (*po jĩxwa*). The bean has markings similar to the deer, and the shell of the annatto fruit is sharp and pointy, similar to deer toenails that are often used in making ritual belts (*krat-re*). While jaguars (*Panthera onca* [L.]) are rarely seen in the Canela territory nowadays, some crop varietals reference the animal's markings or body parts, namely jaguar head yam (*krêrô rop-*

krā), small jaguar bean (*pàt juhtõi-re kroro-re*), and jaguar fava bean (*pànkrỳt kroro-re*). Gardeners especially appreciate the markings of these beans, ad miring the black and brown spots and recalling past sightings of the animals in the forested area in the southeast of their territory. Crop names some-times reflect Canela engagement with or knowledge of other regional land-scapes as well. Monkey from Pará sweet potato (*jàt jõtep-ti*), for example, resembles a type of monkey from neighboring Pará State (known as *cuput* in Canela) that has a yellow bottom. Other crop names reference riverine animals found in local waterways. The chief anaconda yam, which circles around itself as the anaconda does, references the large snake (*sucuri* in Por-tuguese; *Eunectes* sp.) that is also the subject of mythical stories. The other chief, electric eel yam, is long and straight, resembling the native electric eel (*poraquê*; *Electrophorus electricus*) that is often caught in streams nearby the village and eaten. Meanwhile, tortoise arm bitter manioc (*kwỳr caprãn jũkee*) resembles a tortoise arm in size and shape, and tortoise egg true/original yam (*krẽrô pej caprãn cre-re*) and tortoise egg sweet potato (*jàt caprãn cre*) have a rounded shape similar to the animal's egg. While all of these crops bear a physical resemblance to forest and riverine animals that is primarily visu-ally appreciated, other sensory experiences are also involved in crop naming. Cobra bitter manioc (*kwỳr awari*), for example, has delicious, meaty pulp that resembles the flesh of the false water cobra (*Hydrodynastes gigas* Duméril, Bi-bron & Duméril) in texture and taste. It is a favorite type of bitter manioc for many families, and Liliana enjoys it for its taste, texture, and the beautiful yellow toasted manioc flour (*farinha*) it produces.

Similarly, naming crops after local birds involves visual appreciation as well as other sensory modalities. Most varietals are named after a particular bird's body part or markings. Ema shinbone bitter manioc (*kwỳr māã tehkà*), for example, has a stick that is long and white similar to the shinbone of this large native bird (*Rhea americana*) that commonly is found in the *chapada* and either hunted for meat or kept in the village for its large eggs. Small red par-rot tail sweet manioc (*kwỳr caprêc-re/krỳi-re japỳ*) has leaves that resemble a parrot's tail, while *kàkàre* bird squash (*cuhkõn cahàc kàkàre*) has the same half-yellow, half-green coloring as this native bird. Many bean varietals also ref-erence birds, such as color-of-hawk fava bean (*pànkrỳt krẽhkrẽpti*), which is large and white with a violet-black marking that resembles a hawk's feathers. King vulture fava bean (*pànkrỳt cuhkryt-ti*) resembles the king vulture with its white, purplish-black, and red coloring, and two black beans resemble the vulture: vulture fava bean (*pànkrỳt xôn*) and large vulture fava bean (*pàn-krỳt xôn-ti*). Small twisted beak fava bean (*pànkrỳt kãjkãj-re jahkat*), with its swirled black and white markings, resembles a bird's beak and the circling of an anaconda (*kãjkãj-re* means twisted or encircled as an anaconda). Six types of beans in the *pànkrỳt* category reference native bird eggs in size, shape, and color, including hummingbird egg fava bean (*pànkrỳt jũnren cre*), *jõkrãire* egg fava bean (*pànkrỳt jõkrãire cre*), and four varieties named after the *hipêj* bird's egg.

In addition, there are crop names that reference intimate perceptual encounters between birds and people. Common *têhtê* bird fava bean (*pànkrỳt têhtê cahàc*) has markings similar to the bird that "advises" people when animals are nearby with its call. Hunters hear and understand the bird's message, and it often notifies people in the village when cattle or donkeys are in the area. Meanwhile, parakeet fava bean (*pànkrỳt krêwre*) references parakeets (*krẽ-re* in Canela) who were formerly people in the mythical past. In a popular mythical story recounted to me by Leandro, Fernando, and others, a family of Canela people transforms themselves into various animals and they eventually become parakeets. These birds "enjoy" eating the rice crop as it matures in the garden space because they "used to be people," Liliana and her husband explained to me. These last two names in particular highlight the complex multispecies engagements that are encoded in Canela ethnobotanical classification. The fact that two crop names can reference simultaneously the relationships between people and birds who can communicate aurally (and were even formerly human), and between people and beans identified with birds through primarily visual appreciation, demonstrates the depth of Canela environmental knowledge based on intimate engagements.

Noticing the complexity of the local landscape and the plants and animals within, it is therefore a multi-sensory endeavor, involving not only seeing a particularly striking marking on an animal or plant but also paying attention to its meaty pulp or brittle texture, its floral or pungent smell, its delicious or bland taste, and the sounds of its calls as it communicates with you. Drawn from these sensory experiences of noticing, naming solidifies particularly significant human–nonhuman engagements as valued and meaningful. While weeding the garden plot, a woman notices the leaves of small red parrot-tail sweet manioc that resemble a parrot's brilliantly colored tail. Harvesting electric eel yam in forest gardens reminds women and men of the times they have fished for the eels in nearby streams, often using the *tepja-re* fish poison vine to stun them in the water. Near the riverbank, elder men such as Fernando appreciate the long, white stick of growing ema shinbone bitter manioc, recalling long-ago hunts and the savory taste of the bird's flesh and eggs. Elder women such as Liliana are reminded of the mythical story of people transformed into birds while sorting parakeet fava bean and sometimes recount the story to their younger female relatives (and the anthropologist, if she is sorting beans nearby.) Crop names encode collective and individual memories of living and being or becoming with nonhumans in the life-world. Named and remembered, cultivated crops are valued for the memories of past human–environment engagements they invoke, as well as for the potential intimate relationships that gardeners can form with them over time. The art of noticing, categorizing, and naming is also an art of living and "becoming with" (Haraway 2008) nonhumans in the unfolding life-world.

Sorting: Coming to Know Pànkrỳt Bean Seed Infants

While all crops are noticed, named, and remembered, bean varietals from the *pànkrỳt* category are given particular attention during sorting sessions (see the photo insert featuring all fifty-two beans in alphabetical order by name). Gardeners find particular enjoyment in sorting the beans, feeling their smooth or rough textures, seeing their brilliant colors and markings, remembering the ritual songs they have sung to growing bean children, and describing their flavors and aromas when cooked into *beribu* pies or stewed alongside rice. Learning and remembering the names of the fifty-two types of *pànkrỳt* beans is the mark of an expert gardener and admired throughout the community. Men can acquire this knowledge, such as Ademar, one of the participants in a June 2012 gardening survey, who identified seven named types of bean that were missing from the ethnobotanical lists. Sifting out individual seeds from the plastic 2-liter soda bottle that serves as a storage container, Ademar proudly listed the names of each and the reasons behind the naming practices. He described how the swirled black and white coloring of small twisted beak fava bean resembles both a bird's beak and the encircling of an anaconda, and how the white and red markings of another type (*pànkrỳt mẽ hupkre têp*; translation unclear) resembles a person being painted with bright red annatto body paint. Ademar's interest in bean seeds, however, was seen as unique for a Canela man within the community. On the whole, women are the primary seed savers and are the knowledge-bearers of bean naming, varietal diversity, and maintenance from one season to the next.

Women named most of the beans for me throughout sorting sessions where they meticulously sorted through large piles of seeds to find those they had remembered. Sitting or squatting in groups, either next to, behind, inside, or occasionally in front of the house, women spread out brightly colored cloths (*panos*) on which they piled their saved beans for sorting. On one occasion in May 2012, Liliana and her sister Camila lay down a large, bright blue cloth on the dusty red earth in between their houses. As the sis-

Figure 4. Liliana, daughter Aline, and granddaughter Beta sort through a pile of beans, including red child fava beans (*pànkrỳt ahkrare caprêc-re*), July 2012.

ters began sorting their beans, neighbor women came to visit, sitting next to them and touching the seeds as they discussed the names and admired the markings. During another sorting session in July 2012, Liliana, her daughter Aline, and her granddaughter Beta sorted through large piles of recently harvested beans on a yellow tarp inside the house (see figure 4). As the two adult women separated varietals and commented upon the beauty of particular types such as the pink-and-white red child fava bean (*pànkrỳt ahkrare caprêc-re*), the toddler Beta played with the seeds, handling them with interested curiosity. Five years later, in November 2017, Beta continued to play with the bean seeds during another sorting session. As Liliana, Aline, and I once again crouched around a pile of beans spread onto a checkered tablecloth on the ground to admire their shapes, sizes, and colors, Beta, now a young girl, was more actively involved in the handling, sorting, and naming process. Touching, visually appreciating, and naming the beans aloud are ways in which women and young girls come to know bean seeds, which are considered infants or fetuses, and initiate the intimate engagements with them that develop throughout the plant's life course.

More than any other crop, *pànkrỳt* bean names link the seed infants to their human families through shared physical characteristics or activities. Names often reference Canela people at various life stages. Child fava bean (*pànkrỳt ahkrare*) and red child fava bean, for example, are both associated with a child and the umbilical cord (*ahkrare*), yet differ in their coloring, the former being white and black, the latter with brilliant reddish-pink markings. Another type called young/unripe children fava bean (*pànkrỳt mēhkra tetet*), is white with black stripes and associated with children who have not yet matured (*mēhkra* = children; *tetet* = "unripe"). Four types of beans are associated with Canela girls and women who are using different types of body paint. Mature strong young girls fava bean (*pànkrỳt mēcuprỳ catia/tỳjtu*), for example, is white with brownish-yellow coloring on one side that is said to resemble an older girl who is wearing "lipstick." Annatto fava bean (*pànkrỳt mēcuprỳ-re*), with its bright red coloring, is thought to resemble younger girls whose bodies are painted entirely in red annatto, while large annatto fava bean (*pànkrỳt pyhti*), which is white with purplish-red "lipstick" on one edge, is named after a woman who paints her mouth with annatto prior to visiting her garden while menstruating. Messily painted fava bean (*pànkrỳt mēhkra tàmtuw*), which is white with brown markings, references the messy, disorganized body paint design for a woman who has recently given birth to a child and/or already has two or three children.

Boys and men wearing particular body paint are also referenced in bean naming, albeit with less frequency than their female counterparts. Strong black face child fava bean (*pànkrỳt ahkrare kuctỳi tyc*) has black markings that resemble a boy whose forehead is painted with black *pau de leite* (*aràmhôc; Sapium gladulatum* [Vell.] Pax) or *jenipapo* (*pôl-ti*), and warriors fava bean (*pànkrỳt mēhaprār*) resembles "courageous" warriors who paint their cheeks with red body paint. There is also a type of bean named after the elderly: old people fava bean (*pànkrỳt mēhkàa*) has wrinkled brown skin that resembles that of elderly Canela men and women. Beans can be named after people outside the community as well, such as white woman fava bean (*pànkrỳt cupēkwỳj*), which is white with red "lipstick" similar to the makeup worn by non-Indigenous Brazilian or foreign women (the *cupēn*).

Bean names directly reference particular human activities as well. One of the varietals kept by Ademar, *pànkrỳt mē hupkre tễp*, references a person being painted with annatto. Similarly, the red-colored younger child painted with annatto fava bean (*pànkrỳt mēhkra tetet cucràn*) directly refers to the activity it describes (*cucràn* = act of painting with annatto). Another type named the strong and happy ones fava bean (*pànkrỳt mēhtỳi*) is white-colored and larger and is said to resemble "strong" and "happy" (*ihtỳi*) Canela people. A number of beans reference human ritual activities, such as the five types named after the *tohcaiwêu* mask in the Mask festival, part of the Canela annual ceremonial cycle (see Crocker 1990:276–277, n.d.). All of these beans have swirled markings that resemble that of the ritual mask, albeit in different color combinations and sizes. Small mask fava bean (*pànkrỳt tohcaiwêu-re*) is smaller with black and white swirls, large mask fava bean (*pànkrỳt tohcaiwêu-ti/pàn jahkat*) is larger with the same black-and-white markings and also resembles a macaw's beak, and very large mask fava bean (*pànkrỳt tohcaiwêu-re catia ita*) is the largest of these three with similar coloring. There is also a small red mask fava bean (*pànkrỳt tohcaiwêu-re tep-re*), which has swirled red and white markings, and small grey mask fava bean (*pànkrỳt tohcaiwêu jipro-re*), which has swirled brown, grey, and white coloring. Another type called ritual headdress fava bean (*pànkrỳt hàc jarati*) is dark red with white markings and resembles the *hàc jarati* (literally "large hawk's wing") woven headdress worn by the ritual girl associates (*wuh-tỳ*) during the Khêêtuwajê festival, one of the three male initiation ritual periods (see Crocker 1990:272–273).

With these complex names, Canela gardeners and especially women seed savers are connecting the nascent lives of their bean seeds with those of humans, including children, girls and boys, women and men, and the elderly. The beans named after children invoke smiles, laughter, and comments upon their "prettiness" or "cuteness," as they are associated with human infants who are treated with similar parental indulgence. Similarly, discussing old people fava bean usually leads to laughing comparisons between this bean and elderly neighbors, and some elderly research assistants themselves have told me they are beginning to resemble the bean. White woman fava bean also invokes laughter and smiles, as women describe this varietal's pale "skin" and bright red "lipstick" that resembles non-Indigenous women in the nearby towns of Barra do Corda and Fernando Falcão (where lipstick is available to purchase). On the other hand, the type of warriors fava bean is treated with respect and honor as is due to a brave Canela warrior. Fernando and Ademar called this bean "courageous" in its likeness to warriors of the past. Beans that are named after ritual activities are given similar respect, such as ritual headdress fava bean, which is valued for its connection with a highly prized ritual ornament. Naming bean seeds gives them value and meaning to Canela gardeners and allows them to begin establishing the embodied connections that are more fully developed with growing plants.

When women see, hold, and speak aloud a bean's name, they are creating and maintaining a space for these seed infants in their multispecies families. This is similar to human infants, who are given names at birth (and throughout their lives) that connect them to their family home and their relatives. Boys are given between two and eight Canela names by their mother's brother (*kêt*), and girls are given names by their father's sister (*tùy*) (Nimuendajú 1946:77; Crocker 1990:234–249). The named human infant has an intimate bodily connection with his or her parents, which is created and maintained through bodily acts of eating, sleeping, and living together. With bean seed infants, the bodily connection is maintained through acts of sorting, handling, and remembering and saying the names, usually along-side other human family members. The seemingly mundane activity of sorting and naming seeds therefore becomes a crucial multispecies encounter between seed infants and their human mothers (and occasionally fathers). Sorting seeds is often undertaken for the sheer pleasure of taking stock and coming to know one's current seed infants. At other times, it is the precursor to saving the seed infants, the final step before they are planted and can grow into crop children.

Saving: Motherly Love and Agro-Biodiversity Conservation

In addition to noticing, naming, and sorting, saving seeds and cuttings is necessary so that they may continue to live and grow in the unfolding lifeworld. Canela seeds and cuttings are considered infants or newborns (*filhotes* or *recém-nascidos* in Portuguese) in need of sustained care and attention. As Fernando explained during one of our conversations in August 2012, the lives of seed (and cutting) infants began while they are being saved, similar to a fetus inside its mother:

> [The seed] is like an infant; it is stays saved, just as a child who stays inside his mother, and when he is born people will take care of him. The mother takes good care of him and does not let anything bad mistreat him.

Saving seeds ensures they are kept in a safe space until they are planted, the moment from which they can begin growing and developing. As Liliana has told me repeatedly, saved seeds and cuttings are the "same as people" and need to be "well protected" to stay alive during storage. Women are primarily responsible for saving their family's seeds and cuttings for the next season's harvest. To prepare seeds for storage, Liliana and other female gardeners usually prepare seeds with *malagueta* pepper (*Capsicum frutescens* L.) and/or with animal or vegetable oil, all of which prevent the accumulation of extra moisture that can ruin the seeds by making them sprout. Once prepared, women store the seeds in hollowed-out gourd (*cuhkòn*) and bottle gourd (*cuhtōj*) varietals or, more commonly nowadays, in plastic 2-liter soda bottles. They typically keep different species separate but freely mix varietals in one container. Varietals are typically separated for planting, often during the sorting sessions described above. According to Liliana, the seeds of *pànkrỳt* bean, *pàt juhtòi-re* bean, rice, squash, gourd, watermelon, and peanut usually remain in storage for four to six months. If stored any longer than six months, the seeds will not germinate or "birth themselves" after planting.

Rice is initially hung from the rafters to dry, as Camila often showed me in her house, and afterward can be stored in large sacks for saving or consumption. It should be kept separate from other crops, as it is prone to insect damage during storage. Women typically store maize in a similar manner, hanging the dried-out ears from the rafters inside the house and making sure to protect the kernels from the smoke of cooking fires during storage. Species propagated by vegetative methods, such as manioc, sweet potato, and yam, are typically kept in the earth until harvesting and stored in the house for short periods before planting again. Liliana usually keeps her bitter, sweet, and half-bitter/half-sweet manioc varieties growing in the gardens, and once harvested, stores the roots for around five days before planting. She stores yam and sweet potato varietals for only three or four days after harvesting, and then plants the cuttings in a new garden plot. She maintains that these are the best ways to help keep the seed and plant cutting infants alive during storage.

Indeed, during this period the seeds and cuttings are alive yet waiting, in a transient period throughout which the caring acts of their gardener mothers help nurture and protect them. Through acts of rubbing bean seeds with oils and hot chili pepper, handling manioc roots and yam tubers, and ensuring that drying maize kernels are kept away from the smell and presence of smoke, Canela women ensure the well-being of their seed and plant cutting infants. Similar to the care of a fetus inside the womb, women are the primary caretakers of seeds and cuttings during this waiting period. Planting also emphasizes the role of seed mothers. Typically, women place the seeds or cuttings into the holes that men have dug in the garden space. While both gardener parents are involved, women are the planters of their own seed and plant cutting infants, demonstrating the intimate bodily connection between mother and child.

As seeds and cuttings grow into plant children, women continue to be the primary caretakers through frequent visits, weeding and tending, and ritual singing, among other activities. As the plants mature into adults and become ready to harvest, they have reached the end of their natural life cycles. No longer children in need of care and affection, harvestable plants already have passed through adulthood and their lives have "ended," as Fernando explained to me (see chapter 3, "Understanding Plant Children"). Plant life cycles are cyclical, however, in that some of the seeds and cuttings from the "dead" harvest become "live" infants as they are saved for the next planting season. Liliana explained the cyclical nature of plant lives in the following way:

> It is like this—[harvesting crops] is the same as death. However, if I harvest a seed that I want to increase, I protect it well. During the first

harvest, I have already set aside a separate part [of the seeds] to save and to not die. I have to save them well . . . I do not want the seeds to die as people die and not have any more of them. The harvest of crops is the same as people. Just as people become ill with some problem and the family, the mother or father has to protect them [by] finding a remedy to make them better. If I did not take care of the seeds that I harvest, it would be the same as an illness! [. . .] If I take good care of the seeds, keeping them saved well, then the crops . . . stay alive! All the time and year after year.

For Canela gardeners, the crops that people eat are dead, and if the entire harvest of a particular varietal is consumed, then that varietal will be dead forever. Conversely, saving a particular seed or cutting ensures that the varietal lives, for the saved seeds become "alive" through the act of seed saving itself. Ademar and his wife Osvalda expressed similar thoughts on the subject of maintaining their beloved bean seeds. Osvalda explained that Ademar tells his family not to "disturb" (mexer in Portuguese) or consume all the bean seeds before they have dried out, in order to save some for the following season. "I think it is pretty—all the seeds together," Ademar explained as a reason for his pursuit of bean diversity. While men are typically less interested in seed maintenance, Ademar's sentiments are shared by women gardeners such as Liliana and her daughters. Liliana has often told me that she "enjoys" the "beautiful" diversity of her saved seeds, cuttings, and plants growing in her garden plots. Her daughters agree, often commenting on the beauty of particular varietals and seeking out moments to sort through and admire the seeds they are currently saving in plastic bottles in a corner of the house.

By rubbing the seeds with oils and placing them in a dry container, by drying maize or rice from the rafters, or by storing cuttings underground, Liliana and other women gardeners bring cultivated crops to life and can maintain beloved, passed-down varietals for future generations to come. For example, Liliana continues to save bean, yam, maize, and peanut varieties that her grandmother Manuela Célia and her classificatory maternal grandparent Dirceu gave her. As a man who became a woman (mam hũmre hapuhna cahãj) in old age, Dirceu was known for seed saving, which was one of the primary ways that Dirceu became a Canela woman (see chapter 3, "Gendering Gardening: Traditions and Transgressions").

Liliana especially values the varietals passed down from her family members and told me she does not want to "leave behind" these saved seeds and cuttings. These include eleven types of pànkrỳt beans, seven from Manuela Célia and four from Dirceu, six types of yam, three from each, and five types of maize and a few kinds of peanut and pàtjuhtoi-re bean from Dirceu.[1] Other than one type of large black maize (*põhy tyc-ti*) that has been lost, Liliana continues to save all of these varietals. Sorting through and saving these seeds and cuttings are reminders of Liliana's past social relationships with her grandparents. She recounted to me how Dirceu saved beans in a number of gourds and glass bottles, including the *pànkrỳt càà pê-xuùre* (translation unclear) type passed down to her. Dirceu linked seed saving and familial love and care, explaining to Liliana that the gifted seeds demonstrated how "I took care of you, I treated you well; [now] be this way with your family." For Liliana and other female gardeners, these seeds and cuttings are artifacts of past social relationships, materially embodying connections to deceased family members. By keeping them alive, therefore, women are maintaining these past connections to other humans, as well as ensuring future nurturing engagements with the living nonhuman plant children themselves.

In this way, the motherly love of Canela women toward their seeds and cuttings directly affects varietal diversity maintenance or loss. Women strive to love as many seed and plant cutting infants as possible, including those passed down by past generations, and to nurture and care for them throughout their infancy, childhood, adulthood, death, and re-birth as infants once again. While men also interact with plant children in caring and affectionate ways, overall they are less involved in the lives of seeds and cuttings during their infancy. This is similar to the role of Canela fathers, who traditionally are prohibited from holding or carrying their infants until they are around six months old. Just as the mother and her female relatives are responsible for nurturing, touching, and holding their newborn babies during this period, so too are women in charge of caring for, rubbing, handling, and saving their seed and plant cutting infants. Women even maintain seed infants in storage for four to six months, the same amount of time as that of the initial intimate period between human mothers and newborns seen in the food and sex restrictions. By keeping seeds "saved well," as Liliana described, Canela women can maintain robust plant children that contribute to the overall agro-biodiversity in their garden plots.

Expanding Multispecies Families

Adopting Plant Children through Exchange

The overarching Canela preference for agro-biodiversity results in many gardeners seeking to acquire new types of seeds and cuttings for their gardens. As part of her role as a plant mother, a female gardener is typically responsible for expanding her plant family by adopting new varietal infants through exchanges both inside and outside the community. Inside the village, women typically trade their seeds and cuttings for varietals they do not currently maintain. Since women and men frequently discuss the diversity of their saved and growing crops each season, community members are typically aware of one another's expertise in saving particular seeds and cuttings. For example, during a visit at my naming-aunt (tùy) Ivanete's house to photograph her well-known store of yam varieties, Ivanete offered to give Liliana and myself cuttings of her favorite type of anaconda yam in exchange for some of Liliana's renowned collection of pànkrỳt bean seeds. Both women were pleased with the exchange—Ivanete was acquiring beans that were new to her garden plots and Liliana was increasing her relatively smaller store of anaconda yam. Similarly, Liliana exchanged some of her bean varietals with Noemi in order to obtain large curved root sweet potato (jàt jikôt-ti), which Noemi had revealed she was cultivating during an ethnobotanical survey with me. Liliana was particularly excited to acquire this sweet potato, since she did not currently save or grow it. If a relatively equal exchange is not available, women sometimes purchase desirable varietals, often using funds provided by the monthly stipend of the Bolsa Família governmental social assistance program. Noemi purchased a few types of yam from Liliana around the same time they were trading sweet potato and bean varietals, as part of their ongoing exchange relationship. Liliana explains that she even grows varietals specifically for the purpose of "giving, trading, or selling" to others in the village because her seed and plant cutting infants "should not be left behind" to disappear.

Women usually exchange or sell varietals in a leisurely manner, visiting each other's houses to chat and share gardening tips. In addition to the enjoyable social relationships that these visits enable, exchange within the village allows for individual women to increase the diversity in their own plots. The seeds and cuttings will become newly adopted children within a particular couple's garden space, through the activities of noticing, naming, sorting, and saving. Exchange within the village also supports the community-wide maintenance of agro-biodiversity as a whole, as more individuals, couples, and families work to keep alive a wide array of seeds and cuttings.

Outside the village, women often seek out exchanges with people in neighboring Indigenous communities. Noemi's acquisition of mixed-color peanut (caahy kror-ti) from a relative in the neighboring Krĩkatí community, as mentioned earlier, is a good example of this type of exchange. Noemi brought this seed, its name, and whatever knowledge she acquired from the Krĩkatí villagers back to the Canela community. She subsequently cultivated it and exchanged her harvested peanuts with other Canela women, and the

varietal now exists in multiple Canela gardens. In this way, mixed-color peanut, though coming from the outside, has become part of Canela garden
spaces and the multispecies relationships that emerge within them. While
Noemi was the original adopter of this seed infant, other gardener mothers
followed suit, so much so that the peanut is now fully embedded in Canela
human–plant engagements and the life-world as a whole. Wander's relative
Teodora exchanged crops with people in a Krĩkatí village as well, trading bitter manioc roots for small black sweet potato (*jàt tyc-re*). Teodora and her
family are the main cultivators of this varietal, and other gardener couples
are gradually adopting it into their garden plots over time. Similarly, Renato's
relative Urânia was the original adopter of a type of rice (either small-winged
red fast-growing rice [*arỳihy jarare caprêc-re kênpei*] or small-winged white
fast-growing rice [*arỳihy jarare jaka-re kênpei*]) that she acquired from a relative who had married into a Jê-speaking Apinayé community. Through multiple exchanges and seasons of growing and saving this varietal, it is now a
popular type of rice that everyone in the Canela community maintains, Renato informed me.

Indeed, exchange with outsiders highlights how easily new crop species
and varieties become incorporated into Canela gardens, ethnobotanical
classification, and intimate human–plant entanglements. Overall, Canela
gardeners differentiate between crop species and varieties that are "aboriginal" to their community, and those that are "introduced." This categorization is a dynamic process and bears similarity to the Tupi-Guaraní-speaking
Ka'apor's "artificial" dichotomy between "domesticates" and "nondomesti-
cates" (Balée 2013:97). While the categorical distinction has existed since
at least the 1920s, modern-day gardeners include crops in the "aboriginal"
category that previously were thought of as "introduced." In addition to the
aboriginal crops of maize, yam, sweet potato, sweet and bitter manioc, *pànkrỳt* beans, squash, gourd, peanut, annatto, and cotton as recorded by Nimuendajú (1946:58), contemporary gardeners also include all types of cashew (*ahkrỳt*), the two types of half-sweet/half-bitter manioc, the general
category of *pàt juhtõi-re* bean (*feijão* in Portuguese), and sometimes the general category of rice (*arỳihy*) as aboriginal crops today. Interestingly, some
of these aboriginal crops have known links to people or communities from
the "outside." Four types of maize, for example, were acquired through a
government-sponsored seed exchange with other Indigenous communities
in September 2012.[2] Although coming from other Indigenous communities,
the varietals were immediately given Canela names, incorporated into the
aboriginal general category of maize, and planted in many families' gardens

a few months later. As of 2017, gardeners frequently grow these maize varietals and consider them to be integrated fully into Canela gardening and crop childcare. Similarly, the type of stranger/outsider sweet manioc (*kwỳr cahkrit-re*), was originally obtained through a "stranger" (*cahkrit*) from the neighboring Jê-speaking Apaniekra village of Porquinhos. Many gardeners currently cultivate and maintain this type of sweet manioc, which is preferred for making *beribu* pies. A number of families currently grow *mineira* sweet manioc (*kwỳr mīnêr*) as well, which is named after an exchange with a person from the state of Minas Gerais in southeast Brazil (*mīnêr = mineiro/a*, a person from Minas Gerais). It has a beautiful white pulp that women admire as they process it into dough for *beribu* pies. Although linguistically marked as coming from the outside, both types of sweet manioc are considered authentically part of contemporary Canela crop cultivation.

Additionally, Guajajara tree bean (*pàt juhtõi-re pàràre/pryjĩ; Cajanus cajan*), currently a favorite bean that has a visually appealing appearance and a delicious taste, originates from the neighboring Tupi-Guaraní-speaking Guajajara community, on whose territory the Canela lived between 1963–1968. Forced to flee their own territory after a messianic movement that invoked violence from their non-Indigenous neighbors, the Canela relocated to the Guajajara territory in 1963 without many of their beloved seeds and cuttings (see chapter 2, "Gardening: A Brief History, 1814–Present"). Canela families eagerly added this bean into their gardens and took it with them when they returned to their territory a few years later. Originally domesticated in Africa, this species of bean was most likely brought to Brazil by Portuguese colonists and/or African slaves. It is now found among many different Tupi-speaking groups in northeast and central Brazil, such as the Assurini, who received it through exchange from the Tupi-speaking Tapirapé and similarly named it "tree bean" (Balée 2013:20). While the bean's name (*pryjĩ* = Guajajara) in Canela marks it as coming from the outside, it has become an integral part of Canela gardens today. In addition, Canela gardeners most likely obtained rice, either the African species (*Oryza glaberrima*) or Asian species (*Oryza sativa*), from non-Indigenous settlers in the late nineteenth–early twentieth centuries, including perhaps freed African slaves who brought *Oryza glaberrima* to northeast Brazil as they created their own settlements (*quilombos*) in the region (Carney 2001). Although the crops' status as originating from the outside is sometimes marked, including linguistically, the general categories of maize, sweet manioc, *pàt juhtõi-re* bean, and rice have become fully integrated into contemporary Canela gardens, often being known as aboriginal crops and connected to Star-Woman's mythical horticultural teachings. In this way, the types of maize, sweet manioc, bean, and rice varietals have been adopted into Canela multispecies families as plant children in need of the same loving, affectionate care as other aboriginal crops.

Other crops that originally were acquired through exchange with outsiders remain classified as introduced to the Canela community. Nevertheless, they are also welcomed into Canela gardens as adopted plant children. These include types of mango (*mac*), papaya (*mamão*; same as in Portuguese), banana (*pypyp-re*), sugarcane (*cãn*), the *tingí* fish poison vine (*tepja-re*), and tobacco, all of which Nimuendajú (1946:58) documented, as well as types of watermelon (*praxĩ*), pineapple (*prôprô*), coconut (*rõrti*), orange (*ràràj*), lime (*rĩm*), avocado (*bacat*), and jackfruit (*potukà*), among other fruits. Certain introduced varietals are associated with particular exchanges. Green-shelled coconut (*rõrti te krãnti*) was acquired from CTI (a nongovernmental organization that works with Jê-speaking communities in northeast and central Brazil). The two types of orange trees, known as orange (*ráráj*) and regular orange (*ráráj cahàc*), originally were acquired from non-Indigenous *cupẽn* (whites) in the neighboring settlement of Buriti in the 1970s. Many of those original plantings failed, however, and Canela gardeners acquired additional orange trees from other white neighbors more recently. Large black sugarcane (*cãn tyc-ti*), also known as *cana de São Paulo* in Portuguese, is said to originate from outsiders coming from southeastern São Paulo State. Other introduced crops generally are associated with outsiders, such as sprawling tree banana (*pypyp-re jakàhtetet-re*), which Fernando and Liliana described as coming from an exchange with their *cupẽn* neighbors at some point in the recent past.

When a Canela gardener receives an introduced crop through exchange, she quickly incorporates it into her gardening practices through the processes of noticing, naming, sorting, and saving the seed or cutting. A number of banana varietals, for example, are named for certain characteristics and qualities that Canela gardeners noticed after acquiring them through exchange with outsiders. One type that is commonly called apple banana (*banana maçã*) in Portuguese was renamed as cobra bitter manioc banana (*pypyp-re awarxô*) in Canela, because gardeners found a similarity between the banana fruit (*xô*) and the root of cobra bitter manioc (*kwỳr awari*). Fernando explained that both the fruit and the root are "small, full, and tasty." Canela gardeners named another type babaçu fruit banana (*pypyp-re rõrxô*) because the fruit is smaller and more rounded, similar to the native babaçu (*rõrõxô*; *Attalea speciosa* Mart.) fruits found in the Cerrado biome. Naming introduced varietals after crops and native fruits that already exist in the territory is practiced by other Indigenous groups as well, including many Tupi-speaking communities in Brazil and throughout lowland South America (Balée 2013:20). For the Canela, these naming practices help incorporate the "outsider" plants into the "inside" of their life-world, where they can be treated as plant children in need of care and affection. After generations of naming, sorting, and saving, banana trees are now seen as especially beautiful (*impej*) in Canela gardens. Women often plant the trees in backyard gardens behind their houses and eagerly await their fruiting in July or August. They admire the growing trees and connect them to human life cycles. While pregnant with her second child, my sister Joaquina insisted that I photograph her next to the banana trees in her backyard, so that she could show off her growing belly next to her growing trees. In this photograph (figure 5), Joaquina's care and affection for her human and plant children are displayed and celebrated.

Through exchange within and outside the village, agro-biodiversity increases for individual gardeners and their families and for the community as a whole. Exchanges among women within the village highlight the importance of biodiversity maintenance and increase in individual garden plots, as women seek out varieties that are new to their own forest and riverbank gardens. While these new types are already children to the women who have maintained them over generations, they are newly adopted into another woman's multispecies family. In this way, the beans that Liliana has maintained from her grandparents will find new life as part of the crop children that Ivanete and Noemi care for in their garden plots. Exchanges with outsiders underscore different types of crop children adoption. In some cases, such as with the general categories of *pàt juhtoi-re* bean and rice, the adopted crops can be fully incorporated into Canela gardens as "aboriginal" to the community. The outside origins of certain aboriginal crops remain linguistically marked, demonstrating that the adopted status of these plant children is known and encoded in naming. Still other crops are marked as adopted through their classification as "introduced" from exchanges with outsiders. Classifying crops as introduced does not imply that they are less important to Canela gardens than aboriginal crops, however. Rather, the introduced crops are given Canela names and are sorted and saved alongside their aboriginal counterparts. After a few seasons, they rapidly become part of Canela ethnobotanical classification and are engaged with in multi-sensory, affectionate ways as seed and plant cutting infants and growing crop children. Crops acquired through all these types of exchange therefore become authentically part of Canela human–plant families, garden plots, and the unfolding life-world.

Figure 5. Pregnant Joaquina with her banana tree, May 2012.

Discovering New Plant Children in the Garden Space

While exchange is the primary way that new crop children are adopted into the Canela life-world, gardeners occasionally discover new crops growing within their own garden plots. Liliana in particular has discovered beans in her saved seed collections and in the garden space. During one of her sorting sessions with me in July 2012, Liliana found one seed of jaguar fava bean hidden amongst a large pile of diverse bean types. Unaware that she currently had this variety in her saved stores, Liliana explained that a seed which "appeared" like this had "turned" or "became by itself" (*virou por si mesmo*). She likened the process to Canela infants who are sometimes born with slightly different skin colors than their parents, in that both seed and human infants have "become" different colors on their own without their parents' intervention. Later in the season, in February 2013, Liliana noticed that three new varieties of bean had appeared in her forest garden plot. Once again, Liliana compared the new variety to an infant with "changed" skin color from that of its parents. In this way, she told me, "plants are the same as people. They change colors; there are many colors of people. And crops are the same thing. Even today, I see it. [With] my produce, there are so many types of fava bean!"

Excited over the discovery of new beans, Liliana immediately named them. She called one *hipêj* egg bean (*pàt juhtõi-re hipêj cre*) because it has markings similar to *hipêj* egg fava bean (*pànkrỳt hipêj cre*), and she named another type jaguar bean (*pàt juhtõi-re kroro-re*) because it is spotted white and black, similar to the markings of jaguar fava bean, which she had found the previous year. The third type of bean with a brilliant red color had not yet been named, but Liliana vividly described it to me, saying, "I like this bean. It is the same type as that fava bean that has the little red markings. Similar to that fava that we call *mẽcuprỳ-re* [annatto fava bean]; it is a little girl. It is similar; the same kind of coloring as that little fava bean." Through noticing the bean—likening its color and size to another type of named bean and to "little girls" (*mẽcuprỳ-re*; which the fava bean is named after), Liliana was in the process of giving the little red bean a name that accurately displayed its characteristics and traits. She would ask other gardeners if they had already found and named this type of bean as well, which is a common occurrence when a gardener finds a new type in their plot.

In the case of the little red bean, however, Liliana found that other gardeners, especially her family members, did not already grow and save this type. Instead, her family was just as surprised to see the appearance of this new bean as she was. Although Liliana told me she had seen this bean in her garden around seven years ago, she and her family were amazed at its (re-)appearance. She explained to me, "at the moment this year when we cultivated beans, I never knew that there was a different type of bean like this one. And now, we are all shocked!" Liliana then emphasized the importance of separating out and saving this varietal for years to come, through a conversation she had with her daughter Nilda:

> Nilda asked me, "mother [*inxê*], where did you get this bean? Where can I get it?" [I responded], "No, I did not even get it somewhere! I save it like this, with the seed protected. Save it, and it will transform all the time. And when the planting season [begins], I will give it to you for you to plant."

Gardeners' understandings of the appearance of new varietals are multiple and overlapping. On the one hand, gardeners express shock and wonder at the appearance of new beans, as Liliana described for herself and her family. Those who are evangelical Christians, such as Liliana, sometimes attribute their discoveries to God as well. "These things are from our father, God," Liliana explained to me. "He is doing these things. He changes all of us. That is my understanding. And some [beans] already; it is not a lot, but we separate them out so that I can plant them." On the other hand, gardeners' seed saving and planting practices indicate a general knowledge of seeds' abilities to "transform" from one season to the next. As Liliana indicated above, she has knowledge of seeds "transforming all the time" while they are saved and then "appearing" as new types in the garden space. While gardeners often save multiple varietals in the same plastic bottle or gourd, they generally sort them out in order to plant varietals in separate holes. Expert gardeners in particular prefer to separate varietals for planting whenever possible. Occasionally, gardeners such as Liliana and her daughters mix different varietals together in the same hole if they are in a hurry to finish planting or when planting in small backyard plots where there is not enough space for long rows of each type. Mixing varietals can lead to a new phenotypically distinct variety (although it may not be genetically distinct) and to processes of inter- and intra-specific hybridization (see Harrison and Larson 2014). Planting similar species next to one another also can lead to introgression, or the flow of genes from one species to another, particularly with beans from the *Phaseolus* genus to which at least two-thirds of Canela bean types belong (see Blair et al. 2010). Canela gardeners' preference to keep varietals separate when possible may indicate a general understanding of these processes, which can lead to visible transformations and appearances of varietals with new colors, shapes, and sizes that are similar to yet distinct from those already existing in garden plots.

The new beans that appear in gardeners' plots also may be the result of outcrossing with wild relatives that exist throughout the Cerrado biome. Wild and cultivated beans from the *Phaseolus* genus are self pollinating and easily hybridize with each other, "producing viable and fertile individuals" (Singh et al. 1991:379). Gardeners note the presence of wild legumes in their territory, sometimes giving them names such as the inedible bitter fava bean (*pànkrỳt ihkên*) and cobra fava (*pànkrỳt cahàc-ti*), the latter of which is planted in the corners of garden plots to deter snakes (see chapter 2, "Loving Forest and Riverbank Gardens in the Twenty-First Century"). Bitter, inedible (and most likely wild) beans can accidentally surface in Canela cooking, and my family told me a story of a woman who had once died from eating the poisonous bitter fava. Some types of named cultivated beans also have a slightly bitter taste, although Liliana assured me that the beans that are "only a little bitter" are safe for human consumption. As bitterness is an indicator of a wild origin, it is possible that these beans are in fact semi-domesticated "weedy" hybrids of cultivated and wild types (Chacón et al. 2007:178). The jaguar bean (*pàt juhtõi-re kroro-re*) that Liliana discovered and named in early 2013 may be an outcrossed hybrid as well. In addition to its similarities with jaguar fava bean, Liliana told me that jaguar bean is of the "same type as a seed of the forest that has a red part, and a black part, [known as] *pàt juhtõi-re ikhên tep*." Since plants categorized as "of the forest" (*do mato*) are typically wild, and since its name includes *ihkên*, similar to the wild fava bean, the *pàt juhtõi-re ikhên tep* seed to which she refers is presumably a wild, nondomesticated type. By linking the new bean in her garden with this wild legume, Liliana is displaying her understanding of the bean's origin and giving clues to the ways in which gardeners may passively allow or even actively encourage hybridization in their garden plots.

Whether human gardeners are active or passive participants in processes of crop introgression, hybridization, or outcrossing, they thoroughly enjoy and appreciate any new types discovered in their gardens. Liliana often told me how much she enjoys the "changing" (*mudança*) of new varieties, and she and her family expressed amusement and happiness with the new additions to their gardens' agro-biodiversity. Explaining why she takes pleasure in discovering new crops, Liliana stated:

> I want to increase more [crops] for me to cultivate, to leave for my family, my grandchildren. Perhaps someone will be interested and increase more than what I have! That is why I like the new things that have appeared. Because I do not want to lose the things that appeared.

Even though the new beans had just recently appeared in her forest garden, Liliana had already become committed to the seeds, stating she did not want to lose them over time. Through noticing their different colors and sizes, naming them after similar beans that are already categorized, and sorting and saving them for herself and her daughters to cultivate and keep in seasons to come, Liliana was fully accepting jaguar bean, *hipêj* egg bean, and the little bright red bean into her agro-biodiversity maintenance practices and into her multispecies family. She sees herself as the mother of these newly adopted seed infants, linking them to human infants and to the processes of care and affection that both human and plant children need.

Through processes of exchange and introgression, hybridization, and outcrossing, Canela gardeners can increase the agro-biodiversity that is essential to the creation and maintenance of strong, happy, and healthy multispecies human–plant families. While the origins of adopted plant children may be marked and remembered, gardeners strive to incorporate myriad new crops fully into their ethnobotanical classification, gardening, and seed-saving practices. Canela gardeners value the intimate relationships of care and affection that they develop with all their crop children, be it a recently discovered "weedy" hybrid bean child or an "aboriginal" one passed down through generations. Whether coming from a village neighbor, an Indigenous Apaniekra "stranger," a white person from the south of the country, or from a hybridization of wild and cultivated plants, new seeds and cuttings are highly valued and appreciated as plant children that are integral to their multispecies families' ability to survive and thrive.

Writing: Plant Childcare in the Twenty-First Century

Noticing, naming, sorting, and saving seeds and cuttings is a traditionally oral process. Sitting side by side on the reddish earth, women teach the names of their saved varietals to their daughters and granddaughters. Sorting through a pile of saved seeds, maize kernels, yam cuttings, or manioc roots, girls learn how to identify and name varietals based on their physical characteristics as well as their ecological, nutritional, sociocultural, sociopolitical, cosmological, and aesthetic aspects. Passing down these names through sustained, multi-sensory interactions among women, girls, and seeds and cuttings remains the primary way that Canela ethnobotanical classification is maintained across generations. Oral crop-naming practices have been maintained at least since the 1920s, as Nimuendajú (1946:58–61) documented, and most likely since the early nineteenth century as recorded by Ribeiro ([1819] 1841). For at least the past two hundred years, then, crop names have been passed down through familial conversations, relationships, and encounters with seed and plant cutting infants themselves.

Yet when younger generations do not develop long-term, intimate engagements with seeds, cuttings, and growing plants, the names of these crop children (as well as the knowledge associated with them) can be lost. The *kupá* vine (*Cissus* sp.), for example, was a significant crop for the community in the early twentieth century, as it was for many Jê-speaking communities in the region (Ribeiro [1819] 1841:188). Nimuendajú (1946:58) documented the crop as "aboriginal" to the Canela in the 1920s, and the community lived in a village named Kupá-Khĩa (*Kupá* Vine Oven) at the turn of the century, highlighting the crop's importance to everyday life. By the 1950s, the vine was still available and consumed, but it was grown less commonly than in the past. After the 1963 messianic movement, however, the cuttings were lost when the community fled their territory to the Guajajara community's lands (Crocker, personal communication; see chapter 2, "Gardening: A Brief History, 1814–Present"). Recently there have been attempts to begin growing *kupá* again, especially by Fernando, who is keenly interested in revitalizing Canela agro-biodiversity. In 2012, Fernando met with representatives of FUNAI and EMBRAPA at their offices in Brasília and received cuttings of the *kupá* vine to bring back to the village. While it is as yet unknown whether this attempt to revitalize *kupá* will be successful, the knowledge of storing, planting, cooking, and consuming the vine is no longer actively passed down, nor are any varietal names that may have existed in the past. Without active sensory engagements with the cuttings for half a century, gardeners have largely lost their abilities to interact and come to know the *kupá* vine as a plant child in the Canela life-world.

Other crop children are becoming less well-known over time as well. While still considered aboriginal crops, cotton varietals are grown much less frequently than they were in the past. In the mid-twentieth century, cotton was still a commonly cultivated crop, processed into string for belts and other ritual ornaments (Crocker, personal communication). When he was a young boy during that time, Fernando remembers his mother making string from the fluffy cotton pulp by rolling it out until it became smooth. She used the string to make ritual bracelets for girls, and occasionally to make hammocks to sleep in. While a few expert gardeners such as Liliana continue to grow cotton today, it is no longer commonly found in Canela gardens. The plant has become less useful, since many women today prefer to make string out of the tucum (*ronre*; *Bactris setosa*) plant or purchase cotton or plastic cords from markets in nearby towns. And although gardeners can still name the two varieties of large cotton (*caxàt catia ita*) and small cotton (*caxàt kryi-re*), it was one of the last crops that Fernando, Renato, and Liliana remembered to include in our plant lists after months of interviews and research. Concerned over the cotton crop children's survival, Fernando hopes that gardeners will increase their cotton cultivation. He passionately told me during a conversation in June 2012, "my mother made the [cotton] cords herself, and nowadays, no one does that! We have to return to this ... we have to revitalize and produce more!"

There is also concern over the maintenance of gourd varietals, especially large types that traditionally were used as containers for food or to carry and store water. Gardeners currently name fifteen types of gourd belonging to at least two species: twelve varieties of gourd (*cuhkõn*; *Cucurbita* spp.) and three varieties of bottle gourd (*cuhtõj*; *Lagenaria siceraria* and/or *Crescentia cujete*). Many of these gourds are not edible yet were especially useful for collecting water from nearby streams and bringing it back to the house for consumption. Since 2003, piped-in water has been available to Canela families in Escalvado village, which is connected to a well that the government created and maintains. Many community members now use large plastic containers (*baldes*) purchased from nearby towns for collecting water from the tap installed behind their houses. Consequently, crops such as neck gourd (*cuhkõn put-tyt*), with a long neck that was traditionally used to carry water, are now infrequently cultivated and maintained. Another type called largest gourd (*cuhkõn catia ita*) that is not currently cultivated was also used to carry water, as well as to store bean seeds, rice, and *farinha*. Purchased metal pots and pans have also largely replaced gourds as food receptacles. As a result, not-bitter gourd (*cuhkõn xenre*) and large long gourd (*cuhkõn japjêh-ti*), which were traditionally used as bowls for food and for ritual purposes, are not currently cultivated. Fernando, Renato, Liliana and many other elder Canela gardeners expressed concern that younger generations are no longer interested in saving gourd seeds or cultivating the plants in their gardens. They all agreed that "gourds are children" and should be treated with care and affection. Fernando elaborated:

> The gourd is a child, yes. That is why all old people plant gourds. Yesterday, Ademar and his wife [Osvalda] were planting, and he said that all their children complained—"gourds are so much work ... they are not good! Let's leave them behind! Now we can buy [plastic] *baldes* to bring water." So, he said that they left behind [the gourds]. But not me. I wouldn't think of it. [...] On the one hand, there are *baldes*, but we can also preserve gourds. I like them. I really love gourds! I can take gourds

with me—in the garden, I can bring a gourd to carry water. When I am on a journey, this gourd will bring water along.

While the older generations such as Fernando, Ademar, and Osvalda are continuing to respect and care for their gourd varietals, some of the younger generations are uninterested in coming to know large gourd children. The varietal names remain, yet those too could be lost if the long-term engagements between people and gourds are no longer sought out and developed. As older gardeners such as Liliana and Fernando point out, varietals can only remain alive as infants or children if they consistently are cared for through saving, planting, tending, harvesting, and saving again. Without human parental nurturance and assistance, then, gourd children's ability to survive and thrive will be threatened.[3]

Fernando's love for gourds and other plant children led him to begin writing down crop names on his ancient typewriter in 2011. When he initially showed me his ethnobotanical lists on that sunny July afternoon, he made a point of emphasizing the importance of gardening to the modern-day community and connected his list making to the recent loss of certain varieties such as types of gourds. Maintaining agro-biodiversity was therefore at the forefront of the ethnobotanical project I developed the following year with Fernando, Renato, Liliana, Wander, and other gardeners. By creating a comprehensive series of written crop lists, the first of their kind for the community, we aim to provide a written record of the oral process of learning about and remembering ethnobotanical classification, gardening knowledge, and human–plant engagements. During fieldwork in 2011, 2012–2013, and 2017, we developed a process for compiling the written lists that includes frequent revisions and expansions, as described above. While Fernando, Renato, Liliana, and Wander can name the majority of varieties themselves, we learned about (or were reminded of) additional crop types from Noemi, Lorena, Osvalda, Ademar, and sixteen other male and female gardeners who participated in the ethnobotanical survey. With direct input from these twenty-four Canela gardeners (and indirect input from other community members), I documented the Canela names of 266 cultivated crop varietals belonging to at least 45 species, as well as 54 native tree and plant types.

These written lists are "living lists" (Miller 2016) that are changing over time to reflect the dynamic relationships that develop between Canela gardeners and various plants in their territorial landscape. In 2017, less than five years after our original list making, gardeners were already changing the plant lists, adding new varietals they had acquired through exchange, remembering others that were not included in the previous lists, and indicating which varietals they are no longer cultivating but which they still name and seek to revitalize (see appendices A and B for more detail). Nevertheless, the lists documented here provide a recorded snapshot of Canela agro-biodiversity maintenance (and loss) in the early twenty-first century. For example, the list making revealed that contemporary gardeners seek out and value bean diversity of both the *pànkrỳt* and *pàt juhtõi-re* categories, with fifty-two and eighteen named types in each respective category (see table 4). Rice follows with the second-highest number of varietals at twenty-eight named types, then manioc and yam with eighteen named varietals each, and sweet potato with fifteen named types. Other crops have noticeably less varietal diversity, and in some cases, such as with cotton, this may reflect a recent decrease in cultivation. Still other aboriginal crops such as *kupá* and arrowroot are noticeably absent from the lists, reflecting the loss of these crops and any named varietals that may have been cultivated in the past. Through writing down crop names and quantifying each crop category, gardeners such as Fernando were able to glean a better picture of their current agro-biodiversity maintenance and of what they wish to revitalize in the future.

As a new activity for Canela gardeners, the act of writing down crop names bears similarities and differences to the traditionally oral process of crop naming. Just as orally naming crops is a pleasurable activity, compiling the lists is enjoyable for Canela gardeners. They pore over the names and spelling of different varietals and enthusiastically display samples of seeds and cuttings for me to photograph. Whenever someone has found or remembered an additional crop name to write down, the joy is palpable. When Ademar and Osvalda showed us their seven additional types of *pànkrỳt* beans, for example, Liliana, Fernando, and Renato were overjoyed. Liliana sorted through the seeds with Osvalda as Fernando and Renato asked Ademar about their names. Instructed by the gardeners, whose enthusiasm for the writing process was evident, I wrote down the names on a piece of scrap paper, making sure that the descriptions and spellings were accurate. In this instance, writing down the names was an additional stage tacked on at the end of the process of noticing, naming, sorting, and saving.

Indeed, writing on the whole has been incorporated throughout the twentieth and twenty-first centuries as a supplementary activity to Canela daily life. Writing was initially introduced to the Canela in the early 1940s by SPI agents, who established a local schoolhouse where a few Canela boys became literate in Portuguese (Devine Guzmán 2013:32). By the 1950s, some of these literate men were communicating to outsiders via written messages, and their literacy enabled them to become research assistants to Crocker in the late 1950s and early 1960s (Crocker, personal communication). In the late 1960s, Canadian SIL missionaries Jack and Josephine Popjes began living with the community and documenting the Canela language. From 1968 to 1990, they worked on translating the Bible into Canela and creating the first comprehensive grammar of the language (Popjes and Popjes 1986; Crocker and Crocker 2004:35). German missionaries from the Christian Evangelical Mission of Brazil (*Missão Cristão Evangélica do Brasil*), Bernhard and Elke Grupp, who have been living in Escalvado since the mid-2000s, have updated a Canela dictionary that the Popjes began, with the input of Canela assistants (Grupp 2015). While no standardized orthography was created for the Canela language, in the 1990s the local schoolhouse began employing Canela teachers who could instruct their pupils in writing Canela and Portuguese. Nowadays most young boys and girls attend the school and become literate, to varying degrees, in their own language and in Portuguese. While attending school and becoming literate are important to many Canela families, writing in particular remains an optional supplement to daily processes of learning, knowing, and living in the village and garden spaces, dependent on one's preferences, abilities, and the availability of the purchased materials of paper and pen or pencil.

Although a supplementary activity, the act of writing and composing written documents generally are accorded special significance and meaning. One of Crocker's main research assistants in the 1960s, for example, sought out a notebook in order to write down a diary of his daily life, as he considered this an important activity (Crocker, personal communication). The man's writing activities, undertaken on his own initiative, formed the basis of the decades-long written and audio-recorded diary program that Crocker later developed (Crocker 2007:34). Similarly, Fernando approached me with his typed plant list in 2011, also describing them as important for Canela gardening and seed-saving practices. The writing up of agreements with anthropologists and other outsiders is also common, especially when gift giving is involved. Crocker hand-wrote agreements of participation in an agricultural project with the Canela in 2003, for example, which community leaders co-signed (Crocker, personal communication). Photographs show the men sitting at a table in the town of Barra do Corda, poring over the paper documents together. When I began my ethnobotanical research in April 2012, Fernando, Renato, Liliana, and Wander also asked me to write out paper contracts in order to make their work with me official. I used paper with actual carbon copies that I purchased in Barra do Corda, as they wanted copies for their records.

The materials of paper and pen are also highly valued in the community. They are relatively expensive and must be purchased at stationery stores in

Barra do Corda, located 65 km from the Canela territory. It is difficult to obtain transportation between the village and the town, with truck drivers' schedules frequently changing, poor weather and road conditions common, and mechanical breakdowns of trucks often significantly delaying the journey.[4] Women who need to make the journey into town in order to receive and/or spend the monthly Bolsa Família governmental social assistance payments are restricted in their ability to travel, for it is considered inappropriate and dangerous to travel alone, especially without a male companion. Even if a woman or man has acquired enough money to purchase a truck journey and shop in town, writing materials are usually at the end of one's shopping list, after essentials such as soap, coffee, salt, sugar, cooking oil, bread, cloth, and gardening tools. Considered luxury goods that are associated with the *cupẽn*, writing materials are sought after and desired, much like larger items such as stoves, refrigerators, and television sets. Many people often requested I bring them paper and pen from my journeys into town, as part of the gift-giving practices of an outside researcher "giving happiness" (*dando alegria*) to the community. Fernando, Renato, Liliana, and Wander in particular asked that I bring each of them paper notebooks, pens and pencils, and printed versions of our most recent list compilations each time I returned from a journey into town.

The value of writing activities, written documents, and writing materials is largely derived from their status as originally coming from "outside" the traditional Canela life-world. Learned from foreign missionaries and in a government-sponsored schoolhouse, using materials available from only non-Indigenous towns, writing comes from "outsiders," or the *cupẽn*. Yet just as gardeners have incorporated crops introduced through exchange with outsiders into their gardens, so too is the community including writing and written materials into their highly transformational contemporary life-world. This transformation of "outside" elements into the "inside" is common among Jê-speaking communities in central and northeast Brazil (Gordon 2006; Ewart 2013). Similar to the Panará, for whom the division between themselves (*panará*) and the "enemy/others/white people" (*hipe*) is an inherent part of their transformational sociality (Ewart 2013:232), the Canela approach interactions with outsiders as opportunities for transformation and adoption—of crops, of gardening practices, and of written documents, writing materials, and the very activities of writing in Portuguese and Canela. Although writing techniques and materials still are associated with outsiders (similar to the crops that remain categorized as introduced), Canela men and women have been using them for their own valued and meaningful activities, such as writing unprompted diaries, documenting agreements with outsiders that are beneficial to them, and, more recently, composing typewritten plant lists and written ethnobotanical lists (along with myself, an outsider). The written lists therefore form part of the emergent Canela life-world, as a new transformation of coming to know plant names and lives.

Additionally, just as originally *cupẽn* crops are now considered Canela plant children, so too is writing down plant lists currently being transformed into another activity of plant childcare. By writing down the names of beloved crop children, gardeners are providing an additional way to remember, take care of, and keep alive these nonhuman beings. While the written lists cannot replace the intimate sensory engagements that develop between gardener parents and crop children each season, they are a useful supplement to understanding processes of knowing and becoming with plants. In written form, the lists provide another visual sensory experience with which gardeners can connect with their plant children, alongside speaking about and listening to plant names, handling seeds, observing growing plant children, and tasting them at the end of their life cycle. Overall, the written lists aim to emphasize the importance of diverse plant children to the Canela life-world, by accurately documenting their wide array of names, characteristics, sociocultural and sociopolitical organization, cosmological associations, and lives as they unfold.

The written lists serve as another way to pass on the education of affection for plant children to younger generations as described in chapter 3. Elder gardeners such as Fernando and Liliana were enthusiastic about using the printed ethnobotanical booklets (including photographs and names and descriptions in Canela and Portuguese) that I gave them in February 2013 as teaching tools for younger gardeners (see figure 6).[5] Liliana expanded on the importance of the written lists to herself and her family:

This research [on gardening] opened my eyes, my ears, and my mouth. My research, your research, is for me more than the light of the world! [Laughs] . . . [And] I am very happy. I am going to stay happy all the time, every year; I am never going to feel weak, I am never going to feel sad. I want to be happy all the time, every year, every month. Do you know why? Because I have education! I have knowledge! . . . I have to have courage, to have happiness, to have strength . . . and this work is very important for me. It is not negative; it is not false. It is true what you are doing. In my understanding, it is like this. It is very important; it is very *impej* for me. [. . .]

This book [of ethnobotanical lists] that you prepared; I am going to

Figure 6. Liliana and family looking through photographs and ethnobotanical booklet given to community by author, February 2013.

read all of it. I will never leave this work that you did. I will remember all the time; I will pass it on to my grandchildren. It could be that I become a little old lady, but I will pass it on to those who are interested ... our research is very important! You are seeing my case; that we always lack something, [even though] I always try. I cannot lose the [crops] that you photographed ... I want to increase what I cultivate!

In this view, the written lists and their incorporation into ethnobotanical knowledge transmission can help multispecies Canela families of humans and plants survive and thrive for generations to come. Written plant lists also have the potential to help increase crop diversity, through the written documentation and remembrance of new varietals acquired through exchange with others or discovery in one's own garden plots.

This new form of plant childcare is dynamic and transformative, drawing from activities, materials, and people adopted from the outside and open to noticing changes in the composition and characteristics of plant children over time. As such, it is uniquely situated to address agro-biodiversity maintenance, increase, and loss in the Anthropocene. By documenting crops in the territorial landscape in written form, Canela gardeners will have another tool to understand and come to know their crop children, in addition to noticing, orally naming, sorting, and saving. Gardeners therefore will be especially attuned to any changes their crop children are experiencing and can develop strategies to better care for their seed and plant cutting infants and plant children in years to come.

Multispecies Loving, Open Taxonomies, and Living Lists

Canela ethnobotanical classification is complex, drawing from the intertwined web of relations that emerge between and among humans, animals, wild plants, cultivated seeds and cuttings, and even cosmological entities such as Star-Woman. It is also processual, open to incorporating myriad human–plant relations as they unfold or change over time. Despite its complexity and dynamism, Canela ethnobotanical classification exhibits key themes: the pursuit of multispecies love and diversity. It is grounded in an overarching pursuit of caring, affectionate, and loving relationships between an ever-expanding diversity of people and plants. Canela women, men, girls, and boys from different families and across generations participate in these relationships. People from other Indigenous groups and even non-Indigenous communities implicitly participate as well, through the adoption of crops that were originally their own plant children. Of course, seed and plant cutting infants in need of loving care and affection are active participants, whether good (*impej*) or bad (*ihkên*), aboriginal or introduced, coming from other Indigenous groups or from strangers, enemies, or foreigners, or even appearing somewhat mysteriously in the garden plot. Ethnobotanical classification is about a love of diversity *and* a diversity of love. Gardener mothers seek out and enjoy the relationships they form with as many seed and plant cutting infants as possible and distribute their love to each and every crop they hold, caress, name, sort, and save. This is similar to Tsing's (2010:201) description of "multispecies love" that is focused on a "passionate immersion in the lives of the nonhuman subjects being studied." Yet as Tsing (2010:200) also notes, the "forms of love" that develop between humans and plants can be "diverse, even contradictory," dependent on particular circumstances and human and plant life stories. In the Canela lifeworld, the love required by seed and plant cutting infants in preparation for storage is distinct, dependent on their unique needs. Similarly, the love of a gardener mother for her plant children is distinct from a gardener father in terms of the active perceptual engagements that each pursues. Focused on the pursuit of diversity and the pursuit of love, Canela ethnobotanical classification is crucial to understanding and coming to know plants and the emergent territorial landscape within which human and plant lives unfold.

Recognizing the contingency of human and plant lives, Canela ethnobotanical classification is inherently fluid and dynamic. Rather than focusing on static traits or abstract concepts, gardeners categorize and name crops based on their living attributes—what color, size, and shape they appear—and based on the types of ecological, social, and cosmological relationships they form over time. The relational aspect of crop-naming practices results in an open taxonomy, one that can easily incorporate new crops and can change over time. At first glance, the openness and dynamism of Canela ethnobotanical classification may seem contradictory to standardized Western Linnaean taxonomy as it is commonly understood. Indeed, certain Canela crop categories such as those for beans do not easily correspond with Linnaean species categories. The *pànkrỳt* category of beans, with fifty-two named "varietals," most likely includes at least five species belonging to three genera: lima bean (*Phaseolus lunatus* L.), common bean (*Phaseolus vulgaris* L.), and other species in *Phaseolus*; species in *Vigna*; and fava bean (*Vicia faba* L). The *pàt juhtõi-re* category also includes the common bean species, pigeon pea (*Cajanus cajan*) and other unidentifiable species. The Canela categorization of these beans may seem incommensurable to Linnaean classification, especially if taxonomy is construed "as a project of emphatic, absolute dominion of life forms, tyrannically steering them all into tiny boxes" as social theorists often do (Hartigan 2015a:70). As John Hartigan points out, however, "taxonomists are continually open both to new data and new visions, sharing in a recognition that deep time, with its barely perceptible shifts and transformations or hybridizations of species, could prove their formulations wrong." This is strikingly similar to Canela gardeners, who gladly embrace new "data" (when collaboratively naming and categorizing newly adopted crops, for example) and new "visions," in terms of envisioning the potential for new loving relationships that can be formed with seeds, cuttings, and growing plants. And while the concept of "deep time" may be different for the Canela (centered more on historical and mythical storytelling and ancestral knowledge), modern-day Canela gardeners are keenly aware of transformations or hybridizations of species that have occurred or are currently occurring in their gardens. The categories for beans in particular reflect this knowledge, as gardeners name and incorporate hybridized beans that have appeared in their plots. Noticing, naming, and saving these semi-domesticated "weedy" hybrids for future cultivation, Canela gardeners may be engaging in processes of neo-domestication of beans that blur the lines of Linnaean species categories.[6] An open taxonomy such as that of the Canela can address and incorporate these new hybrids and is in fact akin to Western taxonomy in its recognition of the "philosophical and metaphysical conundrums" (Hartigan 2015a:67) involved in species identification.

Indeed, there is growing evidence that Indigenous communities in lowland South America come to know and classify their local environment in ways that overlap with those of Western taxonomists and natural scientists. Laura Rival (2014:224) demonstrates this in her comparative "fieldwork on

fieldwork" study analyzing interactions between Western-trained natural scientists and the Indigenous Huaorani and Makushi in Ecuador and
Guyana, respectively. Focusing on three different scientific fieldwork experiments involving Western scientific experts and Indigenous people, who are
"to a greater or lesser extent expert knowers" (Rival 2014:229), she shows that
the commensurability of these two sets of knowledge lies in similar ways of
thinking about ecological relations. By focusing on ecological relations, "expert knowers" coming from diverse backgrounds can find common ground
in their understandings and classifications of the environment, what Rival
(2014:229) terms "ecological reasoning." The divergences in conceptualiz-
ing ecology that do exist arise from the "moralization of ecological relationality," which is different among every Indigenous group and many Western-
trained scientists as well (Rival 2014:231).[7] Canela gardeners' emphasis on
making sense of and classifying *relationships* in their open taxonomy shows
a similar approach to ecological reasoning. In a similar vein, the uniqueness
of the Canela open ethnobotanical taxonomy lies in its inclusion of sociocultural, cosmological, and aesthetic/moral relationships and reasoning along
with (and equivalent to) the ecological. Recognizing the convergences and
divergences between Indigenous and Western scientific ways of coming to
know and classify plants is central to ethnobotany, the study of human–plant
relationships with "frictions at its heart" (Ellen 2016:25). The frictions that
arise between overlapping yet disparate Canela and Western Linnaean crop
categories can lead to new ways of knowing about and becoming with plants
for both classification systems. The creativity and experimentation of the Canela taxonomy could provide new "data and visions" for the Western taxonomy of hybrid wild and cultivated beans (*Phaseolus* spp.). In turn, the Canela
open taxonomy gladly welcomes and adopts outside crop categories with ties
to Western classification, such as the many fruit tree species and varieties
that were obtained from non-Indigenous outsiders. Maintaining the categories of banana, mango, and papaya while giving the varietals new Canela
names demonstrates the transformative potential of Canela ethnobotanical classification, able to incorporate crop categories from the "outside" and
make them "insider"-named intentional beings with whom one can form
a simultaneously ecological–sociocultural–cosmological–aesthetic–moral
relationship.

The openness of Canela ethnobotanical classification is derived from
its oral tradition of noticing, naming, sorting, and saving in multi-sensory
ways. This is common with Indigenous ecological knowledge, which offers,
as Rival (2014:228) points out, "many opportunities to study the relationship between thinking about and acting on nature, as well as to consider im-

plicit bodies of practical and experiential knowledge that are memorized in forms other than linguistic." In some cases, the written documentation of Indigenous oral knowledge can supplant the original embodied oral practices, leading to an "orthodoxy" of the written word (J. Goody 2004:94). With the Bagre of northern Ghana, for example, Jack Goody (2004) found that traditionally oral performative recitations were replaced with readings of written text. He maintains that the process of creating written text from oral recitation "changes the nature of the work by giving a permanent shape to something that is otherwise undergoing continuous change" (J. Goody 2004:92). Issues also can arise when using written documentation to safeguard traditional Indigenous knowledge in a meaningful way. As Nic Eoin and King (2013:10) point out in their study of residents in Metolong, Lesotho, near a dam construction site, local people were much more interested in "physical archives" of the plants, animals, and fish that would be impacted by the dam than the textual documentation of their ecological knowledge. While written documentation of Indigenous knowledge should be treated with caution, for the Canela the process of writing down crop names differed from these contexts in three main ways. In the first place, the written plant lists do not supplant oral tradition but rather serve as a supplement to it, which echoes the supplementary role of writing throughout the community. Secondly, the lists themselves are not, and never were intended to be, permanent entities as other textual documents can be. Rather, they are living lists that grew and changed over years of documentation (in 2011, 2012–2013, and 2017) and will undoubtedly undergo additional revisions in the future. Finally, the original intention of the written lists, as outlined by Fernando, Liliana, and other Canela gardeners, was to safeguard agro-biodiversity in complement to the existing oral tradition. Canela gardeners are dealing with different environmental threats and destruction than the residents of Metolong and are therefore interested in the written documentation of human-plant engagements that are not rapidly disappearing yet may be threatened in the near future.

Overall, the written plant lists, with an openness similar to the oral tradition, provide an additional way to protect and care for Canela plant children. Concerned over the negligence toward certain crop children such as gourd and cotton varietals, gardeners are choosing to address agro-biodiversity maintenance and environmental knowledge transmission in a new transformative way. The living lists are significant not only in terms of documenting plant lives but also of passing on the importance of plant childcare to younger generations. They constitute a new, dynamic tool that women and men can use (alongside other more traditional techniques) to teach the younger generations about engaging in affectionate, caring relationships with cultivated crops. In this way, gardeners are re-conceptualizing the "education of affection" that chapter 3 explores in a new, twenty-first century format. This caring, affectionate approach to agro-biodiversity management will be uniquely useful in the threatened Cerrado biome. Through noticing, naming, and engaging with plants, as well as writing down one's observations, gardeners will be able to tell if their plant children are being affected by the environmental destruction currently underway and the threats to come, such as drought, deforestation, pollution of land and water, and climatic changes. While some crop children may be lost over time, gardeners continue to pursue relationships with a diversity of old and new seeds and cuttings. As Liliana explained to me regarding the new beans that she discovered in early 2013, "we will save it; we will experiment. To plant more for the next season—plant and see." With a love of multispecies diversity and a diversity of their forms of love, Canela women and men will continue engaging in the intimate acts of sorting, saving, and naming in order to keep alive as many crop children as possible for generations to come.

CHAPTER FIVE

Becoming a Shaman with Plants

Friendship, Seduction, and Mediating Danger

Talking with Plants

"Sweet manioc talks with me," the shaman Reinaldo informed me during a conversation in August 2012. I had heard from many gardeners about the unique encounters between shamans and plants and asked Reinaldo to describe his own experiences in the garden space. He continued in sweet manioc's own voice: "Shaman [*kay*]! I will live here! In the place where you cleaned." "Okay, okay, you can live here," Reinaldo told me was his response. After this interspecies conversation, the sweet manioc crop begins its life in the garden. Its roots grow rapidly, it develops an intimate relationship with its gardener mother throughout its life cycle, and eventually the crop becomes part of an abundant harvest. Reinaldo explains that his initial interaction with sweet manioc results in the crop being "ready"—to "enter into the ground" after speaking with the shaman, to grow its roots, to interact with its gardener mother, and to present itself to her when mature. Essentially, the shamanic interaction has prepared sweet manioc to live, grow, and become with human gardeners in the garden plot.

Indeed, Canela shamanic engagements with plants are crucial to modern-day gardening practices, yet they are markedly different from those relationships of parental care and affection that develop between gardeners and their crops. With their heightened sensory capacities, shamans (*kay*) are able to enter into distinct communicative relationships with cultivated plants and their gendered master spirits, known as Plant-People. Shamanic encounters with plants and male and female Plant-People can be understood through three main affective modes that I explore in this chapter: friendship, seduction, and potential danger. Through these various encounters, shamans mediate people–plant relationships and support the ever-emergent Canela life-world comprised of living humans, plants, animals, objects and artifacts, master spirits, and *mẽkarõn*, the souls or spirits of deceased Canela people. Shamans potentially can engage with all these entities. Yet maintaining the heightened sensory abilities necessary to engage with nonhumans is an ongoing process, as encapsulated in the term *kay*, which denotes the processual state of acquiring shamanic abilities and the profession itself. One cannot simply *be* a shaman but is rather constantly *becoming* a shaman through particular perceptual experiences with a soul teacher and with other nonhuman beings that are pursued throughout one's life. The essence of *kay* abilities, then, is centered on affective relationships with a variety of nonhuman beings that play out in three shamanic modalities: the ability to communicate with nonhumans, including animals, objects and artifacts, and plants and Plant-People master spirits; the ability to transform into nonhumans, especially animals; and the ability to cure illnesses through a laying of hands and blowing smoke technique. While the shamanic abilities to converse with and transform into animals previously defined the profession, as seen in mythic storytelling, these abilities are less available to contemporary shamans. Rather, these powers largely have been replaced by shamanic engagements with plants and Plant-People in the transformational, unfolding life-world.

Friendship is an affective mode that develops between shamans and plants and takes on similar qualities as those found in discussions of formal and informal friendship throughout lowland South America (Santos-Granero 2007). In this chapter, I explore the heightened sensory communicative relationships that shamans develop with a diversity of growing plants. As a friend and confidante, a shaman listens to the plants as they describe their lived experiences in the garden space, be they happy and strong (*ihtỳi*) or sad and weak (*ihpêc*). The conversations between shamans and plants continue throughout the course of the plant's life, from when it is preparing to live in the ground through the harvest season at the end of its natural life cycle. Shamans, who are predominately male, also interact with male Plant-People master spirits through a gendered mode of friendship. Acting as advisors, friends, and trusted confidants, the male Plant-People and shamans take on similar roles as that of Canela male "formal friends" (*hapĩn*) who are responsible for the safety and well-being of one another.

Meanwhile, shamanic encounters with female Plant-People take on a seductive affective mode. Female Plant-People attract the male shaman with their beautiful appearance and entice the shaman with flirtatious remarks. Shamans desire the diverse Plant-Women, who appear as anthropomorphized versions of the crop species or variety they represent, and therefore seek out frequent engagements with them in the garden space. Through seductive interactions, the Plant-Women are able to advocate for the strength and happiness of their representative crops to the shaman. Shamans, in turn, learn about and become attuned to crop well-being (or lack thereof) through encounters of seduction and friendship. They are responsible for advising individual gardener mothers and fathers, and the entire community, of their plant children's sickness or health.

Shamanic encounters with plants in the garden space can be potentially dangerous, however. Occasionally, deceased Canela souls transform themselves into growing plants, particularly bitter manioc. The souls-transformed-as-manioc will "grab" (*pegar*) the souls of living humans, especially of women, girls, and young children, in order to bring them back to the land of the dead. The dangers for humans whose souls are "grabbed" are immense, including illness and death. While plants that are occupied by souls are sometimes said to produce an abundant harvest, they too face the potential danger of neglect from their gardener mothers and fathers, who refrain from visiting and caring for plants that have been possessed by souls. Only shamans can engage with these souls-transformed-as-plants and send them away from the spaces that healthy, living humans occupy, including the forest gardens, riverbank gardens, and the village. Shamanic healing techniques of laying hands and blowing smoke can remove the deceased soul's power over the infirm person. Encountering souls in this manner is a difficult and potentially dangerous process for the shaman. Yet his prowess in engaging with souls, including souls transformed into plants, is essential for maintaining the safety and well-being of people and plants in the contemporary Canela life-world.

The modern-day importance of shamanic engagements with plants is a recent development that has corresponded with the community's increased emphasis on horticulture for subsistence. Shamans who develop the ability to communicate with plants and Plant-People master spirits emphasize the importance of these beings to the contemporary Canela community in terms of their perceptual abilities. While other nonhuman beings with similar perceptual abilities, such as animals, continue to form relationships with shamans, the plants and Plant-People have become significant intentional actors within what I term a Canela "scalar view of animacy" (Nuckolls 2010). Shamanic heightened sensory encounters with plants and Plant-People help mediate future gardener–crop relationships. As Fernando once explained to me, "[crops] only talk to shamans themselves. Only he knows." In this way, I maintain that shamans and shamanic abilities today are part of the emergent Canela life-world that centers on paying attention to, caring for, and becoming with plants in myriad ways.

Becoming a Shaman: Engagements with Nonhumans

Learning from Soul Teachers

Learning how to become a shaman and cultivate shamanic abilities is a life-long process that involves extended perceptual entanglements with myriad nonhuman beings. The term for a shaman in Canela, *kay*, refers to the shamanic occupation and the ongoing state of being, or rather *becoming*, that enables shamanic abilities. Being in a state of *kay* is not constant and will vary throughout the shaman's lifetime depending on various factors such as age, commitment to food and sex prohibitions (*mē ipiyakri tsà*; *resguardo*), and the types of relationships that the shaman develops with a particular deceased soul (*karõ*) or souls (*mēkarõn*). Younger shamans tend to exhibit more potent shamanic powers than their older counterparts, although extensive periods of training throughout one's life can increase *kay* abilities again. In this sense, the process of becoming a shaman is never-ending, and shamanic abilities easily can be lost, gained, or subject to debate concerning quality and effectiveness. There are variations in *kay* abilities throughout one's life and between shamans, with a key difference between an especially powerful *kay pej* ("good" shaman; variant of the term *impej*—that which is good, beautiful, and true/original) and a *kay cahàc* ("regular" shaman). Women can develop shamanic abilities, and female shamans have existed in recent history and in mythic storytelling (Crocker and Crocker 2004:87–88). In 2012–2013, two women were known to have developed shamanic abilities. The vast majority of shamans are male, however. I encountered several younger and older men who were known to have shamanic abilities, and Fernando, Renato, Liliana, and Wander described the shamanic abilities of their living or deceased male relatives.

Shamans typically experience an initial calling to the profession through a life-threatening illness or accident that makes them attuned to learning shamanic powers from Canela soul teachers. While it is possible to pursue shamanic abilities actively without first experiencing trauma, this pursuit can be in vain if one is unable to develop a relationship with a soul teacher. Ultimately, it is the souls themselves who decide with which living Canela person they will interact and help develop heightened perceptual abilities. A soul often approaches someone who recently has experienced a traumatic illness or accident, offering to heal his wounds or cure his illness and then teach him how to become a shaman. In mid-June 2012, for example, the final celebrations of the Pep Cahàc male initiation ritual complex were underway, including various log races for the boys and men participating in the initiation cycle. During one of the afternoon log races, the leader (*ihcapõn catê impej*; *chefão* in Portuguese) of the young men, Pedrinho, was seriously injured after a log fell onto his shoulder. A large crowd of men and women ran from their houses where they had been watching the race to attend to him. The race continued, yet Pedrinho returned to his mother's house to nurse his wounds. Sleeping outside in front of the house that night, Pedrinho was approached by a soul that promised to cure him. The following day, Pedrinho's arm, initially thought to be broken because of the weight of the heavy hardwood log, was now found to be only wounded. News quickly spread around the village that Pedrinho was on the mend due to the assistance of a deceased soul and that he already was undergoing the process of becoming a shaman. Similarly, Liliana described to me how her grandparent Dirceu initially was approached by a soul after sustaining a serious injury from a log during a ritual log race. Liliana's father Paolo Eduardo, who also developed powerful shamanic abilities, first encountered a soul after becoming ill from a serious snakebite near his forest garden plot. The soul of his deceased father approached him and healed the wound, and immediately afterward Paolo Eduardo began developing his shamanic abilities. There is often a familial connection between the soul and the shaman-to-be, with deceased grandfathers and fathers teaching their sons and grandsons.

With or without a familial connection between deceased soul and living person, the souls must "like" the person they are training. They are especially attracted to a neat and clean physical appearance that can be achieved through the strict food and sex prohibitions that mothers and fathers of human and plant children also undergo (see chapter 3, "Understanding Human–Plant Bodily Engagements"; see also Crocker n.d.:3–5, 13). The restrictions are thought to temporarily prevent pollutants from entering the body through abstaining from consuming "polluting" heavy foods and engaging in sexual intercourse. The purifying effects of the restrictions fundamentally change a person's appearance, making him or her more beautiful (*impej*) and physically attractive to other living humans, deceased souls, and nonhuman beings such as plants, animals, and objects and artifacts. Fernando described someone who frequently undergoes the restrictions as having "clearer eyes, teeth that do not break, and hair that stays black and never turns grey." In another conversation, Fernando added that the person "becomes very beautiful, with soft, smooth hair; his color becomes beautiful too. […] He walks in a beautiful way, because he is undergoing *resguardo*." He or she appears cleaner and tidier and becomes *ihtỳi*, or strong, healthy, happy, and able to experience pleasure. There is also a correlation between physical strength and staying awake, so that those who often partake in the prohibitions do not require more than a few hours of light sleep each night and can endure long walks in the forest during the day without becoming tired. Conversely, those who refrain from undergoing the restrictions develop an unattractive physical appearance. According to Renato, their skin becomes the undesirable yellowish color of squash or large red-yellow maize (*põhy caprêc-ti*). They are thought to experience weakness and sadness (*ihpêc xà*), which manifests itself in sleeping heavily for long periods and staying at home instead of visiting the gardens. Being sad and weak is unattractive to deceased souls (and to plants, animals, and oftentimes other living humans as well).

In addition to making a person more beautiful, undergoing the restrictions allows for the development of certain skill sets such as parenting, gardening, hunting, log racing, ritual singing, and, of course, shamanic abilities. Overall, the prohibitions allow oneself to become open to intimate relationships with others, be they fetuses, infants, children, plants, animals, or souls. For shamans, the restrictions improve the aspiring novice's senses so that, as Fernando describes it, he can "smell as well as a dog" and "listen" to and "see" souls, Plant-People, plants, animals, and objects. The purpose of the restrictions for shamans are twofold: firstly, to make the shaman more desirable in order to initially attract the souls and other nonhumans with whom he wishes to engage; and secondly, to heighten his perceptual abilities further so that he can continue to develop and maintain multi-sensory relationships with these nonhuman beings.

Since the purifying effects of the restrictions are not permanent, undergoing longer restrictive periods throughout one's life typically results in developing better or stronger abilities. Shamans especially should maintain food and sex restrictions for ten to twelve months at a time in order to develop the heightened perceptual abilities specific to their profession, yet a minimum length of three or four months can also suffice. Reinaldo, for example, initially underwent a ten-month restrictive period without eating meat or "touching women" (*encostar às mulheres*) in order to achieve *kay* abilities. During this time, men such as Reinaldo must avoid sexual intercourse with women and heavy foods, including most meats and animal organs, *beribu* meat and manioc pies, and *farinha d'água*, a wetter type of the staple toasted manioc flour. He subsists mainly on *farinha seca*, or dry toasted manioc flour, peanuts, and true/original maize (*põhy pej-re*). In addition, he must keep the water he drinks and uses to bathe separate from those who are not partaking in the prohibitions. Translating for Reinaldo (who is not fluent in Portuguese), Fernando described the necessity of frequently undertaking the restrictions in order to become a skilled shaman:

He [Reinaldo] says that the person that perceives as a *kay*, if he does not continue enduring the *resguardo*—and eats heavy things, *beribu* [meat and manioc pie], or some kind of heavy meat—he says that this knowledge disappears; it leaves him, and he is no longer a *kay*. He says that the person did perceive, but he did not take good care of it, and the knowledge left him. But the person who does take good care of it, enduring, enduring [the restrictions], he becomes an expert!

A shaman also may recruit his family members living in the same household to participate in the restrictive period, since the activities of one person can affect or leave traces on other living people with whom one has developed an embodied connection. This is similar to the shared restrictive period that pregnant women and their husbands undergo to protect the fetus and infant. For shamans, however, sharing restrictions with family members is centered not on protecting another living body but rather on strengthening the shaman's own perceptual abilities through these interpersonal embodied connections. When the snake first bit Paolo Eduardo and his father's soul approached him, for example, he and his wife and children all abstained from eating game meat for three months. Although a young girl at the time, Liliana vividly remembered the restrictive period of eating only rice, *beiju* manioc pancakes, and *farinha seca*. After three months, the family began eating some types of meat but continued to refrain from eating heavy deer and paca meat. As Liliana explained, "if we were to eat [the meat], he would get worse, his leg would rot [from the snakebite], and then he would be injured and even die." In this view, the embodied connection shared amongst family members helped Paolo Eduardo's snakebite wound heal and allowed him to develop shamanic abilities. Shortly afterward, Paolo Eduardo underwent a six-month period of food and sex prohibitions on his own and developed an intimate connection with his soul teacher. Liliana recounted her father's telling of his experience:

> He said that the soul cured his wound as well. So he took a large *resguardo*. He passed six months following the *resguardo*. From there, he transformed into a shaman. The soul encountered and met with him. Because his father, he was called Rodrigo, he was a big shaman; he was a master. [...] So everyone transformed into a shaman; Rodrigo delivered *kay* to him. Afterward, [Paolo Eduardo] was always being a good *kay*, a *kay-pej*.

By frequently undergoing the food and sex prohibitions, Paolo Eduardo allowed himself to become more attractive to and to engage perceptually with his deceased father's soul, who became his primary soul teacher. In order to "always be" or become a *kay-pej* like Paolo Eduardo, it is necessary to interact continually with a soul teacher. Initially, the soul teacher helps the novice shaman develop his heightened sensory abilities, especially the abilities to heal illnesses through a laying of the hands and blowing smoke technique and to communicate with plants, Plant-People, and animals. Just as a novice gardener becomes skilled in gardening through teachings from her or his living elders, a novice shaman learns the unique skills necessary to become a *kay* through lessons from his soul teacher, who is often a deceased relative. Ultimately, the type of relationship a shaman is able to develop with his nonhuman soul teacher is the defining characteristic of creating and maintaining shamanic powers. This is especially true for the ability to cure illnesses, since the soul teacher assists the shaman in removing the presence of dangerous souls that bring illness to living people in the village and garden spaces. While the other shamanic modalities of conversing with and transforming into nonhumans do not directly involve the soul teacher, the shaman is able to develop these abilities through the heightened perceptual powers learned from his soul teacher.

Not all shamans acquire the same level of shamanic powers, however, as the terms good shaman (*kay pej*) and regular shaman (*kay cahàc*) indicate. Shamans who develop particularly intimate relationships with their soul teachers are more likely to become *kay pej*, as are those who are more attractive and likeable to a deceased soul. Those who become skilled in other areas such as hunting and log racing also may have a higher likelihood of becoming especially good shamans. Paolo Eduardo, for example, was a particularly skilled log racer and hunter who regularly killed wild game for his family before he began developing shamanic abilities. Community members lament the decline of good Canela shamans in recent years, much as they point out the lack of skilled hunters. Fernando lamented to me one day that modern-day shamans lacked the powerful abilities and intimate connections with soul teachers that great shamans of the mythical–historical past developed:

> In the past, the shaman underwent a large, serious *resguardo* for eight to nine months, or even a year or fourteen months, to become very skilled. People who work in health become like this. They say that, back then, the shaman was very knowledgeable, very skilled, because he undertook a large *resguardo*. That is why the *mẽkarõ* gave the knowledge to these people. [...] This type of person cured illnesses and saved people at the same time, and they say that he could see thieves and find

things that had been stolen. Nowadays, shamans say, "I can see, I can imagine," but I do not think it is as it was before. These first shamans were transformed by the *mēkarõn*; the *mēkarõn* handed them their knowledge.

In this view, the shaman's relationship with his soul teacher is essential to developing and maintaining *kay* abilities. The shaman and soul teacher relationship is often friendly and helpful, similar to shamanic engagements with "spirit friends" found throughout lowland South America (Santos-Granero 2007:7–8). Yet while a shaman can make himself more attractive to the soul teacher by undergoing prolonged food and sex prohibitions, it is the souls who decide with whom they will become friendly and "hand their knowledge." The soul teacher's agency and intentionality are therefore of paramount importance to Canela shamanism. Novices and experts alike must strive to please and attract their soul teachers continually throughout their lives, in an ongoing process of becoming shamans in the Canela life-world.

Understanding Shaman–Animal Relationships

Through developing a close relationship with the soul teacher, expert shamans can develop the shamanic modality of transforming into non-humans, especially animals. This ability commonly is found in mythic story-telling yet is rarely available to contemporary shamans. Shamanic transformation into animals in the mythic–historical and recent past supported the well-being of individuals and the multispecies community as a whole. The transformative abilities of the great shaman Yah-wuh, for example, are highlighted in the mythical story of his life. In her telling of the mythic story, Liliana described his transformation into a bird:

> Yah-wuh was a great shaman who transformed [with the help of] a soul [*alma*; *karõ*], and that soul was also a master. Yah-wuh flew to another village, another Indian tribe. He brought back ornaments, artisanal crafts from the other Indians to our village. *Hàc jarati*—that headdress made from macaw feathers, he brought back from another village. He transformed into a parrot. The story of Yah-wuh is very beautiful. He talked with another shaman from another village. The other shaman had been saying, "I am more of a master than Yah-wuh. Call for him, I want to try out our master! I have the power of being a master, and he has the power as well. We will see who has more power!" The other shaman was from another village, from Porquinhos [the Apaniekra village], and he could see as well. [. . .] Yah-wuh made the same move-

ments as a bird that flies [flapping his arms]. Shortly after, Hukryc [the other shaman] also performed the same movement, and made baby bird feathers on his skin, similar to the feathers of a baby parrot. Yah-wuh waited to see the other shaman's power; his feathers had not emerged yet. When Hukryc was already covered in feathers, Yah-wuh saw his power. Then, Yah-wuh's feathers emerged on his arms and his entire body, all of a sudden. Shortly after, he began to fly. Hukryc remained rooted in the center, in the same manner, with only a small amount of feathers.

In Fernando's version of the mythic story, Yah-wuh transforms into multiple animals, including a bat, a hawk, and a rodent. He provided a similarly vivid description of the shaman's transformational abilities:

Yah-wuh opened his arms and flapped them, and they say that Yah-wuh's legs became covered in feathers, and then his whole body, until he had hawk feathers. He transformed into a hawk. He jumped and rose into the air, circling and circling, until he disappeared. His friend [the other shaman] also opened his arms and flapped, but only a few feathers covered his legs—he did not fly or disappear, and only became a real fool! While Yah-wuh's people remained there, Yah-wuh had already arrived at the other group's village. Yah-wuh lay peanuts in the sun, transformed into a parrot, and grabbed some food. "Ah, now that I already took different foods, now I have strengthened myself," [Yah-wuh said]. He saw the large *cocá*, [type of ornament]. "There, that is mine; I am going to grab this *cocá*." Then, Yah-wuh transformed into a type of small rodent, and next he transformed back into a hawk. He passed once, twice, and the head of the household said, "that hawk is passing by; I know that he will grab this *cocá*!" Yah-wuh grabbed the large *cocá* and flew away to a very tall palm tree to sit on a large branch. Everyone began shooting at him with arrows, until Yah-wuh brought this *cocá* to our people.

The great shaman was able to develop this transformational ability through the relationship with his soul teacher, the "master" that Liliana mentioned, and through extensive restrictive periods that Fernando described:

Yah-wuh underwent a large *resguardo*—he did not eat anything heavy, only sweet potato, peanut, and white maize—these are the foods that he ate. That is why Yah-wuh perceived a great amount of knowledge. [...] Those who undergo a great *resguardo* can perceive. They see everything; only they know.

With his heightened ability to perceive and "see," Yah-wuh was able to transform into animals to assist the Canela human community. By becoming a parrot, hawk, and rodent, Yah-wuh accesses each of these animals' perspectives in order to bring back ritual ornaments that remain significant to the Canela community today. This type of shamanic ability is characteristic of the shamanic "perspectivism" of accessing the point of view of another being, typically an animal, that can be found throughout lowland South America (Viveiros de Castro 1998, 2011). Yet this kind of perspectival engagement with animals is rare in the contemporary Canela life-world. The perceptual abilities necessary to transform are so great that few modern-day shamans can achieve this transformational state. When I asked if Reinaldo had ever possessed the shamanic modality of transforming into nonhumans, he responded, "no, not me, I do not have the ability," reiterating that his powers included conversing with nonhumans, especially plants and Plant-People, and curing illnesses. He did maintain that contemporary shamans continue to "talk about" transforming into animals and even plants (although this is the only instance I found of the possibility of shamanic transformation into plants). Similar to Reinaldo, other shamans in the village typically were known for their healing powers and communicative relationships with plants.

In the recent past, only Paolo Eduardo was known for developing the transformative power. Through the training and assistance he received from his father's soul, and through undergoing many long restrictive periods, Paolo Eduardo acquired the ability to transform into a snake. Liliana recounted that her father transformed into a snake on two separate occasions. Each time, he first entered into a trance-like state, appearing to be lightheaded and "crazy" (*tonto* in Portuguese), and fell to the ground while foaming at the mouth. Then, he transformed into a snake. By accessing the perspective of the snake in this way, Paolo Eduardo became a master healer of snakebites. In 1984, for example, he cured his son-in-law João Miguel's rattlesnake bite, which is usually fatal. Liliana and João Miguel have recounted this dramatic experience to me many times, for they are still amazed that he survived. As Liliana described in October 2012:

> He [Paolo Eduardo] was the one who saved João Miguel. The snake bit him in 1984, and he was bad—his voice was not coming out, his eyes were blind, his mouth was dry. But when he [Paolo Eduardo] arrived in the middle of the road, he cured him. [...] My father became tired and was breathing slowly: "eh, eh, eh." He passed his hands all over João Miguel's skin. His skin was very tough. I did not think that João Miguel would escape death. [...] We made a [medicinal plant] remedy

of *krucare* that we put in the pan and cooked, and he drank the *kru-tuware* tea. And we passed *malagueta* pepper on the wound. In these ways, Paolo Eduardo removed the snake [from João Miguel's body]. And João Miguel escaped death, and even today he is still walking and working in the gardens.

Having gained access to the snake's perspective through transformation, Paolo Eduardo was able to "remove the snake" (*tirou a cobra*) from João Miguel's body, thereby curing him. Paolo Eduardo's shamanic transformation into a snake promoted the well-being of an individual and his family by enabling a man who likely would have died to continue living and working with his family in the gardens for decades. The physical toll of the transformation was great, and Liliana thinks that particular shamanic ability shortened her father's life span. Nevertheless, Paolo Eduardo was proud of his highly developed shamanic abilities, and Liliana recounted him telling her, "my daughter, I am doing this other transformation [because] I want to be a good *kay*. I want to help people."

In addition to perspectival transformations into animals, shamanic communication with animals also is intended to support individual and communal multispecies well-being. Shamans in mythical storytelling frequently converse with animals, especially during visits to animal villages. After their travels to animal communities, shamans often bring certain species' knowledge and ceremonial activities back to the Canela people. In one well-known story, for example, the mythical shaman Kruwapure visits the underwater village of the alligators and learns about the ritual songs and activities associated with the Wuh-tỳ festival from the alligators, including the alligator chief. With his heightened abilities of perception, Kruwapure is able to interact with the nonhuman alligators and bring their valuable ritual knowledge back to his own village. Fernando told me another story of a shaman in the past who discovered cashew trees by conversing with the parakeet (*krẽ-re*), to whom the trees belonged. This is similar to the mythical story of the discovery of annatto by a Canela man who conversed with macaw (see chapter 2, "Learning from Star-Woman: Origins of Horticulture and Biodiversity Maintenance"). Indeed, in the mythical–historical past everyone could converse with animals, plants, and objects and artifacts without developing particular heightened shamanic abilities.

In the contemporary Canela life-world, shamans who have developed their communicative abilities can converse with animals, although it is becoming less common than in the past as shamanic communication increasingly is focused on relationships with plants and Plant-People master spirits.

Contemporary shamans cannot visit animals in their otherworldly villages as in the mythical–historical past, but they can develop the ability to converse and interact with different animal species they encounter in the forest while hunting, fishing, or working in the garden plot. Reinaldo explained that "all animals, including large and small ones" can converse with a shaman. Shamanic encounters with animals typically are meant to support hunting activities, with the shaman able to speak with and listen to game animals in the forest. Shamans can hear the animals' responses to hunters, especially those who undergo their own restrictive periods to improve hunting abilities. Similar to how shamans can attract soul teachers through the food and sex prohibitions, hunters can become more attractive to animals by maintaining the restrictions and through the practice of steaming their eyes with herb-infused boiling water to develop the ability to "see" well (*intoo-kapôk*; literally "eye-flaming" [Crocker n.d.:3–4]) and engage with the animals they seek to kill. Shamans describe the animals' affectionate reactions to these skilled hunters, as Fernando described:

> They [the animals] say, "ah-ha! He is our father!" [...] The animals— the brocket deer [*Mazama gouazoubira* Fischer], the ema, they say, "our father is walking toward us. I am going to present myself; I am going to nestle up next to him." And another says, "no, I want to go first!" They [shamans] say that the animals are going to the presence of him [their father] in the forest. Those who do not maintain *resguardo* ... they say that the animals stay away in the distance, and say, "no one wants that person! I do not like him." And they stay away from him.

While the hunters themselves are attracting the animals with their beautiful and good appearance due to the restrictions they have undergone, only shamans can understand the animals' conversations and pass along this information to the hunter. Over the past century and especially over the past few decades, however, there has been a marked decline in Canela hunting activities. Fernando, Renato, and Wander explained the recent decline of hunting in terms of a sharp decrease in game animals in the territory and the loss of intergenerational hunting knowledge transmission. They maintained that non-Indigenous neighbors had invaded their lands and killed off most of the wild game. In addition, young people no longer are learning how to hunt from the older generations, preferring to purchase cow meat in town or from local cattle ranchers. Other young men also expressed to me their disinterest in hunting due to the threat of snakebite. Snakes live throughout the territory and hide in the thick brush of hunting areas. In January 2012, for example, a Canela man was killed by a snakebite while hunting in the forest alone, and his body was recovered days later. Only three or four men in the entire community were known as expert hunters in 2012–2013, and game meat rarely was found in daily meals. The consumption of game meat was still in decline as of late 2017. A similar decline in shaman animal encounters has followed suit, since shamanic abilities no longer are needed to mediate between human hunters and their animal prey. Instead, shamans increasingly are focusing their attention on plants and Plant-People master spirits. With the community relying almost entirely on garden produce for subsistence, shamanic communicative abilities with plants and mediation between gardeners and plants have become crucial to the survival and well-being of humans and nonhumans in the Canela life-world.

Shamanic Caring

Becoming Friend to Plants and Plant-People: Shamanic Friendship

Similar to human gardeners, shamans pay attention to the needs of plants growing in the garden space by developing sensory engagements with diverse crops throughout their life cycles. Shamanic care and affection for plants is markedly different than that of gardeners, however, due to the shaman's heightened sensory abilities that allow him to communicate with plants and Plant-People master spirits (the latter of whom do not appear to gardeners). In addition, the care and affection that shamans develop for plants and Plant-People is not modeled on the parent–child tie that connects human gardeners and their seeds, cuttings, and growing crops. Instead, shamans typically interact with plants and Plant-People through an affective mode of friendship. Canela shaman–plant engagements accord with Santos-Granero's (2007:2) understanding of friendship in native Amazonia, which he defines as "a type of interpersonal relationship in which the individuals involved—who may or may not be related by other kinds of ties—seek out each other's company, exhibit mutually helping behavior, and are joined by links of mutual generosity and trust that go beyond those expected between kin or affines." Canela shamans, plants, and Plant-People are friends in these ways, for they actively seek out trusting, generous relationships with each other that are centered on helping individual plants and people and the entire community as a whole survive and thrive. Moreover, with their unique sensory abilities, shamans are able to assist plants in ways that gardener parents, the consanguinal kin of plants, are unable to achieve.

As seen in Reinaldo's conversation with sweet manioc, plants speak directly with their shaman friends who have developed the shamanic modality of communicating with nonhumans. Since gardeners cannot converse with their plant children directly, plants typically tell the shaman the ways in which they are satisfied or dissatisfied with their lives in the garden space. Bitter manioc, for example, cries out to the shaman if it feels neglected. Reinaldo explained that bitter manioc cuttings, especially the root infants, tell him they "do not enjoy" being left lying on the ground by their gardener mothers. Similarly, the shaman Dirceu told their family that manioc would cry out in pain if ignored in this way, saying, "my mother treated me badly, I am in pain, I am sick, [the] mother left its child!" Sweet potato also complains to the shaman if carelessly left in the ground. Liliana recounted that Paolo Eduardo described newly planted maize crying "like a baby with a fever" when its parents ignored it and elicited the shaman for help. Plants also talk amongst themselves, and shamans can overhear these conversations if they are nearby. Different crop species and varieties "converse with each other," Reinaldo informed me. Fernando added that the crops "get together and discuss things; same as us!"

Plants that have become objects and artifacts around the house also converse with each other and with the shaman. These include especially objects and artifacts made from wood, palm, or other plant materials, such as wooden sticks, wooden mortars and pestles, the buriti palm roof and walls of a house, palm mats, tucum and other plant fibers, and gourd bowls and maracas. Dirceu told their granddaughter about their abilities to hear and converse with these processed plant objects in the middle of the night. The gourd bowls and maracas would greet Dirceu and each other with a *"hopââ"* (hello). Similar to growing plants, these objects inform the shaman of their needs or desires. The wooden pestle complains that it is "hungry" for rice, and the empty gourd bowl says it is thirsty because its mother (*inxê*) did not refill it with water. Dirceu was responsible for sharing the grievances of the object friends with other people in the household, and they in turn would heed the shaman's advice to improve the objects' satisfaction. While women and men do not consider these processed plant objects to be children as they do with growing plants, there is an element of the multispecies familial connection mediated by a shamanic friend that is found between gardeners and crops. Gardeners recognize the objects' intentionality and, with the assistance of the shaman's friendship with objects, strive to create a household environment that promotes their overall happiness and well-being.

As a friend to plants, it is the shaman's responsibility to listen to the growing crop species and varieties and bring their complaints to their gardener parents. Shamans usually visit the gardens of their close relatives, including those of their or their wife's family and nearby neighbors. When plants are unhappy or unwell, the shaman typically advises the gardener parents to pay more attention to and actively care for their plant children. This can usually be achieved through regular visits to the garden to weed, sing to, and perhaps engage in a food-sharing ritual with the growing crops (see chapter 3, "Sharing Food with Plants"). Sometimes certain species or varieties make particular requests that the shaman passes on, such as the manioc roots that wish to avoid the pain of lying in the hot sun and the sweet potato's preference to be stored in well-constructed holes underground. Shamans also advise gardeners to maintain a well-kept and tidy garden plot in order to prevent the unhappiness and suffering of their crop children. Heeding the shaman's advice, gardener parents can often re-establish the nurturing engagements that their crop children desire and thrive upon. When gardeners are truly negligent, ignoring the shaman's instructions and failing to engage in affectionate relationships with their growing crops in the long term, the plants can choose to relocate to another gardener's plot. Especially unhappy crops, including all the species and varieties, from one garden plot approach the shaman together. Reinaldo explained to Fernando that the crops tell him, "we are suffering a lot from our father [or mother]! Our father is not taking care of us. And there in the distance, in another location, there are others [crops] like us that are happier and cleaner! We are going to move there." In these cases, the dissatisfied crops will physically relocate to another garden plot where they will be happier, leaving their dried-out stalks and vines behind. Maize and manioc also leave behind their "hair." None of the crops will return to the plot during the growing season, leaving the gardener parents without a harvest. The shaman can see them walking by in the forest, and Reinaldo describes them walking and talking as people do.

To prevent a widespread relocation of crops and subsequent failed harvests, a shaman sometimes visits multiple gardens at a time to assess the overall happiness (or lack thereof) of crop children in general. He typically advises the male elders in the ceremonial center before and after his visit, as Fernando explained:

> The shaman tells the entire community in the patio [ceremonial center]: "look, no one should go to the garden today. I am going to review all the crops from every garden. Afterward, tomorrow, you all will see your own crops again." Everyone hears him and no one visits [his or her] garden. When it is the rice or maize season, or the season of anything new, the shaman goes to the gardens and grabs the [crops]. The maize has already sprouted and is already grown, and he pulls on the point of the leaf. He grabs it . . . [and] he says that Maize-Woman is

beautiful! He says that she has smooth, beautiful hair. Shamans who do these things see yam, sweet potato, everything. The shaman passes through the gardens until the afternoon, and then he returns to the patio, saying, "I have reviewed all your crops, and everything is well." […] He says that Cobra Bitter Manioc-Woman is also beautiful. He says that they are just like people! Without being a shaman, one cannot see [these things]. Only a shaman can see.

Both plants and Plant-People master spirits can converse with the shaman during his garden visits, as Fernando described. Indeed, the input of both plants and Plant-People is helpful for the shaman to determine the well-being of a garden's inhabitants. While the crops themselves relay specific, individualized complaints of feeling pain or sadness to the shaman, the Plant-People usually give him generalized advice on the caretaking of an entire species or variety. The Plant-People speak on behalf of the species or variety they represent and appear to the shaman as anthropomorphized, gendered versions of their particular species or variety. Shamans typically engage in communicative relationships with a diverse array of male and female Plant-People. As Reinaldo told me, all crops have a Plant-Man and Plant-Woman master spirit with whom the shaman can converse. Similarly, Paolo Eduardo told Liliana that he could "see" the Plant-Man and Plant-Woman associated with "every cultivated crop" in the garden. These include all crops that are currently grown in Canela gardens, whether they are classified as "aboriginal" or "introduced" (see chapter 4, "Expanding Multispecies Families"). As Reinaldo maintained, shamans can see and communicate with the Plant-People of aboriginal crops, such as maize, sweet and bitter manioc, sweet potato, yam, peanut, squash, rice, *pànkrỳt* bean, and cashew, as well as with the master spirits of crops considered to be introduced, including banana, pineapple, watermelon, and avocado. According to Reinaldo, all of the Plant-People are friendly and beautiful (*impej*) in their distinct ways. "They are both beautiful. The Plant-Men are handsome, and the Plant-Women are pretty," he said.

Overall, the Plant-Men are taller and larger than the shaman, while the Plant-Women are smaller. The Plant-Men and Plant-Women of maize in general and of different varieties such as true/original maize (*põhy pej-re*), large mixed-color maize (*põhy tohrom-ti*), and large red-yellow maize (*põhy caprêc-ti*) have all appeared to Reinaldo in different forms. These Plant-People exhibit characteristics similar to their representative species or variety. For instance, Paolo Eduardo explained to Liliana that True/Original Maize-Woman (*põhy pej-re cahãj*) has long blonde hair, similar to the crop's light-yellow tassel, while Red-Yellow Maize-Woman (*pōhy caprêc-ti cahãj*) has red hair similar to the red tassel of this type. He described another type of Maize-Woman as being very small, likely referencing the small maize variety (*pōhy kryi-re*). Paolo Eduardo also described in detail how the master spirits of manioc can be differentiated by their size, shape, and the "decorations" (*enfeites*) they wear. For example, Cobra Bitter Manioc-Woman (*kwỳr awari cahãj*) is known as being tall and beautiful with distinctive bright red "bracelets" around her leaf-arms, referencing the reddish color of this variety's leaves and stick. Meanwhile, Tortoise Arm Bitter Manioc-Woman (*kwỳr caprãn jũkee cahãj*) is short and stocky, similar to the short stick of this variety. Rice-People too appear with similar coloring as their particular varieties, such as small red rice, striped rice, and large white rice,[1] as Reinaldo described. He has "conversed" with all of these master spirits, as well as with the general Rice-Man (*arỳihy hũmre*) and Rice-Woman (*arỳihy cahãj*) of the species as a whole. Reinaldo also described one type of Fava Bean-Woman as having a painted face, which refers to many *pànkrỳt* bean varietals that are known as being "painted" (*pintado*).

The Plant-Men and Plant-Women of the same species or variety often interact with the shaman at the same time. Yam-Man and Yam-Woman, for example, both appear to the shaman in the garden plot. Yam-Man informs him where the yam crop has been planted in the ground, and they both tell him when the plants are born. When the yam crop is mature for harvesting, the master spirits tell Reinaldo, "we want to be cooked in the earthen oven." Bitter Manioc-Man (*kwỳr cahàc hũmre*) and Bitter Manioc-Woman (*kwỳr cahàc cahãj*) also appear in the garden together, although the male master spirit always speaks to Reinaldo before the female master spirit. Reinaldo described in detail his interactions with Maize-Man (*pōhy hũmre*) and Maize-Woman (*pōhy cahãj*):

> Reinaldo: [Maize-Woman says], "shaman! We are called maize and you will have a complete [harvest] . . . there will be the taste of maize for people to harvest, and there will be the [corncobs] for you to harvest, and the 'teeth' [*dentes*; corn kernels.]"
> Me: Does Maize-Man also speak to the shaman?
> Reinaldo: He speaks, he speaks with the shaman as well. "Shaman, do you know that we are here? You can speak, you can speak." So the shaman talks and talks. He waits until it is his time to say something and learn.

The purpose of these conversations, as Reinaldo states, is for the shaman to learn about the lives and well-being of the master spirits' representative crops. When Maize-Woman informs the shaman that there will be a good harvest, the shaman knows that the growing crops in that particular garden are being treated well by their gardener parents and are happy, strong, and overall well (*impej*). Similarly, Maize-Man alerts the shaman to the growing crop's presence to inform him that the maize is alive and well in the garden space. The Yam-People also alert the shaman to the crop's well-being throughout its birth, life, and even death by informing him of the crop's desire to be cooked after its natural life cycle has ended.

While the advice and instructions from the male and female master spirits are often similar, the relationships that the shaman forms with them typically fall along gendered lines. With Plant-Men, the shaman forms close friendships that are grounded in mutual respect and admiration, which are markedly different from the seductive affective mode between shamans and Plant-Women that the following section explores. Yam-Man shows the shaman where the yam crop is growing in a straightforward manner and Manioc-Man confidently approaches and speaks to the shaman first, telling him about the crop he represents. Meanwhile, Maize-Man directly informs the shaman of the crop's existence and asks him to engage in a long conversation in which both master spirit and shaman talk, listen, and learn from one another in friendly ways. The physical appearance of the Plant-Men draws respect and admiration from shamans as well—they are extremely tall, handsome, and attractive, having a beautiful (*impej*) anthropomorphized physique similar to an ideal Canela male warrior, hunter, log racer, ritual singer, or shaman who has undergone the appropriate food and sex prohibitions. Plant-Men approach the shaman as a master who can assist the crop species or variety they represent, and the shaman in turn shows his respect for the mastery of these male master spirits by listening to their requests and learning from them.

The serious, responsible relationships between Plant-Men and shamans are akin to Canela male formal friends (*hapĩn*). Formal friendships between men (and women, known as *pĩnxwỳj*) are serious relationships that are grounded in mutual respect and friendly care. Formal friends can be of different genders and of different generations, and nowadays Canela people often use the terms "godfather" (*compadre*) and "godmother" (*comadre*) in Portuguese as a gloss for formal friend relationships. Transformations in these relationships continue to take place, especially concerning the formal initiation of the friendship through a gift-giving ritual that is sometimes called a "baptism" (*batismo*) nowadays. Yet the essence of formal friendships remains the same—namely, a "great respect" for and "defense" of one's formal friend, as Liliana described. Formal friends are serious with one another, they "do not play, they do not speak badly, they do not look at each other in the face ... they have to keep their heads down, they cannot look" at one another, Liliana told me. Formal friends practice empathy toward one another, to the point of sharing in another's pain or suffering. As Liliana explained, if a formal friend becomes hurt or wounded from a burn or bee sting, the other friend also should wound himself in an act of solidarity with the other's suffering. Additionally, a formal friend is responsible for arranging his counterpart's funeral and burial in the cemetery, underlining the respectful nature of the relationship (see also Crocker 1990:177, 299–301). The relationships that form between shamans and Plant-Men broadly follow the parameters of formal friendship, namely the focus on serious, respectful interactions and mutual empathy. Shamans and Plant-Men do not joke with one another and engage mainly in direct conversations about the serious matter of crop life and death. Shamans show empathy and friendly care for Plant-Men with their interest in and advocacy for the well-being of the crop species or variety that the master spirit represents. In turn, Plant-Men display empathetic care for the shaman by asking him questions and inviting him to speak. As friendly shamanic engagements with plants in general have become more significant to the Canela life-world, so too have the formal friendships that develop between shamans and Plant-Men master spirits. Both of these friendly relationships are necessary for successful harvests and the overall happiness and well-being of Canela people and plants.

Seducing Shamans: The Plant-Women

Seductive engagements between shamans and Plant-Women master spirits are also essential for human and plant well-being and abundant harvests. The relationships that shamans form with Plant-Women are distinct from the formal friendships they develop with Plant-Men in terms of the physical connection and in terms of the type of communication that develops. Firstly, while shamans engage with Plant-Men's "bodies" in terms of physical qualities and characteristics they respect and admire, their engagements with Plant-Women are usually centered on the female master spirits' physical beauty and sexual attractiveness. Indeed, shamans describe and emphasize their encounters with sexually attractive Plant-Women's bodies. Renato's father Edcar, who became a shaman later in his life, vividly described to Renato his experience with beautiful female master spirits. While planting sweet manioc in his forest garden one afternoon, Edcar suddenly fainted. When he awoke, three beautiful Sweet Manioc-Women had appeared in front of him and began talking to him. The Sweet Manioc-Women seduced him with their beauty and flirtatious remarks, all the while informing him of the happiness and well-being of each of their representative varieties. Reinaldo also described the physical attractiveness of Sweet Manioc-Woman (*kwỳrỳre cahãj*), with her very white, almost transparent skin and hair, and of Bitter Manioc-Woman with similar long, white hair. He commented on the tall height and attractive darker skin tone (*morena*) of Peanut-Woman (*caahy cahãj*) as well, perhaps referencing the length of the peanut vine and the brownish color of harvested peanuts. Banana-Woman (*pypyp-re cahãj*) is also tall and beautiful, referencing the height of many banana varietals. For many shamans, including Reinaldo and Paolo Eduardo, Maize-Woman is the "most beautiful," with long, shiny hair similar to the corn tassel. Liliana recounted Paolo Eduardo's descriptions of Maize-Woman's beauty with long, flowing white hair and perfect teeth, referencing the corn tassel and straight rows of kernels. The Plant-Women of certain varietals also display unique beauty and charms that attract the shaman. Cobra Bitter Manioc-Woman elegantly wears her red "bracelets" around her leaf-arms to display her connection with the varietal she represents, while Tortoise Arm Bitter Manioc-Woman displays a different kind of attractiveness with her short height and full figure. Meanwhile, True/Original Maize-Woman and Large Red-Yellow Maize-Woman show off their brilliant blond and red locks, respectively. The type of Painted Fava Bean-Woman that Reinaldo described has a unique beauty with her "painted face," and he laughed and smiled when fondly remembering this Plant-Woman in particular. Overall, the Plant-Women display diverse beauty that reflects the wide array of crop species and varieties they represent. Shamans are attracted to the diversity of these master spirits, whether they are tall and darker-skinned as Peanut-Woman appears, short and stocky as Tortoise Arm Bitter Manioc-Woman is described, or anything in-between.

Secondly, the type of communication between shamans and master spirits develops along gendered lines. While the shaman and Plant-Man engage in serious, direct conversations, the shaman and Plant-Woman converse in flirtatious, indirect ways. Reinaldo described the coy, flirtatious way that Sweet Potato-Woman (*jàt cahãj*) typically interacts with him:

> Sweet potato also has a woman, and she is beautiful! "Hey, shaman, I am going to be sweet potato. I live here too" [she says]. "Good, you can live there" [the shaman responds]. She enters the earth, and the tuber grows well ... until there is a huge sweet potato. The woman of sweet potato [says], "hey, shaman, I am going to be sweet potato. Do

you think I am pretty?" "Yes, I am thinking you are pretty!" [the shaman answers]. "I am tasty (*gostosa*), same as sugar itself" [she says].

Playfully asking for compliments from the male shaman, Sweet Potato-
Woman describes herself as *gostosa*, which is a euphemism in Portuguese for
being sexually attractive that plays on the dual meaning of the word "tasty."
Reinaldo also described Squash-Woman (*cuhkõn cahàc cahãj*) as *gostosa*, again
referring to the master spirit's sexual desirability as well as the tastiness of
the squash crop's pulp. Through indirect, joking conversations with the shaman, the Plant-Women entice the shaman to listen to their suggestions and
instructions regarding their representative species and varieties. In the instance described above, Sweet Potato-Woman reminds the shaman where
her crop is living while simultaneously pointing out her sexual desirability.
Through coy and playful flirtations, Sweet Manioc-Woman similarly advises Reinaldo where she and her crop are going to live before disappearing
into the earth. Sweet manioc plants themselves, which are categorized as
feminine, are also seen as beautiful, calm, soft, and sexually attractive (see
chapter 3, "Sharing Food with Plants"). Yet encounters with Plant-Women
are more memorable than with feminine plants on account of the master
spirits' anthropomorphized bodies that shamans can easily desire. Their soft
hair, tall or short stature, elegant decorations, or beautiful skin tone initially
entice the shaman, and their joking, flirtatious conversations seduce him
further. When describing these joking conversations, Reinaldo smiled and
laughed as he remembered the Plant-Women's beauty and bold, sexualized
behavior. He and other shamans express their excitement at encountering
and flirting with a stunningly beautiful Plant-Woman in the garden, and
they seek out future engagements with her more frequently than they do
with their Plant-Men formal friends.

Rather than a formal friendship, the relationship between shamans and
Plant-Women is more akin to that of Canela classificatory spouses or "other
spouses" (*mẽ prõ-nõ* = "wife others"; *mẽ mpyên-nõ* = "husband others"; see
Crocker 1990:258). These relationships form between men and women who
are not related as consanguines, affines, or as formal friends. Unlike the relationship between spouses, which is typically more serious and formal, other
spouses freely engage in playful, sexualized joking with one another. They
also engage in extramarital sex, usually in and around forest gardens at a
distance from the village space. While there are certain times when sexual
relationships with other spouses are discouraged, for example when a couple
is undergoing food and sex prohibitions for their fetus or infant, these rela-

tionships are common and pursued by both men and women. During certain ritual periods such as the male initiation ritual complex, extramarital affairs are publicly encouraged by the male leadership council, who mandate that husbands and wives must leave aside their "jealousies" to allow for sexual relationships with other spouses to take place (see Crocker 1990:270–275). The Plant-Women are other wives to shamans in that they engage in sexualized joking relationships in forest and riverbank garden spaces, away from the village where the relationship between husbands and wives, and the husband's connection to his wife's household, are more pronounced. And while the Plant-Women do not engage in sexual relations with the shaman, their engagements are often described in similar ways as romantic trysts in garden plots. Just as men walk toward their garden plots alone for a romantic encounter with their other wives, shamans seek out and can even faint from being in the presence of the beautiful Plant-Women with their desirable anthropomorphized master spirit bodies. As sexually attractive other wives who entice the shamans to listen to their requests and return for future conversations, the Plant-Women are effective master spirits for the crop species and varieties they represent. Plant-Men can also effectively communicate their crops' needs to the shaman through formal friendships, but the seduced shaman may be more likely to listen to the beautiful, "tasty" Plant-Women's instructions and advice.

Caring for Plants and Their Masters

The intimate relationships that develop between and among shamans, plants, and Plant-People are grounded in care, affection, and mastery. The shaman develops care and affection for plants, Plant-Men, and Plant-Women in distinct ways. Shamanic care for growing plants is grounded in friendship with "familial others" (Santos-Granero 2007:2), since both plants and people form part of Canela multispecies families. While shamans with their heightened sensory capacities do not form parental bonds with growing plants (although they do so when acting in their capacities as male gardeners in their own plots), their friendships with plants support and help maintain individual human and plant families and the entire Canela community, also considered a family in a broad sense. Meanwhile, shamanic care for Plant-Men master spirits incorporates a ritualized component through formal friendship. Jê formal friendships are included in the "familial others" sphere, since people forming these bonds are often related through consanguinity or affinity. Shamans and Plant-Men are related as kin in a broad sense, as part of the overarching multispecies family of Canela people and plants. Finally, Plant-Women enter into relationships with shamans not as friends but rather as other wives, those who are not related as consanguines and therefore appropriate for engaging in flirtatious sexual joking.

The relationship between the Plant-People master spirits and the plants they master is grounded in care and affection yet also incorporates an element of mastery and control. Relationships of mastery or ownership are found throughout Indigenous lowland South America, including master spirits of "the forest, the animals, the rivers, and lakes, but also of an animal species, a plant species, or that bamboo grove, that curve of the river, a certain tree, or a particular mountain" (Fausto 2008:340; my translation). Yet as Carlos Fausto points out, the relationship between master and mastered is asymmetrical (Fausto 2008:333; my translation): "the masters (donos) control and protect their creatures, being responsible for their well-being, reproduction, mobility. The asymmetry implies not only control, but care." Master spirits that control and care for plants in particular can be found across the region. The Paumari of Amazonas State, for example, consider all entities, including plants, to have the potential to adopt human form, which is considered a type of owner or master (dono-mestre; Bonilla 2007:51; Fausto 2007:346). In many communities of northwest Amazonia, there are "master plants" that own or control plants with hallucinogenic or psychotropic properties, including ayahuasca (Banisteriopsis caapi [Spruce ex Griseb.] C. V. Morton) and tobacco (Nicotiana rustica L.) (see Fausto 2008; Barbira Freedman 2010). There are also master spirits for cultivated plants, such as the spirit-goddess Nunkui, who is the mother and owner of manioc gardens and the plants themselves among the Jivaro Achuar of the Ecuadorian Amazon (Descola 1998; Taylor 2001). Shamanic engagement with these master spirits is often necessary to facilitate the use of the mastered plants. For the Yekuana of Venezuela and Brazil, the master spirit (or collective of spirits) Yododai controls and "jealously guards" the type of cane used to make baskets (Fausto 2008:340). While people can identify the presence of Yododai by its distinctive smell and song, the master spirit is invisible to anyone but shamans, and shamanic intervention is therefore required to obtain the plants used for the community's basket-making purposes safely (Guss 1989: 127–128, 131–132). Meanwhile, shamans among the Lamista Quechua of the Peruvian Upper Amazon form relationships with the "mother spirits" of certain medicinal plants, including "water plants" that require the shaman to form a seductive relationship with a "water wife," a female water spirit (Barbira Freedman 2010:156–159).

Engagements between Canela Plant-People master spirits, their representative crop species and varieties, and shamans display another variation

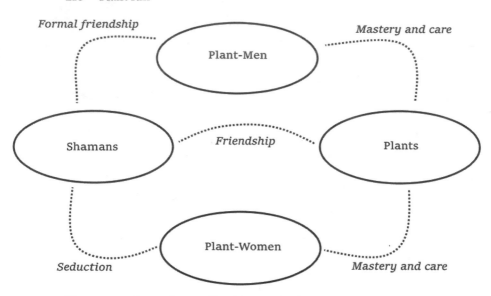

Formal friendship

Mastery and care

Plant-Men

Shamans

Friendship

Plants

Plant-Women

Seduction

Mastery and care

Diagram 5. Shamanic care, friendship, and seduction.

on the Amazonian master spirit–plant theme. The Plant-Men and Plant-Women exhibit care and affection for the growing crops they represent and master, and they form communicative relationships with shamans in order to support their crops' happiness and well-being. Nevertheless, the Plant-People are not considered the mothers or fathers of the growing crops. And although shamanic involvement with plants and Plant-People is necessary for abundant harvests, the Plant-People do not guard their plants from human use or consumption. Rather, the Plant-People seek out engagements with the shaman to encourage plant–human relationships that will result in happy, healthy, and holistically well plants and people. Moreover, while the Plant-Women as "other wives" to the shaman is strikingly similar to the La-mista Quechua "water wives," the spirits themselves are more closely tied to their mastered plants in appearance and likeness. The "water wives" are "mermaids" and underwater animals such as phosphorescent fish, anacon-das, and boas (Barbira Freedman 2010:159), while Canela Plant-Women are anthropomorphized versions of the plants they master. Canela shamans, plants, and Plant-People develop intimate, caring relationships that are distinct among lowland South American communities. Their engagements emerge along relational pathways of multispecies care and kinship that support and maintain the unfolding Canela life-world as a whole (see diagram 5).

Shamanic Mediating: Dangers in the Gardens

Approaching Dangerous Forests and Dangerous Souls

The affective modes of friendship and seduction are central to caring shamanic engagements with plants and their master spirits in forest and riverbank garden spaces. Indeed, gardens themselves are places where multispecies care is broadly developed and maintained between human gardener parents and their plant children. The village also is understood as a place of consanguinal and affinal kinship and care, developed mainly through consubstantial relationships among human adults and children, as well as between human gardeners and seed infants. Yet unlike the village, which is generally understood as a safe space for multispecies inhabitants of the Canela life-world, gardens are also potentially dangerous spaces for humans and plants. Garden plots, and especially forest gardens, can be home to dangerous animals, people, and deceased souls. The live forest (*ivẽntũm*), old forest (*iromtũm*), old land (*pjêhtũm*), and true forest (*caxàt-re kô*) areas in the territory, and the forest gardens maintained within them, are rife with potentially dangerous beings. Shamans engage with some of these entities through the affective mode of danger to protect the multispecies Canela community from ongoing threats. Other entities are considered too dangerous even for shamanic intervention, and relations with them should be avoided in the forested areas where they reside.

Forest gardens and the vicinity of forested areas are home to animals that can pose real danger to humans. Jaguars have been known to roam the real forest land type, and João Miguel told me he saw a jaguar in this region when he was a young man. Snakes are also commonly found in the forested areas, and the threat of snakebite is ever present. Gardeners take great care in planting the *fava danta* plant, which is thought to repel snakes, in the corners of their forest garden plots, and they usually burn small paths leading to the plots since snakes prefer to hide in long grasses. Nevertheless, snakes can still enter garden areas. In November 2017, for example, João Miguel found and killed a baby rattlesnake in the garden during one of my visits there, telling me that this was a common occurrence in garden plots. Hunters are also at risk of encountering a snake in the grasses, and indeed many young men have told me they do not like hunting in densely forested areas for fear of snakes. Shamans are responsible for mediating between snakes and humans through curative healing techniques that remove the snake venom from a person's body, as Paolo Eduardo's healing of João Miguel's rattlesnake bite demonstrates. Without shamanic mediation, snake–human encounters can have deadly effects, an example being the man who died from a snakebite while walking alone in the forest in early 2012. While shamans are not always immediately available to heal snakebite, their potentially curative abilities give comfort to many women and men who regularly visit their forest garden plots.

In these same forested areas, danger also lurks in the form of non-Indigenous white people (*cupēn*). While not all whites pose a threat to Canela people, centuries of violence in the region continues to inform contemporary *mēhĩn–cupēn* relations. For example, in 2002 there was an ongoing violent dispute over the death of a white man who was supposedly killed by a Canela man in a neighboring white village (the Canela man fled the territory shortly after the killing occurred). Canela families became afraid of visiting their forest gardens for fear of retribution by the white man's family. Their fears were confirmed in 2005, when, as Renato vividly described, someone from the dead white man's family killed a fourteen-year-old Canela boy to avenge the relative's death. Owing to the real danger present in forest garden plots during this time, some families had not visited nor cared for their crops, and a widespread period of half-hunger (*meia-fome*) occurred as a result. Since 2012, some whites (with the assistance of a few Canela people) have been illegally logging native hardwood tree species from live forest areas throughout the territory. In 2017, the logging had spread to a prime forest garden area in the northern part of the territory, and gardeners were afraid to return to their plots for fear of disturbing the loggers' activities. Although some Canela people showed me where the logging was taking place on a map, it is difficult to discuss the issue without putting one's own and others' lives in danger, as logging cabals are notoriously violent in the region. The dangerous reality of violence with impunity against Indigenous peoples and others working on territorial land rights and environmental issues in the northeast reflects national trends in Brazil. The rate of assassinations of Brazilian environmental and land defenders has increased exponentially over the last decade and a half, with the main perpetrators of the killings loggers, local landowners, and their hired hitmen (Global Witness 2015:18–19). In 2016 alone, forty-nine land and environmental defenders were assassinated in Brazil, many of them members of Indigenous communities, and the logging industry was definitively linked to sixteen of these murders (Global Witness 2017). Hitmen for loggers and landowners are active in the interior of Maranhão, and the Canela are aware of their presence and the violent acts they regularly commit for hire. In these ways, the presence of living whites brings substantial danger and the threat of violence to Canela forested areas. Shamans are not seen as responsible for mediating *mēhĩn–cupēn* relations; indeed, some *cupēn* are seen as too untrustworthy, deceitful, and "stingy" (*hõ-xỳ*) for sustained interaction and generally should be avoided. Yet powerful political leaders sometimes demonstrate their shamanic *kay* abilities in their engagements with non-Indigenous outsiders. Chief Doroteo Hàktookhot, who led the community from 1935 to 1951 during an intense period of contact with government officials and the anthropologist Curt Nimuendajú, was also a well-known shaman who displayed his shamanic prowess to outsiders through individual and communal healing rituals (Nimuendajú 1946: 237). The shaman Reinaldo led the 1982 messianic movement and used his shamanic authority to dictate how the Canela should be interacting with outsiders, as well as to predict future *mēhīn–cupēn* relations (see chapter 2, "Gardening: A Brief History, 1814–Present"). Thus, while shamanic intervention with living *cupēn* is rare, shamans occasionally mediate between the Canela and outsiders when they conceive it as beneficial to the Canela community.

In contrast, shamans should avoid the deceased souls of white people at all costs. Known as *pehjarohti*, these deceased white souls are understood as being especially dangerous and deceitful. Canela encounters with them, while uncommon, occasionally can take place in remote forest regions. Pursuing ongoing relationships with these white souls, as some shamans have been known to do, almost certainly will have dire consequences for the individual shaman, his family, and the entire community. Liliana explained that the white souls particularly "enjoy" deceiving and disturbing (*mexendo* in Portuguese) living Canela people, especially shamans who have developed the perceptual capabilities to see and listen to the white soul's false promises of wealth and power. Shamanic encounters with white souls usually result in the deaths of the shaman's family members and/or himself. Liliana told the story of her grandfather Rodrigo's encounter with a white soul long ago:

Rodrigo was a great shaman. One day, he was hunting in the forest. There is a large hill there that is very beautiful, and there is a large hole inside it. Rodrigo was hunting inside the hole of this hill. The peccary was running in the middle of the brush, and Rodrigo grabbed his knife to kill this animal; he cut the peccary, but did not catch it. [Suddenly], a can of money appeared! I do not know why the animal transformed into a can of money. Rodrigo said to himself, "what is this?" He grabbed it, wrapped it in a cloth, and began walking away. The owner of the money whispered, "*psiu, psiu!*" "Who is doing that?" Rodrigo asked himself. [...] Then, a white person appeared—he seemed like a living person, but he was a *pehjarohti*. "Ah-ha, you have my money! Give it to me and I will take care of it for you. You will receive it; I will not take it from you. Go home; build and renovate your house, and then I will mark a day for you to take all the money." Rodrigo gave the money to the white soul, and the soul said, "now you are *mine!*"

Despite the white soul's promise that he would return the money, Rodrigo visits the same hill multiple times to collect it and comes back to the village empty-handed. When he finally receives the money and brings his family to a nearby white town to purchase meat, his sons spend it on *cachaça* liquor and get into an altercation with their father. Rodrigo and his daughter died shortly thereafter, and the family blamed both deaths on Rodrigo's encounter with the deceptive white soul. Liliana describes the effect the white soul's relationship with her grandfather had on her family:

> Rodrigo died, and then his daughter died. It is very sad; it is a great sadness. There are people that speak about these things; that the ways of the white souls are like this. They enjoy deceiving people. [. . .] If people trust them, their whole family will die! The white soul receives the family. It is frightful! Because the white soul will give the money, but soon after he will want to receive payment. He does not want the family's things; he wants the family itself!

Through its false promises of wealth and power, the white soul enticed Rodrigo into a dangerous relationship that came with a high price to himself and his family. Crocker (n.d:12) similarly describes how white souls tend to engage in trickery and deceit and often kill the shaman's relatives. There is no chance of mediation between the Canela community and the *pehjarohti*, for these entities thrive on the destruction of the Canela life-world writ large. In a sense, they are hyper-*cupẽn*, seeking complete control and eventual annihilation of living Canela bodies and social relations that the centuries of structural violence perpetrated by living *cupẽn* have not achieved. Avoiding the *pehjarohti* and the deep forested regions they occupy is the best defense against these dangerous beings for Canela shamans and the community as a whole.

The souls of deceased Canela people (*mẽkarõn*), on the other hand, hold a more ambiguous place in the life-world (or rather life-and-death-world). The *mẽkarõn* are certainly dangerous entities, especially for living Canela who do not possess shamanic abilities. Canela souls also reside in forested areas, including forest garden plots, and they desire to bring living souls back with them to the "land of the dead," a world that is understood as existing in parallel to the Canela life-world. In this death-world, the deceased souls exist in a manner similar to living Canela, engaging in everyday activities such as eating and having sexual intercourse. However, as Crocker and Crocker (2004: 86) note, the souls perform these activities with "less pleasure" than their living counterparts do. Reinaldo expanded on the human-like attributes of deceased souls, explaining that the souls appear to a shaman as the "same type as a person"; that is, with similar attributes as living Canela people. Unlike living humans, however, the souls do not possess bodies per se. As disembodied entities, they can exist in multiple locations simultaneously. Fernando described the omnipresent and transformational nature of souls the following way:

> The "life" of *mẽkarõn*—the shaman says that today, they are here [in the territory]. However, if they want to travel, at the same time as they are here, they are in Barra [do Corda]; they are in São Luís perhaps. The life of the *mẽkarõn* is like this—it is similar to energy, a telephone, a phone call—it is quick and light.... They can walk. In addition, they say that *mẽkarõn* observe from a long distance. [...] They fly as well. They transform into birds; they transform into any type of thing in any way. [...] Even if the door is closed or locked with a key, they pass through and enter [the house]! Nothing impacts them; nothing interferes with them.

As Fernando described, the *mẽkarõn* can transform into anything, anytime—including animals, plants, and objects. This transformational ability is perhaps their most dangerous aspect to living people, since those without shamanic abilities rarely can detect which animals or plants are transformed souls. Only shamans with heightened perceptual abilities can see the deceased souls as transformations of plants and animals or as disembodied soul entities that appear "similar to people." The souls often seek out engagements with living people in their transformed states, and shamans are responsible for informing people when a particular animal or plant is a transformed *mẽkarõn*. Shamans in Liliana's family, for example, taught her that a hunted game animal that is dry inside is a transformation of a deceased Canela soul. Liliana and Fernando also described how souls often transform into the *têhtê* bird and sing its song, "*têh-tê, têh-tê*" at midnight to "invite" the souls of living relatives to the death-world.

Canela souls also can transform into plants, including all cultivated crops.[2] Souls often transform into sweet and bitter manioc, and in this form attempt to take living women, girls, and infants with them to their death-world. Liliana and her daughters are well aware of the dangers that souls transformed into manioc pose. Women carrying infants, they explained, should not walk nearby sweet manioc because the plants will take the child's living soul. Nor should women with infants harvest sweet manioc roots, for the "milk" is dangerous to the child. If a woman has planted only bitter manioc in her forest or riverbank garden plot, she should refrain from walking in the middle of the row because the *mẽkarõn* will grab her and make her ill. Bitter manioc leaves can also grab small children if they are nearby, causing serious illness. In these instances, the soul occupies the bitter manioc plant, using its plant body parts (stalk and leaves) to grab women and children's souls. Manioc plants also can suffer from being occupied by souls, since gardeners, upon advice from shamans, will actively avoid taking care of crops that are thought to be currently transformed souls. Held temporarily hostage by the souls and their desires, the manioc plant children do not receive the caring, affectionate relationships they require from their gardener parents.

At the same time, soul occupation of garden plants also can be beneficial to people and plants through improving crop harvests. Souls that temporarily transform or "enter" into one's crops, Liliana informed me, can result in a "famous garden" (*roça famosa*); that is, one with an abundant harvest.

> They say that [the souls] transform [into crops] and then leave, and the crops become very famous. [...] I asked my father, "why do these souls enter into the middle of these crops?" "The *mẽkarõn* only make movements within our crops. Even sweet potato—the *mẽkarõn* transform into sweet potato and shortly thereafter, they leave. They only transform and then leave again for other places. Because the *mẽkarõn* are very different, they are very complicated. They will transform in one place, and at the same time, they will go somewhere else. And you will never see it." My father told me this!

In garden spaces, the *mẽkarõn* are therefore ambiguous entities that can use their abilities, particularly their transformation into plants, in two main ways. Either the souls-transformed-into-plants support the health and well-being of Canela people and plants by creating abundant harvests or they inflict bodily harm, illness, and even death of people, by grabbing their souls, and of plants, through neglect by gardeners who are avoiding soul-filled gardens. Even when the *mẽkarõn* help improve crop harvests, however, their presence in the garden is still potentially dangerous to people without shamanic abilities. To protect oneself from being grabbed by the *mẽkarõn* in forest garden plots and other forested regions, living people typically paint themselves prior to visiting these areas. Liliana explained how the body paint changes the souls' perception of living bodies:

> [My father] always said . . . if you visit the garden, you have to paint [yourself] with *pau de leite* [*aramhôc*]; you have to cut your hair; you

have to paint your whole family. If you all do not do this, a soul [karõ] will see you there and think, "ah-ha! Another karõ is here without body paint, let us take the children with us!" Then, it will grab the children [the children's souls], and you will never know—you cannot see it, because you are blind to it.

With body paint, the souls recognize the integrity of the living body and typically do not approach the person. Conversely, visiting forested areas without the protective body paint puts a person in danger of being "seen" by the souls as of the same kind, another soul who belongs in the land of the dead. Although people such as Liliana who do not possess shamanic abilities cannot see the deceased souls themselves, shamans such as her father warn them of the dangers posed by souls, and souls-turned-plants, in forested areas.

Aware of the risks involved in visiting forest gardens and growing crops, especially manioc, gardeners know they can call on shamans for assistance if someone in their family is grabbed by a soul or transformed soul-turned-manioc-plant. Those who have been affected by soul-grabbing will become ill as their soul travels to the death-world. If the deceased souls who reside there convince the living soul to stay with them and, especially, eat with them, the person's living body will die. Fernando explained the serious effects of a "missing" or "traveling" soul for a living Canela person:

> It is dangerous. That is why, when a person's soul is far away, he feels weakness, he only likes to sleep, and when he sits up, soon after he will be almost asleep again. People say that when the karõ is far away, a person becomes like this. He is partly weak, and becomes sad and angry, because his karõ is not with him.

Shamans are responsible for returning the living soul to the person's body through performing the healing techniques of laying hands and/or blowing tobacco smoke. In the shamanic healing ritual, a shaman calls upon the assistance of his soul teacher to bring back the ill person's soul from the death-world, underscoring the ambiguous nature of the mẽkarõn as agents of illness and death as well as healing. Reinaldo described his experiences of healing as difficult encounters with both dangerous souls and his helpful soul teacher. With his heightened perceptual abilities, Reinaldo can see the souls who are trying to take the ill person's soul with them to the land of the dead. He tells the patient's family they must take special care of the ill person because his or her soul is not currently in the body. During the curing ritual, Reinaldo places his fingers and hands over the person's body and blows tobacco smoke to "remove the sickness and throw it away," as he described. Reinaldo then invites his soul teacher to help him search for the patient's living soul in the death-world, while telling the other deceased souls to "stay away and leave us [the living *mẽhĩn*] alone." The powerful force of his soul teacher's assistance in curing the ill patient is physically challenging for Reinaldo, throwing him to the ground and making him appear temporarily dead. Afterward, the shaman regains consciousness and both he and the patient should be healed and well (*impej*) again. The deceased souls' ambiguity is ever present in shamanic healing, since the shaman must engage with both dangerous *mẽkarõn* that seek to kill the living soul (and potentially the shaman himself) and the helpful *karõ* soul teacher that assists the shaman in a beneficial yet physically taxing encounter.

Shamanic healing is an integrated soul–body experience, involving both the soul (*karõ*) and the body or flesh (*hĩn*) of the shaman and of the ill person. Shamans engage all of their bodily senses during the curing ritual, including heightened vision to see the patient's living soul and deceased souls in the death-world, hearing to listen to and converse with the souls, touch to lay hands on the infirm person's body, and taste and smell to inhale and blow tobacco smoke. A shaman's own soul is involved in this curative process as well, and it must be strengthened through regular interactions with his soul teacher in order to visit the death-world without becoming ill. At the final moments of healing, the shaman's integrated soul–body is thrown to the ground by the sheer force of the connection between himself and his soul teacher.

The infirm person also experiences shamanic healing in both embodied and "ensouled" ways. The experience of Liliana's sister Marlena attests to this integrated body–soul connection in shamanic curing rituals. Over the first few months of 2012, Marlena became very ill, being unable to retain food for months on end. Her body was weak (*ihpêc*), and her physical frailty prevented her from leaving her house, visiting her relatives or gardens, and generally engaging in activities that promote happiness and strength (*ihtỳi*). Near the end of April, Liliana and her sister Camila decided that Marlena needed treatment by a young shaman named Wilson. Marlena's physical weakness was immense; she was skin and bones and unable to walk the short distance to Wilson's house. Her sisters transported her there in a wheelbarrow, concerned that she was near death. Once inside, Wilson placed his hands on Marlena's body and dripped water on her. Next, he blew smoke over her body while chanting. After performing these curing techniques, Wilson ran around the outside of his house a few times. He informed the family that the soul of their father, the famed shaman Paolo Eduardo, had taken Marlena's soul with him to the death-world, thereby leading to her physical weakness. Through the curing ritual he had performed, Wilson assured them he had returned Marlena's soul to her body. Sure enough, after that evening Marlena slowly recovered from her illness. Within weeks, she began eating, visiting her sisters' houses, and even making trips to her garden plots once again. The shaman's curing ritual healed her soul and her body by putting them back together again, as an integrated *karõ-hĩn* soul-body that defines a living person's existence.

While physical illnesses are often long term and caused by the soul's lengthy trip to the death-world, at other times a person's physical illness can occur rapidly due to the onset of a "sickly soul" (*adoentada de alma* in Portuguese). Wander recounted his wife Vilma's experience of a sickly soul to me, including the shamanic healing that quickly cured her. While watching a ritual log race one afternoon, Vilma suddenly collapsed, unconscious. Vilma's uncle, the shaman Antônio, rushed over to perform the curing ritual. He began smoking tobacco and fell to the ground, lying next to her. Antônio then touched Vilma's body with his hands while sweating profusely. Afterward, he quickly jumped up to a standing position, and she did the same. Vilma then had a drink of water and was immediately well (*impej*) again, as Wander described. Antônio explained that Vilma had been near death but that he had cured her by traveling to the land of the dead and retrieving her soul. By mimicking her collapse, laying his hands on her, and smoking, he was able to follow her soul and bring it back to her body. In this instance, Vilma's collapse represented a rapid break in her body–soul connection that could be repaired only through the shaman's expert curing techniques.

Although both of these shamanic healing experiences occurred in the village, souls do not usually visit the village space. Full of men, women, and children who often have their bodies painted in the protective deep black *pau de leite* and *jenipapo*, and brilliant red annatto (*urucum*) paste, the village is a space for the living and their combined body-souls. Initial encounters with deceased souls typically occur in distant garden plots and forested areas where the souls reside. Living people's souls more often are grabbed in these distant forest spaces by deceased souls transformed as birds, plants, or other nonhuman beings that live here. Afterward, the ill person returns to the village space, physically weakened by the temporary loss of his or her soul from the body and in need of shamanic healing. In the forest lurk dangerous deceased souls, as well as other beings that are threatening to people, plants, and the multispecies Canela community. Yet the forests and the deceased Canela souls also have the capacity for supporting multispecies well-being—

the forests as spaces where caring human–plant engagements can be created and maintained, and the souls as entities that can promote abundant harvests through transformations into cultivated crops. Incorporating qualities of both badness or danger, that which is *ihkên*, and goodness and well-being, that which is *impej*, the forests and the Canela souls who reside there are ambiguously part of the emergent life-world. Able to perceive the dangers of forested spaces and engage with dangerous deceased souls, shamans mediate between people and the potentially threatening forests and souls for the sake of the Canela life-world's ongoing continuation and survival.

Understanding Dangerous Shamans

Yet shamans themselves are also ambiguous figures, able to use their unique perceptual abilities to help or harm their own and other communities. Canela shamans today typically are celebrated for their ability to help and support the life-world, through communicative engagements with animals, objects, plants, Plant-People master spirits, and deceased souls and through curative healing rituals that draw upon shamanic relationships with soul teachers. These same abilities, however, potentially can be used to inflict harm, illness, and even death on a shaman's enemies. Whether helpful or harmful, the shamanic profession and shamanic abilities are known by the same term, *kay*, underscoring the ambiguity of the shaman's role. Although shamans who inflict harm on others are often known as "witches" (*feiticeiros* in Portuguese), there is only one term in Canela to describe both good and bad shamans. Revealing oneself or another as a bad shaman or witch is rare, since *kay* abilities intended for harmful purposes typically are developed in secret. Those who choose to use their *kay* abilities for witchcraft throw or blow "spells" (*hũũtsùù*) at their victims, which will cause an unknown illness and eventually death (see Crocker and Crocker 2004:91). Because of the emergent nature of *kay* abilities, which must be actively cultivated and maintained through intimate encounters with a soul teacher, the potential for developing harmful *kay* powers is ever present throughout one's shamanic career. Soul teachers sometimes assist shamans in becoming witches by giving them a disease to "rear" and then "blow" toward their victims (see Nimuendajú 1946:238). A helpful shaman known for powerful curative rituals could therefore turn on individuals and the community to bring illness and death or use his same powers against an enemy group. Even though contemporary shamans use their abilities for individual and communal well-being, they maintain an ambiguous status as potentially dangerous figures in the Canela life-world.

Modern-day Canela people are reminded of the potential dangers of shamans and their ambiguous *kay* abilities through mythic-historical story telling. Leandro recounted the story of Peliga Prai-re, a shaman from the neighboring Apaniekra village of Porquinhos:

> Peliga Prai-re came from the nearby village of Porquinhos; he was Apaniekra. He was log racing and lost to a Canela man. He cried with rage and began singing. Peliga Prai-re put a sick armadillo in the Canela village. He also performed witchcraft on someone in the Canela village, but another [Canela] healer saved the person. Peliga Prai-re treated the Canela village badly on a number of occasions.

In this story, the external forces of Peliga Prai-re negatively affect the entire Canela village, and a Canela shaman uses his abilities for healing purposes only. In another story Leandro told me, the Canela shaman Bajilim is a witch (*feiticeiro*) who performs both harmful and helpful acts:

> Bajilim was a master with vegetables—maize, sweet manioc, among others. He could also cure all illnesses. He was friends with Seberinho, also a master, who was from a different Timbira tribe. Both of them were witches, and they killed many people, both men and women. Seberinho arrived in his Chinela[3] village, and someone killed him. Bajilim was Canela, and he could transform himself into any type of animal. He would transform into a cobra, a jaguar, a giant anteater, a deer, just as a game to show people what he could do. Bajilim removed the deceased souls from the village—this is what a good healer does.

Bajilim is an ambiguous figure; on the one hand, he is a powerful healer and gardener who protects Canela people from the dangerous deceased souls, and on the other, he is a known witch who freely kills people. He is simultaneously an awe-inspiring master shaman (*kay pej*) and a potentially threatening witch who has the potential to both look after and wreak havoc on the Canela life-world. Bajilim's transformations into various large and dangerous animals "as a game" is a display of this ambiguous shamanic power and authority, just as the legendary shaman Yah-wuh transformed into birds and animals to demonstrate his mastery of *kay* abilities. Even Yah-wuh, the most powerful *kay pej* known in mythic storytelling, has the capacity for inflicting harm on others. In Leandro's version of the mythic story, Yah-wuh transforms into a type of dove (*juriti* or *Leptotila*) bird to spy on his wife, who is making love to another man in the forest. With the assistance of his grandfather's soul, who is his shamanic soul teacher, Yah-wuh then casts a spell on his wife and her lover. Leandro vividly described the scene:

Meanwhile, Yah-wuh saw his woman in the forest, making love to her lover. His grandfather's soul came near them as well, transforming into an ant and biting her. Yah-wuh's woman suffered much pain. [...] The woman came back [to the village] moaning and suffering. At the same time, Yah-wuh's brother-in-law killed a paca, took a leg, and roasted it in the fire. He also removed the liver and roasted it, but did so badly, and without washing his hands—his hands were covered in paca blood. He put his hands in the water to take a drink, and then his stomach began to hurt. The woman was suffering, her "friend" [lover] was suffering, and the brother-in-law was suffering from pain. They were all ill. The brother-in-law was ill from stomach pains, and the woman and her "friend" were suffering from Yah-wuh's spell [hūūtsùù] cast upon them.

Yah-wuh then heals his brother-in-law and his wife's lover, despite being responsible for the latter's suffering. The entire community recognizes his expert curative abilities, as Leandro's description displays:

Yah-wuh was beautiful, with long hair! Everyone was watching him. "Yah-wuh is a master!" everyone said. Yah-wuh removed the paca from his brother-in-law's stomach and threw it aside. [The brother-in-law] calmed down; Yah-wuh had healed him.

When he sees his wife, however, Yah-wuh decides not to heal her but rather inflict more pain and suffering with his powerful shamanic abilities:

At daybreak, Yah-wuh went to see his woman ... she was all by herself. At this point, she was already pregnant, for her lover had impregnated her. Yah-wuh had been nearby, waiting there in silence. Yah-wuh's woman became angry with him. "You went to calm the pains of the two men first, and when you came to heal me it was nearly daybreak! I am angry with you," she said. Yah-wuh told her, "calm down; I do not wish to speak about this. Leave it be." "I will not leave it be that you healed your brother-in-law and his friend before me! That is why I am angry," she said. Yah-wuh got up from the buriti mat and became angry too. "You are a liar! Who impregnated you? I know it was your lover who did so! Who was there above you, in the buriti palm? It was I! You said, 'Oh, it's the *juriti* bird!' And your lover said, 'if I had a bow, I would shoot it for you!'" Yah-wuh hit his woman's belly with the buriti stick, and the child fell out, along with much blood. Yah-wuh was already a master. He could already fly. That was that. "I will not see you anymore.

We are separated. I am going to my father's house, and you will never enter my father's house." Then, Yah-wuh left her.

Yah-wuh's callous treatment of his wife and her unborn child is explained by Leandro as part of his shamanic abilities—he is "already a master" who can "fly" and transform into animals and is therefore able to use his *kay* powers how he chooses. The element of choice is crucial in understanding a shaman's ambiguous role in the Canela life-world. As the story of Yah-wuh displays, shamans can choose to use their abilities to heal and cure in one instance and to injure and kill in the next. The shaman is capable of choosing to use his (or her) abilities in helpful or threatening ways at any moment.

Historical accounts of dangerous shamans or witches also attest to the shamanic capacity for violence and destruction. Shamans are unlikely to reveal themselves as perpetrators of illness or violence against people within or outside the community, as Peliga Prai-re, Bajilim, and Yah-wuh freely admitted to Canela people and neighboring groups. Typically, a shaman is accused of using his *kay* abilities for witchcraft by other community members, becoming generally feared and avoided for the potential threat he poses to the community. These accusations often have been lodged against people originating from neighboring Timbira groups. In 1903, for example, a man from the neighboring Fox tribe was accused of killing his Canela wife with witchcraft. Her relatives then killed the accused witch during a log race, which angered the chief and led to the community's split into two villages (see chapter 2, "Gardening: A Brief History, 1814–Present"; Nimuendajú 1946:239). There are also instances of Canela community members being accused of committing violent acts against their own kin. In the late 1950s–1960s, a Canela man was known for being a witch and throwing spells at other community members, causing illness and in some cases death (Crocker and Crocker 2004:91). When witches use their *kay* abilities in negative, dangerous ways, it is the responsibility of the helpful shaman to cure the illness caused by harmful spells. If the shaman is successful in his curing rituals, then the illness will be thrown back to the witch, causing his illness and perhaps death while simultaneously revealing him as a dangerous element of the community (see Crocker and Crocker 2004:90–92). In the contemporary life-world, accusations of witchcraft are extremely rare. The last accusation of witchcraft documented by Crocker dates from 1978 (Crocker and Crocker 2004:91). No shaman has been accused of using his *kay* abilities negatively during my fieldwork (in 2011, 2012–2013, and 2017), and the only discussions of witchcraft were from mythic-historical storytelling. Explanations and performances of shamanism were consistently centered on the helpful, healing, and communicative aspects of *kay* abilities that strengthen and support the community. Modern-day shamans and community members emphasize the shamanic role of helpful mediator between living people and deceased souls, forest spaces, plants, Plant-People master spirits, animals, and objects over the harmful role of witch that shamans could possess if they so desired. Nevertheless, modern-day shamans' *kay* abilities make them inherently ambiguous, capable of both ensuring safety and promoting danger in the multispecies Canela community and beyond.

Becoming Friends to Plants in Canela Scalar Animism

Shamanic engagements with nonhumans are well documented across Indigenous lowland South America and beyond. Shamans commonly are known to use their unique perceptual abilities to transform into and communicate with powerful animals (Viveiros de Castro [1986] 1992, 1998, 2011; Fausto 2008; Wright 2013) and to both cure and inflict illnesses on people through engagements with nonhuman entities, often understood as kinds of "souls" or "spirits" (Whitehead and Wright 2004; Rubenstein 2012; Taylor 2014; Cepek 2015). Studies of shamanic encounters with objects and artifacts show the breadth of shamanic engagements with nonhuman or other-than-human entities (see Santos-Granero 2009). Shamanic engagements with medicinal and hallucinogenic plants, especially *ayahuasca* and their master spirits also abound (Milliken and Albert 1997; Shepard 2004; Labate and Cavnar 2014; Labate et al. 2017). Yet shamanic encounters with cultivated crops and their master spirits are less understood, with some notable exceptions (Descola 1998; Taylor 2001). In the Canela life-world, the importance of shamanic engagements with plants and Plant-People master spirits is a recent transformation that has emerged over the past half-century. Canela shamanic engagements with deceased soul teachers remain integral to becoming a *kay* and curing illnesses, still a defining aspect of the shamanic profession. While mythical and historical storytelling attest to the importance of shamanic transformations into and communications with animals in the past, when hunting was more central to Canela subsistence, shamans are known now for their abilities to engage with plants and Plant-People in a community that practices and values subsistence horticulture. As gardening and agro-biodiversity maintenance have become central to the Canela life-world, a shaman's helpful role as mediator between human gardeners, diverse cultivated crops, and their master spirits is becoming a key component of developing and maintaining shamanic abilities. Rather than accessing an animal's perspective, as perspectival thinking often emphasizes (e.g., Viveiros de Castro [1986] 1992, 1998, 2011), Canela shamans now are seeking to access and understand the point of view of plants and their master spirits. The encounters with cultivated crops and Plant-People master spirits are now a defining aspect of being or becoming a Canela shaman. Shamans enthusiastically describe and look forward to their friendly engagements with cultivated crops, their relationships of male formal friendship with Plant-Men master spirits, and (perhaps especially) the seductive encounters with their more-than-human other wives, the Plant-Women master spirits. Without shamanic mediation, gardeners would not fully understand their crop children's needs, desires, or dissatisfactions. Many more unhappy crop children would leave garden plots, resulting in poor harvests. The caring relationships of friendship and seduction between shamans and plants and their master spirits are not antithetical to the more "traditional" shamanic powers of healing and engagements with animals but have rather unfolded as another transformation of becoming a *kay* in the vibrant and dynamic Canela multispecies bio sociocultural life world.

As subsistence patterns have shifted toward an emphasis on agro-biodiverse horticulture, so too has the intentionality or subjectivity of plants and Plant-People become more significant. Cultivated crops and their master spirits have become significant nonhuman subjects within a Canela "scalar view of animacy," as Nuckolls (2010:353) describes for the Ecuadorian Runa. Within Canela scalar animism, however, possessing a "soul" is not necessary to develop or maintain intentional capacities. While Descola (2009; 2013) argues that shared "inner vitalities" or "interiorities" amongst humans and nonhumans form the basis of the "animist ontology," this is not the case for the Canela. Animals, plants, objects and artifacts, and supernatural entities such as Plant-People are not thought to possess souls (*mēkarõn*) as Canela humans do. When the deceased, disembodied souls transform into animals, plants, and objects, they are essentially occupying the bodies of these soulless nonhuman beings. Despite their soullessness, however, animals, plants, objects, and supernatural entities are intentional actors with varying levels of agentive capacities. For the Canela, the soul is not the site of consciousness or the intentional "mind." Rather than being grounded in an unchanging soul, the intentionality, animacy, or perhaps "mindfulness" of these nonhuman beings is emergent, unfolding through emotive and communicative engagements with each other and with humans, particularly shamans.

Through this emergent phenomenological approach, Canela scalar animism becomes clearer. While all human, nonhuman, and other-than-human beings possess some level of intentionality that emerges through relationships with others, there is a hierarchy of animacy based on potential and realized agentive capacities. The deceased Canela souls (*mēkarõn*) are at the most animate end of the scale, having highly developed agentive capacities of movement, transformation, and communicative powers. As disembodied entities, they are omnipresent, able to move freely and instantly, capable of occupying or transforming into other beings at will, able to inflict harm onto human bodies and to communicate and assist with a shaman's *kay* abilities. In a sense, the *mēkarõn* possess hyper-intentionality, capable of agentive capacities far beyond what embodied living humans can achieve. The white souls (*pehjarohti*) also would fit into this hyper-agentive category, capable of inflicting harm and destruction in the Canela life-world that far surpasses the capacities of living whites. Shamans are next on this animist scale, possessing less agentive capacities than deceased souls yet more than the average living human. While occasionally capable of transformational capacities similar to that of souls, shamans nowadays more commonly develop powerful perceptual and agentive capacities that enable communicative engagements with deceased souls, animals, plants, objects, and Plant-People. Humans without shamanic abilities have slightly less agentive capacities—they possess their own souls and can think, move, and express emotion yet cannot perceive or converse with the nonhuman beings that shamans can. Nevertheless, humans are capable of developing multi-sensory engagements with nonhumans, and especially plants. Human gardeners can observe, touch, sing to, and feed their crops, using their agentive capacities to care for diverse plant children affectionately.

Plant-People master spirits are next in the hierarchy of intentionality. They do not possess souls, yet they can speak, express various emotional states, and manifest themselves to shamans whenever they choose. As Reinaldo described in detail, the Plant-Men and Plant-Women talk with the shaman, display friendly and seductive emotions, and appear and move around in various locations within forest and riverbank garden plots. The master spirits' complete freedom of movement, including appearing out of nowhere, and their ability to represent and speak for entire crop species and varieties, place them as "more animate" than plants and animals in Canela scalar animism. Plants and animals possess the same level of animacy, as they are soulless yet possess similar embodied agentive powers of thought, emotion, consumption of food, and physical movement. Different animal species talk with one another (and occasionally with the shaman) and express emotion toward their hunter fathers, as Fernando described. Animals need and consume food by hunting their prey and can move freely around throughout the forest, *chapada*, and other land types in the territory. Similarly, diverse plant species and varieties converse with shamans and with each other in forest and riverbank garden plots. They express various emotional states to the shaman, including distress, sadness, hunger, anger, satisfaction, and happiness. Plants are thought to need food in the form of *beribu* manioc–meat pies during the food-sharing ritual with their human families (see chapter 3, "Sharing Food with Plants"). And while plants cannot move as freely as animals can, they are capable of relocating to a different garden plot if dissatisfied with their treatment by gardener parents. Objects and artifacts are slightly "less animate" than plants and animals on this scale. They can think, express emotions, and consume food. Household objects converse with one another and with the shaman, and they can become happy, sad, or hungry, as displayed by Dirceu's interaction with a wooden pestle that complained it was "hungry" for rice. Yet objects and artifacts cannot move of their own accord and are therefore slightly more limited in their agentive capacities than plants and animals are. Few, if any, things in the unfolding life-world are considered "inanimate" within Canela scalar animism. Even "materials" (*materiais*) such as fire and water are thought to have intentionality, being able to communicate with shamans as Dirceu described to their family.

Animacy in Canela scalar animism is therefore the result of ongoing processes of movement, growth, and multi-sensory encounters amongst myriad human, nonhuman, and more-than-human supernatural entities that have differing intentional potentialities. While there is a definite hierarchy of intentionality, the animate scale is not vertical but rather operates across space and over time. Ingold's (2000, 2008) phenomenological "meshwork" that enmeshes all sorts of persons and things through time and space is an analytically useful concept here. The communicative relationships amongst humans and diverse nonhuman beings emerge along the "threads" of the meshwork (Ingold 2007a: 81). Taken together, these threads form a fluid and dynamic bio-sociocultural life-world that develops its own shape and consistencies yet is constantly open to new threaded patterns as they emerge. In this sense, certain threads, such as those between gardener parents and crop children and between shamans, plants, and Plant-People master spirits, are becoming more meaningful and valued as they are reinforced and emerge into consistent patterns in the unfolding life-world. With their heightened perceptual abilities, shamans are able to create unique threads of engagement and mediation among humans and nonhumans. Shamans are becoming increasingly valued for the specific threads they develop with diverse plants and Plant-People master spirits. Shamanic friendships with plants, formal friendships with Plant-Men, and seductive trysts with Plant-Women promote the safety, strength, happiness, and well-being of plants and people in forest, riverbank, and village spaces. By becoming friends to plants, shamans are ensuring the reproduction and continuation of the Canela multispecies community and all its emergent transformations.

Exploring Futures for People and Plants in the Twenty-First Century

Advocating for Sensory Ethnobotany in Multispecies Futures

The realities of the Anthropocene are bearing down on the Canela and other communities worldwide, bringing combined ecological and sociocultural change and instability. The challenges the Canela face are multifold, including climate change, drought, deforestation, pollution, and violence brought on by legal and illegal agricultural and extractive industries. Nevertheless, they continue to seek out and develop caring, meaningful relationships with myriad assemblages of multispecies beings that compose the environment, even in the wake of dramatic change. In this epoch defined by human-mediated environmental change, the importance of understanding sustainable human–environment engagements has never been more pressing. The first victims of the structural violence of Western expansionism and capital accumulation that has produced the Anthropocene, Indigenous peoples are at the forefront of contemporary environmental activism and advocacy. From the Standing Rock Sioux water protectors demonstrating against oil pipeline development in North Dakota (Montoya 2016; TallBear 2016; Whyte 2017) to the Kayapó and Munduruku activism against mega-dams in the Brazilian Amazon (Fearnside 2015, 2017; Alarcon et al. 2016; Watts 2018), Indigenous communities are enacting their resistance and resilience in the face of structural violence, environmental destruction, and climate change. Indigenous relationships with and valuation of the environment increasingly are found to be crucial to conservation initiatives and adaptation to climate change, seen especially in ethnobiological studies of traditional environmental knowledge (TEK) (see Gill et al. 2014; Reid et al. 2014; Fang et al. 2016; Herman 2016; Ziker et al. 2016). Through multispecies ethnographic approaches, Indigenous world-making practices with nonhumans and the environment are also being explored (Kohn 2007, 2013; Bird Rose 2011; Cassidy

2012). Both approaches have been criticized for glossing over the diversity and dynamism of Indigenous lived experiences: TEK for its conceptual tendency to become a "bureaucratic object" that can lead to pigeonholing Indigenous knowledge and peoples as "irrelevant" relics of the past (Anderson 2011:8–9) and multispecies ethnography for its emphasis on abstract theoretical and philosophical concepts that can obscure heterogeneity and political and ecological change (Bessire and Bond 2014).

Combining and expanding on both approaches, sensory ethnobotany attends to these criticisms by incorporating historical, political, and ecological change into studies of ethnobotanical classification, environmental and landscape management, and multispecies human–nonhuman perceptual entanglements. As such, it sheds light on previously unseen processes of human–plant lived experiences and their transformations over time. The focus on plants in sensory ethnobotany highlights the importance of human–plant engagements in many life-worlds, both Indigenous and non-Indigenous, that until recently have been underrepresented in multispecies ethnography (see Locke and Muenster 2015; recent exceptions include Kohn 2013; Myers 2014, 2015, 2017; Kawa 2016; Lewis-Jones 2016; Battaglia 2017). It also takes seriously recent advances in plant science that recognize the communicative and intentional abilities of plants as they relate to each other and to humans in the landscape (see Gagliano 2015; Gagliano and Grimonprez 2015). With trees good to "think with" in symbolic or cognitive anthropology (Bloch 1998) and approaching "how forests think" integral to multispecies ethnography (Kohn 2013), it follows that plants — key to combined biological, sociocultural, material, and symbolic processes — should be examined more fully by themselves and through their engagements "becoming with" humans, whether as kin, friends, lovers, or another relation. Sensory ethnobotany takes seriously the variability, dynamism, and resilience of multispecies Indigenous life-worlds as they face ongoing environmental destruction and climate change. The sensory ethnobotany framework that I put forward throughout this book reveals the specific ways in which the Canela life-world supports human–nonhuman and specifically human–plant engagements through multispecies kinship and care. While other Indigenous life-worlds unfold in distinct ways from that of the Canela, a sensory ethnobotany approach allows for a deeper understanding of varied multispecies relationships, including environmental classification and management and their value to human and nonhuman participants.

Additionally, sensory ethnobotany allows for speculation on human and plant multispecies futures. Given the high rates of biodiversity loss and species extinction that continue worldwide (see Pretty et al. 2009; Sodikoff 2012), multispecies futures may involve significantly fewer species and vari eties than the multispecies engagements of the present. Moreover, the cli- matic changes already occurring or expected to occur in the next few de- cades and century will present unprecedented challenges requiring myriad human and nonhuman adaptations, many of which remain unknown or un- foreseen. As the Anthropocene unfolds through biological–sociocultural– geological processes, scholars are grappling with its material and concep- tual emergence in the present and future. By "thinking through definite material relationships in order to read the signs of the future," Whitington (2013:310) advocates for a speculative materialist approach to the Anthropo- cene. Focusing on "thinking with care about open futures," he concludes that the material relations of climate change have "forced" a questioning of the human and its future, and therefore climate change is a form of speculative anthropology (Whitington 2013:324–325). Meanwhile, Swanson et al. (2015) speculate on the Anthropocene as "science fiction" to understand its recent emergence as a scientific and philosophical concept. They maintain that the Anthropocene conjures different "science fiction worlds," such as "thinking politics after the nature–culture divide; genuine kinds of transdisciplinarity; novel ways of imagining what it is to be 'human,' and the hope of survival in a world with other species" (Swanson et al. 2015:163). The Canela are similarly dealing with the emergence of the Anthropocene by attending to material re- lationships with the environment, especially plants, in order to care for and survive in a multispecies future. Canela gardeners' intimate kinship engage- ments with plants underscore their ability to conceptualize humanity as one of many valued species and to overcome natural–cultural divides through intimate perceptual experiences. In a sense, the Canela are practicing their own speculative anthropology, by paying attention to, considering, and re- considering human engagements with the environment as it continues to change. While specific kinship engagements with cultivated crop species and varieties may change over time along with the Cerrado climate, the Ca- nela can envision and "think through with care" their multispecies futures with plants in the Cerrado.

Multispecies futures are possible, I argue, if Indigenous ontological posi- tionings that support care and resilience are taken seriously. Canela intimate, caring multispecies relationships that support the well-being of people and plants will be pursued in the future as the Cerrado landscape and climate continue to change. While specific gardening activities and even the culti- vation of certain crops may change, the focus on paying attention to and developing kinship relationships with plants is likely to remain for the fore-seeable future. Diverse plant species and varieties are the "companions" of Canela humans, bound up with each other through caring acts in the process of "making worlds" (Haraway 2008).

Canela multispecies care and kinship in the present and speculative future also sheds light on Indigenous multispecies futures worldwide. As Indigenous anthropologists Kim TallBear (2011) and Zoe Todd (2016) point out, Indigenous world-making practices and approaches to nonhumans are integral to understanding multispecies relatedness in the past, present, and future, as is the importance of engaging with Indigenous scholarship on multispecies relatedness itself. And with an overarching focus on human-nonhuman relatedness, Indigenous world-making practices offer a promis-ing alternative to the use and destruction of natural resources for capitalist accumulation. As Julian Brave NoiseCat (2017) argues:

> While Indigenous values, beliefs and practices are as diverse as Indige-nous people themselves, they find common roots in a relationship to land and water radically different from the notion of property. For In-digenous people, land and water are regarded as sacred, living rela-tives, ancestors, places of origin or any combination of the above.

Across the globe, Indigenous peoples currently are creating multispecies futures of resilience and hope, through advocating for legal recognition of the personhood of nonhuman entities such as water (Salmond 2014), engag-ing in environmental sustainability initiatives on their own terms (Whyte et al. 2016; Zanotti and Palomino-Schalscha 2016), and through pursuing everyday activities of loving, caring for, and paying attention to cultivated crop children, as the Canela undertake. Sensory ethnobotany is applicable to understanding these life-worlds, as diverse human communities are grappling with their interactions with plants and the changes that will occur owing to the destruction, loss, and possibly extinction of the Anthropocene. Sensory ethnobotany highlights these processes of loss and change, but it also focuses on the resilience of human and plant communities as they con-tinue to live with, grow, and make multispecies futures together. For the Ca-nela, multispecies futures start with the present-day activities of becoming with plant kin. Facing future environmental challenges head-on, the Canela continue to undertake and be committed to caring activities that promote human and plant well-being. And through careful planning and attentive en-gagement with the changing Cerrado landscape, the Canela will continue to create multispecies futures full of diverse crop children. In Liliana's words, her ongoing commitment to human and plant Canela multispecies families and their present and future well-being is clear.

> I want to find more seeds that I can leave for my family, [for] my grand-children, seeing as I am always saving the seeds that I have. I do not want to lose crops; I want to increase them. [...] I will start; I will do it. I will not be weak. I have to do it. It is my part, under my watch; [it is] my turn to be strong.

EPILOGUE

If the world ends, it ends.
But I want to keep working in the garden.
—Jacinto

Returning to the Canela village in November 2017, I was struck by both its continuity and change. Nearly five years had elapsed since my last visit, and many things remained the same—my mother Liliana's house stood in the same spot in the first ring of houses, and she and her entire family were still alive and thriving, adding new members to the family through birth and marriage. The village population had skyrocketed, with nearly three-thousand people now living in the territory, and the gardens remained robust and plentiful. In many ways, the community was vibrant and well (*impej*). Yet there were worrisome changes. A drought, affecting the region since 2012, has had powerful effects: streams and rivers were low, small lakes have disappeared completely, fires were more uncontrollable than in the past, and cultivated crops have suffered, particularly during 2015–2016 when the rainy season brought practically no rain. Illegal logging is rampant inside the territory, affecting forest gardening practices and bringing violence and instability. Meanwhile, eucalyptus expansion looms nearby, a monocrop monster that threatens to exacerbate drought, uncontrolled fires, water pollution, and deforestation. A newly paved asphalt road to the territory facilitates the extraction and removal of both illegally sourced hardwood and legally planted eucalyptus.

Driving past the eucalyptus plantation on the way to the village, my driver and I stopped to taste ripe cashew fruit dangling from trees on the side of the road. Symmetrical stands of eucalyptus surrounded us as far as the eye could see, having replaced the native Cerrado landscape from a few years earlier. In the distance, a charcoal plant belched out smoke as it burnt the freshly harvested eucalyptus trees. The charcoal, my driver informed me, would be sent to cities around Brazil and the world for energy consumption, further contributing to greenhouse gases worldwide (see also Bailis et al. 2013). A dismal scene of the Anthropocene, showing a cycle of environmental change and destruction with seemingly no end.

Yet on my return to the Canela gardens, the continued love and care for biodiversity and plant kin and the bio-sociocultural life-world as a whole were clear. Spending time in the forest and riverbank gardens with Liliana and her human and plant family, I found the resilience of human–plant engagements in the changing Canela life-world undeniable. Although she temporarily lost some of her seeds during a great drought in 2015–2016, Liliana is already recovering many of these plant children through exchange and through renewed appearances in her garden plots. Although her forest garden was burnt by a neighbor's uncontrolled fire, exacerbated by the drought, she was able to recover most of the crops growing there and continued to plant new ones. Despite the environmental and climatic challenges of years ahead, Liliana and Canela gardeners in general remain committed to getting to know and caring for their plant kin. Expanding on the importance of caring for plant kin, Liliana told me during this visit that losing a beloved plant variety is "the same as losing a child; you feel sad, as if your child died." Gardener parents must therefore be alert to a garden's changes and do everything in their power to prevent the loss of plant children. "All plants are our family," Liliana reminded me.

For this multispecies family of Canela people and plants, the loving, affectionate multi-sensory engagements they form over time will keep them alive and thriving even as shocking change, loss, and destruction occur. While the Anthropocene involves scenes that may seem apocalyptic, this does not deter Canela gardeners. Liliana's father Jacinto made it clear to her, telling her during a messianic movement that predicted the world's end, "if the world ends, it ends. But I want to keep working in the garden." If the Anthropocene changes the Canela life-world or even brings about an "end" to certain aspects of it, Canela gardeners will remain, continuing their work of caring for plant children in their gardens.

ACKNOWLEDGMENTS

First and foremost, I thank the Canela people who welcomed me into their community with open arms, including Fernando, Renato, Leandro, and especially my Canela family: Liliana, Camila, Joaquina, João Miguel, Belém, Vítor, Nilda, Aline, Davi, and their children and grandchildren. They made this book possible with their ongoing creativity and curiosity for their environment and the people and plants within it. I also thank the Canela plants, for inspiring Canela community members and myself to become better caretakers of our multispecies kin.

The research that enabled this book was made possible through funding support from the Rausing Scholarship for doctoral studies through Linacre College and the Institute of Social and Cultural Anthropology at the University of Oxford (2010–2013); individual research grants for doctoral field work from the University of Washington–Whatcom Museum (2011–2013) and the BioSocial Society (2012); the Peter Buck Postdoctoral Fellowship for postdoctoral research at the National Museum of Natural History, Smithsonian Institution (2015–2017); the Betty J. Meggers Research Grant for continued research from the Americas Research Network (2017); and the Field Museum (2017–2018).

While at Oxford, my doctoral supervisor, Laura Rival, was a constant source of support both professionally and personally, and she continues to be a mentor and friend. I thank her for her close readings of my work and innovative approach that have pushed me further to consider new ways of researching human–environment engagements. Thanks also go to my doctoral dissertation examiners, Elizabeth Ewart and William Balée, for their thorough review and suggestions to expand the breadth and scope of the dissertation for this book. At Oxford, Dan Hicks helped me deepen my approach to aesthetics, material culture, and animacy; Bob Parkin edited and commented on my work on the materiality of maize; and Lewis Daly, Luíseach Nic Eoin, and Katerine French were excellent conference-organizing and editorial partners to consider "botanical ontologies" from an interdisciplinary perspective.

In Brazil, Carlos Fausto served as my *orientador* at the Federal University of

Rio de Janeiro. I thank him for his support starting my fieldwork and devising my research proposal and especially for his advice on thinking through perspectivism, animism, and mastery with plants. Thanks to Fábio Freitas at EMBRAPA in Brasília for his collaboration and interest in Canela plants, especially gourds, and for searching for gourd seeds with me in seed banks and markets. In Maranhão, Bernhard and Elke Grupp have greatly assisted me with organizing my fieldwork with the Canela, and I thank them for their logistical support, their knowledge and appreciation of the Canela, and their friendship. Thanks also to Joel Alacantra da Silva, for the interesting conversations and for transportation of myself (and cows!) to Escalvado village.

The Peter Buck Postdoctoral Fellowship at the National Museum of Natural History, Smithsonian Institution, enabled me to spend even more time with Canela people and plants and approach their changing engagements from a historical archival perspective. My postdoctoral advisor, Joshua Bell, gave me valuable advice and input on incorporating political–ecological analyses into my work, for which I am grateful. Ashley Egan of the Smithsonian Botany Department collaborated with me on interdisciplinary work, and I thank her for her interest in the Canela, her enthusiasm for Brazilian legumes, and for teaching me the basics of plant DNA extraction, another way of getting to know our beloved legumes. Barbara Watanabe greatly assisted me as I delved into the anthropological archives, and I am thankful for her assistance, kindness, and in-depth knowledge of the Canela material. William Merrill organized meetings of South Americanists, and I thank him, Emi Ireland, Phil Tajitsu Nash, and Eduardo Ribeiro for our valuable discussions on Indigenous life-worlds in past and present. I also thank Gabriela Pérez-Baéz, Stéphanie Caffarel, and Kristina Douglass for fruitful exchanges during our environmental reading group meetings, especially conversations on the Anthropocene as a concept and epoch. In addition, thanks to the late Betty Meggers for reading my master's thesis and pushing me to reconsider past human–environment engagements in South America.

My co-advisor at the Smithsonian, William Crocker, has been a friend, colleague, and inspiration since our first meeting in 2011. His generosity and kindness are unwavering and seen especially during our visit to the Canela community in July 2011, his last fieldwork trip and my first. For introducing me to the Canela, and especially my adoptive family, I am forever grateful. Our frequent meetings on Canela history, language, ritual, and everyday life continue to be a source of ever-expanding knowledge and enjoyment. He has become something of an anthropological grandfather to me, for which I am greatly appreciative. His enthusiasm for and dedication to the Canela over six decades of research and study are truly inspiring. I am honored to know him and to have had the opportunity to delve into his expansive archives with him during my postdoctoral fellowship.

Thanks also go to the members of the Amazonianist anthropologist community in the Washington, DC, area for our collaborative exchanges and for commenting upon my work in the Center for Research and Collaboration in the Indigenous Americas (CRACIA) meetings at the University of Maryland. These include especially Janet Chernela, Javier Carrera-Rubio, Lucas de Carvalho, Courtney Stafford-Walter, Emily Colón, Kit Allen, Christopher Hewlett, William Fisher, and Laura Mentore. I particularly thank Janet Chernela for her friendship and support during my time as postdoctoral associate at the University of Maryland and for inviting me to participate and collaborate with students and colleagues working on Amazonian anthropology. Other Amazonianists in the Society for the Anthropology of Lowland South America have also provided valuable comments on my work and engaged in lively discussions on Amazonia over the years, including especially Laura Zanotti, Jeremy Campbell, James Welch, and Nick Kawa. Thanks also go to Colin Hoag and Chitra Venkataramai with whom I co-edit the Anthropology and Environment Society's *Engagement* website, our work together to expand the scope of environmental anthropology and for its engagement in the world. Additionally, I thank Greg de St. Maurice for being an incredible editorial partner and friend through thick and thin. And thanks to those who have commented on versions of my work: John Hartigan, for helping me envision multispecies futures with plants; Beth Conklin, for thinking through Amazonian multispecies engagements in new ways; and Dana Lepofsky and Steve Wolverton, for their commentary on living lists and editorial support at the *Journal of Ethnobiology*.

In addition, thanks to the members of the Andes–Amazon and Chicago teams in the Keller Science Action Center at the Field Museum for providing a space to think through community-led conservation in the Anthropocene, including especially Nicholas Kotlinski, Alaka Wali, Tita Alvira, Corine Vriesendorp, Ana Lemos, Lesley de Souza, Amy Rosenthal, Nigel Pitman, Lex Winter, and Jacob Campbell.

Finally, I thank my friends and family for their support and encouragement while I have followed the unfolding pathway of coming to know Canela people and plants. Barbara and Marv Miller have always supported me to be curious and dive into new experiences. During fieldwork and writing, I am grateful for all their words of encouragement and care packages, and especially for the writer retreat at their home. I thank Mel Miller-Yule for her support as sister and friend. Eileen Stillwaggon and Larry Sawers have encouraged me throughout this journey. And while they are no longer with us, I have carried with me the memories of Carol and Sandy Jenks, Pauline Miller, Steven Jenks, and David Jenks throughout the research and writing of this book. Edith and Ramona, and Michael, Andrew, and Daniel, inspire me to work toward a better future. And to Rob Sawers, for his never-ending encouragement and inspiration, and for joining me on this path—words cannot express my gratitude, *Lāālac*.

APPENDIX A

Living Lists of Canela Cultivated Crops

Table 1. Maize / Põhy (*Zea mays* L.)

Canela name	Translation	Description
Põhy caprêc-ti	Large red-yellow maize	Large reddish-yellow kernels; produces a large harvest and used to make *beribu*
Põhy caprôô-ti	Large bright-red maize	Large bright-red kernels the color of blood or *urucum* (annatto)
Põhy jaka-ti	Large white maize	Large white kernels
Põhy jĩi-re	Hairy tail maize	Has a hair "tail" off the end of the ear; not very tasty (*jĩi-re* = hairy tail)
Põhy jɪproh-tɪ[1]	Large grey maize	Grey kernels
Põhy kror-ti	Large mixed-color maize	Kernels have mixed colors of white, brown, and black
Põhy kryi-re	Small maize	Yellow kernels and has a short stalk; "friend" of *põhy pej-re* (*kryi-re* = small)
Põhy pej-re	True/original maize	Small, white kernels; eaten as part of young men and women's *resguardo* food and sex prohibition period
Põhy tatap-re[1]	Small bright-yellow maize	Bright-yellow kernels the color of cotton flowers
Põhy tàtà-re[1]	Small yellow-brown maize	Yellowish-brown kernels
Põhy tep-re[1]	Small red maize	Reddish kernels
Põhy tohrom-ti	Large mixed-color maize	Kernels are mixed purple and white
Põhy tyc-ti	Large black maize	Large black kernels

[1] Acquired at government-sponsored seed exchange with other Jê communities in September 2012.

Table 2. Manioc / *Kwỳr* (*Manihot esculenta* Crantz; *Manihot* Mill. spp.)

Canela name	Translation	Description
	Sweet manioc—*kwỳrỳre* (*macaxeira* in Portuguese).	
Kwỳr cahkrit-re	Stranger/outsider sweet manioc	Comes from a strange man from the Apaniekra village of Porquinhos; used to make *beribu* (*cahkrit-re* = stranger/outsider)
Kwỳr caprêc-re (*kwỳr kryi-re japỳ*)	Small red parrot tail sweet manioc	Leaf resembles parrot's tail; has red skin and white pulp; used to make juice (*japỳ* = tail)
Kwỳr kàntep-re	Red sweet manioc	*Macaxeira cacau*; has grey skin, white pulp, and red membrane or "cytoplasm"
Kwỳr mẽhcapôt	Infants sweet manioc	Resembles chubby arms of infants; use to make *farinha seca, beiju*, and *beribu* (*mẽhcapôt* = infants or babies)
Kwỳr mĩnêr	Mineira sweet manioc	*Macaxeira mineira*; from Minas Gerais State; has white pulp
Kwỳr xa jõkõn-re	Curved vine sweet manioc	Vine winds around itself (*xa* = vine or tree; *jõkõn-re* = curved)
Kwỳrỳre hôhpore	Long-leaf sweet manioc	White skin and tasty (*hôhpore* = long leaf)
	Half-sweet/half-bitter manioc.	
Kwỳr xenti	Not-bitter manioc	Has a little bit of poison in pulp; used to make *beribu* (*xen* = not bitter)
Waíputre	Hugging vine manioc	Vines wrap around; unique variety that can remain in ground for 5 years and vines can grow 3–5 m; tapioca has poison but pulp does not
	Bitter manioc—*kwỳr cahàc* (*mandioca* in Portuguese).	
Kwỳr awari	Cobra bitter manioc	*Mandioca naja*; pulp resembles flesh of cobra (*naja*); makes beautiful, tasty yellow *farinha* (*awari* = cobra)
Kwỳr cacôhti	Bitter manioc of the water	*Mandioca d'água*; very watery pulp (*cacôhti* = very watery)
Kwỳr caprêc-ti	Large red-yellow bitter manioc	Makes beautiful reddish-yellow *farinha* but is not very tasty
Kwỳr hêhtyi	Strong vine bitter manioc	Takes 3 years to grow and used to make *farinha* (*hêhtyi* = strong wood, tree, or vine)
Kwỳr mãã tehkà	Ema shinbone bitter manioc	White and resembles shinbone of ema (*mãã*; *Rhea americana* L., large, native South American bird)
Kwỳr pakran-re (*kwỳr caprãn jũkee*)	Tortoise arm bitter manioc	*Mandioca babuzinha*; resembles tortoise arm; has short vine and takes 1.5 years to grow (*caprãn* = tortoise; *jũkee* = arm)
Kwỳr pytẽc jõkrekà	Rooster wattle forest tree bitter manioc	Resembles rooster's wattle and the *jacú* tree; makes yellow-red *farinha* (*pytẽc* = native tree; *jõkrekà* = rooster wattle)
Kwỳr tyc-ti (*kwỳr krã jimoctyc*)	Black hair bitter manioc	Has black hair on its head (*krã* = head; *jimoctyc* = black hair); connected to Tyc-ti, Star-Woman's Canela husband
Kwỳr xatyc-re	Small black vine bitter manioc	*Mandioca manipeba*; red skin and makes beautiful white *farinha*

Table 3. Yam/ *Krêrô* (*Dioscorea* L. spp.)

Canela name	Translation	Description
	True/original yam—*krêrô pej.*	
Krêrô caràmpa caxwỳn tatap-ti	Deer liver bright-yellow membrane yam	Shaped like a deer liver (*caràmpa*); has bright-yellow pulp and membrane; grows vertically on the vine similar to types of common bean "on the vine"; yam vice-chief
Krêrô pej caprãn cre-re	Tortoise egg true/ original yam	Shaped like a tortoise egg; has grey skin and white pulp (*cre* = egg); yam vice-chief
Krêrô pej caxwỳn jaka-ti	Large white membrane true/ original yam	Small and round, similar to a potato; violet and grey-colored skin with white pulp and membrane; consuming it causes wounds in heel of foot (*caxwỳn* = membrane); yam vice-chief
Krêrô pej caxwỳn kukum-ti	Large brown-violet membrane true/ original yam	Small and round, similar to a potato; brown-violet-colored membrane; consuming it causes wounds in heel of foot; yam vice-chief
	Regular yam—*krêrô cahàc.*	
Krêrô crêhô	Pubic hair yam	Has small hairs that resemble pubic hair; grey skin and white pulp (*crêhô* = testicles)
Krêrô crô cre	Pig testicle yam	Round and resembles a pig's testicle (*crò* = pig)
Krêrô kàhcaprôti	Reddish-pink skinned yam	Red/pink-colored skin (*kà* = skin, shell, bark)
Krêrô kàjakẽn	Breast yam	Resembles a human breast in shape (*kàjukẽn*); white pulp
Krêrô kaj-re	Small basket yam	Resembles a small Canela basket (*kaj*); has white pulp
Krêrô kryi-re	Small yam	Small with white pulp and grey skin
Krêrô parpóhti	Long foot yam	Round and has "toes"; grey-skinned (*parpóhti* = long foot)
Krêrô pỳp-re	Electric eel yam	"Yam of the water"; shaped like electric eel (*pỳp*; *poraquê*; *Electrophorus electricus* L.); white-colored, long, and thin; can grow for 5–6 years; one of the yam chiefs and more true/original than others
Krêrô pytĩxwa	*Dente de prego* yam	Resembles insect that burrows inside the skin; grey-skinned (*pytĩxwa* = type of insect)
Krêrô rop-krã	Jaguar's or dog's head yam	Round and resembles jaguar's or dog's head (*rop*)
Krêrô rõrxô	*Babaçu* yam	Round and shaped like *babaçu* fruit (*rõrõ* = *babaçu*)
Krêrô teamjijapê (*krêrô tum pram*)	Yam that multiplies/ grouped yam	Many yams grow together in a cluster on vine; has many "children" who "happily" stay together and have "festivals" (*teamjijapê* = group/together)
Krêrô tekãjkãj/ rorti	Anaconda yam	Circles around itself similar to an anaconda; white-colored; also a "yam of the water"; one of the yam chiefs and more true/original than others
Krêrô xa jĩ-re	Spiny/hairy yam	Vine spiny/hairy; yam very large and white with yellow pulp

Table 4. Squash / *Cuhkõn cahàc* (*Cucurbita* L. spp.)

Canela name	Translation	Description
Cuhkõn cahàc cràà-ti	Large dry squash	Pumpkin with green skin, yellow pulp, and white seeds (*cràà* = dry)
Cuhkõn cahàc japjêhti	Long squash	Green-colored skin and orange pulp (*japjêhti* = long)
Cuhkõn cahàc jiproh-ti	Large grey-skinned squash	Very tasty; grey skin and orange pulp
Cuhkõn cahàc kàhtỳire	Hard/resistant skin squash	Hard skin and orange pulp (*kàhtỳire* = strong/hard skin)
Cuhkõn cahàc kàkàre	*Kàkàre* bird squash	Resembles *kàkàre* bird that is half yellow, half green-colored; maraca-shaped, pretty and small
Cuhkõn cahàc krã[1]	Head squash	Divided into two parts with a head; green skin
Cuhkõn cahàc pej	True/original squash	Tasty with orange pulp
Cuhkõn cahàc-ti	Large squash	Very large and not tasty; similar to a gourd; yellow skin and orange pulp

[1] Identified solely by Liliana in February 2013.

Table 5. Gourd / *Cuhkõn* (*Cucurbita* L. spp.) / *Cabaça* (Portuguese)

Canela name	Translation	Description
Cuhkõn catia ita	Largest gourd	White skin and pulp; inedible but pulp used as fever remedy (rub on skin); not currently cultivated
Cuhkõn jajõ	Round gourd	Rounded in shape (*jajõ* = round)
Cuhkõn jakot[1]	Translation unclear	Smaller and rounded; used to save seeds; not currently cultivated
Cuhkõn japjêh-ti[1]	Large long gourd	Large with small neck; was used to carry water and ritual food; not currently cultivated
Cuhkõn pàrte[1]	Tree gourd	Plant grows like a tree (*pàr*); has long neck and used for musical instruments; not currently cultivated
Cuhkõn pàt-wỳ	Flute gourd	*Pàt-wỳ* = type of flute used by old men and warriors; also used to store things; Star-Woman hid in this type of gourd; is long and fine with a neck
Cuhkõn pàt-wỳ-re[1]	Small flute gourd	Smaller type of flute gourd with long neck; used as musical instrument and in necklaces
Cuhkõn put japjē[1]	Long neck gourd	Has a long, curved neck; used as a bowl by interned boys during Khêêtuwajê festival; cultivated by a few families
Cuhkõn put-tyt	Neck gourd	Traditionally used to carry water (*put-tyt* = neck); not currently cultivated
Cuhkõn put-tyt-re[1]	Small neck gourd	Small gourd with small neck; used as flute
Cuhkõn-re	Smallest gourd	Used to make *krãn-re* ritual adornment for *wuh-tỳ* girls (girls with ritual roles in festivals)
Cuhkõn xenre	Sweet/not-bitter gourd	Traditionally used as bowl; has a fine skin; not currently cultivated

[1] Added to list in November 2017 by Canela gardeners.

Table 6. Bottle Gourd / *Cuhtõj* (*Lagenaria siceraria* (Molina) Standl. and/or *Crescentia cujete* L.) / *Cuia* or *Cabaça* (Portuguese)

Canela name	Translation	Description
Cuhtõj jajõti	Round, ball-shaped gourd	Very round
Cuhtõj japjêhti	Long gourd	Long in shape
Cuhtõj kryi-re	Small gourd	Very small

Table 7. Common bean / *Pàt juhtõi-re* (*Phaseolus vulgaris* L.; *Cajanus cajan* (L.) Millsp.)

Canela name	Translation	Description
Pàt juhtõi-re amcô[1]	Pest bean	Resembles pest insect (*amcô*); also known as *feijão carioca*; brown and white striped
Pàt juhtõi-re caprêc-re[1]	Small red bean	Small and red-colored
Pàt juhtõi-re hipêj cre[2,4]	*Hipêj* egg bean	Resembles *pànkrỳt hipêj cre*
Pàt juhtõi-re ihkũkũm-re[1]	Small purplish-brown bean	Small bean with long vine; a type of "vine bean" (*feijão de corda*) and resembles *hipêj* bird's egg; also known as *feijão barriguda*
Pàt juhtõi-re intep-re[1]	Small bright-red bean	Brilliant red color
Pàt juhtõi-re jaka-re[1]	Small white bean	Small and white-colored
Pàt juhtõi-re jaka-ti[2]	Large white bean	Larger, white-colored
Pàt juhtõi-re jipro-re[1]	Small grey bean	*Feijão manteiga*; butter bean
Pàt juhtõi-re krô japjêh-ti jaka-ti[1]	Long-vined big white bean	Larger, white-colored; type of *feijão de corda* (*krô* = another word for vine)
Pàt juhtõi-re krô japjêh-ti tep-ti[1]	Long-vined big red bean	Larger and red-colored with long vine; a type of *feijão de corda*
Pàt juhtõi-re kroro-re[1]	Small jaguar bean	Has spots that resemble a jaguar
Pàt juhtõi-re pàràre/pryjĩ[3]	Guajajara tree bean	*Pryjĩ* = Guajajara; acquired bean from Guajajara in 1960s; also known as *feijão anduzinho*; only bean that has "tree" (*pàràre*) instead of vine
Pàt juhtõi-re pryti jiwrỳhhi[1]	Cow rib bean	Long and white bean that resembles a cow's rib (*pryti* = cow; *jiwrỳhhi* = rib)
Pàt juhtõi-re tàtà-re[1]	Small yellow-brown bean	Small and yellowish-brown-colored; a type of *feijão de corda*
Pàt juhtõi-re tyc-re[1]	Small black bean	Type of black bean used to make Brazilian *feijoada* stew; not currently cultivated
Pàt juhtõi-ti ihkũkũm-ti[2,5]	Large purplish-brown bean	Larger bean with long vine; type of *feijão de corda*; also known as *feijão barriguda*
Pàt juhtõi-ti intep-ti[1]	Large bright-red bean	Also known as *feijão barriguda*; *feijão vinagre*; *feijão sempre verde*; very important (*pej*) and tasty
Pàt juhtõi-ti tyc-ti[1]	Large black bean	Another type of black bean used to make *feijoada*; not currently cultivated

[1] Identified as *Phaseolus vulgaris* L. by Stephen Harris, PhD, Department of Plant Sciences, University of Oxford, May 2014.
[2] Species unidentifiable given current data.
[3] Identified as *Cajanus cajan* (L.) Millsp. by Stephen Harris.
[4] New variety that appeared in Liliana's garden in February 2013.
[5] Added to list in November 2017 by Canela gardeners.

Table 8.   Fava bean / *Pànkrỳt* (*Phaseolus* L. spp.; *Vicia faba* L., *Vigna* Savi spp.)

Canela name	Translation	Description
Pànkrỳt ahkrare[1]	Child fava bean	Small with white and black coloring; associated with a child (*ahkrare*) and the umbilical cord
Pànkrỳt ahkrare caprêc-re[2]	Red child fava bean	White with brilliant reddish-pink markings; matures quickly in 5–6 months
Pànkrỳt ahkrare kuctỳi tyc[1]	Strong black-face child fava bean	White with some black coloring; resembles male child whose forehead is painted black (*kuc* = face)
Pànkrỳt càà pê-xuùre[1]	Translation unclear	White and "charcoal" colored (*càà* = center, field, party/celebration)
Pànkrỳt carêntohkà pó[3]	Translation unclear	Pink and resembles larger version of *pànkrỳt mēhkàa*; prepared with sweet manioc dough (*kà* = skin/shell; *pó* = broad or wide)
Pànkrỳt catêc-re hy[1]	*Catêc-re* seed fava bean	Red and white markings; resembles seed (*hy*) of native *catêc-re* plant
Pànkrỳt cuhkryt-ti[1]	King vulture fava bean	White with purplish-black and red coloring; resembles king vulture (*cuhkryt-ti*)
Pànkrỳt cupēkwỳj[1]	White woman fava bean	White with pinkish markings; resembles white woman wearing lipstick
Pànkrỳt hàc jarati[1]	Ritual headdress fava bean (or hawk's wing fava bean)	Dark red with some white coloring; resembles *hàc jarati* woven headdress worn by ritual girls (*wuh-tỳ*) during the Khêêtuwajê boys' internment festival (*hàc* = hawk; *jarati* = large wing)
Pànkrỳt hipêj cre[4]	*Hipêj* egg fava bean	White with black/brown coloring; resembles *hipêj* bird's egg
Pànkrỳt hipêj cre catia[4]	Large *hipêj* egg fava bean	White and dark brown; larger and resembles *hipêj* bird's egg
Pànkrỳt hipêj cre jarkwa tep[1]	Another type of *hipêj* egg fava bean	Red and white coloring; resembles *hipêj* bird's egg and woman wearing lipstick; is "old" and used in the past
Pànkrỳt hipêj cre tep-re[4]	Red *hipêj* egg fava bean	White and red; rounded and resembles *hipêj* bird's egg
Pànkrỳt jaka-re[4]	Small white fava bean	Small and white
Pànkrỳt jaha-ti[4]	Large white fava bean	Large and white
Pànkrỳt jōkrāire cre[4]	*Jōkrāire* egg fava bean	Red and striped with white; resembles *jōkrāire* bird's egg
Pànkrỳt jūnren cre[3]	Hummingbird egg fava bean	White and small; resembles hummingbird's (*jūnren*) egg
Pànkrỳt kājkāj-re jahkat[2]	Small twisted-beak fava bean	Small with black and white design that twists/swirls around; resembles bird's beak (*kājkāj* – twisted or encircled like anaconda)
Pànkrỳt krēhkrēpti[1]	Color-of-hawk fava bean	Large and white with violet-black color that resembles color of hawk
Pànkrỳt krêwre[1]	*Krē-re* bird fava bean	Dark red with some white coloring; resembles parakeets (*kre-re*) that eat rice growing in garden plots

Table 8. Continued

Canela name	Translation	Description
Pànkrỳt kroro-re[1]	Jaguar fava bean	Brown with black spots that resembles jaguar's markings
Pànkrỳt kror-ti[1]	Large mixed-color fava bean	Mixed coloring of white, purplish-black, and red
Pànkrỳt kryi-re jaka-re[5]	Very small white fava bean	White and small
Pànkrỳt kwỳrkà[3]	Manioc skin fava bean	Violet-black color that resembles hawk; also similar to bitter manioc
Pànkrỳt mē hupkre têp[1]	Translation unclear	Small with white and red coloring; resembles being painted with *urucum* (annatto)
Pànkrỳt mēcuprỳ catia (tỳjtu)[1]	Mature strong young girls fava bean	White with tan marking; resembles young woman wearing lipstick (*mēcuprỳ* = plural young girls; *tỳjtu* = very strong)
Pànkrỳt mēcuprỳ-re[3]	Annatto fava bean	Round and red-colored, similar to annatto (*urucum*); related to little young girls (*mēcuprỳ-re* = smaller/younger girls)
Pànkrỳt mēhaprār[1]	Warriors fava bean	Red with white markings on the "cheeks" that resemble those of brave warriors (*mēhaprār*)
Pànkrỳt mēhkàa[6]	Old people fava bean	Smaller with brown, shriveled skin that resembles that of old Canela people (*mēhkàa* = old men in the center and/or all old people)
Pànkrỳt mēhkra tàmtuw[1]	Messily painted fava bean	White with brown markings; resembles "messy" body paint of woman who has recently had 1–3 children; eat this type for "sustenance" (*tàm* = raw and/or menstruating woman; *tuw* = recently fresh)
Pànkrỳt mēhkra tetet[1]	Young/unripe children fava bean	White with black stripes; eaten during food and sex prohibitions
Pànkrỳt mēhkra tetet cucràn[1]	Young children painted with annatto fava bean	Red with some white; resembles children painted with red annatto (*urucum*; *pym*) (*mēhkra* = children of Canela/Timbira people; *tetet* = light-colored or unripe; *cucràn* = act of painting with *urucum*)
Pànkrỳt mēhtỳi[5]	The strong and happy ones fava bean	White and larger (*mē* = plural; *ihtỳi* = strong, happy, healthy)
Pànkrỳt po cahàc[3]	Common Cerrado deer fava bean	Black with white stripes and a bit of red coloring; resembles pampas deer native to the Cerrado (*po*; *veado-galheiro*; *Ozotoceros bezoarticus* L.)
Pànkrỳt pyhti[1]	Large annatto fava bean	White with red lipstick; resembles women who paint their mouths with red annatto (*urucum*) to visit the garden while menstruating
Pànkrỳt pyytà[1]	Annatto root fava bean	White with brownish markings; resembles weak brownish-red color of annatto root and common annatto
Pànkrỳt tatap-re[1]	Small bright-yellow fava bean	Smaller and brighter-yellow-colored

Table 8. Continued

Canela name	Translation	Description
Pànkrỳt tàtà-re[6]	Small yellowish-brown fava bean	Yellowish-brown when ripe/dried out; yellowish-white when fresh/green
Pànkrỳt tàtà-ti[6]	Large yellowish-brown fava bean	Yellowish-brown with white stripes when ripe/dried out; yellowish-white when fresh
Pànkrỳt têhtê cahàc[5]	Common têhtê bird fava bean	Black and white markings; resembles native têhtê bird that advises people when animals are nearby
Pànkrỳt tic-re intep-re[4]	Small bright-red fava bean	Smaller; bright red with white stripes
Pànkrỳt tic-re tep-re[5]	Small red fava bean	Smaller and completely red colored
Pànkrỳt tic-ti catia ita[4]	Large bright-red fava bean	Larger; bright red with white stripes
Pànkrỳt tohcaiwêu jipro-re[5]	Small grey mask fava bean	Smaller with swirled brown/grey-and-white design; resembles Tohcaiwêu mask
Pànkrỳt tohcaiwêu-re[3]	Small mask fava bean	Very small with swirling white-and-black markings; resembles lively Tohcaiwêu mask figure in mask festival
Pànkrỳt tohcaiwêu-re catia ita[1]	Very large mask fava bean	Swirled black and white; largest bean that resembles Tohcaiwêu mask
Pànkrỳt tohcaiwêu-re tep-re[1]	Small red mask fava bean	Smaller with swirled red-and-white design; resembles Tohcaiwêu mask
Pànkrỳt tohcaiwêu-ti (pàn jahkat)[2]	Large mask fava bean (or macaw's beak fava bean)	Swirled black and white; large and pointed—resembles Tohcaiwêu mask figure and macaw beak (pàn = macaw; jahkat = beak)
Pànkrỳt tyc-re[1]	Small black fava bean	Small; black-and-red-striped
Pànkrỳt tyc-ti[1]	Large black fava bean	Large; black-and-white-striped
Pànkrỳt xôn[4]	Vulture fava bean	Black and smaller in size (xôn = vulture)
Pànkrỳt xôn-ti[1]	Large vulture fava bean	Black and larger in size

[1] Identified as *Phaseolus vulgaris* L. by Stephen Harris, Department of Plant Sciences, University of Oxford, May 2014.
[2] Identified as *Phaseolus lunatus* L. by Stephen Harris.
[3] Identified as *Vigna* Savi sp. by Stephen Harris.
[4] Identified as *Vicia faba* L. by Stephen Harris.
[5] Species unidentifiable given current data.
[6] Identified as *Phaseolus* L. sp. by Stephen Harris.

Table 9.   Sweet potato / Jàt (*Ipomoea batatas* L.)

Canela name	Translation	Description
Jàt ahkrare jõntot	Child's umbilical cord sweet potato	Resembles navel of newborn baby; small, white, and round; potatoes hang from the vine
Jàt caprãn cre	Tortoise egg sweet potato	Round and resembles tortoise egg; grey-skinned
Jàt caxwỳn tatap-ti	Large yellow membrane sweet potato	Yellow pulp, membrane, and skin; comes from afar and starting to cultivate
Jàt cràà-ti	Large dry sweet potato	Yellow-skinned and dry pulp
Jàt jakat jajõh-re	Small round white sweet potato	Smaller, rounded, and white-skinned
Jàt jakat jajõh-ti	Large round white sweet potato	Very round and ball-shaped; white-skinned
Jàt jaka-ti	Large white sweet potato	White skin; sweet-tasting
Jàt jarxê	Translation unclear	White-skinned and longer in shape
Jàt jikôt-ti	Large curved root sweet potato	Grey-skinned (*jikôt* = curved)
Jàt jĩtehtu-re	Small human-faced sweet potato	Shape resembles human cheeks (*jĩtehtu*); long vine and potatoes grow in a line on the vine
Jàt jõtep-ti	Monkey from Pará sweet potato	Resembles *cupût* monkey from Pará State that has a yellow bottom; half orange, half yellow-colored skin
Jàt kàhcaprêc	Red-skinned sweet potato	Red-colored skin and white pulp; very tasty
Jàt krãjipro	Grey-white sweet potato	Grey and white skin
Jàt tyc-re	Small black sweet potato	Black-colored skin
Jàt tyc-ti	Large blackish-purple sweet potato	Large with blackish-purple-colored skin

Table 10. Rice / *Arỳihy* (*Oryza sativa* L. and/or *Oryza glaberrima* Steud.)

Canela name	Translation	Description
Fast-growing rice—*arỳihy kênpei* / *arroz ligeiro* (Portuguese).		
Arỳihy capêê kênpei	Striped fast-growing rice	Striped black and white (*capêê*)
Arỳihy caprêc-re kênpei	Small red fast-growing rice	Most original (*impeaj*) rice—eaten during new parents' food and sex prohibition period
Arỳihy caprêc-ti jarati kênpei	Large-winged red fast-growing rice	*Arroz de asa*; has "wings" or arms (*jarat* = wings)
Arỳihy caprêc-ti kênpei	Large red fast-growing rice	Large, long, and red-colored
Arỳihy jaka-re kênpei	Small white fast-growing rice	True/original and beautiful (*impej*) rice
Arỳihy jaka-ti japjêhti kênpei	Large long white fast-growing rice	Large, white-colored, and long
Arỳihy jarare caprêc-re kênpei	Small-winged red fast-growing rice	Small and red; has "wings" or arms (*jarare* = wings)
Arỳihy jarare jaka-re kênpei	Small-winged white fast-growing rice	Small and white; has "wings" or arms
Arỳihy jarati kror-ti kênpei	Large-winged mixed-color fast-growing rice	Large and purple-painted/striped; has "wings" or arms
Arỳihy jõhkênture caprêc-re kênpei	Red rooster wattle fast-growing rice	Small, rounded, and red-colored; resembles *jõhkênture* (rooster's wattle)
Arỳihy kranre caprêc-re kênpei	Small short red fast-growing rice	Short (*kranre*) and rounded; red-colored with some white; tasty
Arỳihy kroro-re kênpei	Small mixed-color fast-growing rice (or small jaguar fast-growing rice)	Striped black and white-colored (*kroro* = mixed colors or spotted like jaguar)
Arỳihy kror-ti kênpei	Large mixed-color fast-growing rice	Purple-colored and painted/striped
Aryihy tyc-re kênpei	Small black fast-growing rice	Made into hot beverage and used as remedy for various ailments: diarrhea, fever, menstrual and other pains, gonorrhea

Table 10. Continued

Canela name	Translation	Description
	Slow-growing rice — *arỳihy kênpôc* / *arroz margão* (Portuguese).	
Arỳihy capêê kênpôc	Striped slow-growing rice	Striped black and white
Arỳihy caprêc-re japjêre kênpôc	Small, fine, long, and red slow-growing rice	Longer growing period; very tasty; resembles ema meat (*japjêre* = fine and long)
Arỳihy caprêc-re jõhkênture kênpôc	Red rooster-wattle slow-growing rice	Small and red; resembles rooster's wattle
Arỳihy caprêc-re kênpôc	Tiny red slow-growing rice	Most original (*impeaj*); very small and red; new parents use to make *mingau* during food and sex prohibition period
Arỳihy hônxôti kênpôc	*Hônxôti*-leaf slow-growing rice	Resembles native forest plant that appears dried out when it ripens; long and white; *arroz pai moça*; has 6-month-long growing period
Arỳihy jaka-ti japjêhti kênpôc	Large long white slow-growing rice	White-colored and long
Arỳihy jarati catia kênpôc	Largest-winged white slow-growing rice	*Arroz de asa branca*; large and has "wings" or arms
Arỳihy jõhkênture jaka-re kênpôc	White rooster-wattle slow-growing rice	Small and white; resembles rooster's wattle; hard husk and produces large harvest
Arỳihy jõhkênture kroro-re kênpôc	Rooster-wattle striped slow-growing rice (or rooster-wattle jaguar slow-growing rice)	Small and black-and-white striped; resembles rooster's wattle (and/or resembles jaguar's spots)
Arỳihy jõhôti kênpôc	Hair-on-the-bottom slow-growing rice	*Arroz peba*; has one hair growing off the end (*jõhô*); birds do not eat while growing
Arỳihy krãnre jaka-re kênpôc	Small short white slow-growing rice	Is the "friend" of small, white fast-growing rice (*arỳihy jakare kênpei*)
Arỳihy kror-ti kênpôc	Large mixed-color slow-growing rice	Large and "painted" mixed colors; lumpy in shape
Arỳihy tyc-re kênpôc	Small black slow-growing rice	Burn, grind, and make hot beverage as remedy for aches and pains
Arỳihy xoti japỳ kênpôc	Fox-tail slow-growing rice	Large, short, white, and hairy; resembles fox tail (*xoti* = fox)

Table 11. Peanut / *Caahy* (*Arachis hypogaea* L.)

Canela name	Translation	Description
Caahy capa-re	*Capa-re* plant peanut	Resembles plant that grows near riverbeds; grey skin, white pulp, and sweet; used as remedy for fevers
Caahy catia ita	Largest peanut	Yellow skin, white meat, and red seed coat; true/original (*impej*) peanut
Caahy kàhcaprêc[1]	Red-skinned peanut	Red-skinned with white meat
Caahy kror-ti	Mixed-color peanut	Mixed colors; striped like a watermelon; grey skin, white pulp, pink/painted seed coat; exchanged from Krĩkatí village
Caahy kryi-re	Small peanut	Yellow skin, white pulp, and red seed coat

[1] Added to list in November 2017 by Canela gardeners.

Table 12. Sugarcane / *Cãn* (*Saccharum* L. spp.)

Canela name	Translation	Description
Cãn ahtu / Cãn jiprore	Grey *ahtu* grass sugarcane	*Cana capim-da-chapada*; resembles *ahtu* type of grass that grows in the *chapada*; grows abundantly and produces large harvest
Cãn capêê	Striped sugarcane	Black-and-white striped; tougher/durable
Cãn peaj-re	True/original sugarcane	*Cana canhana*; soft, yellow, and pretty; used to chew on
Cãn põhy-re	Small maize sugarcane	*Cana do milho*; resembles small maize plant; children like to chew
Can tetet-ti	White/translucent-skinned sugarcane	*Cana piojota*; bright white, almost translucent
Cãn tyo ti	Large black sugarcane	*Cana do São Paulo*, comes from São Paulo State

Table 13. Annatto / *Pym* (*Bixa orellana* L.)

Canela name	Translation	Description
Pym krã caprêc	Red shell annatto	Bright red and very pretty; also called "red-head annatto"; (*krã* = head)
Pym po jĩxwa	Cerrado deer toenail annatto	Pointed shell that resembles the toenail of Cerrado pampas deer (*veado-galheiro*; *Ozotoceros bezoarticus* L.)
Pym peaj	True/original annatto	Bright red and very pretty; tree lives for 9 years
Pyytà	Common annatto	Weak reddish/yellow color; not desirable or used for body paint

Table 14. Sesame / *Hyhcuxwa-re (Sesamum indicum* L.)

Canela name	Translation	Description
Hyhcuxwa-re jaka-re	Small white sesame	Small and white-colored; mixed into *farinha* and *beribu*
Hyhcuxwa-re tyc-re	Small black sesame	Small and black-colored

Table 15. Cotton / *Caxàt (Gossypium barbadense* L.)

Canela name	Translation	Description
Caxàt catia ita	Large cotton	Larger in size
Caxàt kryi-re	Small cotton	Smaller in size

Table 16. Banana / *Pypyp-re (Musa* L. spp.)

Canela name	Translation	Description
Pypyp-re awarxô	Cobra bitter manioc (*kwỳr awari*) banana	*Banana maçã*; fruit resembles cobra bitter manioc; small, full, and tasty (*xô* = fruit)
Pypyp-re intep-ti	Large red banana	Large and red peel
Pypyp-re jakàhtetet-re	Sprawling tree banana	*Banana prata*; white peel and pulp (*jakàhtetet-re* = sprawling tree); from *cupēn*
Pypyp-re pàrkrãnti (*pypyp-re kãncot*)	Short-tree banana (or green-peel banana)	*Banana anão/anais*; small tree with many bananas; peel is always green (*pàrkrãnti* = short tree; *kãncot* = green skin, peel, shell)
Pypyp-re pàrkrãnti catia ita	Large short-tree banana	*Banana aná verdadeira*; larger than *pypyp-re pàrkrãnti* but still short
Pypyp-re pryti jiwrỳhhi	Cow's rib banana	*Banana costela de vaca*; long, white; resembles cow's rib
Pypyp-re rõrxô	*Babaçu* fruit banana	More rounded and resembles *babaçu* fruit
Pypyp-re tyc-ti	Large black banana	*Banana canhana*; black peel
Pypyp-re xô pohti	Long fruit banana	*Banana murici*; banana fruit is long

Table 17. Cashew / *Ahkrỳt* (*Anacardium occidentale* L.)

Canela name	Translation	Description
Ahkrỳt jaka-ti	Large white cashew	Large with white-colored skin and pulp
Ahkrỳt japjêhti	Long cashew	Longer in shape
Ahkrỳt kà kūkūm-ti[1]	Large purplish cashew	Large with purplish skin
Ahkrỳt rerecti	Soft cashew	*Caju manteiga*; long and soft pulp (*rerec* = soft)
Ahkrỳt tatap-ti	Large bright-yellow cashew	Bright yellow; similar to color of cotton flower
Ahkrỳt tàtà-ti (ahkrỳt jajó-ti)	Large round yellowish-brown cashew	Yellowish-brown and green in color; rounded
Ahkrỳt tep-ti	Large red cashew	Large with red-colored skin
Ahkrỳt-ti (ahkrỳt catia ita)	Largest cashew	Largest of the cashews

[1] Brought from Goiana State and added to list in November 2017 by Canela gardeners.

Table 18. Watermelon / *Praxī* (*Citrullus lanatus* [Thunb.] Matsum. & Nakai var. *lanatus*)

Canela name	Translation	Description
Praxī cahàc	Common watermelon	Not currently cultivated
Praxī capê-ti	Large striped watermelon	Striped color and large
Praxī jaka-ti	Large white watermelon	White-colored and large
Praxī tàtà-ti	Large yellow watermelon	Yellow-colored; not currently cultivated
Praxī tyc-ti	Large black watermelon	Black-colored and large

Table 19. Papaya / *Mamão* (*Carica papaya* L.)

Canela name	Translation	Description
Mamão jajóti	Round papaya	Rounded
Mamão japjêhti	Long papaya	Longer in shape
Mamão jêrmū (cakjêrti)	Cut-in-the-middle papaya	Rounded and appears to be cut in the middle (*cakjêrti*); resembles a pumpkin (*jerimum* in Portuguese)
Mamão kryi-re	Small papaya	*Mamãozinho*; smaller than others

Table 20. Mango / *Mac* (*Mangifera indica* L.)

Canela name	Translation	Description
Mac cuhtõj	Maraca-gourd mango	*Manga cujubu*; resembles *cuhtõj* gourd that is used to make maracas
Mac cuxỳhti	Different/distinct-smell mango	*Manga de cheira*; has a unique smell (*cuxỳhti*)
Mac jicacure	Soft mango	*Manga espada*; soft pulp (*jicacure* = another term for soft)
Mac kukum-ti	Large violet-greenish mango	*Manga de mesa*; violet-green-colored skin
Mac peaj-re	True/original mango	*Manga fiaba/manga comum*; true/original mango for Canela, "common" for *cupēn*
Mac prĩn-re	*Prĩn-re* (small *piqui*) mango	Resembles native *piqui* fruit (*Caryocar coriaceum* Wittm.) in shape and smell
Mac rõhkrỳt	Brush-cutter mango	*Manga de fois*; resembles brush-cutter tool or large knife (*rõhkrỳt*); also resembles toucan beak
Mac tep-ti	Large red mango	*Manga de rosa*; red-colored skin
Mac tyc-re	Small black mango	Small and lightweight; grey/black-skinned

Table 21. Coconut / *Rõrti* (*Cocos nucifera* L.)

Canela name	Translation	Description
Rõrti kà tatap-ti	Large yellow-shelled coconut	Yellow shell and large; typical to northeast Brazil
Rõrti pàr japjêhti	Tall tree coconut	Tree is very tall
Rõrti te krãnti	Green-shelled coconut	*Coco da praia aná*; has green shell

Table 22. Pineapple / *Prôprô* (*Ananas comosus* [L.] Merr.)

Canela name	Translation	Description
Prôprô kà tatap-re	Small yellow-skinned pineapple	Small with yellow skin
Prôprô tyc-ti	Large black pineapple	Large and black-colored

Table 23. Acerola / Têc-rà cahàc xô (Malpighia emarginata DC. or Malpighia glabra L.)

Canela name	Translation	Description
Têc-rà cahàc xô	Common acerola	Resembles têc-rà cahàc, type of native Cerrado fruit (Psidium sp.); is the "normal" type of acerola
Têc-rà cahàc xô jêrmũ	Pumpkin acerola	Resembles pumpkin and têc-rà cahàc fruit

Table 24. Lime / Rĩm (Citrus L. sp.)

Canela name	Translation	Description
Rĩmcahhàc-re	Common lime	Normal lime; green skin and white pulp
Rĩmcahpopoc-re	Tangerine lime	Resembles tangerine (popoc-re)
Rĩm catia ita hĩ tep-ti	Largest reddish-orange pulp lime	Green skin with reddish-orange pulp (hĩ); resembles an orange

Table 25. Orange / Ràràj (Citrus L. sp.)

Canela name	Translation	Description
Ràràj	Normal orange	Regular or "normal" orange
Ràràj cahàc	Common orange	Laranja da terra; "earth orange"

Table 26. Avocado / Bacat (Persea americana L.)

Canela name	Translation	Description
Bacat catia ita	Large avocado	Larger in size
Bacat kryi-re	Small avocado	Smaller in size

Table 27. Jackfruit / Potukà (Artocarpus heterophyllus Lam.)

Canela name	Translation	Description
Potukà catia ita	Large jackfruit	Larger in size
Potukà kryi-re	Small jackfruit	Smaller in size

Table 28. Passion fruit / *Ahkrôhti-xô* (*Passiflora edulis* Sims)

Canela name	Translation	Description
Ahkrôhti-xô catia ita	Large passion fruit	Larger in size
Ahkrôhti-xô kryi-re	Small passion fruit	Smaller in size

Table 29. Guava / *Cwaj-jap* (*Psidium guajava* L.)

Canela name	Translation	Description
Cwaj-jap catia ita	Large guava	Larger in size
Cwaj-jap kryi-re	Small guava	Smaller in size

Table 30. Cultivated crops with only one type

Canela name	Translation	Species
Awar cahàc	*Pupunha*	*Bactris gasipaes* Kunth
Carampá	Deer liver plant	N/A; known as *planta de fígado de veado* in Portuguese; resembles a deer's liver
Catëëere-xô	*Ata* or *pinha*	*Annona squamosa* L.
Cupuaxu	*Cupuaçu*	*Theobroma grandiflorum* (Willd. ex Spreng.) K. Schum.
Curuware	*Coquinho* (*alho-do-mato* or *jerivá*)	*Cipura paludosa* Aubl. or *Syagrus romanzoffiana* (Cham.) Glassman
Hyjorore	*Pitomba*	*Talisia esculenta* Radlk.
No translation	*Graviola*	*Annona muricata* L.
Pôj kõc-jõjre cahàc	Tamarind	*Tamarindus indica* L.
Pôl-ti pàr	*Jenipapo*	*Genipa americana* L.; fruit (*pôl-ti xô*) used to make ritual black body paint; cultivated and also found in the *põ* (*chapada*)
Rãrãj kà popoc-re	Tangerine	*Citrus* sp.
Rimi	Another type of lime	*Citrus* sp.
Tepja-re	*Tingui*	N/A; fish poison vine that shocks/immobilizes fish; cultivated and also found in the *parkô* (closed *chapada*)
Tomat	Tomato	*Solanum lycopersicum* L.

APPENDIX D

Living Lists of Canela Native Plants in Savannah, *Chapada*, and Riverbank

These lists include species identified by Canela research assistants in the savannah (*irom*), chapada (*põ*), and riverbank (*coh-cahêhnã*) eco-regions in 2012–2013 and 2017. As living lists, there are likely many more species and varieties that Canela gardeners will add to these lists during subsequent research.

Table 1. Trees and plants native to the savannah eco-region (*irom*)

Canela name	Translation	Species and description
Capôcre pàr	Tuturubá, taturuba, or cutite	Pouteria macrophylla (Lam.) Eyma; also found in chapada
Caprãn jõõ pàr	Tortoise tree; maçaranduba	Manilkara huberi (Ducke) A. Chev.; hunters eat fruit (caprãn jõõxô) while hunting
Critĩn-re cahàc pàr	Guabiroba or gabiroba	Campomanesia pubescens (DC.) O. Berg and/or Campomanesia sp.; in the forest and/or in the caatinga
Cuhtà pàr	Sucupira	Bowdichia virgilioides Kunth; hardwood tree found in savannah and chapada
Cũmxêre pàr	No translation	N/A; medicinal remedy for various illnesses; also found in chapada
Cutẽre pàr	Murici	Byrsonima crassifolia (L.) Kunth
Cuuhẽ kàhtyc pàr	Purple tree (pau roxo)	N/A
Hôhcatõtõc-re pàr	No translation	N/A
Papôrôre pàr	Type of guava	Psidium sp.; pulp of fruit is similar to jenipapo
Pàt jĩnka-re pàr	Hiáre	Animals eat the fruit (pàt jĩnka-re xô)
Pjêrêre krô	Small babaçu (babaçuzinho)	Attalea sp.; vine grows near the ground (krô = vine)
Pôikôre pàr	Jatobá de mateira	Hymenaea sp.
Prycatàt-re pàr	Small jatobá (jatobázinho)	Hymenaea sp.
Pyyrija pàr	Cajá	Spondias mombin L.; also found in chapada
Ronhàc pàr	Macaúba	Acrocomia aculeata (Jacq.) Lodd. ex Mart.; also found in chapada
Rônti pàr	Tucum of the forest	Bactris setosa Mart.
Rõrõ pàr	Babaçu or babassu	Attalea speciosa Mart.; also found in riverbank (coh-cahêhnã)
Rõrõ pej-re pàr	True/original babaçu	Attalea sp.
Têc-rà cahàc pàr	Guava of the forest	Psidium sp.
Tehti pàr	Jatobá de socalho	Hymenaea sp.
Tu-re pàr jaka-ti	White ipê (ipê-branco)	Tabebuia roseoalba (Ridl.) Sandwith

259

Table 1. Continued

Canela name	Translation	Species and description
Tu-re pàr tyc-ti	Black-purple ipê (*ipê roxo*)	*Handroanthus impetiginosus* (Mart. ex DC.) Mattos
Wajõtot cahàc-re pàr	No translation	N/A; also found in *chapada*
Wôôre pàr	Pati	*Syagrus botryophora* (Martius) Martius; also found in *chapada*
Xut-re pàr	Jacaranda	*Jacaranda brasiliana* Pers. and/or *Jacaranda* sp.

Table 2. Trees and plants native to the *chapada* (*põ*)

Canela name	Translation	Species and description
Ahkrỳt-re pàr a) *Ahkrỳt-re pàr intep-re* b) *Ahkrỳt-re pàr jaka-re*	Cashew of the *chapada* a) Small red *chapada* cashew b) Small white *chapada* cashew	*Anacardium* sp.
Ahtu	Type of native *chapada* grass	N/A
Aràmhôc pàr	*Pau de leite*	*Sapium gladulatum* (Vell.) Pax; fruits used to make black body paint
Catēti intep-re pàr	Red *bruta*	N/A
Catēti jaka-ti pàr	White *bruta*	N/A
Crĩtĩn-re pàr	Soft *puçá*	*Mouriri pusa* Gard. and/or *Mouriri* sp.
Crotot-re pàr	Hard *puçá*	*Mouriri pusa* Gard. and/or *Mouriri* sp.
Cucrànre pàr	No translation	N/A; medicinal remedy for wound
Cũmxê pàr	Bacuri	*Platonia insignis* Mart.; also found in the *parkô* (closed *chapada*)
Cutēre põ tekjê pàr	*Murici* of the *chapada*	*Byrsonima* sp.
Hĩ kà krõ	No translation	Use fruit (*hĩ kà xô*) as remedy to stop menstruation
Hôckà / ahkrô krô	*Timbó* or *cipó-timbó*	N/A; type of fish poison vine traditionally used by "another tribe"; causes fish to rot while still alive
Mã jatõti pàr	No translation	N/A; large tree; bats eat the fruit (*mã jatõti xô*)
Pênxôô pàr	Mangaba	*Hancornia speciosa* Gomes
Pjêrêti catia ita pàr	Type of *babaçu*	*Attalea* sp.; also found in *irom* (savannah)
Pôj pàr	*Jatobá da chapada*	*Hymenaea* sp.; also found in *irom* (savannah)
Prĩn pàr	Piqui	*Caryocar coriaceum* Wittm.
Prykà cacô pàr	Type of *pau de leite*	*Sapium gladulatum*; use "milk" as remedy for skin rashes
Ronre pàr	Tucum of the *chapada*	*Bactris setosa* Mart. and/or *Bactris* sp.
Têc-ràire pàr	Araçá	*Psidium guineense* Sw. and/or *Psidium* sp.
Tecrêj (põjõhpôj) pàr	*Jatobá vaqueiro*	*Hymenaea* sp.
Tuhhôhôre pàr	Type of wild manioc	*Manihot grahamii* Hook. and/or *Manihot* sp.
Woporore	Another type of native *chapada* grass	N/A

Table 3.   Trees and plants native to the riverbank (*coh-cahêhnã*)

Canela name	Translation	Species and description
Ahkrôhti pàr	Type of passion fruit	*Passiflora* sp.
Awar pàr	*Najá* or *inajá*	*Attalea maripa* (Aubl.) Mart. and/or *Attalea* sp.
Capêr pàr	Bacaba	*Oenocarpus bacaba* Mart.
Crowa pàr / Hõrcuràhti	Buriti	*Mauritia flexuosa* Mart.; *crowa xô* = fruit; *crowa pàr* or *hõrcuràhti* = tree
Crowarà pàr	Buritirana	*Mauritiella armata* (Mart.) Burret and/or *Mauritiella aculeata* (Kunth) Burret
Kõc-jõiti pàr	Ingá	*Inga* sp.
Mrĩti krô	Potato of the riverbank	*Ipomoea* sp.; *krô* = vine
Têrêre pàr	Juçara or açaí	*Euterpe edulis* Mart. and/or *Euterpe oleracea* Mart.

APPENDIX C

Star-Woman (Caxêtikwỳj) Mythic Story

Told by Leandro, June 2012

Tyc-ti is Caxêtikwỳj's husband. Caxêtikwỳj chose Tyc-ti to be with him, teach him, and show him the food of the forest, because the "ancient" Indians [ancestors] did not know about this food. Caxêtikwỳj came down from the sky and turned into a small frog and sat on top of Tyc-ti's stomach. He threw the frog off his stomach, and Caxêtikwỳj, as a frog, fell to the ground. When Tyc-ti was sleeping, she sat on top of his stomach once again, and he threw her off him—this happened two times. Caxêtikwỳj then said to him, "why do you not like me?" Tyc-ti responded, "I did not know; you are a person!" Caxêtikwỳj told him, "yes I am; I came down from the sky. My name is Caxêtikwỳj [Estrela Dalva, Star-Woman]. You can call me this, and now let us get together!" The two of them got together [slept together], and they talked about many things; they were talking and talking. Afterward, Caxêtikwỳj advised Tyc-ti: "you should hide me again, wherever you want, in secret, so that no one sees me." Tyc-ti responded, "I have my sheath for storing arrows, I will clean it out so that you can hide in there." He removed the bow and arrows, and put Caxêtikwỳj inside. It was becoming light outside; the day was almost dawning. Tyc-ti took Caxêtikwỳj with him, and she was hidden inside the *cuhkõn-ti* [or *cuhkõn pàt-wỳ*] gourd. He hid her and carried the gourd around with him.

All morning, Tyc-ti opened the lid of the gourd, saw Caxêtikwỳj, and laughed. He laughed for her, and she laughed for him. She liked him, and he liked her too—they both liked each other. Tyc-ti's youngest sister saw him laughing into the gourd and thought, "my brother is opening the lid of this gourd and laughing all the time; I do not know why." When the day dawned, everyone began eating rotten wood, which was the people's food. The Indians ate this rotten wood; it was soft enough to eat. They did not know about "good" food.

Afterward, Tyc-ti went to his house, which was large and long. He advised his sisters, "do not tamper with this gourd, it is beautiful! I am going along with my group to search for a log." Tyc-ti and his brothers [from the same male age group] went hunting for rotten wood to eat. They sat, they thought. Meanwhile, everyone [in the house] saw this gourd. Tyc-ti's sister opened the lid and looked inside, but when Caxêtikwỳj saw a different face than Tyc-ti's, she hung her head in shame. She hid in the gourd once again. When Tyc-ti arrived, he opened the lid and saw that Caxêtikwỳj was still hanging her head. Tyc-ti said, "who tampered with my gourd?" His sister replied, "it was me." "Did you see the nice thing there?" Tyc-ti asked. "Yes, I saw her face is pretty," responded his sister. Tyc-ti told Caxêtikwỳj, "do not be angry, do not be upset with your youngest sister." Caxêtikwỳj responded, "now, with the afternoon arriving, I will come out, for everyone to see me." Tyc-ti asked his sister to bring a mat for him and his wife to sleep on. "I will remain lying on the ground itself, next to the fire," he said. Later in the afternoon, Caxêtikwỳj came out of the gourd and sat on a log in the doorway of the house. She was beautiful, with white, almost clear-colored skin and very long hair that was very pretty. There she was, in the house. The brothers said, "we do not know where her tribe comes from; she is so white!" Tyc-ti's sister said, "no one knows. Only they know [Tyc-ti and Caxêtikwỳj]."

The next morning, at seven in the morning, Caxêtikwỳj said to her husband, "let us go bathing. Bring the large basket." They came to the stream and saw a large amount of tucum fruit [rônti xô or ronre xô; *Bactris setosa*; a type of native palm]. "Pick this tucum," Caxêtikwỳj told Tyc-ti, and he did so. She began chewing it, and asked him, "Are you going to eat it?" "No, if I eat that, I will die," Tyc-ti answered. He did not want to eat it; he became angry. "No, you will not die. This is what feeds you; it is your food. I am going to find everything for you to know about," Caxêtikwỳj told him. She gave him the tucum fruit, and he chewed it, swallowed it, and found it tasty. Once they were in the water, there were many buriti [crowa pàr; *Mauritia flexuosa*] palms next to the stream. Caxêtikwỳj gave the buriti fruit to Tyc-ti for him to taste it as well. Again, Tyc-ti said, "I am not going to eat this because it is raw, and very red." Caxêtikwỳj told him, "no, it is not raw; it is fruit, buriti fruit! People are not accustomed to eating it, you do not know. I am still going to find other fruit in the *chapada*, and in the forest." Caxêtikwỳj gave Tyc-ti the fruit for him to swallow, and he liked it. She made juice and showed him how to drink it.

Another day, Caxêtikwỳj took Tyc-ti to a different stream. They went into the stream, and there were many ears of corn falling into the water. Tyc-ti asked her, "what is in here, these tall stalks and big ears?" "It is maize!" Caxêtikwỳj told him. "This is what I am discovering for you all to know about. Let us go to the village, to show people." They had to roast it, because it was still raw. There were so many ears of corn, and they arrived to the house with all the ears. Caxêtikwỳj's sisters-in-law were seated, and she told one of them, "my sister-in-law, this is food; it is an ear of corn. I am going to roast it for you to see." Caxêtikwỳj said this; she had this knowledge. Together, they made a grater to grate the ears of corn. Then, they made a fire, roasted the ears, and ate them. All the sisters-in-law were chewing the food. "Are you seeing it; is it tasty?" Caxêtikwỳj asked. It was so tasty! "You have never seen this; it was I who discovered it, and I still have other things to discover," Caxêtikwỳj told them. "The fruits of the riverbank, and there are other plants too."

Caxêtikwỳj grated the ears of corn, made an earthen oven, and brought the maize husks with her as well. She wrapped the grated maize meal in the husks, covered them, and baked them in the oven. When it started smoking, she opened the oven. Everyone smelled the nice smell of the maize *beribu* pie and thought it was beautiful. She distributed the pie to the children and to the adults, in the same house. In the afternoon, the men's groups put the pies in the village street and performed the log racing. Everyone was together. One grandson, a little boy, took a piece of the maize pie and began eating it. "What are you eating?" people asked him. The little boy ran away and sat [near Caxêtikwỳj]. In this way, everyone found out about Caxêtikwỳj. People said, "Caxêtikwỳj is finding this food for us to know about! We are going to cut down the maize tree; it is very tall and is heavy with ears of corn." The next morning . . . the Indian, he never learned to be intelligent, he did not know, and he asked the Christians [*cupẽn*; non-Indigenous white people] to cut down the maize tree. The Christians took the largest ears of corn and left the smaller ones for us. That is why the whites plant maize with large ears and the Indians plant maize with smaller ears, because the Christians stole the large ears and left the smaller ones.

Another day, Caxêtikwỳj said, "let us go to the forest so I can show another fruit to you." It was *mangaba* [*pênxôô pàr*; *Hancornia speciosa*]; it was a large, tall tree with fruit this size [about the size of a fist]. Caxêtikwỳj was in the forest and presented the *mangaba* tree to the people, saying, "this is for you all to know about and to eat. Stop eating rotten wood; that is not food! This is the food that I came here for everyone to know about." An Indian climbed up the tree to cut down the fruit, and it fell to the ground. They collected all of it. Caxêtikwỳj herself showed them how to do everything—how to make the earthen oven. They dug a hole and arrived with the *mangaba* fruit. "Light this earthen oven," Caxêtikwỳj told them, and when they heated up the stones, Caxêtikwỳj took off the stones and put water in the hole. She heated it up and put in the fruit, which turned soft that very moment. When she was done teaching them, Caxêtikwỳj took away the cooked fruit and returned to the village. They made the food, ate it, and enjoyed it. "[Look at] all of my discoveries of these fruits of the forest! Stop eating rotten wood now; do not remember it anymore," Caxêtikwỳj told the people.

On another day, she said, "let us go again to the forest, so that I can show you another fruit." She took only women with her, and there were many of them. They arrived in the forest, and there were many sweet potato vines, right there in the forest. She started digging up the sweet potatoes, and the women took them back to the village. They made another earthen oven and baked the sweet potatoes, and after cooking them, they were soft as well. All the teachings of Caxêtikwỳj, everything that she taught them, the ancestors learned as well.

Another day, Caxêtikwỳj showed them sweet manioc in the forest. There was so much of it! They harvested the sweet manioc, and they ate it—it was tasty. Caxêtikwỳj showed them bitter manioc too, and told them, "This bitter manioc is not for making *beribu* pies. The sweet manioc is feminine, and the bitter manioc is masculine. You cannot make pies with the bitter manioc, only with the sweet manioc—[because] it is a woman. Bitter manioc is a man; it is bitter, and if you make pies with this, it will kill you, and you will die. You have to grate it, squeeze it in the *tap-ti* [*tipití*], and make *beiju* [a type of pancake] or *farinha* [toasted manioc flour] with it, and you can eat it this way." She showed all of these crops for the Indians to know about. Slowly, they became accustomed to this new food; they began to know about it until they knew everything well. Caxêtikwỳj told her husband, "I am going now. I only came to show this food to you all for you to learn about it. Now I already showed you everything. I am going to return to the sky." Tyc-ti did not want to let her leave. "I am going with you," he said. "No, you are not," she told him. Nevertheless, he convinced her, and Caxêtikwỳj took Tyc-ti with her to the sky. She told him, "let us go together. They already found the fruits in the forest, and the food from the crops as well. They will make gardens and harvest the crops—the *maniva* [roots] of sweet manioc. They will plant sweet potatoes, and buriti, and watermelon, and all the seeds." Caxêtikwỳj went into the sky with her husband.

Introduction

1 Indigenous is capitalized throughout the book following Anderson (2011:11), who identifies the increasing practice of using Indigenous as a proper noun in Canada and elsewhere. Here, the usage of Indigenous as a proper noun also signifies the importance of recognizing the agency of Indigenous peoples throughout the world.

2 Cerrado with a capital C refers to the entire savannah biome that comprises nearly a quarter of Brazil's territory. Within the Cerrado biome, the "cerrado sensu lato" eco-region is the "dominant savannah vegetation type" (Simon and Pennington 2012:712) and includes savannah woodlands, or "cerrado sensu stricto," as well as other land types (Hoffman 2000:63; Felfili et al. 2004:38).

3 Burning fossil fuels, deforesting the land for industrialized agriculture and livestock, and polluting the air, land, and waterways with toxic chemicals have all resulted in an accumulation of the greenhouse gases carbon dioxide, methane, and nitrous oxide (Zalasiewicz et al. 2011:838).

4 The term was originally coined by Paul Crutzen and Eugene Stoermer (2000) and more widely publicized in Crutzen's 2002 article in Nature.

5 There are debates as to whether the Anthropocene was initiated 5,000–8,000 years ago with the development of intensified agriculture during the Neolithic Revolution (Ruddiman 2003, Kutzbach et al. 2010), around the late eighteenth–early nineteenth centuries with the advent of the Industrial Revolution (Crutzen 2002; Steffen et al. 2007, 2011:849), or after 1950 with the "Great Acceleration" of rapid population growth, petroleum consumption, fertilizer use, dam creation, and other large-scale human activities (Steffen et al. 2015).

6 As outlined by the Anthropocene Working Group that recommended the recognition of the Anthropocene as a geological epoch by the International Commission on Stratigraphy and the International Union of Geological Sciences at the 2016 International Geological Congress (Carrington 2016; Waters et al. 2016).

7 The Carbocene draws from a neo-materialist perspective to decenter humanity and recognize "the powerful co-starring role played by coal and hydrocarbons like oil and gas in creating our current era" (Le Cain 2015:23). The Capitalocene was formulated by numerous scholars independently and is understood as signifying "capitalism as a way of organizing nature—as a multispecies, situated, capitalist world-ecology" (J. Moore 2016:6). The Chthulucene, meanwhile, reckons with the past, present, and future by entangling "myriad temporalities and spatialities and myriad intra-active entities-in-assemblages—including the more-than-human, other-than-human, in-human, and human-as-humus" (Haraway 2015:160).

8 Sensory ecology has been incorporated into anthropological studies, most notably by Glenn Shepard (2004) in his cross-cultural analysis of the sensory properties of medicinal plant classification among the Matsigenka and Yora Indigenous communities of the Peruvian Amazon. Shepard's (2004:264) sensory ecology approach focuses on "cross-cultural variation and similarities and ... incorporate[s] physiological understandings and cultural constructions of sensory perception within a broad, biocultural model addressing human–environment interactions."

9 The Canela territory, known as the TI Kanela, is 125,212 hectares and was legally demarcated in 1982. The community is currently working with governmental authorities to demarcate another territory called the TI Kanela/Memortumré of 100,000 hectares that encircles the current territory. This territory was identified in 2012 but has not yet been declared and "homologated" (*homologada*), which are the next steps necessary for legal recognition and status. See Instituto Socioambiental (2018b) for more information.

10 Canela names have been changed from their originals. Canela men and women typically acquire between two and eight Canela names throughout their lives from their naming-uncle and naming-aunt, respectively (see Nimuendajú 1946:77; Miller 2015: 120), and parents usually give a child a Portuguese name as well. Since Canela names may easily identify certain individuals, I have chosen to substitute both Canela and Portuguese names with Portuguese pseudonyms throughout.

11 One's mother and mother's sister are both called "mother" or *inxê* in the first person or as a form of address and *nàà* in the second person (i.e., you). One's mother's mother (maternal grandmother) is called *tùy*, the same term as one's father's sister (aunt), including the naming-aunt who gives names to a Canela girl, and one's father's mother (paternal grandmother; see Crocker 1990:234).

12 Dirceu was known in old age as a man who became a woman (*mãm hũmre hapuhna canãj* in Canela). As gender non-binary, Dirceu is referred to throughout the book with the pronouns "they/them."

Chapter 1: Tracing Indigenous Landscape Aesthetics in the Changing Cerrado

1 Liliana's husband, João Miguel, described seeing a jaguar in the *caxàt-re kô* region as a young man. The story of Liliana's grandfather Rodrigo's encounter with a *pehja-rohti* (a deceased "white soul"), described in chapter 5 ("Approaching Dangerous Forests and Dangerous Souls"), also takes place in a densely forested region that is most likely the *caxàt-re kô*.

2 While Fernando referred to the soil pairs as a couple in a general sense, known by the term *amji catê*, certain soil pairs are specifically known as complementary couples (also known as *amji catê*) and others as oppositional (*amji kajnã*).

3 Eucalyptus plantations commonly are used to meet Brazil's growing demand for charcoal, which is used mainly for industrial processes (Bailis et al. 2013). Brazil is the world's largest charcoal producer.

Chapter 2: Loving Gardens

1 The mythical story of Awkhêê is found among a number of Eastern Timbira groups (see Azanha 1984). In Canela versions, Awkhêê has shamanic powers and is killed by his relatives, only to be reborn and transformed into a god-like mythical figure. He offers the community the choice of taking a shotgun to become like the whites (*cupẽn*) or a bow and arrow, to remain themselves (*mẽhĩn*). The community chooses the bow and arrow, and Awkhêê, angry with them for not choosing to transform as he has done, curses them and their future descendants. In the version of the myth recounted by Leandro to me in 2012, Awkhêê tells the community, "'Why do you not want the riches? Well, you will receive poverty then! I am throwing you out of here; go walk the earth! Suffering from thirst, from hunger, from necessity! You will never become rich; all the time you will suffer from poverty and steal cattle from the whites. The cattle are no longer yours, the money is no longer yours, the baked goods are no longer yours; they belong to the whites now." For a more detailed discussion of this mythic story, see Miller (2015:107–111; 404–411).

2 Crocker and Crocker (2004:33–34) make a distinction between the "messianic" and "agricultural" solutions to the future, the former of which centered on messianic predictions and the latter of which was initiated by younger men who had cultivated crops in the Guajajara forests and wanted to farm for commercial purposes. While certain commercialized agriculture projects were undertaken throughout the 1970s to 1990s, the majority of families continued to cultivate plots solely for subsistence purposes. In addition, resistance to messianic movements centered on the valuation and appreciation of subsistence gardening work, not of working on large commercial farms "based more on the backland way of life" as Crocker and Crocker (2004: 34) suggest. I therefore argue that the messianic approach to the future of the Canela life world is in contrast to the subsistence gardening (rather than commercial farming) approach.

3 *Caxàt-re kô* refers to both the true forest eco-region in general, and specifically to older garden spaces found throughout the territory.

4 Whether female or male, a person's mother and mother's sister are both called "mother" (*inxê* or *nàà*) in Canela. An elder woman and her sister usually build houses next door to each other in the village, and the women in their families often garden together.

5 After my naming-aunt (*tùy*) named me Toaxêkwỳj in July 2011, everyone in the village has referred to me by this name. Liliana and I converse in Portuguese with Canela vocabulary, as seen here.

6 In 2012–2013, all of these situations were evident. The 2012 municipal election, in which some Canela community members were running for office, was fraught with corruption and cronyism. When purchasing cattle for ritual festivities, people often became indebted to ranchers, who would increase interest payments and obscure debt amounts. Furthering the exploitation, ranchers sometimes convinced Canela women to loan their conditional cash transfer payments (in the form of debit cards) to pay their "debts." Professional hitmen and their violent attacks were well known in

the region. In mid-2012, for example, a hitman was serving as a truck driver between Escalvado and nearby towns and would frequently visit Liliana's house.

Chapter 3: Educating Affection

1 An ear-piercing specialist may perform the ritual on behalf of the naming uncle, as noted in Crocker (1990:291).

2 It is interesting to note the similarities between Canela and Panará peanut cultivation, including the food restrictions undertaken during the growing season, although growing peanuts and the restrictions associated with them are exclusively male activities in the Panará case (Ewart 2005:25).

3 Traditionally, the male leadership council (pró-khãmmã) chooses which man becomes the owner of the maize ceremonies, but nowadays the person often nominates himself for the role.

4 Fernando explained that the men's Red (Kàà-mã-khra) Regeneration moiety traditionally circles around the center while the maize owner sings, and the young men bring mats out to the center where the symbolic maize house is located. Meanwhile, the men of the Black (Atùk-mã-khra) Regeneration moiety grab leaves and place them on the heads of those men in the opposing group.

5 These include true/original sugarcane (cãn peaj-re), true/original maize (põhy pej-re), largest peanut (caahy catia ita), electric eel yam (krẽrô pỳp-re), and anaconda yam (krẽrô tekãjkãj/rorti).

6 Becoming ihpêc is often linked to times of mourning and is parallel to the Panará state of being suangka as compared with its opposite, suakiin, which is similar to the Canela term ihtỳi, meaning happiness and strength (see Ewart 2013:179). The Canela concepts of ihtỳi and ihpêc as linked to gardening are explored in more detail in chapter 3, "Becoming Strong, Becoming Happy, Becoming Well".

7 EMBRAPA's extensive seed bank has provided seeds to and sponsored seed exchanges for a number of Indigenous communities, including the Jê-speaking Krahô (see Ávila 2004; Moraes et al. 2017).

8 Siqueira (2007:104–109) provides an account of the difficulties implementing the "Cerrado Fruits Project" for the Wyty-Catë pan-Timbira association in the 1990s. The Canela appear to have been marginally included in this project, less so than their Krĩkatí and Gavião-Pykobjê Timbira neighbors.

9 Viveiros de Castro (1996:188) originally included a third theoretical mode, the "political economy of control" that focuses on communal institutions of human kin such as moieties and age classes. As Santos-Granero (2007:1–2) pointed out, however, this third mode is often left out of theoretical analyses such as that of Taylor (1996), which has created a somewhat entrenched opposition between two "inflexible models of native Amazonian sociality": the "moral economy of intimacy" and the "symbolic economy of alterity."

Chapter 4: Naming Plant Children

1 Manuela Célia gave Liliana the following beans: large vulture fava bean, small mask fava bean, young/unripe children fava bean, very small white fava bean (*pànkrỳt kryi-re jaka-re*), small white fava bean (*pànkrỳt jaka-re*), large white fava bean (*pànkrỳt jaka-ti*), and *pànkrỳt carêntohkà pó* (translation unclear), as well as the yam varieties reddish-pink-skinned yam (*krẽrô kàhcaprôti*), large white membrane true/original yam (*krẽrô pej caxwỳn jaka-ti*), and long foot yam (*krẽrô parpóhti*). Dirceu gave her four beans: large mask fava bean, annatto fava bean, large black fava bean (*pànkrỳt tyc-ti*), and *pànkrỳt càà pê-xuùrè* (translation unclear); three yams: anaconda yam, breast yam (*krẽrô kàjakẽn*), and *dente de prego* yam (*krẽrô pytĩxwa*); five maize varieties: large red-yellow maize (*põhy caprêc-ti*), true/original maize (*põhy pej-re*), large mixed-color maize (*põhy tohrom-ti*), large bright-red maize (*põhy caprôô-ti*), and large black maize (*põhy tyc-ti*).
2 These include small yellow-brown maize (*põhy tàtà-re*), small red maize (*põhy tep-re*), large grey maize (*põhy jiproh-ti*), and small bright-yellow maize (*põhy tatap-re*).
3 These conversations about gourd loss have led to my working with Canela community members including Liliana, Renato, and others to revitalize gourds that are not currently cultivated. This applied research, initiated in November 2017, connects digital photographs of gourd artifacts from the Smithsonian Institution's National Anthropological Archives, collected by Crocker in the 1960s to 1970s, with Canela gardeners to identify gourds for revitalization. I am also working with colleagues from EMBRAPA in Brasília to send gourd seeds to Canela gardeners for future planting in their garden plots.
4 In my experience in 2012–2013, on more than one occasion my journey from Barra do Corda to the Canela territory took eight hours to complete owing to a combination of engine trouble, poor weather, and difficult road conditions. As of 2017, the road leading to the territory is almost entirely paved (the roads inside the territory remain sandy pathways carved out by truck tracks). In the best conditions, the drive of 65 km can take three hours to complete.
5 When I returned in November 2017, I brought color photo field guides, with Canela plant names, of all the plants I had photographed in 2012–2013. Gardeners were excited to receive these new versions of the ethnobotanical booklet, commenting that the glossy laminated sheets were *impej* and would be useful in the local primary school. Photo field guides (e.g., Field Museum 2018) can be a useful tool for Indigenous and traditional communities to create and use in order to document and maintain their ethnobiological knowledge.
6 Processes of domestication and neo-domestication in lowland South America are complex and deeply bio-sociocultural and deserve further fleshing out through anthropological, archaeological, and historical ecological research. For more details on domestication as a combined biological, sociocultural, and historical concept, see Rival (2007) and Balée (2013).
7 In this study, for example, the Western-trained scientists were Ecuadorian, European, and Indigenous Mayan (Rival 2014:219). Despite being trained in similar

methods and approaches to ecological relations, they all came to their fieldwork experiences with different understandings of moral relations, just as the Indigenous Huaorani and Makushi experts did.

Chapter 5: Becoming a Shaman with Plants

1 In these cases, Reinaldo is referring to either the fast- or slow-growing types of rice: small red fast-growing rice (*arỳihy caprêc-re kênpei*) or small red slow-growing rice (*arỳihy caprêc-re kênpôc*); striped fast-growing rice (*arỳihy capêê kênpei*) or striped slow-growing rice (*arỳihy capêê kênpôc*); and large long white fast-growing rice (*arỳihy jaka-ti japjêhti kênpei*) or large long white slow-growing rice (*arỳihy jaka-ti japjêhti kênpôc*).

2 My research has found the transformational capabilities of Canela souls to be more fluid than the descriptions found in Crocker (1993:72) and Crocker and Crocker (2004:86), in which the souls are described as transforming in a linear fashion, first turning into large animals and then smaller ones and finally into plants before ceasing to exist. While Fernando once explained to me that male and female souls have "infants" (*mẽhkra; filhotes*) that transform into animals, overall the *mẽkarõn* are described as able to transform quickly in and out of animal and plant forms at whim. This immediate transformational ability has implications for human–plant relationships, for there is always the possibility that growing crops in gardens have been occupied temporarily by souls (and should be avoided, rather than affectionately cared for as one regularly does with crop children).

3 The Chinela people referred to in this story are most likely the Khéncatêjê, a group that lived near the Chinela stream in Maranhão until a 1910 massacre forced them to disperse as a group (Azanha 1984:49; see chapter 2, "Gardening: A Brief History, 1814–Present"). The remaining survivors are thought to have joined neighboring Krahô and Apaniekra villages.

Alarcon, Daniela Fernandes, Brent Millikan, and Mauricio Torres, eds. 2016. *Ocekadi: Hidrelétricas, Conflitos Socioambientais e Resistência na Bacia do Tapajós.* Brasília: International Rivers Brazil; Santarém, Brazil: Programa de Antropologia e Arqueologia da Universidade Federal do Oeste do Pará.

Alexander, Catherine. 2002. The Garden as Occasional Domestic Space. *Signs: The Journal of Women, Culture and Society* 27(3):467–485.

Altieri, Miguel A. 2009. The Ecological Impacts of Large-Scale Agrofuel Monoculture Production Systems in the Americas. *Bulletin of Science, Technology, & Society* 29(3):236–244. https://doi.org/10.1177/0270467609333728.

Anderson, A. B., and Darrell A. Posey 1989. Management of Tropical Scrub Savanna by the Gorotire Kayapó of Brazil. *Advances in Economic Botany* 7:159–173.

Anderson, Eugene N. 2011. Ethnobiology: Overview of a Growing Field. In *Ethnobiology*, edited by Eugene N. Anderson, Deborah Pearsall, Eugene Hunn, and Nancy Turner, 1–14. New York: Wiley-Blackwell.

Annaes da Biblioteca e Archivo Público do Pará. 1902–1913. 8 vols. Belém do Pará, Brazil.

Archambault, Julie Soliel. 2016. Taking Love Seriously in Human-Plant Relations in Mozambique: Toward an Anthropology of Affective Encounters. *Cultural Anthropology* 31(2):244–271.

Atkinson-Graham, Melissa, Marth Kenney, Kelly Ladd, Cameron Michael Murray, and Emily Astra-Jean Simmonds. 2015. Care in Context: Becoming an STS Researcher. *Social Studies of Science* 45(5):738–748.

Ávila, Thiago Antônio Machado. 2004. "Não é do Jeito o que Eles Quer, é do Jeito que Nós Quer": Os Krahô e a Biodiversidade. Master's thesis, University of Brasília.

Azanha, G. 1984. A Forma "Timbira": Estrutura e Resistência. Master's thesis, University of São Paulo.

Bailis, Rob, Charissa Rujanavech, Puneet Dwivedi, Adriana de Oliveira Vilela, Howard Chang, and Rogério Carneiro de Miranda. 2013. Innovation in Charcoal Production: A Comparative Life-Cycle Assessment of Two Kiln Technologies in Brazil. *Energy for Sustainable Development* 17:189–200.

Balée, William. 2013. *Cultural Forests of the Amazon: A Historical Ecology of People and Their Landscapes.* Tuscaloosa: University of Alabama Press.

Barbira Freedman, Françoise. 2010. Shamanic Plants and Gender in the Healing Forest. In *Plants, Health, and Healing: On the Interface of Ethnobotany and Medical Anthropology*, edited by Elizabeth Hsu and Stephen Harris, 135–178. New York: Berghahn.

Barth, Friedrich G., and Axel Schmid, eds. 2001. *Ecology of Sensing.* New York: Springer.

Battaglia, Debbora. 2017. Aeroponic Gardens and Their Magic: Plants/Persons/Ethics in Suspension. *History and Anthropology* 28(3):263–292. https://doi.org/10.1080/027572 06.2017.1289935.

Bell, Joshua A., Paige West, and Colin Filer, eds. 2015. *Tropical Forests of Oceania: Anthropological Perspectives*. Acton: Australian National University Press.

Bellacasa, Maria Puig de la. 2011. Matters of Care in Technoscience: Assembling Neglected Things. *Social Studies of Science* 41(1):85–106.

———. 2015. Making Time for Soil: Technoscientific Futurity and the Pace of Care. *Social Studies of Science* 45(5):691–716.

Berlin, Brent. 1992. *Ethnobiological Classification: Principles of Categorization of Plants and Animals in Traditional Societies*. Princeton, NJ: Princeton University Press.

Bessire, Lucas, and David Bond. 2014. Ontological Anthropology and the Deferral of Critique. *American Ethnologist* 41(3):440–456.

Beuchle, René, Rosana Cristina Grecchi, Yosio Edemir Shimabukuro, Roman Seliger, Hugh Douglas Eva, Edson Sano, and Frédéric Achard. 2015. Land Cover Changes in the Brazilian Cerrado and Caatinga Biomes from 1990 to 2010 Based on a Systematic Remote Sensing Sampling Approach. *Applied Geography* 58:116–127.

Biedrzycki, Meredith L. and Harsh P. Bais. 2010. Kin Recognition in Plants: A Mysterious Behavior Unsolved. *Journal of Experimental Botany* 61(5):4123–4128.

Bird Rose, Deborah. 2011. *Wild Dog Dreaming: Love and Extinction*. Charlottesville: University of Virginia Press.

Blair, Matthew F., Laura F. González, Paul M. Kimani, and Louis Butare. 2010. Genetic Diversity, Inter-Gene Pool Introgression and Nutritional Quality of Common Beans (*Phaseolus vulgaris* L.) from Central Africa. *Theoretical & Applied Genetics* 121:237–248. https://doi.org/10.1007/s00122-010-1305-x.

Bloch, Maurice. 1998. Why Trees, Too, Are Good to Think With: Towards an Anthropology of the Meaning of Life. In *The Social Life of Trees: Anthropological Perspectives on Tree Symbolism*, edited by Laura Rival, 39–55. Oxford, UK: Berg.

Bonilla, Oiara. 2007. O Bom Patrão e o Inimigo Voraz: Predação e Comércio na Cosmologia Paumari. *Mana* 11(1):41–66.

Brand, Fridolin Simon, and Kurt Jax. 2007. Focusing the Meaning(s) of Resilience: Resilience as a Descriptive Concept and a Boundary Object. *Ecology & Society* 12(1):23.

Brown, Cecil H., Charles R. Clement, Patience Epps, Eike Luedeling, and Søren Wichmann. 2013. The Paleobiolinguistics of Domesticated Manioc (*Manihot esculenta* Crantz). *Ethnobiology Letters* 4:61–70.

———. 2014a. The Paleobiolinguistics of Maize (*Zea mays* L.). *Ethnobiology Letters* 5:52–64.

———. 2014b. The Paleobiolinguistics of the Common Bean (*Phaseolus vulgaris* L.). *Ethnobiology Letters* 5:104–115.

Bustamante, Mercedes Maria da Cunha, G. B. Nardoto, A. S. Pinto, J. C. F. Resende, F. S. C. Takahashi, and L. C. G. Vieira. 2012. Potential Impacts of Climate Change on Biogeochemical Functioning of Cerrado Ecosystems. *Brazilian Journal of Biology* 72(3):655–671.

Cahill, James F. 2015. Introduction to the Special Issue. Beyond Traits: Integrating Behavior into Plant Ecology and Biology. *AoB PLANTS* 7.plv120. https://doi.org/10.1093/aobpla/plv120.

Campbell, Jeremy. 2015. *Conjuring Property: Speculation and Environmental Futures in the Brazilian Amazon.* Seattle: University of Washington Press.

Canguilhem, Georges. [1965] 2008. *Knowledge of Life.* New York: Fordham University Press.

Carney, Judith A. 2001. *Black Rice: The African Origins of Rice Cultivation in the Americas.* Cambridge, MA: Harvard University Press.

Carranza, Tharsila, Andrew Balmford, Valerie Kapos, and Andrea Manica. 2013. Protected Area Effectiveness in Reducing Conversion in a Rapidly Vanishing Ecosystem: The Brazilian Cerrado. *Conservation Letters* 7(3):216–223. https://doi.org/10.1111/conl.12049.

Carrington, Damian. 2016. The Anthropocene Epoch: Scientists Declare Dawn of Human-Influenced Age. *The Guardian*, 29 August 2016. https://www.theguardian.com/environment/2016/aug/29/declare-anthropocene-epoch-experts-urge-geological-congress-human-impact-earth.

Cassidy, Rebecca. 2012. Lives with Others: Climate Change and Human–Animal Relations. *Annual Review of Anthropology* 41:21–36.

Cepek, Michael. 2015. Ungrateful Predators: Capture and the Creation of Cofán Violence. *Journal of the Royal Anthropological Institute* 21:542–560.

Chacón, Maria Isabel Sanchez, Barbara Pickersgill, Daniel. G. Debouck, and J. Salvador Arias. 2007. Phylogeographic Analysis of the Chloroplast DNA Variation in Wild Common Bean (*Phaseolus vulgaris* L.) in the Americas. *Plant Systematics and Evolution* 266:175–195. https://doi.org/10.1007/s00606-007-0536-z.

Chamovitz, Daniel. 2012. *What a Plant Knows: A Field Guide to the Senses.* New York: Scientific American/Farrar, Straus, and Giroux.

Coelho de Souza, Marcela. 2002. O Traço e o Círculo: O Conceito de Parentesco Entre os Jê e Seus Antropólogos. PhD dissertation, Federal University of Rio de Janeiro.

———. 2004. Parentes de Sangue: Incesto, Substância e Relação no Pensamento Timbira. *Mana* 10(1):25–60.

Corteletti, Rafael, Ruth Dickau, Paulo DeBlasis, and Jose Iriarte. 2015. Revisiting the Economy and Mobility of Southern Proto-Jê (Taquara-Itararé) Groups in the Southern Brazilian Highlands: Starch Grain and Phytoliths Analyses from the Bonin Site, Urubici, Brazil. *Journal of Archaeological Science* 58:46–61.

Crocker, William. 1978. Estórias das Épocas de Pré e Pós-Pacificação dos Ramkókamekra e Apâniekra-Canelas. *Boletim do Museu Paraense Emílio Goeldi* 68:1–31.

———. 1990. *The Canela (Eastern Timbira), I: An Ethnographic Introduction.* Smithsonian Contributions to Anthropology 33. Washington, DC: Smithsonian Institution Press.

———. 1993. Canela Relationships with Ghosts: This-Worldly or Otherworldly Empowerment. *Latin American Anthropology Review* 5(2):71–78.

———. 1994. Canela. In *Encyclopedia of World Cultures*, edited by Johannes Wilburt, 94–98. New York: G. K. Hall & Company.

———. 2007. The Canela Diaries: Their Nature, Uses, and Future. *Tipití* 5(1):33–57.

———. n.d. Canela Shamanism: Delimitation of Shamanic Terms, Shamans' Accounts, and an Application of the Harner Method, 1–23. Unpublished manuscript.

Crocker, William, and Jean Crocker. 2004. *The Canela: Kinship, Ritual, and Sex in an Amazonian Tribe*. Belmont, CA: Wadsworth/Thomson Learning.

Crutzen, Paul J. 2002. Geology of Mankind: The Anthropocene. *Nature* 415:23. https://doi.org/10.1038/415023a.

Crutzen, Paul J., and Eugene F. Stoermer. 2000. The Anthropocene. *Global Change Newsletter* 41:17–18.

Daly, Lewis. 2016. Cassava Spirit and the Seed of History. *Commodity Histories*, The Open University. February 2016.

Da Matta, Roberto. 1973. A Reconsideration of Apinayé Social Morphology. In *Peoples and Cultures of Native South America: An Anthropological Reader*, edited by Daniel R. Gross, 277–293. New York: Doubleday/The Natural History Press.

———. 1982. *A Divided World: Apinayé Social Structure*. Cambridge, MA: Harvard University Press.

Degnen, Catherine. 2009. On Vegetable Love: Gardening, Plants, and People in the North of England. *Journal of the Royal Anthropological Institute* 15(1):151–167.

Descola, Philippe. 1998. *The Spears of Twilight: Life and Death in the Amazon Jungle*. New York: The New Press.

———. 2009. Human Natures. *Social Anthropology/Anthropologie Sociale* 17(2):145–157.

———. 2013. *Beyond Nature and Culture*. Chicago: University of Chicago Press.

Despret, Vinciane. 2004. The Body We Care For: Figures of Anthropo-Zoo-Genesis. *Body & Society* 10(2–3):111–134.

Devine Guzmán, Tracey. 2013. *Native and National in Brazil: Indigeneity after Independence*. Chapel Hill: University of North Carolina Press.

Dudley, Susan A. 2015. Plant Cooperation. *AoB PLANTS* 7:plv113. https://doi.org/10.1093/aobpla/plv113.

Dudley, Susan A., Guillermo P. Murphy, and Amanda L. File. 2013. Mechanisms of Plant Competition: Kin Recognition and Competition in Plants. *Functional Ecology* 27:898–906.

Ellen, Roy. 2016. Is There a Role for Ontologies in Understanding Plant Knowledge Systems? *Journal of Ethnobiology* 36(1):10–28.

Eloy, Ludivine, Catherine Aubertin, Fabiano Toni, Silvia Laine Borges Lúcio, and Marion Bosgiraud. 2016. On the Margins of Soy Farms: Traditional Populations and Selective Environmental Policies in the Brazilian Cerrado. *The Journal of Peasant Studies* 43(2):494–516. https://doi.org/10.1080/03066150.2015.1013099.

Emperaire, Laure, and Ludivine Eloy. 2008. A Cidade, um Foco de Diversidade Agrícola no Rio Negro (Amazonas, Brasil)? *Boletim Museu Paraense Emílio Goeldi. Ciências Humanas, Belém* 3(2):195–211.

Emperaire, Laure, and Nivaldo Peroni. 2007. Traditional Management of Agrobiodiversity in Brazil: A Case Study of Manioc. *Human Ecology* 35:761–768.

Ewart, Elizabeth. 2005. Fazendo Pessoas e Fazendo Roças entre os Panará do Brasil Central. *Revista da Antropologia* 48(1):9–35.

———. 2008. Seeing, Hearing, and Speaking: Morality and Sense among the Panará in Central Brazil. *Ethnos* 73(4):505–522.

———. 2013. *Space and Society in Central Brazil: A Panará Ethnography.* London School of Economics Monographs on Social Anthropology. London: Bloomsbury.

Falleiros, Guilherme Lavinas Jardim. 2005. A Dádiva e o Círculo: Um Ensaio Sobre Reciprocidade A'wẽ-Xavante. Master's thesis, University of São Paulo.

Fang, Wei-Ta, Hsin-Wen Hu, and Chien-Shing Lee. 2016. Atayal's Identification of Sustainability: Traditional Ecological Knowledge and Indigenous Science of a Hunting Culture. *Sustainability Science* 11:33–43. https://doi.org/10.1007/s11625-015-0313-9.

Fausto, Carlos. 2008. Donos Demais: Maestria e Domínio na Amazônia. *Mana* 14(2):329–366.

Fausto, Carlos, and Luiz Costa. 2013. Feeding (and Eating): Reflections on Strathern's "Eating (and Feeding)." *Cambridge Anthropology* 31(1):156–162.

Fearnside, Philip M. 2015. Brazil's São Luiz do Tapajós Dam: The Art of Cosmetic Environmental Impact Assessments. *Water Alternatives* 8(3):373–396.

———. 2017. Brazil's Belo Monte Dam: Lessons of an Amazonian Resource Struggle. *DIE ERDE: Journal of the Geographical Society of Berlin* 148(2–3):167–184.

Feeley, Kenneth J., and Miles R. Silman. 2009. Extinction Risks of Amazonian Plant Species. *Proceedings of the National Academy of Sciences of the United States of America* 106(30):12382–12387.

Felfili, Jeanine M., Manoel C. da Silva Júnior, Anderson C. Sevilha, Christopher W. Fagg, Bruno M. T. Walter, Paulo E. Nogueira, and Alba V. Rezende. 2004. Diversity, Floristic and Structural Patterns of Cerrado Vegetation in Central Brazil. *Plant Ecology* 175(1):37–46.

Field Museum. 2018. *Field Guides.* http://fieldguides.fieldmuseum.org/.

Françoso, Renata D., Reuber Brandão, Cristiano C. Nogueira, Yuri B. Salmona, Ricardo Bomfim Machado, and Guarino R. Colli. 2015. Habitat Loss and the Effectiveness of Protected Areas in the Cerrado Biodiversity Hotspot. *Natureza e Conservação* 13: 35–40. https://doi.org/10.1016/j.ncon.2015.04.001.

Freitas, Fábio de Oliveira. 2006. Evidências Genético-Arqueológicas Sobre a Origem do Feijão Comum no Brasil. *Pesquisa Agropecuária Brasileira* 41:1199–1203.

Friese, Carrie. 2013. Realizing Potential in Translational Medicine: The Uncanny Emergence of Care as Science. *Current Anthropology* 54(S7):S129–S138.

Folke, Carl. 2006. Resilience: The Emergence of a Perspective for Social–Ecological Systems Analyses. *Global Environmental Change* 16:253–267.

Fowler, Cynthia T., and James R. Welch. 2015. Introduction: Special Issue on Fire Ecology and Ethnobiology. *Journal of Ethnobiology* 35(1):1–3.

Gagliano, Monica. 2015. In a Green Frame of Mind: Perspectives on the Behavioral Ecology and Cognitive Nature of Plants. *AoB PLANTS* 7:plu075. https://doi.org/10.1093/aobpla/plu075.

Gagliano, Monica, and Mavra Grimonprez. 2015. Breaking the Silence: Language and the Making of Meaning in Plants. *Ecopsychology* 7(3):145–151.

Gagliano, Monica, Stefano Mancuso, and Daniel Robert. 2012. Towards an Understanding of Plant Bioacoustics. *Trends in Plant Science* 17(6):323–325.

Gagliano, Monica, Michael Renton, Martial Depczynski, and Stefano Mancuso. 2014. Experience Teaches Plants to Learn Faster and Forget Slower in Environments Where It Matters. *Oecologia* 175:63–72.

Garrett, Rachael D., and Lisa L. Rausch. 2016. Green for Gold: Social and Ecological Tradeoffs Influencing the Sustainability of the Brazilian Soy Industry. *The Journal of Peasant Studies* 43(2):461–493. https://doi.org/10.1080/03066150.2015.1010077.

GEF (Global Environment Facility). 2016. Sustainable Cerrado Initiative. Global Environment Facility. https://www.thegef.org/project/sustainable-cerrado-initiative.

Gibbs, Holly K., Lisa Rausch, Jacob Munger, Ian Schelly, Douglas C. Morton, Praveen Noojipady, Britaldo Soares-Filho, Paulo Barreto, L. Micol, and Nathalie F. Walker. 2015. Brazil's Soy Moratorium: Supply Chain Governance is Needed to Avoid Deforestation. *Science* 347(6220): 377–378.

Gibson, James. [1986] 2015. *The Ecological Approach to Visual Perception*. New York: Taylor & Francis.

Gill, Harneet, Trevor Lantz, and the Gwich'in Social and Cultural Institute. 2014. A Community-Based Approach to Mapping Gwich'in Observations of Environmental Changes in the Lower Peel River Watershed, NT. *Journal of Ethnobiology* 34(3):294–314.

Global Witness. 2015. How Many More? Deadly Environment: The Killing and Intimidation of Environmental and Land Activists. Global Witness. https://www.global witness.org/en/campaigns/environmental-activists/how-many-more/.

———. 2017. Defenders of the Earth: Global Killings of Land and Environmental Defenders in 2016. Global Witness. https://www.globalwitness.org/en/campaigns/envi ronmental-activists/defenders-earth/.

Goody, Esther N. 1989. Learning, Apprenticeship and the Division of Labor. In *Apprenticeship: From Theory to Method and Back Again*, edited by Michael W. Coy, 233–256. Albany, NY: State University of New York Press.

Goody, Jack. 2004. The Transcription of Oral Heritage. *Museum International* 56:91–96.

Gordon, Cesar. 2006. *Economia Selvagem: Ritual e Mercadoria entre os Xikrin-Mebêngôkre*. São Paulo: State University of São Paulo Press.

Gorzelak, Monika A., Amanda K. Asay, Brian J. Pickles, and Suzanne W. Simard. 2015. Inter-Plant Communication through Mycorrhizal Networks Mediates Complex Adaptive Behavior in Plant Communities. *AoB PLANTS* 7:plv050. https://doi.org/10 .1093/aobpla/plv050.

Gow, Peter. 1991. *Of Mixed Blood: Kinship and History in Peruvian Amazonia*. Oxford, UK: Clarendon Press.

———. 2000. Helpless—The Affective Preconditions of Piro Social Life. In *The Anthropology of Love and Anger: The Aesthetics of Conviviality in Native Amazonia*, edited by Joanna Overing and Alan Passes. London: Routledge.

Grant, Suzanne. 2012. Fences, Pathways and a Peripatetic Sense of Community: Kinship and Residence amongst the Nivacle of the Paraguayan Chaco. In *Landscapes Beyond Land: Routes, Aesthetics, Narratives*, edited by Arnar Árnason, Nicholas Ellison, Jo Vergunst, and Andrew Whitehouse, 67–82. Oxford, UK: Berghahn.

Greene, Margaret E., and William H. Crocker. 1994. Some Demographic Aspects of the Canela Indians of Brazil. In *The Demography of Small-Scale Societies: Case Studies from*

Lowland South America, edited by Kathleen Adams and David Price, 47–62. Bennington, VT. Dennington College.

Greenpeace Brasil. 2016. Alerta: Ameaças ao Povo Ka'apor se Intensificam. Greenpeace Brasil, 18 June 2016. http://www.greenpeace.org/brasil/pt/Noticias/Alerta-ameacas -ao-povo-Kaapor-se-intensificam/.

Griffiths, Thomas. 2001. Finding One's Body: Relationships between Cosmology and Work in North-West Amazonia. In *Beyond the Visible and the Material: The Amerindianization of Society in the Work of Peter Rivière*, edited by Laura M Rival and Neil L. Whitehead, 247–262. Oxford, UK: Oxford University Press.

Grupp, Bernhard. 2015. *Dicionário Canela*, 2nd ed. Barra do Corda, Brazil: Missão Cristão Evangélica do Brasil.

Guss, David M. 1989. *To Weave and Sing: Art, Symbol, and Narrative in the South American Rainforest*. Berkeley, CA: University of California Press.

Hall Matthew. 2011. *Plants as Persons: A Philosophical Botany*. Albany: State University of New York Press.

Haraway, Donna. 1991. *Simians, Cyborgs, and Women: The Reinvention of Nature*. New York: Routledge.

———. 2008. *When Species Meet*. Minneapolis: University of Minnesota Press.

———. 2015. Anthropocene, Capitalocene, Plantationocene, Chthulucene: Making Kin. *Environmental Humanities* 6:159–165.

———. 2016. *Staying with the Trouble: Making Kin in the Chthulucene*. Minneapolis: University of Minnesota Press.

Haraway, Donna, Noboru Ishikawa, Gilbert Scott, Kenneth Olwig, Anna L. Tsing, and Nils Bubandt. 2015. Anthropologists are Talking About—The Anthropocene. *Ethnos* 81(3):535–564. https://doi.org/10.1080/00141844.2015.1105838.

Harrison, Richard G., and Erica L. Larson. 2014. Hybridization, Introgression, and the Nature of Species Boundaries. *Journal of Heredity* 105(S1):795–809 https://doi.org/10 .1093/jhered/esu033.

Hartigan, John. 2015a. *Aesop's Anthropology: A Multispecies Approach*. Minneapolis: University of Minnesota Press.

———. 2015b. Plant Publics: Multispecies Relating in Spanish Botanical Gardens. *Anthropological Quarterly* 88:481–507.

———. 2017. *Care of the Species: Races of Corn and the Science of Plant Biodiversity*. Minneapolis: University of Minnesota Press.

Hartigan, John, Elizabeth Seccombe, and Eben Kirksey. 2014. How to Interview a Plant. The Multispecies Salon. http://www.multispecies-salon.org/how-to-interview-a -plant/.

Haskell, David George. 2017. *The Songs of Trees: Stories from Nature's Great Connectors*. New York: Viking.

Hecht, Susanna B. 2003. Indigenous Soil Management and the Creation of Amazonian Dark Earths: Implications of Kayapó Practices. In *Amazonian Dark Earths: Origin, Properties, Management*, edited by Johannes Lehmann, Dirse C. Kern, Bruno Glaser, and William I. Woods, 355–372. Dordrecht, The Netherlands: Kluwer Academic Publishers.

Hecht, Susanna B., and Darrel A. Posey. 1989. Preliminary Results on Soil Management Techniques of the Kayapó Indians. *Advances in Economic Botany* 7:174–188.

Heckler, Serena L. 2004. Tedium and Creativity: The Valorization of Manioc Cultivation and Piaroa Women. *The Journal of the Royal Anthropological Institute* 10(2):241–259.

Heidegger, Martin. [1971] 2001. *Poetry, Language, Thought.* New York: Perennial Classics.

Herman, R. D. K. 2016. Traditional Knowledge in a Time of Crisis: Climate Change, Culture and Communication. *Sustainability Science* 11: 163–176. https://doi.org/10.1007/s11625-015-0305-9.

Hoffman, William A. 2000. Post-Establishment Seedling Success in the Brazilian Cerrado: A Comparison of Savanna and Forest Species. *Biotropica* 32(1):62–69.

Holling, C. S. 1973. Resilience and Stability of Ecological Systems. *Annual Review of Ecology and Systematics* 4:1–23.

Horrigan, Leo, Robert S. Lawrence, and Polly Walker. 2002. How Sustainable Agriculture Can Address the Environmental and Human Health Harms of Industrial Agriculture. *Environmental Health Perspectives* 110(5):445–456.

Ingold, Tim. 2000. *The Perception of the Environment: Essays on Livelihood, Dwelling and Skill.* London: Routledge.

———. 2006. Rethinking the Animate, Re-Animating Thought. *Ethnos* 71(1):9–20.

———. 2007a. *Lines: A Brief History.* London: Routledge.

———. 2007b. Materials Against Materiality. *Archaeological Dialogues* 14(1):1–16.

———. 2008. When ANT meets SPIDER: Social Theory for Arthropods. In *Material Agency: Towards a Non-Anthropocentric Approach,* edited by Carl Knappett and Lambros Malafouris, 209–215. London: Springer.

———. 2011. *Being Alive: Essays on Movement, Knowledge and Description.* London: Routledge.

———. 2012. The Shape of the Land. In *Landscapes beyond Land: Routes, Aesthetics, Narratives,* edited by Arnar Árnason, Nicholas Ellison, Jo Vergunst, and Andrew Whitehouse, 197–208. Oxford, UK: Berghahn.

———. 2013. Prospect. In *Biosocial Becomings: Integrating Social and Biological Anthropology,* edited by Tim Ingold and Gisli Pálsson, 1–21. Cambridge, UK: Cambridge University Press.

Ingold, Tim, and Elizabeth Hallam. 2014. Making and Growing: An Introduction. In *Making and Growing: Anthropological Studies of Organisms and Artefacts,* edited by Elizabeth Hallam and Tim Ingold, 1–24. Farnham, UK: Ashgate.

Ingold, Tim, and Gisli Pálsson, eds. 2013. *Biosocial Becomings: Integrating Social and Biological Anthropology.* Cambridge, UK: Cambridge University Press.

Instituto Socioambiental. 2018a. Terras Indígenas no Brasil: Terra Indígena Kanela. https://terrasindigenas.org.br/pt-br/terras-indigenas/3719.

Instituto Socioambiental. 2018b. Terras Indígenas no Brasil: Terra Indígena Kanela/Memortumré. https://terrasindigenas.org.br/pt-br/terras-indigenas/4137.

Jepson, Anne. 2014. Gardening and Well-Being: A View from the Ground. In *Making and Growing: Anthropological Studies of Organisms and Artefacts,* edited by Elizabeth Hallam and Tim Ingold, 147–162. Farnham, UK: Ashgate.

Jepson, Wendy. 2005. A Disappearing Biome? Reconsidering Land-Cover Change in the Brazilian Savanna. *The Geographical Journal* 171(2):99–111.

Karban, Richard, William C. Wetzel, Kaori Shiojiri, Satomi Ishizaki, Santiago R. Ramirez, and James D. Blande. 2014. Deciphering the Language of Plant Communication: Volatile Chemotypes of Sagebrush. *The New Phytologist* 204(2):380–385.

Kawa, Nicholas C. 2016. *Amazonia in the Anthropocene: People, Soils, Plants, Forests.* Austin: University of Texas Press.

Kerner, Susanne, Cynthia Chou, and Morten Warmind, eds. 2016. *Commensality: From Everyday Food to Feast.* New York: Bloomsbury.

Kirksey, Eben. 2015. *Emergent Ecologies.* Durham, NC: Duke University Press.

Klink, Carlos A., and Ricardo B. Machado. 2005. Conservation of the Brazilian Cerrado. *Conservation Biology* 19:707–713.

Kohn, Eduardo. 2002. Natural Engagements and Ecological Aesthetics among the Ávila Runa of Amazonian Ecuador. PhD dissertation, University of Wisconsin–Madison.

———. 2007. How Dogs Dream: Amazonian Natures and the Politics of Transspecies Engagement. *American Ethnologist* 34(1):3–24.

———. 2013. *How Forests Think: Toward an Anthropology beyond the Human.* Berkeley: University of California Press.

Kutzbach, John E., William F. Ruddiman, Steve J. Vavrus, and G. Philippon. 2010. Climate Model Simulation of Anthropogenic Influence on Greenhouse-Induced Climate Change (Early Agriculture to Modern): The Role of Ocean Feedbacks. *Climate Change* 99: 351–381. https://doi.org/10.1007/s10584-009-9684-1.

Labate, Beatriz Caiuby, and Clancy Cavnar, eds. 2014. *Ayahuasca Shamanism in the Amazon and Beyond.* Oxford Scholarship Online. https://doi.org/10.1093/acprof:oso/9780199341191.001.0001.

Labate, Beatriz Caiuby, Clancy Cavnar, and Alex K. Gearin, eds. 2017. *The World Ayahuasca Diaspora: Reinventions and Controversies.* New York: Routledge.

LaDuke, Winona. 1999. *All Our Relations: Native Struggles for Land and Life.* Cambridge, MA: South End Press.

Lapola, David M., Luiz A. Martinelli, Carlos A. Peres, Jean P. H. B. Ometto, Manuel E. Ferreira, Carlos A. Nobre, Ana Paula D. Aguiar, Mercedes M. C. Bustamante, Manoel F. Cardoso, Marcos H. Costa, Carlos A. Joly, Christiane C. Leite, Paulo Moutinho, Gilvan Sampaio, Bernardo B. N. Strassburg, and Ima C. G. Vieira. 2014. Pervasive Transition of the Brazilian Land-Use System. *Nature Climate Change* 4:27–35. https://doi.org/10.1038/NCLIMATE2056.

Laris, Paul, Sebastien Caillault, Sepideh Dadashi, and Audrey Jo. 2015. The Human Ecology and Geography of Burning in an Unstable Savanna Environment. *Journal of Ethnobiology* 35(1):111–139.

Lave, Jean. 1979. Cycles and Trends in Krikati Naming Practices. In *Dialectical Societies: The Gê and Bororo of Central Brazil,* edited by David Maybury-Lewis, 16–45. Cambridge, MA: Harvard University Press.

———. 2011. *Apprenticeship in Critical Ethnographic Practice.* Chicago: University of Chicago Press.

Lea, Vanessa. 1986. Nomes e Nekrets Kayapó: Uma Concepção de Riqueza. PhD dissertation, Federal University of Rio de Janeiro.

Le Cain, Timothy James. 2015. Against the Anthropocene: A Neo-Materialist Perspective. *International Journal for History, Culture and Modernity* 3(1):1–28.

Lehmann, Johannes, Dirse C. Kern, Bruno Glaser, and William I. Woods, eds. 2003. *Amazonian Dark Earths: Origin, Properties, Management.* Dordrecht, The Netherlands: Kluwer Academic Publishers.

Lévi-Strauss, Claude. 1963. *Structural Anthropology*, vol. 1. New York: Basic Books.

———. 1995. *The Story of Lynx.* Chicago: University of Chicago Press.

Lewis-Jones, Kay. 2016. Introduction: People and Plants. *Environment and Society: Advances in Research* 7:1–7. https://doi.org/10.3167/ares.2016.070101.

Lima, Thiago Carvalho de. 2014. Modelagem dos Vetores de Mudança na Paisagem no Bioma Cerrado. Master's thesis, Federal University of Minas Gerais, Belo Horizonte, Brazil.

Locke, Piers, and Ursula Muenster. 2015. *Multispecies Ethnography.* Oxford, UK: Oxford Bibliographies. https://doi.org/10.1093/OBO/9780199766567-0130.

Lúcio, Sílvia Laine Borges, Ludivine Eloy Costa Pereira, and Thomas Ludewigs. 2014. O Gado que Circulava: Desafios da Gestão Participativa e Impactos da Proibição do Uso do Fogo aos Criadores de Gado de Solta da Reserva de Desenvolvimento Sustentável Veredas do Acari. *Biodiversidade Brasileira* 4(1):130–155.

Maffi, Luisa, ed. 2001. *On Biocultural Diversity: Linking Language, Knowledge, and the Environment.* Washington, DC: Smithsonian Institution Press.

Maffi, Luisa, and Ellen Woodley, eds. 2010. *Biocultural Diversity Conservation: A Global Sourcebook.* London: Earthscan.

Marchand, Trevor. 2014. Skill and Aging: Perspectives from Three Generations of English Woodworkers. In *Making and Growing: Anthropological Studies of Organisms and Artefacts*, edited by Elizabeth Hallam and Tim Ingold, 183–201. Farnham, UK: Ashgate.

Marder, Michael. 2013. *Plant-Thinking: A Philosophy of Vegetal Life.* New York: Columbia University Press.

Marimon, Beatriz S., and Jeanine M. Felfili. 2001. Ethnobotanical Comparison of "Pau Brasil" (*Brosimum rubescens* Taub.) Forests in a Xavante Indian and a Non-Xavante Community in Eastern Mato Grosso State, Brazil. *Economic Botany* 55(4):555–569.

Martin, Aryn, Natasha Myers, and Ana Viseu. 2015. The Politics of Care in Technoscience. *Social Studies of Science* 1–17. https://doi.org/10.1177/0306312715602073.

Martin, Gary J. 2004. *Ethnobotany: A Methods Manual.* New York: Earthscan.

Maybury-Lewis, David. 1960. The Analysis of Dual Organizations: A Methodological Critique. *Bijdragen tot de Taal-, Land- en Volkenkunde* 116(1):17–44.

———. 1967. *Akwe-Shavante Society.* Oxford, UK: Oxford University Press.

———. 1979a. Conclusion: Kinship, Ideology, and Culture. In *Dialectical Societies: The Gê and Bororo of Central Brazil*, edited by D. Maybury-Lewis, 301–312. Cambridge, MA: Harvard University Press.

———, ed. 1979b. *Dialectical Societies: The Gê and Bororo of Central Brazil.* Cambridge, MA: Harvard University Press.

———. 1979c. Introduction. In *Dialectical Societies: The Gê and Bororo of Central Brazil*, edited by D. Maybury-Lewis, 1–13. Cambridge, MA: Harvard University Press.

———. 1989. Social Theory and Social Practice: Binary Systems in Central Brazil. In *The Attraction of Opposites: Thought and Society in the Dualistic Mode*, edited by David Maybury-Lewis and Uri Almagor, 97–116. Ann Arbor: University of Michigan Press.

Melatti, Julio C. 1978. *Ritos de uma Tribo Timbira*. São Paulo: Ática Press.

———. 1979. The Relationship System of the Krahô. In *Dialectical Societies: The Gê and Bororo of Central Brazil*, edited by David Maybury-Lewis, 46–79. Cambridge, MA: Harvard University Press.

Melo, Maycon. 2017. A Agonia da Etnia Gavião. *Carta Capital*, 7 March 2017. https://www.cartacapital.com.br/sociedade/madeireiros-invadem-floresta-no-maranhao-e-intimidam-indigenas-gaviao.

Merleau-Ponty, Maurice. [1947] 1974. The Primacy of Perception and its Philosophical Consequences. In *Phenomenology, Language, and Sociology: Selected Essays of Maurice Merleau-Ponty*, edited by John O'Neill, 196–228. London: Heinemann.

———. 1964. Eye and Mind. In *The Primacy of Perception: And Other Essays on Phenomenological Psychology, the Philosophy of Art, History and Politics*, edited by James M. Edie, 160–183. Chicago: Northwestern University Press.

Milanez, Felipe. 2017. Madeireiros Invadem Floresta no Maranhão e Intimidam Indígenas Gavião. *Carta Capital*, 7 March 2017. https://www.cartacapital.com.br/sociedade/madeireiros-invadem-floresta-no-maranhao-e-intimidam-indigenas-gaviao.

Miller, Theresa L. 2010. The Aesthetics of Environment: An Exploration of Indigenous Maize Cultivation and Biocultural Diversity in Central Brazil. MPhil thesis, University of Oxford.

———. 2013. Hunger, Gender, and Social Assistance Programs in the Canela Indigenous Society of Northeast Brazil. Paper Presented at XXXI International Congress of the Latin American Studies Association, Washington, DC, May–June 2013.

———. 2015. Bio-sociocultural Aesthetics: Indigenous Ramkokamekra-Canela Gardening Practices and Varietal Diversity in Maranhão, Brazil. DPhil (PhD) dissertation, University of Oxford.

———. 2016. Living Lists: How the Indigenous Canela Come to Know Plants through Ethnobotanical Classification. *Journal of Ethnobiology* 36(1):105–124.

———. 2017. Valuing the Bad and the Ugly: Tasting Agrobiodiversity among the Indigenous Canela. *Food, Culture & Society* 20(2):325–346. https://doi.org/10.1080/15528014.2017.1305831.

Milliken, William, and Bruce Albert. 1997. The Use of Medicinal Plants by the Yanomami Indians of Brazil, Part II. *Economic Botany* 51(3):264–278.

Mistry, Jayalaxshmi, Andrea Berardi, Valeria Andrade, Txicaprô Krahô, Phocrok Krahô, and Othon Leonardos. 2005. Indigenous Fire Management in the *Cerrado* of Brazil: The Case of the Krahô of Tocantíns. *Human Ecology* 33(3):365–386. https://doi.org/10.1007/s10745-005-4143-8.

MMA (Ministério do Meio-Ambiente). 2016. *Plano de Ação para Prevenção e Controle do Desmatamento no Cerrado: Plano Operativo 2016–2020*. Brasília, Brazil: Ministério do Meio-Ambiente.

MMA (Ministério do Meio-Ambiente). 2018. Política Nacional de Recuperação da Vegetação Nativa. http://www.mma.gov.br/florestas/política-nacional-de-recuperação-da-vegetação-nativa.

Montoya, Teresa. 2016. Violence on the Ground, Violence Below the Ground. Hot Spots. *Cultural Anthropology* (website), 22 December 2016. https://culanth.org/fieldsights/1018-violence-on-the-ground-violence-below-the-ground.

Moore, Amelia. 2015. The Anthropocene: A Critical Exploration. *Environment and Society: Advances in Research* 6:1–3. https://doi.org/10.3167/ares.2015.060101.

———. 2016. Anthropocene Anthropology: Reconceptualizing Contemporary Global Change. *Journal of the Royal Anthropological Institute* 22(1):27–46.

Moore, Jason W. 2016. Introduction: Anthropocene or Capitalocene? Nature, History, and the Crisis of Capitalism. In *Anthropocene or Capitalocene? Nature, History, and the Crisis of Capitalism*, edited by Jason W. Moore, 1–13. Oakland, CA: PM Press.

Moraes, Clara Salas de, Terezinha Aparecida Borges Dias, Sylvania de Paiva Pinto Costa, Rogério da Costa Vieira, Sérgio Eustáquio de Noronha, and Marília Lobo Burle. 2017. *Catálogo de Fava (Phaseolus lunatus L.) Conservada na Embrapa*. Brasília, Brazil: EMBRAPA Recursos Genéticos e Biotecnologia.

Murphy, G. P., and S. A. Dudley. 2009. Kin Recognition: Competition and Cooperation in *Impatiens* (Balsaminaceae). *American Journal of Botany* 96:1990–1996.

Myers, Natasha. 2014. Sensing Botanical Sensoria: A Kriya for Cultivating Your Inner Plant. Centre for Imaginative Ethnography. http://imaginativeethnography.org/imaginings/affect/sensing-botanical-sensoria/.

———. 2015. Conversations on Plant Sensing: Notes from the Field. *Nature Culture* 3:35–66.

———. 2017. From the Anthropocene to the Planthroposcene: Designing Gardens for Plant/People Involution. *History and Anthropology* 28(3):297–301. https://doi.org/10.1080/02757206.2017.1289934.

Myers, Norman, Russell A. Mittermeier, Cristina G. Mittermeier, Gustavo A. B. da Fonseca, and Jennifer Kent. 2000. Biodiversity Hotspots for Conservation Priorities. *Nature* 403:853–858.

Nabhan, Gary, Kimberlee Chambers, David Tecklin, Eric Perramond, and Thomas E. Sheridan. 2011. Ethnobiology for A Diverse World Defining New Disciplinary Trajectories: Mixing Political Ecology with Ethnobiology. *Journal of Ethnobiology* 31(1):1–3.

Nading, Alex. 2012. Dengue Mosquitoes Are Single Mothers: Biopolitics Meets Ecological Aesthetics in Nicaraguan Community Health Work. *Cultural Anthropology* 27:572–596.

Nic Eoin, Luíseach, and Rachel King. 2013. How to Develop Intangible Heritage: The Case of Metolong Dam, Lesotho. *World Archaeology* 45: 653–669. https://doi.org/10.1080/00438243.2013.823885.

Nimuendajú, Curt. 1946. *The Eastern Timbira*. Berkeley: University of California Press.

NoiseCat, Julian Brave. 2017. The Western Idea of Private Property Is Flawed: Indigenous Peoples Have It Right. *The Guardian*, Opinion, 27 March 2017. https://www.theguardian.com/commentisfree/2017/mar/27/western-idea-private-property-flawed-Indigenous-peoples-have-it-right.

Nuckolls, Janice B. 2010. The Sound-Symbolic Expression of Animacy in Amazonian Ecuador. *Diversity* 2.353–369.

Ogden, Laura, Nik Heynen, Ulrich Oslender, Paige West, Karim-Aly Kassam, and Paul Robbins. 2013. Global Assemblages, Resilience, and Earth Stewardship in the Anthropocene. *Frontiers in Ecology and Environment* 11(7):341–347. https://doi.org/10.1890/120327.

Oliveira, Gustavo, and Susanna Hecht. 2016. Sacred Groves, Sacrifice Zones and Soy Production: Globalization, Intensification and Neo-Nature in South America. *The Journal of Peasant Studies* 43(2):251–285. https://doi.org/10.1080/03066150.2016.1146705.

Olson, Valerie, and Lisa Messeri. 2015. Beyond the Anthropocene: Un-Earthing an Epoch. *Environment and Society: Advances in Research* 6: 28–47. https://doi.org/10.3167/ares.2015.060103.

Overing, Joanna. 2000. The Efficacy of Laughter: The Ludic Side of Magic within Amazonian Sociality. In *The Anthropology of Love and Anger: The Aesthetics of Conviviality in Native Amazonia*, edited by Joanna Overing and Alan Passes, 64–81. London: Routledge.

Overing, Joanna, and Alan Passes. 2000a. Introduction: Conviviality and the Opening up of Amazonian Anthropology. In *The Anthropology of Love and Anger: The Aesthetics of Conviviality in Native Amazonia*, edited by Joanna Overing and Alan Passes, 1–30. London: Routledge.

———, eds. 2000b. *The Anthropology of Love and Anger: The Aesthetics of Conviviality in Native Amazonia*. London: Routledge.

Pálsson, Gisli. 2013. Ensembles of Biosocial Relations. In *Biosocial Becomings: Integrating Social and Biological Anthropology*, edited by Tim Ingold and Gisli Pálsson, 22–41. Cambridge, UK: Cambridge University Press.

Passes, Alan. 2000. The Value of Working and Speaking Together: A Facet of Pai'kwene (Palikar) Conviviality. In *The Anthropology of Love and Anger: The Aesthetics of Conviviality in Native Amazonia*, edited by Joanna Overing and Alan Passes, 97–113. London: Routledge.

Petty, Aaron M., Vanessa deKoninck, and Ben Orlove. 2015. Cleaning, Protecting, or Abating? Making Indigenous Fire Management "Work" in Northern Australia. *Journal of Ethnobiology* 35(1):140–162.

Popjes, Jack, and Jo Popjes. 1986. Canela-Krahô. In *Handbook of Amazonian Languages*, edited by Desmond C. Derbyshire and Geoffrey K. Pullum, 128–199. New York: Walter de Gruyter & Company.

Posey, Darrell A. 2002. *Kayapó Ethnoecology and Culture*, edited by Kristina Plenderleith. London: Routledge.

Praet, Istvan. 2013. Humanity and Life as the Perpetual Maintenance of Specific Efforts: A Reappraisal of Animism. In *Biosocial Becomings: Integrating Social and Biological Anthropology*, edited by Tim Ingold and Gisli Pálsson, 191–210. Cambridge, UK: Cambridge University Press.

Pretty, Jules, Bill Adams, Fikret Berkes, Simone Ferreira de Athayde, Nigel Dudley, Eugene Hunn, Luisa Maffi, Kay Milton, David Rapport, Paul Robbins, Eleanor Sterling, Sue Stolton, Anna Tsing, Erin Vintinner, and Sarah Pilgrim. 2009. The Intersections of Biological Diversity and Cultural Diversity: Towards Integration. *Conservation and Society* 7(2):100–112.

Quinlan, Marsha. 2005. Considerations for Collecting Freelists in the Field: Examples from Ethnobotany. *Field Methods* 17(3):219–234.

Reid, Michael G., Colleen Hamilton, Sarah K. Reid, William Trousdale, Cam Hill, Nancy Turner, Chris R. Picard, Cassandra Lamontagne, and H. Damon Matthews. 2014. Indigenous Climate Change Adaptation Planning Using a Values-Focused Approach: A Case Study with the Gitga'at Nation. *Journal of Ethnobiology* 34(3):401–424.

Ribeiro, Francisco de Paulo. [1815] 1848. Roteiro da Viagem que Fez o Capitão ... às Fronteiras da Capitania do Maranhão e da de Goyaz (1815). *Revista do Instituto Histórico e Geográfico Brasileiro* 10:5–79.

———. [1819] 1841. Memoria Sobre as Nações Gentias que Presentemente Habitam o Continente do Maranhão (1819). *Revista do Instituto Histórico e Geográfico Brasileiro* 3:184–196.

———. [1819] 1849. Descripção do Território de Pastos Bons, no Sertões do Maranhão (1819). *Revista do Instituto Histórico e Geográfico Brasileiro* 12:41–86.

Ribeiro, Ricardo F. 2008. Da Amazônia para o Cerrado: As Reservas Extrativistas como Estratégias Socioambientais de Conservação. *Sinapse Ambiental* 5(1):12–32.

Rival, Laura. 1998. Androgynous parents and guest children: the Huaorani couvade. *Journal of the Royal Anthropological Institute* 4(4):619–642.

———. 2001. Seed and Clone: The Symbolic and Social Significance of Bitter Manioc Cultivation. In *Beyond the Visible and the Material: The Amerindianization of Society in the Work of Peter Rivière*, edited by Laura Rival, 57–80. Oxford, UK: Oxford University Press.

———. 2007. Domesticating the Landscape, Producing Crops and Reproducing Society in Amazonia. In *Holistic Anthropology: Emergence and Convergence*, edited by David J. Parkin and Stanley J. Ulijaszek, 72–90. New York: Berghahn.

———. 2014. Encountering Nature through Fieldwork: Expert Knowledge, Modes of Reasoning, and Local Creativity. *Journal of the Royal Anthropological Institute* 20: 218–236.

———. 2016. *Huaorani Transformations in Twenty-First-Century Ecuador: Treks into the Future of Time*. Tucson: University of Arizona Press.

Rival, Laura, and Doyle McKey. 2008. Domestication and Diversity in Manioc (*Manihot esculenta* Crantz ssp. *esculenta*, Euphorbiaceae). *Current Anthropology* 49:1119–1128.

Rivière, Peter. 1969. *Marriage among the Trio: A Principle of Social Organization*. Oxford, UK: Clarendon Press.

Rizzo de Oliveira, Adalberto L. 2005. Projeto Carajás, Práticas Indigenistas e Povos Indígenas no Maranhão. *Revista Anthropológicas* 15(2):135–169.

———. 2007. Messianismo Canela: Entre o Indigenismo e o Desenvolvimento. *Revista Anthropológicas* 18(2):183–214.

———. 2014. Apaniekrá e Ramkokamekra-Canela: Desenvolvimento e Mudanças Socioambientais no Centro-Sul Maranhense. Paper presented at 38th National Meeting of ANPOCS (Associação Nacional de Pós-Graduação e Pesquisa em Ciências Sociais), Caxambu, Minas Gerais, Brazil, October 2014.

Rodrigues, Ayron D. 1999. "Macro-Jê." In *The Amazonian Languages*, edited by Robert M. W. Dixon and Alexandra Y. Aikhenvald, 165–203. Cambridge, UK. Cambridge University Press.

Rubenstein, Steven Lee. 2012. On the Importance of Visions among the Amazonian Shuar. *Current Anthropology* 53(1):39–79.

Ruddiman, William F. 2003. The Anthropogenic Greenhouse Gas Era Began Thousands of Years Ago. *Climate Change* 61: 261–293. https://doi.org/10.1023/B:CLIM.0000004577 .17928.fa.

Salmond, Anne. 2014. Tears of Rangi: Water, Power, and People in New Zealand. *HAU: Journal of Ethnographic Theory* 4(3):285–309.

Santos-Granero, Fernando. 2000. The Sisyphus Syndrome, or the Struggle for Conviviality in Native Amazonia. In *The Anthropology of Love and Anger: The Aesthetics of Conviviality in Native Amazonia*, edited by Joanna Overing and Alan Passes, 268–277. London: Routledge.

———. 2007. Of Fear and Friendship: Amazonian Sociality beyond Kinship and Affinity. *Journal of the Royal Anthropological Institute* 13(1):1–18.

———, ed. 2009. *The Occult Life of Things: Native Amazonian Theories of Materiality and Personhood*. Tucson: University of Arizona Press.

———, ed. 2015. *Images of Public Wealth or the Anatomy of Well-being in Indigenous Amazonia*. Tucson: University of Arizona Press.

Sawyer, Donald. 2009. Fluxos de Carbono na Amazônia e no Cerrado: um Olhar Socioecossistêmico. *Sociedade e Estado* 24(1):149–171.

Schwartzman, Steven. 1988. The Panará and the Xingu National Park: The Transformation of a Society. PhD dissertation, University of Chicago.

Scott, Colin. 1989. Knowledge Construction among Cree Hunters: Metaphors and Literal Understanding. *Journal de la Société des Américanistes* 75:193–208.

Seeger, Anthony. 1981. *Nature and Society in Central Brazil: The Suyá Indians of Mato Grosso*. Cambridge, MA: Harvard University Press.

———. 1989. Dualism: Fuzzy Thinking or Fuzzy Sets? In *The Attraction of Opposites: Thought and Society in the Dualistic Mode*, edited by David Maybury-Lewis and Uri Almagor, 191–208. Ann Arbor: University of Michigan Press.

Shepard, Glenn. 2004. A Sensory Ecology of Medicinal Plant Therapy in Two Amazonian Societies. *American Anthropologist* 106(2):252–266.

Simon, Marcelo F., and Toby Pennington. 2012. Evidence for Adaptation to Fire Regimes in the Tropical Savannas of the Brazilian Cerrado. *International Journal of Plant Sciences* 173:711–723.

Singh, Shree P., Paul Gepts, and Daniel G. Debouck. 1991. Races of Common Bean (*Phaseolus vulgaris*, Fabaceae). *Economic Botany* 45(3):379–396.

Siqueira, Jaime Garcia, Jr. 2007. Wyty-Catë: Cultura e Política de um Movimento pan-Timbira. Master's thesis, University of Brasília.

Sodikoff, Genese Marie, ed. 2012. *The Anthropology of Extinction: Essays on Culture and Species Death*. Indianapolis: Indiana University Press.

Stang, Carla. 2009. *A Walk to the River in Amazonia: Ordinary Reality for the Mehinaku Indians*. New York: Berghahn.

Steffen, Will, Wendy Broadgate, Lisa Deutsch, Owen Gaffney, and Cornelia Ludwig. 2015. The Trajectory of the Anthropocene: The Great Acceleration. *The Anthropocene Review* 2(1):81–98.

Steffen, Will, Paul J. Crutzen, and John R. McNeill. 2007. The Anthropocene: Are Humans Now Overwhelming the Great Forces of Nature? *Royal Academy of Sciences* 36(8):614–621.

Steffen, Will, Jacques Grinevald, Paul Crutzen, and John McNeill. 2011. The Anthropocene: Conceptual and Historical Perspectives. *Philosophical Transactions: Mathematical, Physical and Engineering Sciences* 369(1938): 842–867.

Stevens, Martin. 2013. *Sensory Ecology, Behavior, and Evolution.* Oxford, UK: Oxford University Press.

———. 2016. *Cheats and Deceits: How Animals and Plants Exploit and Mislead.* Oxford, UK: Oxford University Press.

Strassburg, Bernardo B. N., Thomas Brooks, Rafael Feltran-Barbieri, Alvaro Iribarrem, Renato Crouzeilles, Rafael Loyola, Agnieszka E. Latawiec, Francisco J. B. Oliveira Filho, Carlos A. de M. Scaramuzza, Fabio R. Scarano, Britaldo Soares-Filho, and Andrew Balmford. 2017. Moment of Truth for the Cerrado Hotspot. *Nature: Ecology and Evolution* 1:0099. https://doi.org/10.1038/s41559-017-0099.

Swanson, Heather, Nils Bubandt, and Anna Tsing. 2015. Less Than One but More Than Many: Anthropocene as Science Fiction and Scholarship-in-the-Making. *Environment and Society: Advances in Research* 6:149–166. https://doi.org/10.3167/ares.2015.060109.

Tallbear, Kim. 2011. Why Interspecies Thinking Needs Indigenous Standpoints. Theorizing the Contemporary. *Cultural Anthropology* (website), 4 April 2011. https://culanth.org/fieldsights/260-why-interspecies-thinking-needs-Indigenous-standpoints.

———. 2016. Badass (Indigenous) Women Caretake Relations: #NoDAPL, #IdleNoMore, #BlackLivesMatter. Hot Spots. *Cultural Anthropology* (website), 22 December 2016. https://culanth.org/fieldsights/1019-badass-Indigenous-women-caretake-relations-nodapl-idlenomore-blacklivesmatter.

Taylor, Anne-Christine. 1996. The Soul's Body and Its States: An Amazonian Perspective on the Nature of Being Human. *Journal of the Royal Anthropological Institute* 2:201–215.

———. 2001. Wives, Pets, and Affines: Marriage among the Jivaro. In *Beyond the Visible and the Material: The Amerindianization of Society in the Work of Peter Rivière*, edited by Laura Rival, 45–56. Oxford, UK: Oxford University Press.

———. 2014. Healing Translations: Moving between Worlds in Achuar Shamanism. *HAU: Journal of Ethnographic Theory* 4(2):95–118.

Todd, Zoe. 2016. An Indigenous Feminist's Take on the Ontological Turn: "Ontology" Is Just Another Word for Colonialism. *Journal of Historical Sociology* 29(1):4–22. https://doi.org/10.1111/johs.12124.

Tsing, Anna. 2010. Arts of Inclusion, or How to Love a Mushroom. *Manoa* 22(2):191–203.

———. 2015. *The Mushroom at the End of the World: On the Possibility of Life in Capitalist Ruins.* Princeton, NJ: Princeton University Press.

Turner, Terence. 1995. Social Body and Embodied Subject: Bodiliness, Subjectivity, and Sociality among the Kayapó. *Cultural Anthropology* 10(2):143–170.

Vergunst, Jo, Andrew Whitehouse, Nicholas Ellison, and Arnar Árnason. 2012. Introduction. In *Landscapes Beyond Land: Routes, Aesthetics, Narratives*, edited by Arnar Árnason, Nicholas Ellison, Jo Vergunst, and Andrew Whitehouse, 1–14. Oxford, UK: Berghahn.

Viveiros de Castro, Eduardo. [1986] 1992. *From the Enemy's Point of View: Humanity and Divinity in an Amazonian Society*. Chicago: University of Chicago Press.

———. 1996. Images of Nature and Society in Amazonian Ethnology. *Annual Review of Anthropology* 25:179–200.

———. 1998. Cosmological Deixis and Amerindian Perspectivism. *Journal of the Royal Anthropological Institute* 4(3):469–488.

———. 2011. *A Inconstância da Alma Selvagem*. São Paulo: COSAC NAIFY.

Walker, Brian, Stephen Carpenter, John Anderies, Nick Abel, Graeme Cumming, Marco Janssen, Louis Lebel, Jon Norberg, Garry D. Peterson, and Rusty Pritchard. 2002. Resilience Management in Social–Ecological Systems: A Working Hypothesis for a Participatory Approach. *Conservation Ecology* 6(1):14. http://www.consecol.org/vol6/iss1 /art14.

Walker, Brian, C. S. Holling, Stephen R. Carpenter, and Ann Kinzig. 2004. Resilience, Adaptability and Transformability in Social–Ecological Systems. *Ecology & Society* 9(2):5.

Waters, Colin N., Jan Zalasiewicz, Colin Summerhayes, Anthony D. Barnosky, Clément Poirier, Agnieszka Gałuszka, Alejandro Cearreta, Matt Edgeworth, Erle C. Ellis, Michael Ellis, Catherine Jeandel, Reinhold Leinfelder, J. R. McNeill, Daniel de B. Richter, Will Steffen, James Syvitski, Davor Vidas, Michael Wagreich, Mark Williams, An Zhisheng, Jacques Grinevald, Eric Odada, Naomi Oreskes, and Alexander P. Wolfe. 2016. The Anthropocene is Functionally and Stratigraphically Distinct from the Holocene. *Science* 351(6269). https://doi.org/10.1126/science.aad2622.

Watts, Jonathan. 2017. Brazilian Farmers Attack Indigenous Tribe with Machetes in Brutal Land Dispute. *The Guardian*, 1 May 2017. https://www.theguardian.com/world /2017/may/01/brazilian-farmers-attack-Indigenous-tribe-machetes.

Watts, Johnathan. 2018. World Water Day: Deadly Plight of Brazil's River Defenders Goes Unheard. *The Guardian*, 22 March 2018. https://www.theguardian.com/environment /2018/mar/22/world-water-day-deadly-plight-of-brazils-river-defenders-goes -unheard.

Welch, James R. 2015. Learning to Hunt by Tending the Fire: Xavante Youth, Ethnoecology, and Ceremony in Central Brazil. *Journal of Ethnobiology* 35(1):183–208. https://doi.org/10.2993/0278-0771-35.1.183.

Welch, James R., Eduardo S. Brondízio, Scott S. Hetrick, and Carlos E. A. Coimbra Jr. 2013. Indigenous Burning as Conservation Practice: Neotropical Savanna Recovery amid Agribusiness Deforestation in Central Brazil. *PLoS ONE* 8(12): e81226. https:// doi.org/10.1371/journal.pone.0081226.

Whitehead, Neil L., and Robin Wright, eds. 2004. *In Darkness and Secrecy: The Anthropology of Assault Sorcery and Witchcraft in Amazonia*. Durham, NC: Duke University Press.

Whitington, Jerome. 2013. Fingerprint, Bellwether, Model Event: Climate Change as Speculative Anthropology. *Anthropological Theory* 13(4):308–328. https://doi.org/10.1177/1463499613509992.

Whyte, Kyle Powys. 2017. The Dakota Access Pipeline, Environmental Injustice, and U.S. Colonialism. *Red Ink: An International Journal of Indigenous Literature, Arts, & Humanities* 19:1–11.

Whyte, Kyle Powys, Joseph P. Brewer II, and Jay T. Johnson. 2016. Weaving Indigenous Science, Protocols and Sustainability Science. *Sustainability Science* 11:25–32. https://doi.org/10.1007/s11625-015-0296-6.

Wilbert, Johannes, ed. 1978. *Folk Literature of the Gê Indians.* Los Angeles: University of California–Los Angeles Latin American Center Publications.

Wolfe, Amir H. and Jonathan A. Patz. 2002. Reactive Nitrogen and Human Health: Acute and Long-Term Implications. *AMBIO: A Journal of the Human Environment* 31(2):120–125.

Wright, Robin. 2013. *Mysteries of the Jaguar Shamans of the Northwest Amazon.* Lincoln: University of Nebraska Press.

Zalasiewicz, Jan, Mark Williams, Alan Haywood, and Michael Ellis. 2011. The Anthropocene: A New Epoch of Geological Time? *Philosophical Transactions: Mathematical, Physical and Engineering Sciences* 369(1938):835–841.

Zanotti, Laura, and Marcela Palomino-Schalscha. 2016. Taking Different Ways of Knowing Seriously: Cross-Cultural Work as Translations and Multiplicity. *Sustainability Science* 11:139–152. https://doi.org/10.1007/s11625-015-0312-x.

Ziker, John P., Joellie Rasmussen, and David A. Nolin. 2016. Indigenous Siberians Solve Collective Action Problems through Sharing and Traditional Knowledge. *Sustainability Science* 11:45–55. https://doi.org/10.1007/s11625-015-0293-9.

INDEX

aboriginal crops: as classified by Canela today, 116, 130, 150, 164–167, 172, 176, 181, 202; in Nimuendajú's work, 55–56, 87, 135, 173

acerola (*têc-rà cahàc xô*; *Malpighia emarginata* DC. or *Malpighia glabra* L.), 150, 257

adoption of crop children, 148, 167, 178, 181

aesthetics of landscape: in Canela life-world, 3, 17, 21, 33, 41, 45–46; as unfolding phenomenological concept, 23–24. *See also* life-world; phenomenology

agricultural hotspot: for soy in the Northeast of Brazil, 31, 44. *See also* deforestation; eucalyptus; soy

agro-biodiversity: maintenance by the Canela, 11, 77, 79, 80, 86–87, 127, 128, 134, 163, 167, 175–176, 184–185, 224; as multispecies childcare, 103, 141, 147–148, 159–162, 171–173, 180

Amazon/Amazonia: conservation of, 30–31, 229; Indigenous aesthetics of, 22–23; Indigenous peoples of, 1, 266n8; region of, 9. *See also* Amazonian; lowland South America

Amazonian: aesthetics, 22–23; Indigenous peoples, 1, 266n8; multispecies engagements, 209–210, sociality, 93, 144, 199, 268n9. *See also* Amazon/Amazonia; conviviality; lowland South America

Apaniekra Indigenous people, 44, 53, 88, 165, 172, 194, 221, 242, 270n3

apocalypse: in Canela messianism, 61. *See also* messianic movements

annatto (*pym*; *Bixa orellana* L.): classification of, 141, 150–151, 152, 155, 157, 164, 169, 241, 248, 253, 269n1; cultivation of, 56; in mythic storytelling, 83–85, 197; use as ritual body paint, 94, 219; use in ritual, 104–105, 125, 219

annual ritual cycle, 9, 157

Anthropocene: climatic and environmental changes in, 17, 21, 234–235; definition of, 2–4; Indigenous adaptation to, 45, 47, 89,
231–232, 235; Indigenous lifeways in, 7, 19, 180, 229; theoretical conceptualizations of, 4–5, 231. *See also* climate change; resilience

archaeology: of Indigenous plant domestication in Cerrado and Brazil, 29–30, 269n6; as part of sensory ethnobotany framework, 6

avocado (*bacat*; *Persea americana* L.), 150, 166, 202, 257

Awkhêê mythical figure, 58, 60–61, 266n1. *See also* messianic movements

babaçu (*rõrõ pàr*; *Attalea speciosa* Mart.), 166, 243, 254, 259, 260

bacaba (*capêr pàr*; *Oenocarpus bacaba* Mart.), 51, 133, 134, 261

bacuri (*cumxê pàr*; *Platonia insignis* Mart.), 35, 38, 51, 111, 260

banana (*pypyp-re*; *Musa* L. spp.): classification of, 150, 183, 254; as crop child, 167–168; cultivation of, 41, 66, 68, 125, 127; exchange and adoption of, 131, 166–167; food and sex prohibitions associated with, 108; introduction of, 16, 56; master spirits of, 202, 206

bandeiras, 50

Barra do Corda, 12, 14, 37, 43, 44, 56, 122, 127, 158, 177, 178, 269n4

beribu meat and manioc pie: in first harvest rituals, 117; food and sex prohibitions associated with, 108, 191–192; in food-sharing ritual with plants, 113–115, 227; as ritual foodstuff, 12, 155, 165, 241, 242, 254; in Star-Woman mythic story, 78, 80–81, 263–264. *See also* khĩya; manioc

Berlin, Brent, 149–150

bio-sociocultural: as Canela bio-sociocultural life-world, 17, 93, 145, 149, 225, 227, 235; as unfolding concept linking biological and socio-cultural processes and diversity, 24–25, 269n6. *See also* life-world